Advance praise for *Blood Letters*

"*Blood Letters* tells the story of Lin Zhao's martyrdom with the elegance her life demands. Those who tortured her could not prevent the beauty of her life and poetry from testifying to her faith in God. We are in Lian Xi's debt for making Lin Zhao's life and witness available to Christians in the West like myself because we can barely imagine from where a life like that of Lin Zhao comes. Lian Xi's book will surely become a classic not only as we come to understand the struggle of Christians in China but also for how the story he tells helps us understand China."

—STANLEY HAUERWAS, Gilbert T. Rowe Professor Emeritus
of Divinity and Law at Duke University

"*Blood Letters* is a genuinely exciting book. Lian Xi sheds a whole new light on an extraordinarily important Christian figure (and martyr) who has hitherto been utterly unknown outside a narrow band of specialists. Beyond writing an enthralling account of the story of this heroic woman, the author provides a rich historical and international context, and he thoroughly justifies the daring analogy he draws between Lin Zhao and legendary figures like Dietrich Bonhoeffer. A masterpiece."

—PHILIP JENKINS, author of *Crucible of Faith:
The Ancient Revolution That Made Our Modern
Religious World*

BLOOD LETTERS

BLOOD LETTERS

The Untold Story of Lin Zhao,
a Martyr in Mao's China

Lian Xi

BASIC BOOKS
New York

Basic Books
Hachette Book Group
1290 Avenue of the Americas, New York, NY 10104
www.basicbooks.com

Printed in the United States of America

First Edition: March 2018

Published by Basic Books, an imprint of Perseus Books, LLC, a subsidiary of Hachette Book Group, Inc. The Basic Books name and logo is a trademark of the Hachette Book Group.

The publisher is not responsible for websites (or their content) that are not owned by the publisher.

Print book interior design by Jeff Williams.

Library of Congress Control Number: 2018931841.

ISBNs: 978-1-5416-4423-6 (hardcover); 978-1-5416-4422-9 (ebook)

LSC-C

10 9 8 7 6 5 4 3 2 1

TO THOSE WHO LABORED
TO PRESERVE LIN ZHAO'S LEGACY
AND TO KEEP HER SPIRIT ALIVE

CONTENTS

INTRODUCTION

ON MAY 31, 1965, THIRTY-THREE-YEAR-OLD LIN ZHAO—POET, JOUR-nalist, dissident—was tried in the Jing'an District People's Court in Shanghai. She was charged as the lead member of a "counterrevolutionary clique" that had published *A Spark of Fire*, an underground journal that decried Communist misrule and Mao's Great Leap Forward, which caused an unprecedented famine in 1959–1961 and claimed at least thirty-six million lives nationwide.[1]

Lin Zhao had also contributed a long poem entitled "A Day in Prometheus's Passion" to the journal. It mocked Mao as a villainous Zeus trying, and failing, to force Prometheus to put out the fire of freedom taken from heaven. According to the authorities, the poem "viciously attacked" the Chinese Communist Party (CCP) and the socialist system and inspired fellow counterrevolutionaries to "blatantly call for 'a peaceful, democratic, and free'" China.[2] She was sentenced to twenty years in prison.

"This is a shameful ruling!" Lin Zhao wrote on the back of the verdict the next day, in her own blood. "But I heard it with pride! It is the enemy's estimation of my individual act of combat. Deep inside my heart I feel the pride of a combatant! I have done too little. It is far from enough. Yes, I must do more to live up to your estimation! Other than that, this so-called ruling is completely meaningless to me! I despise it!"[3]

It was an unexpected, jarring note in the symphony of Mao's revolution. The Communist movement, which began in the 1920s and which Mao had led since the 1930s, had triumphed with the founding of the People's Republic in 1949. The revolution had turned communism into a sacred creed and a mass religion in China, complete with its Marxist and Maoist scriptures, priests (the cadres), and revolutionary liturgy.

The cult of Mao dated to the 1940s but blossomed with the publication of *Quotations from Chairman Mao*—known in the West as *The Little Red Book*—in 1964. Over one billion copies were printed over the next decade. During the Cultural Revolution, launched in 1966, collective rituals of slogan chanting and of waving *The Little Red Book* were performed daily in front of the portrait of the "great leader." Meanwhile, some 4.8 billion Mao badges were made. The largest was as big as a soccer ball.[4]

Sacrilege was hard to imagine and rare. Even those condemned "counterrevolutionaries" sent to execution grounds had often chanted "Long live Chairman Mao" as shots were fired, in a last-ditch effort to escape the wrath of the revolution and to attest their loyalty to it.[5]

At a time when critics of the party had been silenced throughout China, Lin Zhao chose to oppose it openly from her prison cell. "From the day of my arrest I have declared in front of those Communists my identity as a resister," she wrote in a blood letter to her mother from prison. "I have been open in my basic stand as a freedom fighter against communism and against tyranny."[6]

Lin Zhao's dissent seemed as futile as it was suicidal. What sustained it was her intense religious faith. She had been baptized in her teens at the Laura Haygood Memorial School, a Southern Methodist mission school in her hometown of Suzhou, but drifted away from the church when she joined the Communist revolution in 1949 to help "emancipate" the masses and create a new, just society, as she believed. Her disenchantment with the revolution came in the late 1950s, when she was purged as a Rightist—along with at least 1.2 million others across China—for expressing democratic ideas.[7] Thereafter she gradually returned to a fervent Christian faith.

As a Christian, she believed that her struggle was both political and spiritual. In a postsentencing letter from prison to the editors of *People's Daily*—the party's mouthpiece—she explained that, in opposing communism, she was following "the line of a servant of God, the political line of Christ." "My life belongs to God," she claimed. God willing, she would be able to live. "But if God wants me to become a willing martyr, I will only be grateful from the bottom of my heart for the honor He bestows on me!"[8]

Lin Zhao's defiance of the regime was unparalleled in Mao's China. The tens of millions who perished as the direct result of the CCP rule died as victims, their voices unheard. No significant, secular opposition to the ideology of communism was recorded in China during Mao's reign.[9] Lin Zhao endured as a resister because of her democratic ideals and because her Christian faith enabled her to preserve her moral autonomy as well as political judgment, which the Communist state had denied its citizens. Her faith provided a counterweight to the religion of Maoism and sustained her in her dissent.

THE TITLE OF this book comes from Lin Zhao's impassioned means of expressing that dissent. "During her imprisonment," an official document read, Lin Zhao "poked her flesh countless times and used her filthy blood to write hundreds of thousands of words of extremely reactionary, extremely malicious letters, notes, and diaries, madly attacking, abusing, and slandering our party and its leader."[10] Her letters were addressed variously to the party propaganda apparatus, the United Nations, the prison authorities, and her mother. She called them her "freedom writings."

"As a human being, I fight for my right to live a whole, upright, and clean life—my right to life," she explained. "It shall forever be an irreproachable struggle! Nobody has the right to tell me: in order to live, you must have chains on your neck and endure the humiliation of slavery."[11]

Lin Zhao's prison writings, which total some 500,000 characters, include essays, poems, letters, and even a play. She wrote in both ink and blood, using the latter when she was denied stationery or as an extreme act of protest. She drew blood with a makeshift prick—a bamboo pick, a hair clip, or the plastic handle of her toothbrush, sharpened against the concrete floor—and held it in a plastic spoon, in which she dipped her "pen," often a thin bamboo strip or a straw stem. Her writing was done on paper when it was available and on shirts and torn-up bed sheets when it was not.[12]

At a certain point, having poked the fingers on her left hand so many times, she could no longer draw blood from them. They turned numb when pressed.[13] In a letter to her mother dated November 14, 1967, she wrote:

> The small puddle of blood that I squeezed out for writing is almost all gone now. My blood seems to have thinned lately; coagulation is quite poor. It may be partially due to the weather getting cold. Alas, dear Mama! This is my life! It is also my struggle! It is my battle![14]

The fullest expression of Lin Zhao's political beliefs is found in her 1965 letter to the editorial board of *People's Daily*. She chose July 14, the anniversary of the storming of the Bastille, as the day to begin writing it. It took her almost five months to complete the letter, which ran to about 140,000 characters, 137 pages in all. She did it in ink, but stamped it repeatedly with a shirt-button-sized seal bearing the character *zhao* and inked with her blood.

In the letter, Lin Zhao challenged the theory of a continuous "class struggle," which the Communists saw as intrinsic to human history and from which there was no escape. Since the 1920s, the CCP had looked upon this theory as an immutable truth and had used it to justify the so-called dictatorship of the proletariat after

1949. The doctrine gained new urgency in the 1960s when Mao declared that "class struggle must be talked about every year, every month, and every day."[15]

Lin Zhao scoffed at this. "I do not ever believe that, in such a vast living space that God has prepared for us, there is any need for humanity to engage in a life-and-death struggle!"[16]

The CCP dictatorship was but a modern form of "tyranny and slavery," she wrote in her letter to the party's propagandists. "As long as there are people who are still enslaved, not only are the enslaved not free, those who enslave others are likewise not free!" Those seeking to end Communist rule in China must likewise not "debase the goal of our struggle into a desire to become a different kind of slave owner," she wrote. "The lofty overall goal of our battle dictates that we cannot simply set our eyes on political power—the goal must not and cannot be a simple transfer of political power!" The end was "political democratization . . . to make sure that there will never be another emperor in China!"[17]

Lin Zhao wrestled with the moral question of whether violence was a justified means to that end. Her Christian faith had hardened her for the fight. At the same time, it also tempered her opposition. She acknowledged the occasional "sparks of humanity" even in those who were at the "most savage center" of Chinese communism. As strenuously as she argued against her imprisonment, against Mao's dictatorship, and for a free society, she was unable to sanction violence in that struggle. "As a Christian, one devoted to freedom and fighting under the Cross, I believe that killing Communists is not the best way to oppose or eliminate communism." She admitted that, had she not "embraced a bit of Christ's spirit," she would have had every reason to pledge "bloody revenge against the Chinese Communist Party."[18]

FOR HER REFUSAL to submit to "thought reform" and her unflagging sacrilege against Mao and his revolution, Lin Zhao's sentence was changed to the death penalty. On April 29, 1968, she was shot under the orders issued by the Shanghai Military Control Committee of the People's Liberation Army. She was thirty-six.

Lin Zhao died with unfulfilled wishes: having caused her mother much grief because of her involvement in politics, she had wanted to make amends by caring for her in her old age. She told her mother in one of her last blood letters, written in November 1967: "When the morning light of freedom in a century of human rights shines upon the vast land of this country, we shall pour out our hearts to each other!"[19] That letter, and her other blood writings, were confiscated by the prison and never sent.

She had vowed to make a pilgrimage one day to the tomb of American president John F. Kennedy to pay her respects, for he had taught her—in his "Ich bin ein Berliner" speech of 1963—that freedom is indivisible and that "when one man is enslaved, all are not free."[20]

And she had written an appeal to the United Nations in 1966 asking to testify in person about her torture and about human rights abuses in China. In the event of her death while in detention, she asked the United Nations to "conduct a detailed, rigorous, and true investigation" of her case and make it public. Similar appeals from dissidents in the Soviet Union made it to the United Nations Committee for Human Rights during the 1960s, yet Lin Zhao's letter never reached beyond her prison walls.[21]

Her death sentence began with a "supreme instruction" from Chairman Mao: "There certainly will be those who refuse to change till they die. They are willing to go see God carrying their granite heads on their shoulders. That will be of little consequence."[22]

That would be true, and this book would not have been possible, if her prison writings had not survived.

Lin Zhao had believed—against all hope—that they would. Unimaginably, they did. In spite of the "extremely reactionary" and damning nature of her writings, no prison or public security bureaucrat apparently dared to risk a potentially costly political mistake by ordering their destruction. Instead, her writings were collected and filed away as part of the criminal evidence in her counterrevolutionary case. In 1981, Shanghai High People's Court posthumously revoked Lin Zhao's death sentence and declared her innocent. Her writings were returned to the family the next year.[23]

In 2004, a digitized version of Lin Zhao's 1965 letter to *People's Daily* appeared on the Internet. It quickly became a Promethean fire to political dissent in China today. The late Nobel Peace laureate Liu Xiaobo called Lin Zhao "the only voice of freedom left for contemporary China."[24]

During the past decade, an increasing number of democracy activists in China have visited Lin Zhao's tomb on Lingyan Hill on the outskirts of Suzhou to pay their respects. In recent years, as the government's crackdown on dissidents has intensified, plainclothes as well as uniformed police in riot gear have shown up dutifully on the anniversary of her execution to block access to her tomb and break up gatherings of human rights advocates who traveled from across the country to commemorate her. The result has been an annual ritual of police detaining and roughing up pilgrims at the foot of Lingyan Hill.[25]

Throughout contemporary China, no other spirit of the dead has required such unrelenting exorcism.[26] In death even more so than in life, Lin Zhao has become a nemesis of the Communist state.

To the poet Shen Zeyi, Lin Zhao's friend and classmate at Peking University, she was the "Lamplight in the Snowy Fields," the title of a poem he penned in 1979 when he emerged from his own banishment, only to learn about her death:

For some reason
I always miss the lamplight on the other side of the mountain.
On a desolate night filled with a cold fog
in the middle of the fields covered with white snow

it shone a beautiful, lonely, inviolable light.
Where its radiance touched
it cast as far off as it could
the thick, dark night
of windswept, deep snow.[27]

That lamplight bore witness to human dignity and the tenacity of the human will to be free. In the course of the twentieth century, the giant wheel of totalitarian systems rolled over the lives of untold tens of millions worldwide. Like Dietrich Bonhoeffer and Sophie Scholl during the Nazi era, Aleksandr Solzhenitsyn under the Soviet regime, and Jerzy Popiełuszko in Communist Poland, Lin Zhao attempted—to borrow Bonhoeffer's words—to "drive a spoke into the wheel itself."

Religious faith played a role in the heroic struggles of these individuals. It gave Bonhoeffer the moral clarity to pronounce the Nazi doctrine a heresy, and it inspired Solzhenitsyn to oppose communism as a "spiritual enslavement." To Solzhenitsyn, the immoral totalitarianism of the Soviet Union had demanded a "total surrender of our souls." When Caesar demands "that we render unto him what is God's—that is a sacrifice we dare not make!" he concluded.[28]

In the early 1980s, Father Jerzy Popiełuszko stood with Solidarity, the Polish trade union, in defying the martial law the Communist government in Poland had imposed. "Woe betide state authorities who want to govern citizens by threat and fear," he cried. He believed that "to serve God is to condemn evil in all its manifestations"—and he paid for that conviction with his life.[29]

The connection between religious faith and the extraordinary courage of individuals to resist totalitarianism had been foretold by German theologian and philosopher Ernst Troeltsch, whom Bonhoeffer had read as a student. Because of its own revolutionary principle of "unlimited individualism and universalism," wrote Troeltsch, Christianity has "a disintegrating effect" upon "every form of exclusively earthly authority."[30]

IN 2013, *The Collected Writings of Lin Zhao*—including her returned prison writings and other extant works and correspondence, compiled and annotated by her dedicated friends—was privately printed.[31] I was given a copy.

It was a godsend. A year earlier, I had embarked on my search for Lin Zhao's story. Since 2012 I have retraced her life's journey, from the former Laura Haygood Memorial School in Suzhou where she underwent a double conversion—to Christianity and then to communism—to the picturesque campus of Peking University where she broke with communism after a political awakening. To better understand the mission school's education that left a permanent mark on her mind, I turned to the United Methodist archives in Madison, New Jersey.

I also paid my respects to Lin Zhao at her tomb, above which a surveillance camera was installed in 2008, in the lead-up to the fortieth anniversary of her execution, lest a spiritual and political plague break out undetected from her tomb.[32]

I have come to know Lin Zhao not only through her writings but also through interviews and correspondence with those who knew her intimately—her former fiancé, classmates, friends, fellow counterrevolutionaries, and her sister—and those who knew her prison intimately, namely Tilanqiao's former political inmates.

In my exclusive interview with the now retired judge who reviewed Lin Zhao's case in 1981 for rehabilitation, I asked about his decision to return her prison writings—sheets of manuscripts, numbered and bound with green threads, and four journal notebooks that contain her "battlefield diaries," essays, and ink copies of her "blood letters home." Using a pen, she had meticulously copied onto notebooks and loose sheets of paper all her blood writings after they were handed to the guards so that her words would be preserved.[33]

The returned writings were from her secondary file, he told me. The primary file contains her interrogation records and other key materials, which total about three linear feet on a shelf. It remains to this day locked away at a secret location for classified documents outside Shanghai.

"She is a good poet," he reminisced. "I secretly took some of her poems home and hand copied them," he added with a mischievous smile.

"Did you see the blood writings?"

He did. Only some of them. The blood had turned dark on pieces of yellowed paper.

I asked why he didn't return them to Lin Zhao's family along with the other prison writings.

"*Taichu shenjing le*"—too much for the raw nerves—he answered.[34]

LIN ZHAO WOULD have been consigned to oblivion, like the millions killed as enemies of the revolution. Her story would have been lost but for the constancy of her prison writings and the caprices of history. What follows is that story.

one

TO LIVE UNDER THE SUN

LIN ZHAO FOUND OUT FROM HER PARENTS THAT POLITICS IN TWENTI-eth-century China was a treacherous business. In the late 1920s, her mother, Xu Xianmin, at the time a student at Leyi Middle School in Suzhou, joined her radical brother Xu Jinyuan as agitators in the city's labor movement led by the local branch of the nascent Chinese Communist Party. Xu Xianmin later recalled the moment when she came on the scene as a fifteen-year-old revolutionary neophyte. During a strike by Suzhou's rickshaw pullers, she "wove in and out of the crowd of demonstrators on the street, running around like a lunatic," dressed in red with megaphone in hand. "I did not really know what revolution was all about. I just followed Big Brother Jinyuan, waving a flag and shouting, but that got me the nickname 'the lady in red.'"[1]

The woman in red soon came to know what a heavy price a revolution could exact. In the wee hours of April 11, 1927, the Nationalist (Guomindang) police burst into the house where Xu Jinyuan and a few regional CCP leaders were holding an emergency meeting and arrested them. The next day, Chiang Kai-shek launched his brutal purge of the Communists in Shanghai. Hundreds of activists in Shanghai's General Labor Union, the CCP stronghold in the city, were killed. As the campaign continued, thousands went missing.

The April 12 Incident marked the end of the brief Nationalist-CCP alliance against the warlords. Thereafter the Communists were hunted down, and the bloody struggle between the two parties would continue for over two decades. A few days after his arrest, Xu Jinyuan's murdered body was put into a hemp sack and dumped into the river. He was twenty-one.[2]

The manner of her brother's death apparently dampened Xu Xianmin's heroism. She soon distanced herself from the CCP and aligned instead with a reformist faction within the Guomindang, serving as secretary of its local county branch. But her political loyalties remained divided: to a large extent, her sympathies remained with the revolutionaries.[3]

LIN ZHAO, NÉE Peng Lingzhao, was born on January 23, 1932.[4] She abandoned her birth name in her late teens when she joined the Communist revolution. The adoption of Lin as her new surname, no small sin against filial piety, marked a symbolic break with the Peng family: Peng Guoyan, her father, had not embraced the revolution in his youth. In 1922, he had been admitted to Southeast University in Nanjing, one of the first national universities established after the fall of the Qing dynasty in 1912. He majored in political economy, part of the university's Western-style curriculum, which was designed to advance the modernizers' nationalist dreams of wealth and power for the country. Those were dreams from the late nineteenth century. Battered by the failed reforms of the 1890s, the disaster of the Boxer Uprising at the turn of the century, and the country's descent into warlordism after 1916, the dreams nevertheless remained buoyant.

In 1926, Peng Guoyan graduated from Southeast University. Unlike his fiery future wife, he envisioned the introduction of constitutional politics and efficient, accountable government—what writer and family friend Feng Yingzi called his "Westminster-style democratic ideas"—to China. His bachelor's thesis was entitled "On the Constitution of the Irish Free State."[5]

By 1928, a time of fresh beginnings for China appeared to have arrived. Major warlords either had been defeated or had pledged allegiance to the newly established National government in Nanjing; the radicalism of communism had been contained. National rejuvenation seemed possible under the new Nanjing government, which began a vigorous push to end almost a century of unequal treaties that had been forced on China since the Opium War of 1839–1842. Successful negotiations with Western powers soon led to reclaimed tariff autonomy.[6]

Meanwhile, the Nanjing government sought to introduce reforms in the economy, industry, education, and the army, as well as in government administration and the tax system. In Jiangsu province, examinations were held in September 1928 to select chief executives at the county level, ostensibly a break with the corrupt officialdom of the past. The twenty-four-year-old Peng scored highest in the test and became the magistrate of Wu county, which included the city of Suzhou and the neighboring areas.

Peng's glory was short-lived. Unwilling and unable to play by the intricate rules of local politics, he neither bribed his provincial superior nor appeased the power brokers in areas nominally under his administrative control. He initiated road construction projects and the installation of telephone lines; he also cracked down on gambling and opium dens, to the ire of local police, who earned protection money from murky establishments.

Magistrate Peng apparently also harbored sympathies for Communists and leaked to Xu Xianmin, his future wife, a secret provincial order for the arrest of Suzhou leftists. Within months, he was briefly detained on vague charges of insubordination and indiscretion and removed from office.[7]

In 1930, he and Xu Xianmin were married. By the time of Lin Zhao's birth in 1932, he was in his third short-lived administrative stint, now as the magistrate of the remote, impoverished county of Pi. In May, after only six months on the job, the scrupulous and hardworking Peng was again arrested on trumped-up charges of "wanton taxation" to profit himself. He had tried to stay above factional politics but ended up running afoul of a local strongman. He spent the next three years in jail. The wings of the would-be modernizer had again been clipped. As if this was not enough, the strongman commissioned a stone stele at taxpayers' expense to commemorate the "inferior administrative deeds" of Peng. One could hardly have suffered a more resounding defeat.[8]

LIN ZHAO WAS five when Japan's full-scale invasion of China began. The hostilities, which broke out in July 1937 near Beijing (called Beiping at the time), spread to the Shanghai area in August. Shanghai fell in November, and Suzhou, eighty kilometers west, quickly followed. In December, the Japanese took Nanjing, the then capital of the Republic of China, and unleashed six weeks of horror—the Rape of Nanking, in which some three hundred thousand Chinese were massacred.

As the Japanese army advanced, Lin Zhao's family joined the estimated fifty million refugees who fled coastal China and headed west. In wartime capital Chongqing, Peng Guoyan worked for the Ministry of Finance of the Nationalist government. Xu Xianmin decided to return to occupied Shanghai and Suzhou as an undercover agent for the resistance movement—a Nationalist "commissioner" for Shanghai's surrounding countryside. At one point, she was briefly detained and tortured by the Japanese gendarmes.[9]

From a young age, Lin Zhao found in her mother an example of courage and sacrifice. Many years later, she reflected in a prison poem that it was her uncle Xu Jinyuan who had taught her mother to fight and her mother who passed on to her the same fighting spirit.[10]

After the end of the Japanese occupation, Peng Guoyan returned to the lower Yangzi valley and secured a position at the government's Central Bank in Shanghai. For her part, Xu Xianmin emerged as a progressive socialite in Suzhou. Back in the early 1930s, she had cofounded the Suzhou Women's Association to mobilize public opinion against Japan's takeover of Manchuria. After the war, her activist credentials and connections propelled her into prominent roles in respectable Suzhou society. She served on the board of trustees of a local bank, assumed directorship of *Dahua Daily*, a Suzhou newspaper, cofounded a transportation company, and successfully ran for the National Assembly in 1946 as a representative from Suzhou.[11]

During these years, Peng Guoyan and Xu Xianmin were able to provide a respectable education for Lin Zhao and a comfortable life for their two younger children: Peng Lingfan, their second daughter, born in 1938, and a son, Peng Enhua, born in 1944. In fall 1947, Lin Zhao entered the Laura Haygood Memorial School for Girls, or Jinghai, where she would spend two of the most formative years of her life.[12]

Founded in 1903, Jinghai was named after Laura Haygood (the Chinese name of the school translates to "in admiration of Haygood"), who went to China in 1884 as the first female foreign

Laura Haygood Memorial School for Girls, n.d. (ca. 1910s). Used with permission from General Commission on Archives and History, United Methodist Church.

missionary of the Methodist Episcopal Church, South. She died in 1900, a well-known educator and founder of the prestigious McTyeire Home and School in Shanghai. Three years later, the Southern Methodist mission built the Laura Haygood Memorial School in Suzhou to honor her memory.[13]

Unlike most mission schools in the nineteenth century, which catered to poor families, it was an elite school from the start. "There is the newly built Laura Haygood Memorial School for girls of the higher classes," noted the survey volume of a century of Protestant work in China published in 1907. It offered "exceptional literary advantages" and charged "eighty dollars per annum, not including music"—several times the entire annual income of an average laborer at the time.[14]

The school was built in a quiet eastern corner of Suzhou, next to what was once a moat and the grassy ancient city wall on top of which one could take a stroll in the sunset. Across a narrow street was Soochow University, the pride of Methodist educational missions in China, which opened in 1901. One could look out from the wide, balustraded balconies onto the well-groomed lawn, lined with tall trees. There was a pavilion where students could meet and chat. In autumn, chrysanthemums bloomed in the flower beds and along the school's borders; elegant flower arrangements graced the auditorium, the long hall, and the social room—with carved rosewood tables and a piano—where tea was served.[15]

The rules at Laura Haygood were strict: one's posture had to be decorous, one's gait elegant. School uniforms must be neat. Students filed into the cafeteria to the accompaniment of music, prayed before they dined, and prayed again at bedtime. In its early days, all instruction as well as textbooks were in English, with the exception of the Chinese classes.

In 1917, to meet the growing needs for modern early education in the new republic, Laura Haygood reorganized itself and became primarily a teachers' school. The instructors, American missionaries and Chinese as well, were rigorously trained. The Chinese faculty included some of the bright literary stars of Republican China. Among its graduates were also notable future writers as well as pioneers in modern education such as Wu Yifang, president of Ginling College.[16]

Laura Haygood students distinguished themselves in sports as well. In spring 1948, when Lin Zhao was a junior, the school won championships in basketball and volleyball and received banners for folk dancing and track. Its students also won first and fourth places in an English declamation contest sponsored by the Rotary Club of Suzhou. Its annual concerts featured choruses and a quartet singing such pieces as "Hark, hark! the lark at heaven's gate sings" from Shakespeare's *Cymbeline*. A graduate compared herself to a "plant growing in the big beautiful garden of Laura Haygood" with plenty of "sunshine and good rain" and vowed to also "give sunshine and good rain to other people of the world."[17]

From its early days, Laura Haygood had embodied the reformist spirit in mission education: the biology teacher had girls make charts of mosquitoes and flies for their visits to local homes to promote public health; students devoted their summer vacation to teaching children who had never had opportunities for formal education. The school also cultivated cosmopolitan social mores in its students; for one, Laura Haygood girls formed mixed choirs with male students at Soochow University. Emancipation was on everyone's lips and took tangible form in unbound feet and bobbed hair. Many students also championed coeducation as well as equal inheritance and divorce rights for women.[18]

In the early 1920s, Laura Haygood began publishing a bilingual, semiannual, student-run journal, called *The Laura Haygood Star* (*Jinghai xing*). With an editorial board made up of students and a missionary faculty adviser, it published articles and photographs that portrayed a progressive as well as idyllic campus life—featuring a science lab and a Chinese music band, as well as the school's YWCA chapter. Its literary section was dedicated to translations of Western fairy tales, short stories, and plays, as well as original

creative works by students. The weighty issues that the teenage contributors explored ranged from modern childhood education to
the promotion of vernacular Chinese and women's liberation from
"slavery" and "husbands' oppression." Professionally printed by the
American Presbyterian Mission Press in Shanghai, it had the polish
of a mainstream periodical.[19]

After the disruptions of the Sino-Japanese War, during which
its campus was occupied by the Japanese army, Laura Haygood re-
opened in late 1945 when Jiang Guiyun, the principal since 1927,
returned with a contingent of refugee students. (Jiang's brother,
Jiang Changchuan, had baptized Chiang Kai-shek in 1930 and
served as bishop of the United Methodist Church in China after
1941.) There was a record enrollment by 1947. Its college-preparatory
high school was full, as were the lower grades all the way down to
nursery. Lin Zhao's father, as the former county magistrate, knew
Jiang Guiyun, a connection that apparently secured her admission
to its college-preparatory division.[20]

In its first two decades, Laura Haygood mandated chapel attendance. However, under the rules first instituted in 1925 by the
warlord-controlled Beijing government and enforced by the Nationalist government after 1928, religious affiliation and observance
were made optional. In fact, the school attracted a significant number of students from families with more interest in the career and
marriage prospects of their daughters than the well-being of their
souls. "This year we have to work up from a very small nucleus of
Christians," wrote Annie Eloise Bradshaw, a veteran teacher, in July
1947.[21]

Yet there was fresh interest in Christianity among the students;
thirteen girls joined the church at Easter that year, and a young
Chinese teacher organized a Christian club. A student-faculty group
planned vespers. Worship service was held each day, led either by
a teacher or by students. Not long after she arrived at Laura Haygood, Lin Zhao was baptized by a missionary teacher and joined
the church.[22]

Lin Zhao's existent writings make no mention of how or why she chose to be baptized. In a sense, her conversion was not unexpected: before Laura Haygood, she had briefly attended Vincent Miller Academy, a Presbyterian mission school near her home in the outskirts of Suzhou. A melancholy essay she wrote in May 1947, before her transfer to Laura Haygood, hinted at deep emotions stirred by an image of the Holy Mother.[23]

Many years later, when she was in prison, she would write fondly of the "influence of the humanitarian ideas of liberty, equality, and fraternity" that she came under in mission schools. She also associated mission Christianity with other virtues, such as efficiency and pragmatism. By the time she enrolled in Laura Haygood, her own patriotic flame, passed on from her mother, had already flared up, and the school's Christian concerns with justice apparently appealed to her. For progressive young Christians of the late 1940s, it was not uncommon to identify Christianity with the struggle against the forces of evil in Chinese society. As Wu Yaozong, future leader of the Three-Self Church, put it in 1947, "In this painful and cruel world, the Christian truth has become a force for liberating humanity and moving history forward."[24]

In any event, Lin Zhao put down religious roots during her time at Laura Haygood. As she would discover later in life, they ran much deeper than she initially realized. The many hymns and biblical verses that she called to mind almost two decades later in her prison cell—which was stripped of all materials except party propaganda—were from her mission school years. They would become the imaginary bricks with which she would build her own chapel in her prison cell for weekly "grand church worship" as she put it.[25]

DURING THE TWO years when Lin Zhao was at Laura Haygood, much of the country was ravaged by the war between the Nationalists and the Communists. Inflation skyrocketed as military expenditures exploded. The rise had begun in 1938 following the Japanese invasion. By 1945, more than 80 percent of the Nationalist government's expenditures were financed through "monetary expansion." By 1948, the wholesale price index in Shanghai was 6.6 million times that of 1937.[26]

As the tide of war turned against the authoritarian government of Chiang Kai-shek, it became even more brutal and intolerant of dissent. Conditions deteriorated for ordinary people. For patriotic youths, the country was a sick parent dying from the cancerous growth of the corrupt and repressive yet inept rule of the Guomindang. Only the most extreme treatments—the "new democracy" that the Communists promised and the violent land reform that they conducted in areas under their control—seemed to promise a cure. Before long, Lin Zhao became disenchanted with Laura Haygood's aloofness from radical politics.

For all of the school's reformist spirit, activism at Laura Haygood during the civil war years was well contained within genteel boundaries. The school furnished occasional entertainments for children at a local orphanage and contributed to it "ten per cent of our student church collection." A "flower mission to the hospital" was conducted during the half hour between Sunday school and church; students would put a flower in the hand of each patient.[27]

Indeed, the temperament of the Southern Methodist mission in China as a whole was distinctly Victorian. In 1948, the Methodist Church East China Conference, which oversaw the work in the lower Yangzi valley, including Suzhou, called attention to the importance of "temperance and social service" and urged its pastors to "preach on the subject of temperance" at least once each year. "Special attention should be given to matter of total abstinence from the use of tobacco, opium, liquors, gambling, the wastage of time and money, and from all immoral and excessive practices of both a personal or social nature."[28]

Such social vision had little appeal to the growing number of radical students at Laura Haygood. Communist influence had been felt at the school since the 1920s. The CCP's propaganda against Western imperialism—which also targeted the "cultural invasion" of Christian missions—had long threatened to disrupt its educational program. There was a period after 1927 during which not a single student joined the church in an entire year.[29]

There had also been instances of Communist infiltration at Laura Haygood. For the required course in "party-spirit education" during the early 1930s, the Nationalist government had sent its own teachers to mission schools. One day, the appointed government teacher at Laura Haygood disappeared: he had been arrested. While he had included a standard question—What is the only salvation for China?—on a test he gave his students, the correct answer, he insisted, was communism.[30]

In 1948, another underground Communist who taught at Laura Haygood initiated Lin Zhao into communism. That summer, Lin Zhao secretly joined the CCP. She was sixteen.[31]

LOOKING BACK ON that decision from her prison cell a decade and a half later, Lin Zhao wrote: "In my solemn reflections and painful self-reproach, I always saw my leftist leaning and my pursuit of communism during adolescence as a personal mistake. . . . It could be attributed to both the trend of the time and family influence. Lin Zhao was but treading the same path as most people of my generation! At the time when this young person began following the Communist Party, 'the Communist Party' only meant such things as persecution, arrest, imprisonment, and execution." CCP membership did not carry "the sweet smell of steamed rice and meat broth," she added.[32]

But, to young patriots, persecution, arrest, imprisonment, and execution were part of the glorious price to pay for their heroic struggle against the dark forces of repression and injustice. Lin Zhao's mother, Xu Xianmin, had battled similar forces in Suzhou after the end of the Japanese occupation: two men working for the powerful Bureau of Investigation and Statistics, or *juntong*, the intelligence agency of the Nationalist government, raped and killed a young woman teacher in Suzhou. The victim's mother sought justice but was powerless against the *juntong* system. Xu intervened in support of the prosecution. When a letter of intimidation arrived at her home with a bullet enclosed, she published it in a newspaper. With her help, the plaintiff eventually won the court case against the rapists.[33]

During the civil war years, Xu Xianmin became disillusioned with the Nationalist rule. However, already in her late thirties and a mother of three, she was no longer a revolutionary firebrand. She eventually joined the China Democratic League, a coalition of pro-democracy parties founded in 1941 that sought an alternative to both Chiang Kai-shek's government and the CCP and that included prominent intellectuals such as poet and scholar Wen Yiduo.[34]

Lin Zhao, by contrast, became increasingly enchanted with communism. In early 1947, while she was still a student at Vincent Miller Academy, she helped set up an independent library and reading group—called The Good Earth (Dadi)—in the home of a fellow student. With assistance from an underground CCP branch that targeted teenagers, the group promoted progressive books among local middle school students and even staged street-side dramas to raise funds. They also published their own journal, *The Newborn*, and turned the library into a magnet for pro-Communist youths.[35]

One of Lin Zhao's earliest surviving writings, an essay entitled "Between Generations," was published in *The Newborn* in June 1947, when she was fifteen. It offers a glimpse into her drift toward communism and her break with her parents two years later when they attempted to stop her.

She had found herself drawn to the children in a neighborhood primary school. "They jump and shout under the sun, filled with innocence and life," she wrote. She wanted to see those children "live forever under the sun."

The older generation were "a bunch of rotten wood," she declared. They were "busy making money and grabbing land. They do not wish to see the youths of our generations answer the call of the time; they only wish to see us rot with them." In fact, most young people "have already been poisoned," unable to look into the future. Yet it had fallen precisely upon the young "to change our country and change our society," she added.

When that is accomplished, "there will be no corrupt officials and no dishonest profiteers. There will only be kindhearted people, kindhearted social mores, and kindhearted society." But the new world must be built "with our own blood and sweat as bricks and timber." Those who build it will die, she conceded, "but this kind of death is much better than a silent death at the mercy of others."[36]

Having reached that conclusion, she must have found it a rather simple step to take when she swore the oath of allegiance to become an underground CCP member a year later.

FOR ALL ITS risks, Lin Zhao's choice was not an extraordinary one. Throughout the Nationalist era, patriotic activism of students had increasingly coalesced into Communist-inspired agitation directed at the failures of the Guomindang government to end the civil war and stop Japanese aggression. Theirs was a patriotism fired by the promises of the Communist revolution, whose success in Russia had heralded a bright future. As the dreamy young Qu Qiubai, one of the earliest leaders of the CCP, put it, the Bolshevik victory in 1917 shone "a ray of light, red as blood, that illuminates the whole world."[37]

The Guomindang's savage purge of the Communists in 1927 had driven progressive intellectuals deeper into the arms of the CCP. While many Western-influenced liberal intellectuals heeded the warnings of Hu Shi against *isms* (the student of the American philosopher John Dewey favored independent, critical study of the problems of the day), radical students and intellectuals found promise and urgency in the Communist plan for saving China.

In the 1930s, following the epic, nearly six-thousand-mile Long March of the Communists to Yan'an, a town on the loess plateau in the north, many progressive writers and artists went on their revolutionary pilgrimage to the new base of the CCP. In 1936, American journalist Edgar Snow made a secret visit to Yan'an. His glowing account of Mao's revolution, which he would later call "the most thoroughgoing social revolution in China's three millenniums of history," was published under the title *Red Star over China* in 1937. It was followed by a Chinese edition in 1938 and helped generate an infatuation with the Communists among the young. In 1938 alone, the CCP agency in Xi'an provided papers for more than ten thousand educated youths to make their way to Yan'an, which to them was the cradle of a future China.[38]

Even American general Joseph Stilwell, who during World War II served as commander of the China-Burma-India Theater and was chief of staff to Generalissimo Chiang Kai-shek, was impressed with the Communist program. He described it in simple terms: "Reduce taxes, rents, interest. Raise production, and standard of living." In contrast, the Guomindang government was riddled with "greed, corruption, favoritism, more taxes, a ruined currency, terrible waste of life, callous disregard of all the rights of man," he wrote.[39]

In Lin Zhao's eyes, the Nationalist Party at the time not only was "incapable of controlling and stabilizing the domestic political situation," it was also unable to provide young people with a "peaceful environment for learning." As a result, countless students abandoned their studies and were swept into communism. During the four years of civil war, membership in the CCP more than tripled, to about 4.5 million.[40]

BY THE SUMMER of 1948, the Communists were already on the offensive. Later that year, Communist forces routed the Nationalists in three major battles and came to control almost all areas north of the Yangzi River. "No one will prophesy when the Communists will cross the river, occupy Nanjing, and move on down the railroad to Soochow and Shanghai," wrote Annie Bradshaw, Lin Zhao's teacher at Laura Haygood, in December 1948. "People don't seem to care. There is so much chaos and deprivation now that I believe they would welcome a frying pan as escape from the fire, especially a frying pan so full of Utopian promises."[41]

Throughout the Nationalist period, more than a few mission school students and graduates had in fact welcomed the frying pan of communism, which felt blissfully warm at first. The convergence of communism and Christianity was not as strange as it sounds: both the church and the CCP had decried injustice and oppression. The Communists, like the new generation of Social Gospellers in the Chinese church, sought a new order and a new world.

There was in fact a special affinity between Communist and Christian patriotism for disaffected young students in particular. Lin Zhao's martyred uncle Xu Jinyuan had attended Vincent Miller Academy and Hangchow Christian College (Zhijiang Daxue)— both of them run by the Presbyterian missions—before he joined the Socialist Youth League (later renamed Communist Youth League) in 1923. Under radical Communist influence and spurred on by the anti-imperialist mood in the country, Xu Jinyuan soon joined the anti-Christian movement that had broken out across China in 1922. The campaign demanded the "restoration of education rights" and an end to foreign control of mission schools. In 1924, he cofounded the Suzhou branch of the Anti-Christian Federation. Soon afterward, he joined the Communist Party and, in 1926, became secretary of the party's Suzhou branch.[42]

A few converts to the CCP returned to the church after souring on communism. But in most cases, one hears of the graduation from the church to the party. In his *Red Star over China*, Edgar Snow fondly remembers the underground CCP operative known as Pastor Wang who arranged his trip to Yan'an in 1936. The pastor's real name was Dong Jianwu. Dong had attended the Anglican St. John's University and had become a popular Anglican priest in Shanghai. From 1925 to 1931 he was rector of St. Peter's, a major Anglican church in the city, which drew its membership from the educated middle class in Shanghai's International Settlement.[43]

Unbeknownst to his parishioners, he joined the CCP in 1928, a year after Chiang Kai-shek's coup against the Communists, and turned St. Peter's into a secret hideout and meeting place for Communist leaders in Shanghai who had been driven underground—a "red fortress" with the "sacred aura of St. Peter's" around it, rhapsodizes a historian of the CCP. It was Dong who in the 1930s took care of Mao Zedong's two young sons—their mother having been captured and killed by the Guomindang in 1930—and helped arrange for their safe passage to the Soviet Union in 1936.[44]

Toward the end of her life, Lin Zhao found herself in lone opposition to communism because of her "conscience as a Christian who, once lost, has found her path again." But in 1949, her social conscience was directing her in the opposite direction. The church did not seem to be addressing the systemic evils of an unjust society as boldly as the Communists. Later, she would confront and chastise a rural Catholic priest whose preaching made his flock unresponsive to the CCP's land reform, which redistributed farmland among the poor.[45]

In the Protestant community, the "trend of the time" that Lin Zhao referred to was one of progressive Christians finding communism to be the next sacred step of social commitment. "The Nationalist Party was always a disgrace" is how Lin Zhao later recalled her adolescent views. Wu Leichuan, chancellor of Yenching University—the crown jewel of missionary educational enterprise in China—called Jesus a "revolutionary" and warned the church not to defend the status quo but to seek the kingdom of God in a "new social order." If Christianity were to have a future in China, he argued, it had to accommodate the revolutionary cause.[46]

Wu himself was on the way to joining the CCP when he died in 1944, but many Yenching graduates actually took that step. When Yenching's president John Leighton Stuart met Mao Zedong in Chongqing in August 1945, Mao bragged about the presence of many of Stuart's former students in Yan'an. "I laughingly replied that I was well aware of that and hoped that they were proving a credit to their training," Stuart recalled.[47]

Many missionaries felt a profound ambivalence toward communism—supportive of its noble ends but troubled by its violent means. Some would have been sympathetic to Lin Zhao's decision to join the Communist struggle to create a more just China. Frank Joseph Rawlinson, editor-in-chief of *The Chinese Recorder*, the leading missionary journal in China, found himself "caught just between the old capitalistic system and that of a system in which the goods of life are distributed more equitably," as he told his children in a letter in 1934. He wished to work in support of workers on strike; he also organized discussions among missionaries to address "the question of Russia as a possible guide to a 'Christian' economic order." Rawlinson had arrived in China a fundamentalist Southern Baptist missionary. It was the plight of the Chinese poor that gave him a soft spot for the revolution.[48]

Likewise, conditions in China radicalized the worldview of Maud Russell, who arrived in 1917 as a YWCA secretary but became "a Marxist, committed to socialist revolution in China." Under Russell's influence, Deng Yuzhi, who began working for the YWCA in the 1920s and headed its Labor Bureau in the 1930s, came to identify with the goals of the CCP, which in her view accorded with Christian values. During the 1930s, she assisted Russell in teaching a course on Christianity and communism at a YWCA student conference and, though not a party member herself, helped the CCP arrange to send the party's cultural workers—including Mao's future wife Jiang Qing—to teach in YWCA night schools for women workers in Shanghai.[49]

On October 1, 1949, as a member of the Chinese People's Political Consultative Conference, Deng was invited to join government officials on the viewing platform when Mao declared the founding of the People's Republic.[50]

FOR A WHILE, Lin Zhao was able to hold her twin identities as a Christian and a Communist in an uneasy balance. Still a student at Laura Haygood, she undertook clandestine activities for the party, making and distributing mimeographed copies of the CCP's propaganda materials. "All it took was a tin of oil-based ink. Nothing else was necessary. You pinned the engraved stencil to the desk using thumbtacks. . . . How was it difficult!"[51]

But as she was nearing the end of her senior year at Laura Haygood, she felt torn between her two loyalties. In spring 1949, just weeks before the People's Liberation Army crossed the Yangzi River and captured Nanjing, the Nationalist government's capital, Lin Zhao joined a dozen or so radical students at Laura Haygood in demanding a school holiday to mark International Women's Day on March 8 and to celebrate "the happy life of women in the Soviet Union."[52] The ensuing clash with the school authorities apparently alienated her from Laura Haygood. It likely also led to the fraying of her ties to the church as a whole.

Demands made by mission school students to suspend classes for patriotic reasons had been a constant test for administrators since the Revolution of 1911, which ended the last imperial dynasty in China. They bespoke the unhealed wound to national pride since China's humiliating defeats at the hands of foreign powers in the nineteenth century. John Dewey observed, after spending two years in the country from 1919 to 1921, that "wherever a few are gathered together in China the favorite indoor sport is 'saving China.'"[53]

That was especially the case on school campuses. Like most mission schools, Laura Haygood sought to dampen the revolutionary zeal of its students. "A delicate balance is required," noted Annie Bradshaw, "if the teacher is to show proper sympathy with young people who are convinced that they must 'save our country—now!' and at the same time hold up academic standards."[54]

Progressive students were ever happy to upset that balance. After Japan's seizure of Manchuria in September 1931, for instance, a large contingent of Laura Haygood students made up their mind to go to Nanjing to demand that Chiang Kai-shek declare war on Japan and personally lead an army to Manchuria. At the time, the principal compromised and allowed those who obtained permission from their parents to leave campus.[55]

Laura Haygood's administration had often suspected Communist agitation as being behind these and other eruptions. By and large, the American teachers at Laura Haygood frowned upon communism and, for all their dismay at the economic collapse and deteriorating societal order, tended to side with Chiang Kai-shek and the Guomindang, whose policies "sound as if they had been drafted by Christian statesmen."[56]

Their response to the demand from Lin Zhao's class about International Women's Day was predictably lukewarm. The director of religious education, who had recently returned from a period of training at Scarritt College for Christian Workers in Tennessee, lectured the senior class on the crudity of the idea.

"The Hemp Sack came and gave us a good chiding," Lin Zhao wrote, using the unflattering nickname that she and her friends had bestowed on the director. "She started by claiming that women in America were already completely free and equal (?) and never needed to celebrate March 8." The director also reminded the students that their primary responsibility was to study hard. She added "in a stern voice: you are all hot-blooded youths. Be careful and don't let yourselves be used by other people!"[57]

Lin Zhao could not possibly have imagined that a decade and a half later she would use almost the same words when reflecting on her youthful devotion to the revolution. "Countless hot-blooded youths fell victim to the agitation," she wrote in her letter to *People's Daily* in 1965. "They abandoned their studies, forsook honest work, got swept into the political whirlpool, and became the tools of political careerists!"[58] Perhaps at some level, she was recalling the admonition of Laura Haygood's director of religious education, which she had spurned.

But in early March 1949, Lin Zhao and her friends were unrelenting as they claimed their right to celebrate "our own holiday" and "spread the seeds" of revolutionary womanhood. In the end, the school authorities met their demands halfway: an hour and a half would be set aside for celebrations on March 8, but there would be no cancellation of classes.[59]

The administration apparently also reported the clash to the authorities. Either as a result of this incident or because Lin Zhao's clandestine printing of mimeographed CCP propaganda materials became known, she and a fellow student named Li Biying—also an underground CCP member—were blacklisted by the local security apparatus. The party's intelligence in Suzhou learned of this and warned its local cell of the danger. As a result, two "progressive teachers" at Laura Haygood disappeared one night. The party operatives also ordered Lin Zhao and Li Biying to leave Suzhou for their own safety. Li decamped for Shanghai; Lin Zhao ignored the order, convinced that, as the daughter of a member of the National Assembly, she was safe. For her refusal to obey a direct command from the CCP, her party membership was revoked.[60]

Lin Zhao's disregard for what must have felt like an arbitrary order to leave Suzhou was in character: throughout her life she followed her own judgments. But it was a willfulness that the party could not tolerate. The loss of her party membership on the eve of the CCP's victory in the civil war was to weigh heavily on her. It was "a shameful blemish" in her revolutionary career, as she put it in a letter to a comrade. She was going to do penance later by throwing herself into some of the hardest work the party required of its young devotees.[61]

SUZHOU AND THE Nationalist capital Nanjing fell to the People's Liberation Army in late April 1949. That summer, Lin Zhao graduated from Laura Haygood. A brilliant student (except in math), she had distinguished herself in classical Chinese, having been tutored by her erudite father, who meted out strikes to the palm for any imperfectly remembered passages.[62]

Her parents expected her to go to college, and got a rude shock when they found out that she had secretly applied—and had been admitted—to the South Jiangsu Journalism Vocational School. A party-run institution of dubious academic standards that prepared journalists and propagandists for the revolution, it opened in Wuxi, forty kilometers from Suzhou, in July 1949.[63]

Peng Guoyan was not among those cheering the Communist victory. As the Guomindang's rule unraveled, he made it known to his family that he was prepared to follow in the footsteps of Bo Yi and Shu Qi, princes of a kingdom at the end of the ancient Shang dynasty (ca. 1600–1046 BCE).[64] After the fall of Shang, the two had refused to serve or take food from the ruler of the ascendant Zhou dynasty. They lived as hermits on a mountain, ate tree bark and wild plants, died from starvation, and were immortalized as paragons of unbending loyalty and integrity for the literati throughout Chinese history.

Lin Zhao's mother, Xu Xianmin, cautiously supported the Communist cause. In the final months of the civil war, she used her connections in the Nationalist government to secretly aid the Communists. When two underground CCP operatives were dispatched to Suzhou to "instigate rebellion," she put them in touch with Shi Jianqiao, the famed female assassin of the former warlord Sun Chuanfang. Shi succeeded in obtaining important intelligence on Shanghai's military police headquarters, which she passed to the two CCP agents. Xu Xianmin also helped them instigate the defection of several Nationalist agents, and persuaded some local self-defense groups to submit to CCP leadership.[65]

It was an entirely different matter when Lin Zhao chose a CCP journalism school over college. Xu Xianmin was furious and forbade her to go. Peng Guoyan had warned her about her susceptibility to manipulation by career revolutionaries. "It is the utmost cruelty to use the innocent zeal of young people for political purposes," he told her.[66]

But it was to no avail. Lin Zhao was unyielding, and escaped through her bedroom window one night. She was caught by her mother and brought back home, but her mind was already made up, she announced, and nothing could stop her, not even her mother's threat to expel her from the family. Xu Xianmin told her that she would have to sign an agreement with her parents vowing "no contacts while alive; no mourning in the event of death" if she left the house. She grabbed a pen, signed the paper, and departed.

When Lin Zhao was filling out her enrollment forms at the journalism school and came to the question about the class origins of her parents, she put down "reactionary bureaucrats."[67] She had left them in order to become a revolutionary journalist and to help build a new society, where the children would be able to live under the sun.

two

EXCHANGING LEATHER SHOES FOR STRAW SANDALS

LIN ZHAO'S DEPARTURE FOR THE SOUTH JIANGSU JOURNALISM VOCA-tional School left her parents exasperated, but it must have felt like a liberation from petty bourgeois self-interest for her, as she turned to the glorious task of building a socialist China. As a high school graduate, Lin Zhao was already considered a member of the class of intellectuals in a country in which 80 percent of the population was illiterate. The students' assumption of an outsized public role for themselves was rooted in a Confucian tradition more than two thousand years old: "the scholar takes all under heaven as his responsibility" (*shi yi tianxia wei jiren*). The imperial civil service examination system channeled the aspirations of all scholars (*shi*) into government service and reinforced that sense of calling.[1]

The abolition of the imperial examination in 1905 had released the scholars from their presumptive role of governing, but the tradition did not die. During the 1910s–1920s, as a new generation of Chinese intellectuals turned their back on Confucianism in favor of Mr. Democracy (*de xiansheng*) and Mr. Science (*sai xiansheng*) from the West, they continued to view "all under heaven" as their exclusive responsibility.[2] After the Communist victory, the door to becoming revolutionary *shi* was thrust wide open. In 1949, Lin Zhao was among more than a thousand young people who applied to the South Jiangsu Journalism Vocational School.

The school was located in Huishan, a picturesque suburb of Wuxi. It had emerged from an earlier party-run journalism school that opened in northern Jiangsu in 1946, one of the four training centers for propagandists that the CCP established during the civil war to help shape public opinion and win popular support.

Its prototype was the Resist-Japan Military and Political University—short-term training camps for military and government leaders, which the CCP had started in Yan'an and maintained throughout the war of resistance. Thousands of educated youths swarmed to these camps in the late 1930s, evidence of the success of the CCP in winning the educated over to its revolutionary cause.[3]

In 1949, Lin Zhao was 1 of 220 admitted. "I remember her pretty face, her elegant bearing, and her mandarin Chinese with notable Suzhou accent," wrote Li Maozhang, who first met her in the fall of 1949. "She was talkative, witty and humorous, and often sharp and caustic," Li added. She wore two French braids. "While chatting with others, she would untie each of the braids at the end . . . and braid them again, her head slightly tilted to one side, looking composed and carefree while chatting, laughing, and braiding."[4]

The curriculum consisted of classes in news editing, management of news agencies, and telecommunications. No tuition was collected; room and board were provided free of charge, though conditions were spare. There was no classroom to speak of, or even a blackboard. Students either brought their own stools or sat on the ground; the teachers would cool themselves in summertime with a palm-leaf fan and a large pot of tea.[5]

Students were divided into classes, which were subdivided into study groups. Each study group, made up of nine or ten youths, shared a room: male and female roomed together, with only a mosquito net to divide the genders. "We lived in peace with one another with no troubles; there was no peach-colored news [sexual scandal]

Lin Zhao, front row, first from right, with South Jiangsu Journalism Vocational School classmates, 1950. Courtesy of Ni Jingxiong.

till we graduated," a former student recalled. For all the hardships, their spirits were high. Out of Lin Zhao's class, several eventually became nationally known journalists and writers.[6]

At Huishan, students were trained to become both reporters and fomenters of the revolution. In ten months, they would complete their education and be assigned by the party to the frontline of the propaganda war. Meanwhile, during the fall term, three months were spent in rural areas, where they lived with and learned from the peasants, working hard to obtain "a diploma from the 'University of the Peasants,'" as Lin Zhao put it, echoing a popular phrase of the time.[7]

Lin Zhao's reporting on her class's preparation for the journalistic stint in rural areas was an exercise in revolutionary piety. Entitled "A Few Days before Going Down to the Countryside," it was her first published piece as a journalist. She wrote of the students' mix of excitement and trepidation, and noted that some students had questioned the school's decision, wondering if it was a good idea for them to interrupt their studies and go down to the countryside.

"Let's just obey the [party] organization in all matters," Lin Zhao urged. "The organization is always thoughtful and thorough in its considerations." The most practical issue was backpacks and straw sandals. "It is said that those feet that are unaccustomed to straw sandals will have blisters when the skin is rubbed off," she observed. "Going down to the countryside—this is quite a practical test. Don't fail the test!" she exhorted.[8]

It was genuine piety, matched by a revolutionary humility. "We may make fools of ourselves and run into difficulties, but we are not afraid! We are going to live with the many suffering peasants and get to understand their thoughts and feelings; we are going to learn . . . many things that neither schools nor books can teach. We are going to cut off the last remaining section of the tail in our body."[9]

That strange metaphor required no explanation. The coinage was Mao's, in his characteristically earthy style. The tail to be amputated was the three *isms*: subjectivism, dogmatism, and sectarianism.

On March 9, 1942, the party newspaper *Liberation Daily* had published an editorial, drafted by Mao's secretary Hu Qiaomu and revised by Mao himself, under the title "Dogmatism and Pants." It rebuked the learned, often Russian-trained Marxists within the CCP—whose theoretical sophistication irked the irregularly educated Mao—telling them to "take off the pants" because "the problem lies in their lower, honorable bodies." Since "a tail lies hidden under the pants, you have to take them off to see it." Only then can one cut the tail of dogmatism off "with a knife."[10]

Beginning with the Yan'an Rectification Campaign of 1942–1945, "taking off the pants" for the purpose of exposing the tail of unrectified thinking meant self-scrutiny of the most unforgiving kind.

All those in Yan'an were required to keep "soul-searching notes" (*fanxing biji*) to lay bare their thoughts and renounce their former selves. A special party committee enjoyed "the right to demand to read the notes of every comrade with no prior notice." Mao made it clear that keeping those notes for the party's examination was mandatory. It was the party's iron discipline, "more formidable and harder than the golden headband" of the Monkey King.[11]

Just as the magical headband had subdued the mischievous Monkey King, the protagonist in the classic mythological novel *Journey to the West*, Mao demanded that every follower of the CCP revolution yield to party discipline. "The cruel method of psychological coercion that Mao calls moral purification has created a stifling atmosphere inside the party," noted a Comintern representative in Yan'an. "A not negligible number of party activists in the region have committed suicide, have fled, or have become psychotic."[12]

By 1945 the disciplinary requirement to figuratively undress had resulted in a new clause in the new party constitution, which was passed at the Seventh Party Congress held that year. Now, CCP members were required to use the method of "criticism and self-criticism to constantly examine the mistakes and shortcomings in one's own work."[13] It was to be done in public, and the party was the final arbitrator regarding the adequacy and the consequences of self-criticism.

AT JOURNALISM SCHOOL, Lin Zhao, like her fellow students, surrendered to the party by exposing her hidden failings. She had initially resisted public "examination of thoughts" and was prepared to go only as far as "pouring out my inner thoughts to two or three bosom friends on a night of cool breeze and bright moon." Things changed after her class went to the countryside. In mid-October, her team held a week of intense self-study, and she overcame her own resistance.

It was strange that, after that examination, I felt a special ease in my heart. My burden of thoughts had been laid down; I was released from vexations. . . . When I did my examination, I felt excited; I also felt happy. . . . I now understand that, to release myself from my own thought burden . . . the only way is to completely bare myself, and accept the criticisms of my comrades. Only this way can I attain to the goal of self-reform and make myself walk the path of a new life.[14]

Lin Zhao had become a true believer. As a convert she had been given a new life in a noble, collective body, and the revolution had both evoked and satisfied her passion for self-renunciation.[15]

For Lin Zhao, as for other members of the educated class in the Communist ranks, the loss of individual autonomy was perhaps inevitable. Since their heyday during the May Fourth era of the 1910s–1920s, when intellectuals were the embodiment of enlightenment and the hope for national salvation, their influence had been on a steady decline. During the Northern Expedition of 1926–1927, Communist propaganda teams had galvanized the masses in the countryside with the slogan "Down with the intellectual class" (dadao zhishi jieji).[16]

Under the "revolutionary dispensation" of the CCP, intellectuals were seen as useful collaborators in the great undertaking of the creation of a new society. Like skilled artisans, they were deprived of the "authority of design," and in fact their very selfhood. In the face of national emergencies—the Japanese invasion and the civil war—it became even more imperative for intellectuals to identify with national salvation. Mao had also reminded the party in 1927 that "political power grows out of the barrel of a gun." It was guns, not learning or reason, that would establish the new political order in China.[17]

Over the years, the party had successfully mobilized the distrust and hostility of commoners toward the educated elite. Guilt-ridden about their own privileges, the intellectuals had, in response, found emotional release in self-abasement before the people and the party that claimed to represent them. Since the Yan'an Rectification Campaign, the revolutionary rite of passage for intellectuals was to descend into the pit of remorse, confess their sins against the party, bury the old self, and emerge into a new life as a "new person." These new selves would renounce their former bourgeois class—along with its lifestyle, manners, and literary and artistic taste.[18]

In most cases, the conviction of one's ineffectual old self was accompanied by a yearning to attain to the high ideals that the party represented. Many intellectuals began mimicking revolutionary writers.

Months into her training at journalism school, Lin Zhao had come to repudiate her former literary practice—her writings about herself, her emotions and dreams, in her "narrow circle of life." Those writings had been "exquisitely decorated, filled with bourgeois sentiments, singing praises to 'the smiles of life' and 'the new life of the good earth.'" It was only after she "entered the revolutionary school" that she began to understand that "literature must be popularized." Her reading of progressive writers such as Zhao Shuli helped her understand the spirit of literature for the masses.

She also broke with her earlier reliance on inspiration for writing and saw the need for writing on demand. "As Comrade Qiaomu put it," she wrote, quoting Mao's secretary, "we need to train ourselves to master the skill of completing a news report in ten minutes." And she overcame her former distrust of collective writing, for in it "I see the wisdom of the masses and the strength of the collective."[19]

Lin Zhao's conversion to revolutionary prose resulted in a series of saccharine journalistic pieces, which she produced with diligent zeal. She sang the praises of her revolutionary school as a "big, warm family," where comrades cared for one another like brothers and sisters. She also wrote of the voluntarism of her fellow students who, while in the countryside, dropped their books and rushed to help unload a boatload of firewood and who picked up stray pieces of kindling to make sure that they did not "lose any revolutionary property."[20]

She later wrote a poem dedicated to the year 1950, celebrating the reduction of land rent for the peasants in spring and the harvest and land reform—the overthrow of the landlords and the return of land to the poor—in autumn: "One cannot sing of all the grace and favor of the Communist Party that is higher than the sky and deeper than the earth." After the outbreak of the Korean War that same year, in which China deployed a "volunteer army" of more than 1.3 million to "resist America, aid Korea," Lin Zhao would also produce a glowing report about a young girl who embroidered a giant red star and the characters "It is glorious to join the army" on a satchel she had given her beloved, urging him to be a hero in the war.[21]

THE FORMULAS OF revolutionary writing dated to the late 1920s and early 1930s. In March 1930, with increasing numbers of Communist intellectuals seeking haven in the International Settlement in Shanghai, the CCP orchestrated the formation of the League of Left-Wing Writers in Shanghai, which drew together both dedicated Communist writers and other leftist intellectuals such as Lu Xun and Ding Ling. At a time when the significance of individuals paled in comparison to that of national salvation, literature must be a "fighting tool," as CCP leader Qu Qiubai put it. It must advance the cause of revolution.

Ding Ling's short story "One Certain Night," written in 1931, served as an example: more than two dozen revolutionary prisoners, who had been chained together and marched through snow and sleet to an execution site, burst into singing "The Internationale," the de facto anthem of the global Communist movement, as a machine gun opened fire. As they sang, "darkness fled. Appearing before them was an expanse of radiant light, the establishment of a new country."[22]

The production of revolutionary literature expanded in Yan'an, where, in 1938, Mao Zedong approved the establishment of the Lu Xun Academy of Arts and Literature. Lu Xun had died in 1936, so the CCP had a free hand in appropriating his legacy of "cold ridicule and burning satire," saving them only for the ills under the old society, from which the Communist revolution promised a complete deliverance. Hundreds of revolutionary writers, poets, playwrights, artists, and musicians were trained at the academy. Some went on to create monumental works of revolutionary art such as the opera *The White-Haired Girl*, in which a peasant girl, oppressed and raped by the evil landlord, flees to the mountain caves. Years later, her hair turns all white, and she is reduced to a ghost-like being, until the Communists come and emancipate her.

The boundaries for writers and artists were set by Mao's addresses at the Yan'an Forum on Literature and Art in May 1942. Literature and art must serve the masses—workers, peasants, and revolutionary soldiers—and must be "led by the proletariat," Mao said. Those who chose individualism took "the stand of the petty bourgeoisie" and would be "nothing but a phony writer." Revolutionary writers and artists "must go among the masses," to the "only source, the broadest and richest source, in order to observe, experience, study and analyze . . . all the vivid patterns of life and struggle."[23]

IN LIN ZHAO'S case, close identification with the poor peasants did reveal to her a world she had not known before. Her time in the countryside gave her writing a new earthiness, evident in a narrative poem she coauthored after witnessing a "recounting bitterness" meeting. Entitled "Wearing Out My Eyes with Expecting—Records of a Peasant's Indictment," it was in the voice of an ill-treated, long-suffering peasant in the old society:

> On someone else's soil I trod; over my head was someone else's sky,
> I labored in someone else's fields and thirty years went by.
> . . . . . .
> Not a single grain was left each year for the next,
> My back hurt; my tendons ached; my bones were dry.
> . . . . . .
> My two crumbling rooms were like a pigsty,
> Not big enough for a cow to turn to the side.

When his son contracts typhoid, the peasant has to borrow rice from his landlord at a ruinous interest rate to pay for the treatment. He is then forced to send his son to serve as a long-term laborer at the landlord's house, as payment of his debt. The toil cripples the young man's health; he collapses in the fields, coughs up blood, and breathes his last.

> *Without its wings a bird cannot fly;*
> *All is in vain for a peasant without his land to live by.*
> . . . . . .
> *Even the clay tiles on the roof would be turned over after a while,*
> *I have waited until this day, wearing out my eyes.*
> . . . . . .
> *Thirty years of bitterness, I have now got to its bottom,*
> *Chairman Mao's grace is higher than the sky.*[24]

Lin Zhao felt a fire burning in her heart as she penned writings like this. "Each day that I am alive, I will not cease to serve the cause of people's literature," she wrote in a letter to Ni Jingxiong, her closest friend from journalism school. She wanted her writing to "benefit the people's cause of liberation," not to bring herself "fame and profit. How insignificant are they compared to our cause as a whole!"[25]

Only a few years earlier, when she was fifteen, Lin Zhao had written a potent, if sentimental, piece called "Tears at Dusk." In it she had explored, with sensibility and subtlety, her self-doubts, despair, and the mysterious power of religion to offer solace.[26] Gone now was the voice of a searching, lonely individual, replaced by revolutionary buoyancy.

WHILE IN THE countryside in 1949, living among peasants, Lin Zhao felt that she was shedding her former self—the "spoiled, willful" girl who had been easily offended and quick to anger. Her guilt over her own bourgeois family origins made the scarcity of rural life feel like a welcome penance. Even when she grew tired of the monotonous diet of plain rice mixed with unflavored vegetables, "seeing the ordinary people living on corn and pumpkin all the time, I feel that it is better for me to live like this," she wrote her middle school friend Lu Zhenhua, "because I feel peace inside my heart; I no longer feel guilty toward the people."[27]

And she came to admire the virtue of the masses, in life as in art. At a gala celebrating the Mid-Autumn Festival, with hundreds of local people in attendance, the peasants' association presented a skit called "Liberation," which they created, directed, and acted in themselves. According to Lin Zhao, the peasants—playing the landlord, the usurer, and the head of the village's mutual-responsibility group—were "vivid in their laughs, their fury, and their curses." Since the dialogue was in the local dialect, she found the satire more nuanced. "When they played the peasants, there was nothing of the feigned and strained acting that we arrogant intellectuals get into when we play the peasants," she wrote. "That skit made me understand the boundless wisdom and creativity of the masses. The masses are the real geniuses. And I came to understand more fully what it means to go 'from the masses, to the masses.'"[28]

The quoted words were Mao's. "In all the practical work of our party, all correct leadership is necessarily 'from the masses, to the masses,'" Mao had written in a directive to the Central Committee of the CCP in June 1943.[29] Lin Zhao's conviction of its truth was apparently heartfelt: she was writing to her friend Lu Zhenhua, who was working at the Suzhou branch of the Communist Youth League.

Beneath her revolutionary piety was the unabated shame of having lost her party membership. In fact, she was keeping a distance from Lu Zhenhua, a party member, and from all her progressive friends in Suzhou. As one who had previously "dropped out of the ranks" of the party, she was tormented by a sense of inferiority, she admitted to Lu. "It feels a bit like being too ashamed to see the elders on the east side of the river," a reference to the predicament of Xiang Yu, a mighty third-century BCE warrior whose forces destroyed the Qin dynasty but who lost his bid for the throne to commoner Liu Bang and chose to take his own life rather than return to his village.[30]

For his part, Lu was in love with her. He asked to come to see her, but she made it clear that they would only be comrades and refused him. "Whoever wants to date me, I shall feel sorry for his misfortune," she wrote Lu. "I have a heart of stone; he would most likely just be courting vexations. Moreover, in these circumstances, I tend not to take responsibility for somebody else's vexations." She did ask him to check on her family, to see if they had been placed under "penal control" (*guanzhi*) as enemies of the revolution. *Guanzhi* usually entailed restrictions on personal movement, loss of political rights, and at times forced menial labor.[31]

Lin Zhao's relations with her parents remained fraught. As a seventeen-year-old, she still missed home from time to time, but her shame as a tainted revolutionary was enough to stiffen her toward them.[32] She had often clashed with her parents when she was still living with them, she told Lu. "You know I have always had a rebellious spirit. Now that we live in a postliberation era, would I make the mistake of compromise, surrender to them, and lose my stand?"

Yet, breaking her earlier vow to completely sever ties with her family, she wrote to her parents in early October, three months after she left home, admitting to some mistakes when she renounced them. For some time, there was no response. "I don't quite care," she told Lu. "There is an unbending temperament in me. . . . One lives on after leaving family. In the meantime, I am indifferent to their financial support." As a journalism school student, she received some monthly stipends, "and I earn some royalties for my writing," she added. "Do you think I lack determination?"[33]

Maybe she did. Within months of leaving home, she traveled back to Suzhou twice. On the second occasion, she stayed briefly with her parents. However, relations remained lukewarm. Her parents were unresponsive to her exhortations to join the revolution, and she continued to worry about their "attitude toward the government." Her father Peng Guoyan had lost his job after the Communist takeover. He would have chosen to leave mainland China for Taiwan had not his wife—the center of a "matriarchal family" as Lin Zhao quipped at one point—vetoed the plan.[34]

After 1949, Peng refused to "bow down his head and admit guilt" for his work for the Guomindang, insisting that there had been good people in the Nationalist government, that the Guomindang had done good things, and that, anyway, few people even had the opportunity to work for the Communists rather than the Nationalists before 1949. Early on under the new Communist regime, he often secretly listened to Voice of America, whose broadcast to China had started in the early 1940s. It was an act of "surreptitiously listening to enemy broadcast," which Lin Zhao allegedly found out and reported to the government. In 1955, he was labeled a "historical counterrevolutionary."[35]

Lin Zhao's mother, Xu Xianmin, who had cofounded a bus company in Suzhou in the late 1940s, continued to serve as associate manager and deputy chair of the board of trustees of the company after 1949—remaining, in her daughter's eyes, a member of the exploiting class. "I so much want to win over my mother, but I can't help it: my heart is willing but my strength is weak. I can only sigh when I see other people's parents becoming progressive."[36]

Xu came to visit Lin Zhao at school a few times, bringing her money and supplies. Lin Zhao accepted the gifts with little visible excitement. She was more heartened by the political awakening of her twelve-year-old sister Lingfan, a student at Laura Haygood, who "has more or less come under my influence; she is progressive, and has learned to tell the difference between 'the good' and 'the bad' in other people from a political point of view."

Still, the danger of bourgeois influence lurked in the family. "If my sister stays home all the time, she will be corrupted—she will be brought up as lady material." Her most difficult relationship was with her father. "My father hates me to the bone; we have not corresponded for a long while," she wrote in April 1950.[37]

IN MAY 1950, after three months in the countryside, a few journalism courses, and multiple group sessions devoted to thought examination and the study of government policies, Lin Zhao's class graduated from the South Jiangsu Journalism Vocational School. The year had given her high spirits. "Life at the journalism school is full of vivacity and joy," she wrote to Lu Zhenhua. "It is youthful." At the graduation ceremony, a congratulatory banner given by Wuxi county's party committee read: "Speak for the people; do propaganda for land reform!"[38]

According to her friend Ni Jingxiong, Lin Zhao was a prominent student at the journalism school. She had published some of her reporting, was known for being outspoken, and enjoyed public debate and the limelight. At graduation, the local Federation of Literary and Art Circles expressed interest in recruiting her.[39]

Instead, she volunteered to go to the countryside and experience the rural revolution firsthand. "I have no desire to become a phony writer," she told Ni, echoing a phrase that both Lu Xun and Mao had used. She wanted instead to "participate in land reform, so as to forge and reform myself." Her spirits were robust, even though her health was not. "Occasionally I run a low fever, but as long as I am not sick in bed, I don't count myself sick." It may have been the beginning of tuberculosis, but she did not see a doctor. That would have been a sign of petty bourgeois softness.[40]

Lin Zhao left Huishan in May to join a work team under the Suzhou Rural Work Corps. Over the next year and a half, she would help conduct land reform in four different areas in Jiangsu province. In September 1949, the Chinese People's Political Consultative Conference had passed the "Common Program"—a proto-constitution set of policy guidelines—which outlined an ambitious plan for rural reform through rent reduction and land redistribution. In line with the practices that had been established in Communist-controlled areas during the 1940s, the land reform program was coordinated at the local level by work teams with the assistance of hastily organized peasant associations.

In June, she wrote to Lu Zhenhua, asking him to help her purchase a color portrait print of Chairman Mao from the New China Bookstore in Suzhou. "I fell in love with it the last time I was in Suzhou, but they ran out of stock," she explained. "Since I came to the countryside, my spirits have never been low. . . . By the middle of this month, my term as a provisional Youth League member will expire. After I become a regular, I will try even harder to be a good Youth League member. I am not burdened with any worries now. Very happy. Full of energy in whatever I do."[41] At the time, membership in the league was a stepping-stone toward party membership.

The CCP's rural reform expanded across China in the second half of 1950. In most cases, the work teams, with help from peasant associations, would identify and isolate landlords and set up violent confrontations—denunciation meetings—at which tenant farmers were encouraged to seek vigilante justice. In July 1950, the Government Administrative Council (later renamed State Council) had authorized the formation of "people's tribunals," made up of local activists, against "local tyrants," bandits, and others opposed to land reform. As rural reform got under way, between one and two million people were killed. Several million more were placed under penal control, extra-legal punishments that varied in severity.[42]

In one township selected for a model land reform program, Lin Zhao and her teammates were each put in charge of one hamlet with more than a hundred households. It was difficult work. "I was fearful at first," she told Lu in October, but had found a magic weapon, which was to "consult with the masses" instead of dictating to them. Three months later, she wrote from another "backward" village, where land had been redistributed and the grains requisitions quota was nearly met. She told Lu that "the work is very dangerous," and she was afraid she might not be able to complete it in time.[43]

The danger she faced stemmed from covert resistance to land redistribution and grains requisitions. Across China, more than three thousand work team members on requisitions assignments had been killed in rural areas in the first year after the Communist

Lin Zhao, March 1951, as
a member of Suzhou Rural
Work Corps land reform team.
Courtesy of Ni Jingxiong.

takeover. The big landlords, who typically lived in the cities, often tried to hide their landholdings and wealth. Others resorted to more nefarious measures. Ni Jingxiong, Lin Zhao's journalism school friend and a fellow member of the Suzhou Rural Work Corps, was assigned to a work team in the Lake Tai area. She was warned not to venture out at night, lest she be "plopped into Lake Tai like a wonton," as others had been.[44]

Lin Zhao worked feverishly during the day, and spent most of the evenings writing. "I often stayed up until after 11 p.m., sometimes after 1 a.m." One of the works she completed during this period was a play in the Suzhou dialect, which was well received when it was staged in the countryside. It featured a peasant wife—played by Ni Jingxiong—as protagonist, who exhibited exemplary revolutionary consciousness: she urged her husband to make a prodigious self-sacrifice in contributing "public grains."[45]

Lin Zhao, first from left, with fellow members of Suzhou Rural Work Corps land reform team, 1951. Courtesy of Ni Jingxiong.

Lin Zhao as a member of Suzhou Rural Work Corps land reform team, 1951. Courtesy of Ni Jingxiong.

苏南农工团十一队太仓八里工作组 1951

Lin Zhao, front row, second from right, with fellow members of Suzhou Rural Work Corps land reform team, 1951. Courtesy of Ni Jingxiong.

By early 1951, Lin Zhao was coughing constantly and often running a fever. "Even if I become really sick," she told Ni, "I will work till the last moment. Maybe I will live a shorter life than others, but if my life is fully utilized, I shall have no regret dying young." In March, an X-ray revealed stage 1 tuberculosis, and her work team leader advised her to rest, but she insisted that she had to stay at her post until land reform in the area was completed. "After all, it is not fun to lie in a sickbed in this spring of life."[46]

Over the first two years of Communist rule, the mass campaign of rural reform remade the countryside. It also remade Lin Zhao. "The mass movement has a huge tempering effect on people," she told Lu Zhenhua, and added that, for her, it marked only the beginning of her own thought reform.[47]

That required a renunciation of her upbringing. Throughout her childhood, her father Peng Guoyan had worked to pass on his own classical learning to her, especially in early Chinese literature. He had wanted to rear her as a boy, to see her develop into a scholar in the traditional vein—learned, independent, proud, disdainful of the vulgarity of the worldly, and upholding Confucian values of loyalty, propriety, and personal integrity. To him, these qualities embodied the upright spirit of the Chinese people, which could be traced to the Yellow Emperor.[48]

Yet the spirit that her father had instilled in her and the values she had been taught at Laura Haygood began to dissipate as she threw herself into revolutionary work in the countryside. Her job required a proletarian tough-mindedness she had not possessed before—a disregard for civility and a contempt for the claims or the pain of individuals if they stood in the way of the righteous cause of making a new society.

When Lin Zhao first went to the countryside in 1949 after the autumn harvest—for the three-month stint in a rural area as part of her journalistic training—her team had been asked to help with the government's grains requisitions. At the time, some fellow students had expressed misgivings about demanding grains from the peasants, but Lin Zhao insisted on following the party's dictates. She told one group of peasants that the government was their own and that "what is taken from the people is used for the people." It was for the villagers to sort out how much the extremely poor would have to contribute, but the village collectively had to meet its requisitions quota. "We are not devouring or wasting people's blood and sweat; we are here for the long-term benefits of all the people," she assured them.[49]

Now as a land reform work team member, she found herself facing the landlords themselves. The encounters were tense. In the township of Chengxiang in Taicang county, more than 100,000 kilograms of rice were forced out of the nearly three hundred landlords, "but the masses are still unsatisfied; they said that the strike [against the landlords] was still inadequate," Lin Zhao reported. The screw had to be tightened even more.[50]

"I recalled that, at the first struggle meeting, I felt pity for the landlord and thought the peasants were rough." But, a year into her work, she had forged a new toughness in herself. She now insisted that requisitions had to proceed as directed by the government. "Not a single grain may be withheld!" she wrote to Lu Zhenhua in May 1951. "When I see the wretched, pitiable state of a landlord, I feel only a cruel satisfaction inside."

Lin Zhao's baptism into revolutionary violence had just occurred that same month when she helped prepare a ritual sacrifice to celebrate International Workers' Day (May 1), a major holiday in the CCP's liturgical calendar:

> To mark "May 1," more than a dozen people were executed in our township. One of them was a collaborator [during the Japanese occupation] and an evil tyrant landlord from the neighborhood where I am in charge. From the collection of materials and the organization of denunciations all the way to the public trial, I did my part to send him to his end. After they were shot, some people did not dare to look, but I did. I looked at the executed enemies one by one, especially that evil tyrant. Seeing that they had perished this way, I felt the same pride and elation as those who had been directly victimized by them.[51]

These were orthodox class feelings, long sanctified by Mao. In 1927, after spending a month in five counties of Hunan province, Mao penned "The Report on an Investigation of the Peasant Movement in Hunan," which he lauded as terrific.

It was true, Mao wrote, that local peasant associations had taken matters into their own hands, exacting fines and contributions from local tyrants and evil gentry and "smashing their sedan chairs." Crowds of what some called riffraff had swarmed into the houses of local gentry to "slaughter their pigs and consume their grains. They even loll for a minute or two on the ivory-inlaid beds belonging to the young ladies in the households of the local tyrants and evil gentry. At the slightest provocation they make arrests, crown the arrested with tall paper hats, and parade them through the villages. . . . Doing whatever they like and turning everything upside down, they have created a kind of terror in the countryside."

There were also executions of landlords ordered by special tribunals formed by peasants. Those seeming excesses, Mao wrote, "were in fact the very things the revolution required." For "a revolution is not a dinner party, or writing an essay, or painting a picture, or doing embroidery; it cannot be so refined, so leisurely and gentle, so temperate, kind, courteous, restrained and magnanimous. A revolution is an insurrection, an act of violence by which one class overthrows another."[52]

Mao's glorification of the violent justice meted out by the Hunan peasants set the tone for later CCP policies as it worked to remake the social and economic order in rural China. Many years later, in an essay written in her own blood while she was behind bars, Lin Zhao would reflect on Mao's report on the Hunan peasant movement, which provided the blueprint for the land reform campaign she joined in 1950 and which made revolutionary contempt for the life and property of the landlords imperative:

> "The Report on an Investigation of the Peasant Movement in Hunan" blatantly promotes and grandly extols savage methods of personal insults directed at individuals—dragging people out to be paraded through the streets, putting tall paper hats on them! So on and so forth. The purely spontaneous, plain acts of revenge on the part of the peasants are one thing. At least that is understandable! But when it becomes a component of "Mao Zedong Thought" and is used in a general manner against anyone who refuses to yield to them and anyone whom they want to strike against . . . it's blood! Blood! Blood![53]

In May 1951, when Lin Zhao surveyed the bloodied bodies of the "class enemies," she was likely conscious of the writer Lu Xun's comments on Chinese onlookers at executions. She began reading Lu Xun before 1949 and had often felt his "burning love and hate between the lines." It is a well-known story that, while studying at a medical school in Japan in 1905, Lu Xun had watched a lantern slide show in which a Chinese was being beheaded by Japanese soldiers while other Chinese looked on. There was numbness written on their faces.[54]

That image changed Lu Xun's ambitions in life. Instead of training to be a doctor who would save lives, he would become a writer who could save souls. In "Medicine," a short story he published in 1919, the reader is introduced to a group of onlookers at a nighttime execution, "all craning their necks, as if those were the necks of ducks grabbed by invisible hands and pulled upwards."[55]

Yet Lin Zhao was not craning her neck in soul-less, blank apathy. On the contrary, intense feelings drew her to the bodies of landlords and counterrevolutionaries that had been lacerated by bullets. "Stored in the depth of my heart is a burning love for the motherland, as well as an equal amount of hatred for the enemies," she wrote Ni Jingxiong.[56]

By that time, her land reform work had undone much of her genteel upbringing, but the violence of those days would haunt her years later when she found herself in prison as an enemy of the people. The realization that she had been "more or less splashed with blood" during the land reform period would bring her "shock and deep grief."[57]

LAND REFORM WORK also eroded Lin Zhao's religious loyalties. In the township of Bali in Taicang county, Lin Zhao's work team encountered an obstacle different from that of the landlords. "There were many Catholics in the area, so it was very hard to mobilize the masses," recalled Li Maozhang, who was on the same work team as Lin Zhao.

In spring 1951, land reform in Bali had turned to identifying class enemies. In the CCP's view of the world, the clergy were members of the exploiting class, to be isolated from the masses and ostracized, not unlike the landlords. However, dislodging the local priest proved difficult. Lin Zhao's work team was also frustrated that the congregational life of the Catholics made it hard for them to rouse the peasants, so they set up their base in the village's Catholic church, having invited themselves in. As Li Maozhang recalled,

> the moment the priest came, all the followers of the doctrine went to pay him respects, and served him the most delicious food they had. At worship, the church was filled with those followers. . . . One had to marvel at their piety. . . . They would listen to the priest, and would not listen to us. We were unable to hold the meetings that we wanted to have, and our work plan was in disarray.[58]

The work team decided to put the priest in his place and wake up his flock:

> One day, that priest was again leading the full congregation in worship. Several comrades on our team who were from the army could not take it anymore. They took out their guns in the corridor outside the church, and, "bang, bang, bang," fired into the air. . . . What was even more annoying was that, no matter how you fired your weapons, those believers would not budge a bit.[59]

After the worship ended, the priest calmly reminded the intruders that they had violated the Common Program, which guaranteed the freedom of religious belief.

At this, Lin Zhao spoke up. She acknowledged the clause on religious freedom in the Common Program but added that the CCP Central Committee had recently issued a new directive. It had ordered all religious activities to be suspended in areas where land reform was underway to allow the party's work to be carried out smoothly. "Your religious activities have seriously hampered our land reform work," she warned.

"There was a bit of shock effect in her reasoning," Li Maozhang recalled. "It took the priest by surprise. He did not say a word. After a moment of hesitation, he walked off. We never saw him again until land reform ended."[60]

By then, Lin Zhao's hatreds and passions seemed perfectly aligned with the party's dictates. "I feel a deep love for our work, a deep love for our peasant brethren who have stood up," she wrote Lu Zhenhua in March 1951. "I hope that one day, I will be able to write to tell you: 'I have once again returned to the ranks of the party.'" To her close friend Ni Jingxiong, Lin Zhao sent a cordial challenge: "Let's strive to join the party while we are in the Rural Work Corps. . . . Let's strive to join the party in 1951! My good comrade, give me your hand and accept my challenge!"[61]

RETURNING TO THE party turned out to be a more tortuous journey than she had imagined. Chief obstacles included her parents' political background and her own ambivalence toward them. From the moment she entered the South Jiangsu Journalism Vocational School, she had been pressured to renounce her family. She had dutifully condemned her father's inglorious past as a county magistrate as well as her mother's term in the National Assembly during the Nationalist period, but when her entire work team held a meeting to discuss the "problem of Lin Zhao's stand" and demanded in the name of the party that she draw a clear line with her family, she endured the criticisms with a long silence but in the end "burst into loud crying," one cadre recalled. "I don't understand, why do I have to sever ties with my family just to take a firm stand?" she protested.[62]

As she lamented in her diaries written in 1950, "I want to strive upward, but the vestiges of the old society, the deep-rooted evils of the petty bourgeoisie, are dragging my feet downward like a rock—when can I overcome them?" In another entry, she wrote, "The warm feelings about my family have taken hold of me; I want to go home. . . . I feel an escapist urge inside me. Go home! At least,

I can have a few days of peace at home, and let the wound in my heart heal."[63]

Lin Zhao had taken heart when, in 1951, her mother wrote a long letter to express support for her land reform work. "The Suppression of Counterrevolutionaries work in Suzhou has educated my mother," Lin Zhao told Lu Zhenhua.[64] This was a reference to the other mass campaign that Mao launched in 1950 to ferret out those who he believed posed a threat to the new regime—"bandits," "spies," leaders of "reactionary" religious societies, as well as former officials and army officers of the Nationalist government. About three-quarter million, and possibly as many as one million, were executed to meet the quotas set by Mao and the party's Central Committee. "Mother has become our friend!" she exclaimed.

Not so in the eyes of her comrades in the Rural Work Corps, who finally brought her around to a politically sound view of the matter: "In the past I was quite sure that my parents were not counterrevolutionaries. I based that simply on the fact that they had not been arrested," Lin Zhao reflected in a letter to Ni. The progressive tone in her mother's recent letters had also misled her, she explained. "It was only with the help and illumination from the comrades in the Corps that I realized that, to have worked for the reactionaries and to have held positions that were not low, that in itself was a form of evil. It had absolutely no benefits for the people, and they must be treated as belonging to the class of counterrevolutionaries." This revelation made her feel all the more inadequate. "I still fall far short of the party's standards," she admitted. "Especially for people like us, the old tail is too long."[65]

The party's voice had again prevailed. Since she joined the revolution, that voice had always been the dominant one, more forceful and righteous than her own. It had shamed and diminished her. She had yearned to own that voice to drown out her own petty bourgeois sentiments—her lingering attachment to family, her frequent attraction to men, her impatience with those comrades who extended to her a patronizing helping hand, and her irritation with uncouth suitors in the Rural Work Corps. There was also the nameless melancholy she had known since middle school days, which all the jubilation and euphoria of the revolution had not dispelled.[66]

She spoke hesitantly and with bewilderment in her diaries and her letters to Ni Jingxiong. They had developed a passionate friendship and kept up regular correspondence after joining the Suzhou Rural Work Corps in May 1950 and being assigned to different work teams. "My diaries are full of 'inauspicious words,'" she wrote Ni. "It is as if the moment I start to write an entry, I cannot help but voice some discontent, and vent some backward sentiments. Nobody will know that; nobody will slap a big hat on me. So the diary has become a little world for my soul."[67]

In her own little world—writing for herself or to Ni—she perceived the coldness of society; she felt wounded by her comrades' incessant criticisms of her pride and of her "fragile feelings." "I have only cried three times since the beginning of 1951," she declared to Ni in April of that year.

Despite all this, Lin Zhao was not incapable of happiness. She had often found deep joy in the countryside "walking in the fields, looking up at the blue sky and at the soft clouds drifting by." In springtime, "the sun shone gently; a breeze sent waves through the wheat fields." As she asked Ni, "What reason do we have not to sing joyful songs to this beautiful life?"[68]

WHAT WEIGHED ON her most was "the single remaining issue" of her party membership, she told Ni. By April 1951, she feared that "the party has raised its requirements; the qualifications are now different." And she began to despair of joining the party before the work of the Rural Work Corps was completed.[69]

In the event, it was not the CCP's high standards that made regaining party membership an unattainable goal. Rather, it was her attempt to hold low-level officials to the party's own standards. She had expected basic human decency from the CCP cadres who held power over her, and was woefully tactless in confronting their own failings.

One late night, she went to visit Ni Jingxiong. Instead of finding Ni, she saw the captain of Ni's team reclining in a bed in the women's quarters. Startled, he reprimanded Lin Zhao, asking why she had left her own team late at night. She shot back sarcastically that whatever she had done was not as bad as a man sneaking into the female dorm in the middle of the night. The next day the captain publicly accused her of seeking him out late at night to malign him.[70]

After the success of the Communist revolution, it was not uncommon for CCP cadres of country background—small heroes of the revolution—to court good-looking city girls who worked under them, divorcing their peasant wives when necessary. Among the cadres who did so was the commissar of Lin Zhao's work team. He won over a woman under him by framing her boyfriend and purging him from the land reform team.[71]

Lin Zhao scorned this act as "taking away another's woman with a drawn sword." "Recently a double happiness has come to the commissar of my humble team," she observed wryly to Ni in August 1951. "The first is that he has been selected to go to study at the cadres' school," which usually preceded a promotion. The second was that "he has decided to separate from his yellow-faced wife back in his home village and from his son, in order to marry the slender female comrade on my team who has some faint white freckles on her face—you are going to blame me for my frivolous and caustic remarks, but, for some reason, whenever I mention the cursed business of this sort of guy, no benevolence accumulates on my tongue."[72]

Lin Zhao's acid comments bespoke a deep wound of her own: earlier that year, a cadre on the work team, married and a dozen years or so her senior, had shown special "care" for her. She became romantically involved. Within a few short months he was reassigned to another leadership position elsewhere, and their relations ended.

"In emotional matters, I have been taken advantage of quite a bit," she confided to Ni. In a subsequent letter, she wrote, apparently referring to the same man, "somebody insulted my love, ruined my youth, and left a permanent scar on my emotions."[73]

Ni at the time had already learned of Lin Zhao's sexual encounter with the cadre. Furious and eager to protect Lin Zhao, she had confronted "that turtle's egg . . . an incredibly officious man"—who quickly put her in her place. He made it known to her that she had made an undue fuss.[74]

Lin Zhao's bitterness after the man left may help explain the sarcasm she trained on her own commissar. She would pay a dear price for it. The commissar secretly compiled damaging materials on her and sent them off to the region's party leadership.[75]

On December 21, 1951, at the ceremony held by the Rural Work Corps on the outskirts of Wuxi to mark the conclusion of the land reform work, with about a thousand people in attendance, the head of the party's organization department of the South Jiangsu District dropped a bomb: he did a tally of the people who had gained party membership as a result of their laudable efforts and of those who had joined the Communist Youth League during the same period. "However, there are also those who are incapable of being reformed, such as the famous Peng Lingzhao!" he pontificated, using Lin Zhao's formal name. "Her thoughts and her conduct have always been vile." He cited her drinking, evidence of her bourgeois liberalism and lifestyle. She had been found lying in a dirt footpath in the fields, he added, drunk as a lord, bringing shame to the work team. This kind of person "needs to find another place to be reformed."[76]

Lin Zhao was known among her comrades to have weaknesses for meat and wine. Whenever she had a break from the austere life on the work team, she went to town to seek out a restaurant for a dish of her favorite lamb. She would sometimes borrow money and forget to return it. Once she invited Ni Jingxiong to "improve our diet" in Wuxi. Where was the money? Ni asked. "It's here," Lin

Zhao said, waving in front of her the vest that her mother had just sent her for the winter. She sold the vest, and the two ate their way through local delicacy stalls.

At times Lin Zhao had also drunk a considerable amount of wine, despondent over her tainted political past, the unforgiving scrutiny of her thoughts, life, and family by the party, and her private woes. The public shaming of Lin Zhao was a calculated retaliation, which her commissar later admitted. She no longer had any hope of rejoining the party. "Have I really sunk to an unredeemable level?" she wondered in a letter to Ni. "Yes, I have let the party down, but I also suspect that somebody has let me down."[77]

Years later, in her letter to the editorial board of People's Daily, Lin Zhao would reflect on the years when she worked for the party. When she joined the revolution, the CCP cadres were "taking off straw sandals and changing into leather shoes; we took off our leather shoes and changed into straw sandals!" She went on:

> Where did you not find us the young people, the nameless heroes whom many at the time scorned as "little crazies," opening up virgin land and breaking new ground under the stars and the moon, with calluses growing on our hands and feet! Inspired (deluded!) by such noble ideas as "country," "society," "people," these young people . . . each with "utter devotion to others without any thought of himself" cast the most precious time of their youth upon the soil! And it was precisely because tens of thousands of innocent, zealous youths eagerly shouldered the hardest and the most down-to-earth frontline work at the grassroots level that the Communist Party was able to make up for the serious shortage of political cadres, and this regime was able to effectively consolidate its power from the ground up![78]

What Lin Zhao could not see when she gave her life to the revolution at the age of seventeen was that the CCP regime that hot-blooded youths like her helped to consolidate would serve the interest of the privileged "new class," a term coined by Milovan

Djilas, the former Yugoslav Communist leader who had "traveled the entire road of Communism." As Djilas learned through hard experience, "membership in the Communist Party before the Revolution meant sacrifice. Being a professional revolutionary was one of the highest honors. Now that the party has consolidated its power, party membership means that one belongs to a privileged class. And at the core of the party are the all-powerful exploiters and masters."[79]

Djilas had a warning for people like Lin Zhao, one she never had a chance to hear. She would have to find out its truth on her own. He wrote, "Revolutionaries who accepted the ideas and slogans of the revolution literally, naïvely believing in their materialization, are usually liquidated."[80]

three

THE CROWN

"It has been more than a month since I came to Changzhou," Lin Zhao wrote Ni Jingxiong in March 1952. "My mood has continued to be melancholy."[1]

After the conclusion of her land reform work, Lin Zhao was assigned to the privately owned *Changzhou People News* as a junior editor and reporter. There was no party-run newspaper in Changzhou yet, so the municipal CCP committee dispatched a few party members and several Youth League members to take the ideological helm at *Changzhou People News*. "We kept reminding ourselves that 'we were sent by the party and must do a good job propagating the party's positions,'" wrote the CCP-trained journalists who were posted to the newspaper.[2]

Lin Zhao's initial responsibilities were to assist the investigation of economic wrongdoing in the local, privately owned textile industry.[3] As land reform was winding down in the countryside, the party launched the nationwide Three-Antis and Five-Antis mass campaigns, in December 1951 and January 1952 respectively. The former aimed to root out corruption, waste, and bureaucratism within the party establishment; the latter targeted the remnants of the capitalist class and waged war against "bribery, theft of state property, tax evasion, cheating on government contracts, and theft of state economic information."

The twin campaigns continued until October 1952. At a mid-sized textile company called Fucheng, Lin Zhao was put in charge of the Five-Antis Campaign. She often worked late into the night preparing investigative reports, at times sleeping only two or three hours a day.[4]

Her tuberculosis worsened after she arrived in Changzhou; she was often laid low by the illness. In late February, she requested sick leave, intending to go home. "I feel confused and tormented," she told Ni. "I only wanted a place to hide." The party secretary who oversaw her work was adamant that she should not leave.[5] Perhaps he was concerned about the deleterious influence of her bourgeois family.

As associate manager of the bus company she had cofounded in Suzhou, Xu Xianmin, Lin Zhao's mother, came under investigation during the Five-Antis Campaign. She attempted suicide sometime in 1952 but was saved by doctors at the Soochow Hospital (Suzhou Boxi Yiyuan), a Southern Methodist mission hospital built in 1883. Across China, some 100,000 people killed themselves during the twin campaigns, many by jumping off tall buildings, the easiest and cheapest way. Shanghai's mayor Chen Yi once remarked on radio, "I don't understand why so many bourgeoisie are willing to jump off buildings but refuse to confess." He referred to the estimated 1,300 or so in Shanghai who jumped to their deaths during the Three-Antis and Five-Antis Campaigns as the "paratroopers."[6]

Lin Zhao had apparently contributed to her mother's distress. She had been pressured to write up materials exposing her mother's reactionary past, which were used against Xu Xianmin during the Five-Antis Campaign. Many years later she told her mother: "They drove me to my wit's end" and did not care "whether I would jump to my death in a well or in the river. I had no choice but to satisfy them, and wrote up things that I was clueless about. . . . I did not mean to falsely accuse you." According to Lin Zhao's sister Peng Lingfan, Xu Xianmin's attempted suicide and a subsequent mediation by a family friend, a high-ranking government official, brought about Lin Zhao's reconciliation with her family that year.[7]

In early 1952, Lin Zhao was also beset with romantic problems. Three men who had been her comrades over the previous two years wrote to her after she went to Changzhou and asked to date her. "My only attitude is silence," she told Ni, adding that she in fact preferred the man that Ni had warned her against, one who had "made mistakes." She reminded Ni that she was "not a forward but a backward person," referring to her own political standing. She had also been chastised harshly by party officials as she stumbled along in personal matters.[8]

"Why can a woman not take the initiative in such matters?" she asked Ni. "There have been some (not too many, two or three) on whom I had a crush, but it usually did not work out. On the other hand, there have been some who had a crush on me, but I usually did not care for them."[9]

Her frustrations had led to a wager in 1951 with two comrades: "Will I get married within five years? If I do, I lose the wager. Otherwise, they lose. Whoever loses will treat the other to a feast at the cost of two *dan* of rice," she told Ni. The women had each betted several months' worth of food rationing. They would meet on February 26, 1956, to check on the outcome.

"The reason that I made the wager was to not set my mind on the desires of the flesh," she wrote, evoking a Pauline language she likely remembered from her Laura Haygood years. The biblical exhortation to consider worldly things a loss and to "press on toward the goal" of heavenly reward seemed to apply to her revolutionary strivings as well. She wanted to turn her back on things of the flesh and to give her life to the CCP's cause. Party membership, though still a distant goal, would be her "crown of righteousness."[10]

DESPITE HER POOR health, Lin Zhao was in the end persuaded by the party secretary not to take sick leave. She was moved when he told her that the party organization bore some responsibility for her state. "We have not taken good care of you when you were sick, so that you were unable to feel the warmth in the revolutionary ranks," he said.[11]

That seemed enough to lift her out of her dejection. She threw herself once again into her work. As she saw it, even though some in the party had acted hypocritically or had stabbed her in the back, the party itself was above reproach, and its work as sacred as ever. "My joy increases as the work unfolds," she wrote.[12]

Doing the party's work also became a form of penance for having "let the party down." In a letter to Ni in May 1952, she wrote: "Ever since the beginning of the 'Five-Antis' I have been calling out silently the name of our great leader—our dear father." The work had made her thoughts "cleaner than before," she felt. "I am very happy. Whenever I see my comrades, the party's flag, the national flag, or a portrait of Chairman Mao, I no longer feel too ashamed to raise my head, as I did before. Because I am not entirely undeserving of the rice of the people or wasting it."[13]

For Lin Zhao's generation of progressive youths, calling the chairman "dear father" was a common—and generally sincere—part of the Communist liturgy. To many, he was their spiritual father, the creator of a new China.[14]

During the next two years in Changzhou, Lin Zhao worked furiously to produce news reports that celebrated the dawn of a new China. Some of her pieces glorified the selfless dedication of model textile workers and technicians, or recounted the speechless happiness of an exemplary female yarn joiner who was granted the opportunity to see Chairman Mao in person at a conference in Beijing.

In other pieces, she cautioned against safety violations and industrial accidents in factories (which resulted in "incalculable loss" of state property), as well as the forfeiture of the "red flag" of production whenever revolutionary fervor wilted and the amount of defective cloth increased. She also reported on an advanced weaving team who modeled themselves on the heroes in the Chinese "volunteer army" in Korea who had presumably laid down their young lives for their motherland.[15]

One of her reports told the story of a saintly member of the Youth and Children of China—a program that fed into the Communist Party itself—who before liberation was reduced to scouring the streets after school for cigarette butts to help her family make ends meet. Now she excelled in school, was ever ready with a helping hand for others, and dreamed of becoming a model worker and going to see Chairman Mao. "How happy are you," Lin Zhao rhapsodized, "young children of New China! Under the warm sun of Mao Zedong, you are flourishing like flowers in spring. In you, we see the beautiful future of humanity."[16]

SUCH EUPHORIA WAS harder to maintain in her private life. Her tuberculosis brought violent coughs and constant chest pain. "On December 1, I coughed up blood," she wrote Ni at the end of 1952. "It continued for more than a day." Apart from the weakened constitution, depression was a major factor for her; she cried almost daily. "I hate myself. A backward sort of thing. Naturally I am pained to see others advancing and me lagging behind. . . . Some comrades said that my singing is unhealthy, that 'it is like crying.'"[17]

Communist cadres who had power over Lin Zhao remained a constant source of aggravation. She disagreed with them often and had little interest in the art of obsequious deference. After the public denunciation and humiliation she endured at the Rural Work Corps meeting in late 1951, she had made up her mind to "never make criticisms of the leaders," but she also admitted to Ni Jingxiong that she could not help breaking that vow.[18]

One day, at a meeting held in a factory where she was a work team member, she disagreed with the party leader and was promptly rebuked. When she refused to back down, he "mobilized others at the meeting to denounce her. Infuriated, Lin Zhao left the meeting," a colleague recalled. To her dismay, the man "ordered several male comrades to forcibly hoist her up and carry her back to continue the denunciation. It was hard for Lin Zhao to put up with such an overbearing and rude act," and she wept bitterly as she recounted the incident to a friend.[19]

IN EARLY 1954, *Changzhou People News*, one of the last two remaining papers in the city not owned by the government, closed down. Lin Zhao was transferred to the Changzhou Federation of Literary and Art Circles. Within months, she obtained permission from her new employer to apply to Peking University and was admitted to its Chinese department: she had one of the top scores on the entrance exam in the department. Five years after she chose revolution over college, she found herself on the campus of the most prestigious university in China. She was twenty-two.[20]

"For me, going to college was a sign of the ebbing of my zeal for the party, and of the sense of emptiness and weariness in my political sentiments," Lin Zhao reflected later. "However, after I was admitted to Peking University and found full satisfaction of my personal aspirations, I still felt optimistic and inspired about life in that vibrant new world and new environment. I hoped to start a new page in my life."[21]

Founded in 1898, Peking University, then known as Jingshi Daxuetang or the Imperial University of Peking, was the first national university in modern China. It was the fruit of the self-strengthening efforts of the ill-fated Hundred Days' Reform and offered a comprehensive modern curriculum. After the coup against the young Guangxu Emperor and the modernizers he supported, Empress Dowager Cixi threw out all the reform edicts that Guangxu had issued but did not touch the new Imperial University.

"In the midst of Beijing's dusty skies and feces-filled earth, there is only one ray of light left, and that is the Imperial University," observed an article in a Tianjin newspaper after the debacle of 1898.[22] Throughout the first half of the twentieth century, Peking University remained the center of intellectual life in China. Its students were at the forefront of the May Fourth Movement of 1919, which ushered in the new era of student-led cultural iconoclasm and political radicalism.

Originally located near the Imperial Palace in downtown Beijing, the university moved to the picturesque campus of Yenching University on the northwestern outskirts of the capital in 1952. Yenching, established in 1919 and the leading Christian university in pre-Communist China, was broken up and its faculty moved to various colleges. Its arts and sciences faculty joined Peking University, which took over its iconic buildings and landscape designed in the 1920s by Yale-educated Henry K. Murphy.

Murphy had found inspiration in the grandeur of the Forbidden City, whose architecture and proportions he adapted for Yenching. The campus, converted from the gardens of a Qing dynasty prince, was an architect's dream, combining modern construction materials with the indigenous style of glazed green tiles and upturned flying eaves. Drawing on Beaux-Arts principles, Murphy had used symmetry to produce order and had also preserved the natural beauty of the original garden, including its lotus ponds, an artificial island, and Weiminghu, or the Unnamed Lake.[23]

"The many cultural relics near Weiminghu were preserved for us by Yenching University!" Lin Zhao reminisced later from prison. China had created an "ancient, brilliant Eastern culture" but had "done a poor job preserving it," she would write. "What some (not all) 'imperialists' did really deserve our deep gratitude from the historical point of view!"[24]

Lin Zhao was admitted as a journalism major. Luo Lie, the program director and also vice chair of the Chinese department, had taught her at South Jiangsu Journalism Vocational School. Lin Zhao read voraciously and soon distinguished herself in classical literature. Professor You Guo'en, a doyen of classical Chinese literature and an expert in *Verses of Chu* (*Chu ci*), was impressed with her "literary agility," seeing great promise in her. He recommended that she be made a literature major, a proposal that, for unknown reasons, was not taken up by the Chinese department.[25]

Lin Zhao, third from left, at Peking University, 1955. Luo Lie is first from left. Yang Huarong is second from right. Courtesy of Ni Jingxiong.

In the early 1950s, student life at Peking University was lively, with more than a dozen student societies devoted to choral music, Chinese instruments, poetry, dancing, Peking opera, martial art, photography, and the like. Lin Zhao joined the poetry club and served as an editor for the monthly *Peking University Poetry Journal,* launched in the spring of 1955. Concurrently, she was an editor for the university's official periodical.[26]

According to Zhang Yuanxun, her classmate, friend, and a fellow poetry club member, Lin Zhao was adept in ancient-style poetry, classical regulated verse, and contemporary free verse. "And so arose the nickname and the reputation of 'Maiden Lin,'" Zhang wrote—one that evoked the image of Lin Daiyu, the tragic heroine in the classic novel *A Dream of Red Mansions*, who was known as much for her frail beauty as for her dazzling poetic talent.[27]

The comparison was perhaps irresistible: Lin Zhao was "slender and delicate in her build, her eyes bright, intelligent, and beautiful; [she had] the typical grace of a southern girl," wrote Shen Zeyi, a classmate and poet. He also noted her composure and weathered melancholy. Zhang Ling, another fellow student and future translator of Thomas Hardy's *Tess of the d'Urbervilles*, recalled Lin Zhao wearing two French braids and dressed in "a close-fitting, light cobalt blue overall and white shirt, looking frail; she had a smile in that pair of intelligent, beautiful eyes of a Southerner."[28]

Lin Zhao had an eclectic range of interests. She delighted in solving riddles at the Lantern Festival and reciting obscure ancient texts. She also loved ballroom dancing. "Wearing a wreath made of the flowers she picked, she entered the ballroom and would dance to its very end."[29]

As her classmates soon found out, Lin Zhao's delicate appearance belied a feisty personality. "She loved bantering with others" at gatherings of friends and enjoyed "waging long verbal battles and scoring victories in jokes," Zhang Yuanxun remembered. And she had a wry sense of humor. Horrified by the usual chaos in the dining hall, she composed a rhyme entitled "The March of the Dining Hall" to mock the misplaced valor of her classmates: "Charge, press forward, and advance with bravery; we are the valiant warriors of the dining hall." At times her verbal sparring could turn passionate and adamant. At a dinner hosted by Luo Lie, a debate she had with a fellow student turned into a quarrel; both left the table and "walked off in a huff."[30]

In fall 1956, the party committee of Peking University directed the launch of a new student journal named *The Red Building* (*Honglou*) after the university's historic administration building, in downtown Beijing. It was there, on the drill ground in front of the Red Building, that Peking University's students rallied on May 4, 1919. They then marched on to Tiananmen, the Gate of Heavenly Peace, to rage against the Treaty of Versailles, by which China ceded territories in Shandong province to Japan.

Several leading intellectuals of modern China, including Cai Yuanpei, Chen Duxiu, Li Dazhao, Lu Xun, and Hu Shi, had worked and taught in the Red Building. Mao Zedong himself had worked briefly (and unhappily) in the building when he was an assistant in the university's library from late 1918 to early 1919. The very name of the new journal connected the students' intellectual and political life to the university's glorious past. At the same time *The Red Building* was founded, *Peking University Poetry Journal* ceased to exist.

Lin Zhao, a junior by then, was among a group of about a dozen students named to the editorial board of *The Red Building*. The journal had no office space of its own, so the editors often met in Lin Zhao's room in a newly completed female dorm, to share the work of copyediting and proofreading.[31]

The inaugural issue, published on January 1, 1957, included a poem by Lin Zhao. It was dedicated to a tank on display outside the military museum in Dalian, which had led the Soviet Red Army's capture of the city from the Japanese in August 1945 and, as Lin Zhao put it, "brought the joy of freedom to the masses." Lin Zhao assumed chief responsibilities for the second issue of *The Red Building*, published in March. An editorial she penned at the end called for an outpouring of patriotic literary talents befitting their time: "We hope to hear in *The Red Building* more resounding songs; we hope that our young singers sing not only of love, of the motherland, and of all the rich and colorful life of our time; we also hope that our songs will be like a blazing flame that burns down all the baneful influence of the old society and anything that is deleterious to socialism."[32]

LIN ZHAO'S EXUBERANCE was characteristic, although the reference to a "baneful influence" may have hinted at the darker side of life at the university. In 1955, the clash between writer Hu Feng and the CCP's cultural tsar Zhou Yang, which had been going on for years, turned treacherous. Hu Feng, a noted literary theorist and a key member of the League of Left-Wing Writers in the 1930s, was purged after Mao denounced him as the head of a supposed antiparty clique. Hu had come under Lu Xun's influence and advocated the "emancipation of individuality" in literary creations. He was arrested in May 1955 and would eventually lose his sanity after long years in prison.[33] More than 2,100 people were denounced and scores were arrested during a nationwide hunt for members of the "Hu Feng Counterrevolutionary Clique."

The purge of Hu Feng was followed immediately by another mass political movement called the Elimination of Counterrevolutionaries Campaign. Mao instructed the party in the summer of 1955 that Hu Feng and his clique were by no means the only "bad elements" that had sneaked into the CCP. He asserted that "many counterrevolutionaries have entered deep into our 'liver'" and that they made up about 5 percent of people in the revolutionary ranks. This meant that of the 14.3 million cadres in 1955 more than 700,000 were to be weeded out as counterrevolutionaries. While the exact number of the victims remains unknown, at least 300,000 were arrested.[34]

The repercussions of these campaigns were soon felt at Peking University. One student was caught having corresponded with a poet who made the list of the "Hu Feng Counterrevolutionary Clique." A "struggle session" was held with hundreds of students present to denounce him. As the hunt for "little Hu Fengs" expanded across campus, more than two hundred students were incriminated as counterrevolutionaries and quarantined in a dorm building under the surveillance of student activists and university security personnel; they were interrogated and were tied up with ropes at night to prevent escape. Many were beaten.[35]

Lin Zhao was not among the suspected little Hu Fengs, though she may have been sympathetic with his views (she later wrote of "the wound of the mental slavery that writer Hu Feng had spoken of"). That did not exempt her from being censured. The Elimination of Counterrevolutionaries Campaign, which carried on well into 1956, offered an opportunity for some party members to vent personal grudges against her. She was denounced as having "a pessimistic worldview, dejected thinking, and 'incorrect views about romantic love.'"[36]

It is unclear how she was caught with those "incorrect views," a code phrase for personal conduct that fell outside Communist strictures on romantic relations. Lin Zhao is known to have turned down suitors during her years at the university, while she herself had also known the pain of unrequited love.

Not long after she entered university, she fell in love with the young poet Shen Zeyi. A friend finally helped arrange a date for the two. Shen, himself tormented by his unfulfilled yearning for a girl with a sunnier personality than Lin Zhao, politely but firmly turned her down. "I am standing on a raft that is being washed away by a flash mountain flood," she told Shen. "I don't know where it is washing me." As Shen recalled, "a deep sorrow flowed silently from the darkening look in her eyes. She turned and left. I remained there like a log, my eyes following her slim shoulders as they receded into the distance."[37]

Whatever the exact nature of her romantic blunders, Lin Zhao was given what she called "a baffling penalty" on a "baffling charge." She was put on a one-year probation as a member of the Communist Youth League—yet another slippage in her arduous climb toward party membership.[38]

She did not take the punishment lightly. At a dinner with friends in a small restaurant outside campus, she ordered Lotus White, a premium distilled liquor made from sorghum, and "without waiting for others to toast, emptied several glasses. Before long, she was incoherent and broke down crying." As a fellow student recalled, "I could see that she felt deeply wronged and was in unspeakable despondency."[39]

She was found one late night sitting at the edge of the Unnamed Lake at the eastern end of campus chanting lines from the poem "Encountering Sorrow" (Li sao) by Qu Yuan (ca. 340–278 BCE), the prototype of the wronged, loyal minister in Chinese history:

The way was long, and wrapped in gloom it did seem,
I would go up and down to seek my vanished dream.[40]

Still, in spring 1957, Lin Zhao was unshaken in her faith in the party. No debasement or act of tyranny by petty party officials, which she had encountered repeatedly since 1949, could shake her conviction that communism had taken the Chinese people on a journey of emancipation. When Stalin died in 1953, she had published a poem that mourned the loss of "our dear father" whose face radiated "love and care for humanity," as she put it. "He is freedom, peace, happiness."[41]

In late April 1957, on the eve of the thirtieth anniversary of the death of Li Dazhao, a CCP cofounder and former Peking University head librarian, Lin Zhao paid a visit to the Li Dazhao memorial room in the "revolutionary Red Building" on the university's former campus. Li had been executed by hanging in 1927 after soldiers of the anti-Communist Manchurian warlord Zhang Zuolin raided the Soviet embassy in Beijing, where he was hiding.

In Li's writing, she found "the flashing eyes of a warrior." What resonated most with her, as she explained in a piece called "The Seed," published in the May 1957 issue of *The Red Building*, were Li's "dagger- and spear-like" words hurled into the darkness of tyranny. "True emancipation comes not from begging others," Lin Zhao quoted Li. "We cannot rely on the grace of the authorities to unlock the iron chains around our heads; we have to break them with our own strength, and break through the darkness of the prison to usher in a shaft of light!"

To Lin Zhao, Li embodied the Chinese Communists' vision of liberation and social justice. Despite his atheism, Li Dazhao loved singing the gospel song "Bringing in the Sheaves," written by Knowles Shaw in 1874, which he may have learned through his contact with the YMCA and the Christian general Feng Yuxiang. "He often compared the revolution to sowing the seed," Lin Zhao wrote. He would "repeatedly sing the following stanza . . . 'Bringing in the sheaves, bringing in the sheaves, / We shall come rejoicing, bringing in the sheaves.'" With the birth of the People's Republic, she declared, "now is the time for 'bringing in the sheaves.'"[42] For her, the success of the Communist revolution had brought fresh meaning to that song of Christian labor, perseverance, and untiring, joyous anticipation of harvest.

By 1957, land reform had ended the systemic oppression of the peasants by landlords; agricultural collectivization had largely been accomplished. In urban areas, private businesses had been nationalized as the party proclaimed the working class masters of the new nation. The first Soviet-style Five-Year Plan had also transformed the nation's infrastructure. All of this probably reinforced the "leftist sentiments" that Lin Zhao's friend Zhang Yuanxun found in her until the summer of 1957.[43]

Appearing in the same May issue of *The Red Building* was Lin Zhao's poem "The Stone Lion," addressed to one of the giant pair of lions that guarded the entrance to Tiananmen. For hundreds of years, she wrote, that lion had been witness to the annual ritual of the lowering of the imperial edict, inside a wooden phoenix, from atop the gate. But during the May Fourth student demonstrations of

1919, it "served as the pulpit for the great assembly." It had "roared" to "call back the sunken soul of the nation":

> *Forty years of wind, frost, rain, and snow—and you are still here;*
> *the red flags on Tiananmen flutter on this sunlit, festive day.*
> *You watch the joyous procession swell past you like a wild tide,*
> *and smile with wide-opened eyes at the free people who have cast their*
>   *shackles away.*[44]

By 1957, the old shackles from the pre-Communist era may have been cast away—gone were the landlords and the capitalists—but freedom remained uncertain. Lin Zhao and her fellow students were soon to find out the boundaries that Mao and the CCP set for their thoughts and expression.

In 1956, Mao had launched the Hundred Flowers Movement, with the slogan "Let a hundred flowers bloom and a hundred schools of thought contend," to invite criticisms of, and help improve, the party's work. The initial public response was hesitant.

In February 1957, to reassure would-be critics and to usher in a political spring for his campaign, Mao delivered a rambling address to the Supreme State Conference, a gathering of the country's top leaders, entitled "On the Correct Handling of Contradictions among the People." He advocated openness toward criticisms as well as different ideas in the arts and sciences and even displayed a measure of tolerance toward skeptics of communism. The only way to settle "controversial issues among the people" is "by the democratic method, the method of discussion, criticism, persuasion and education, and not by the method of coercion or repression," Mao said. The precise form of that method was "unity-criticism-unity."[45]

In late April, the CCP Central Committee issued a directive to boost the Hundred Flowers Movement. It urged a new "rectification campaign" that echoed the one in Yan'an in 1942. The stated purpose was to help the party eradicate the "three scourges" of "bureaucratism, sectarianism, and subjectivism."

At first unwilling to speak out, a few Peking University students were eventually convinced that they could criticize the authorities without risking reprisal. On May 19, they put up the first posters outside the main dining hall questioning the university's unfair practices that favored students with politically reliable family backgrounds: they were more likely to be chosen as Youth League representatives or sent to study in Eastern European countries on government expenses.

Inspired by these first petitioners, Lin Zhao's friends Shen Zeyi and Zhang Yuanxun posted their call to arms, a poem entitled "It Is Time," which touched off the May 19 movement at Peking University. "It is time / Young people / Give full voice to your song!" it cried. "My poem / is a torch / that destroys all the / barriers in this world." The fire was unstoppable, it claimed, because "its spark / came from the 'May Fourth' / . . . With tears of wrath in my eyes / I call to my generation: / My brethren who sing to truth / raise the torch without delay / to cremate all the darkness under the sun!"[46]

In the days that followed, hundreds of posters appeared on the wall outside a dorm building along the main thoroughfare. It became known as the democracy wall of Peking University. On the opposite side of the street was another wall that became the apologists' forum, on which the leftists posted their chastisements of the ideological heresies being committed across the street.[47]

Other posters appeared outside the main dining hall and on a makeshift bulletin board made of mats mounted on wooden posts. Some defended Hu Feng and called for his release; others called on the university's party committee to account for wrongful denunciations during the Elimination of Counterrevolutionaries Campaign of 1955 and to make the all-important individual personnel files—which the administration compiled on each student—available to the students themselves for verification.

Some posters went even further. "Abolish the party committee system; adopt a democratic model for the university's administration," one read. Some argued that the roots of the "three scourges" (bureaucratism, sectarianism, and subjectivism) were in China's political system, which also produced the "cult of personality" endemic to worldwide communism, and that "blind obedience" to party leaders enslaved the human mind.[48]

The democracy movements in Poland and Hungary in 1956—and the violent crackdowns that followed—raised many questions about Communist regimes. Some students lamented the killing and imprisonment of innocent people in Eastern Europe. They warned that the concentration of power in the hands of Communist leaders and their reliance on violence to enforce the will of the state threatened to undermine the legitimacy of those regimes.[49]

Lin Zhao's friend Tan Tianrong, a flamboyant and impetuous physics major, put up a series of posters that were defiantly entitled "Poison Weeds," choosing precisely the term Mao had used to refer to ideas he deemed hostile to socialism, which had a questionable license to "bloom." Tan had been denounced as a counterrevolutionary during the Elimination of Counterrevolutionaries Campaign of 1955 and was still smarting from the pain and insult he had endured.

He decried the party members' claimed monopoly on truth and the "dictatorial method" used at struggle sessions to "apply violence to logic" and to treat those who dissented as counterrevolutionaries. The result had been "warped souls" and "crippled spirits." "To hell with those who willingly enslave themselves to prejudice," he wrote. "We do not accept any external authorities. . . . All must stand before the tribunal of reason." It was the first time since the May Fourth Movement of 1919 that such a cultural and political outcry—echoed across China on school campuses and in various work units—was heard.[50]

Some protests were tongue-in-cheek. One poster announced a "Verdict on the Three Scourges" issued by a fictitious Peking

University Rectification Court. It identified the three defendants as "sectarianism, aged 36, born on July 1, 1921," the CCP's founding date, "dogmatism, aged 38, born on May 4, 1919" (tracing the beginning of Marxist influence in China to the May Fourth Movement), and "bureaucratism, aged eight, born on October 1, 1949," the day the People's Republic came into being.

Although all three were found guilty and deserved the death penalty, the court recognized that dogmatism lessened "mental labor" for officials and that bureaucratism "upholds the prestige of leaders" and "lessens physical labor" for them as well. As a result, the three scourges were declared innocent. "From now on, if anybody creates disturbances and stirs up trouble again by bringing charges against those three isms, this court shall find him guilty of defamation, chop off his head, and display his corpse in public as a warning to others."[51]

THE COUNTERATTACK BY leftists was immediate: within hours of the posting of "It Is Time," another poem, "Our Song," written by a student party member and signed by more than a dozen others, appeared. It affirmed the group's unswerving love of the party and denounced the "hysterical means" that the authors of "It Is Time" had employed to attack the CCP's shortcomings.[52]

"Our Song" spurred Lin Zhao into action. In her own poem entitled "What Song Is This?" posted on May 20, she bristled at its "overbearing tone." Maybe the party-member author had never "borne the heavy burden of discrimination, slight, and suspicion," she suggested. As for her, she had not been instructed by the party to sing "coo, coo, coo; cheep, cheep, cheep, / You are so bright, so pretty." Her protest was directed not at the CCP, but only at the self-appointed defenders of the party. "The power of truth / never lies in / the arrogant air / of the guardians of truth," she added.[53]

Her faith in the party remained strong, even as the dissonance between its lofty ideals and the conduct of CCP cadres was increasingly hard to tolerate. On May 22, she completed another poem, this one with the title "Party, I Call Out to You." She remembered calling out to the party "in the deathly, ferocious silence of the long night" of Guomindang rule and "under the shadow of fetters," and she had also called out to it "rapturously," as red flags fluttered at the dawn of a liberated China. But later

I saw dark shadows under the sun;
in some corners, evil emanations were in view;
I was startled, bewildered, and began to doubt,
but, Party, I still call out to you.

. . . . . .

Speak to me, drop me a line of intimate words,
Party, I am grieved as I call out to you![54]

And so she remained torn as the democracy movement unfolded on campus. "As a member of the [Youth League] organization and because of my deep doubts about the true attitude and true intention of the party, I had no choice but to be conservative and prudent in my action," she later explained in her "Review and Examination of My Personal Thought Journey," written when she was held at the Shanghai No. 2 Detention House. "Compared to my friends, it took me longer to complete the journey of understanding."[55]

Still, her sympathies were already with Shen Zeyi, Zhang Yuanxun, and other like-minded friends. She urged them to exercise caution and avoid antagonizing the university's party leaders.[56] As posters went up, public debates soon erupted on campus, often with dining room tables serving as makeshift podiums.

On May 22, the same day she completed "Party, I Call Out to You," a nighttime debate pitted Zhang Yuanxun and a fellow democracy advocate against a large, organized group of leftist students. The event quickly turned into a mob trial that "had the feel of the Elimination of Counterrevolutionaries Campaign" two years earlier. As the two came under waves of angry denunciation, "a girl student ascended the dining room table in the thick dark," Zhang recalled. She spoke in a "vigorous voice," with a "graceful Suzhou accent" in her mandarin Chinese; she reminded the crowd that the CCP had repeatedly called on nonparty members to make criticisms. Why was there such an ideological crusade against Zhang just because of a single poem?

"Who are you?" someone from the crowd roared.

"I am Lin Zhao!" she shot back. "Who are you, that you should assume the tone of an interrogator? Make a note of it! 'Lin' with the two trees, and 'Zhao' for 'the day when the knife is put to the mouth!'"[57]

Later that night, Lin Zhao got drunk. According to Zhang Yuanxun, she soon went silent. Her last extant piece of writing for the democracy movement of 1957 was the poem "Party, I call out to you."[58]

As the movement gained steam, some students began to form their own independent clubs, such as the Hundred Flowers Society, which organized forums and debates.[59] More than half a dozen independent student pamphlets also appeared, the most influential of which was *The Square*. It was launched on May 30 and published selected democracy wall posters, including the poems of Shen Zeyi, Zhang Yuanxun, and Lin Zhao. Several of Lin Zhao's friends joined the editorial board headed by Zhang and Shen.

The foreword to its inaugural issue, prepared by Zhang, proclaimed a new era in China, a "'May Fourth' New Culture movement of the socialist era!" *The Square* evoked the memory of "the democracy square where the torch of May Fourth was raised" at Peking University in 1919. "The May Fourth blood flows in our veins," Zhang wrote. "We must learn to acquire our May Fourth fathers' spirit of bold inquiry and bold creation and strive for a genuine socialist democracy and culture!"[60]

Lin Zhao had no formal association with *The Square*. In addition to her misgivings about the intent and possible consequences of the Hundred Flowers Movement, her decision not to join its editorial board was likely a reflexive one, having suffered repeated punishments since 1949 for her criticisms of party cadres. She also publicly admitted to conflicts between "my sense of the [Youth League] organization and my conscience." Her obligation to bring her own actions in line with the official pronouncements of the Youth League—the organizational extension of the CCP—left her ill at ease with herself.[61]

At times, she found her own loyalty swinging to the leftist camp. In July, after the democracy movement had come to an end, the editorial board of *The Red Building* met to expel Zhang Yuanxun and another student from the board because of their association with *The Square*. Lin Zhao joined in the criticism.[62] By then the Anti-Rightist Campaign, a movement to rein in all the criticisms the Hundred Flowers Movement had unleashed, was in full swing.

Ironically, subsequent denunciations published in special "Anti-Rightist Struggle" editions of *The Red Building* alleged that Lin Zhao was in fact the "wire puller" and "strategist" of the counter-revolutionary journal *The Square*. That was an exaggeration, but it was true that after falling in line briefly with the leftists, Lin Zhao returned to her friends and her "conscience," however muted it had become.[63]

THE DEMOCRACY WALL at Peking University was one instance of the nationwide response to the party's call for the people to contribute to its "rectification campaign" and to air candid criticisms of its work. In early May, the hundred flowers that Mao expressly welcomed began to bloom, in some places with greater abandon than those at Peking University. Leading members of China's powerless "democratic parties"—which had been formed during the Nationalist era and which had been co-opted by the CCP after 1949—joined the chorus to register their discontent, calling for the implementation of "mutual supervision" between the CCP and the hitherto decorative alternative parties, which Mao had repeatedly and publicly advocated.[64]

Zhang Bojun, minister of communications and vice chairman of the China Democratic League, ventured that legislative and political consultative bodies outside the CCP system should play the role of a "political design institute." Chu Anping, another senior democratic party figure and editor-in-chief of *Guangming Daily*, quipped that the country had become "the party's all-under-heaven" and called for empowering intellectuals outside the CCP. Both were veteran gadflies of autocracy from the Nationalist era and could not help fantasizing about liberalizing the Communist rule.[65]

During the five-week period from May 1 to June 7, 1957, hundreds of thousands of people spoke out. Many decried the violation of human rights in earlier mass campaigns, the absence of freedom of speech, and the mindless aping of the Soviet Union; others called for an independent judiciary and the rule of law and democratization of the party and even an actual multiparty system to replace the CCP dictatorship.

Unbeknownst to all except a few trusted cronies such as Shanghai's party boss Ke Qingshi, Mao had laid a trap. He later called it the open conspiracy (*yangmou*) of "enticing snakes out of their lairs." In early April 1957, Mao told the small circle that the Hundred Flowers Movement was changing the mood of the intellectuals from "cautious to more open." As he explained, "One day punishment will come down on their heads," adding, "Let all those ox devils and snake demons . . . curse us for a few months."[66]

On May 15, four days before the first poster went up at Peking University, Mao wrote "Things Are Beginning to Change," an essay he circulated among a small group of top party officials. It would only be made available to provincial and regional cadres a month later. In it Mao lashed out against the Rightists and their revisionism, which "is appreciative of bourgeois liberalism, opposes the leadership of the party . . . and opposes centralization." The Anti-Rightist Campaign officially began on June 8, when a *People's Daily* editorial claimed that "a small minority of Rightists are staging a challenge to the leadership of the Communist Party and of the working class."[67]

On Peking University's campus, the campaign, directed by the university's party committee, was launched on June 16. By that time, the political signal from the CCP Central Committee was already clear. Throughout the country, prominent liberals had begun to make abject public self-criticisms. By late June, *The Square* was forced to shut down after printing some 500 copies of its first and only issue, and the editorial board voted to dissolve itself after existing for only twenty-three days.[68]

In the months that followed, leading participants in the democracy wall movement at the university were forced to recant and denounce themselves publicly. "The people are my parents and have provided for my food and clothing," a contrite Shen Zeyi read from a written confession at a "ten-thousand-people meeting" held on the university's drill ground in July. "I, as a college student, have not in the least bit repaid our motherland and our party"; he had instead "viciously slandered the party." The editorial board of *The Square* was a "base camp" for the Rightists' "furious and savage attacks on the party and on socialism." Shen ended by incriminating fellow editors of *The Square*. Betrayals were common and readily reciprocated, leading to vicious feuds that would outlast the Mao era.[69]

The university's Anti-Rightist Campaign began to mete out punishments in late June, stripping the most prominent participants in the May 19 movement of their Youth League or CCP membership and placing them under administrative surveillance. It was unclear to the students what would happen next. Some of the activists were hopeful that, having been "struggled against" and brought to their knees before the party, they would be allowed to return to normal life. That was what happened to the two hundred or so suspected little Hu Fengs at the university, after the Elimination of Counterrevolutionaries Campaign of 1955 ended.[70]

However, starting in August, some students were secretly arrested. One student cracked under the constant struggle sessions and physical abuse and fought back one day with his pocketknife, causing some minor injuries. He was sentenced to death as a "Rightist murderer." Before his execution, he asked his wife to remarry and to "teach our child to follow the party and Chairman Mao and walk the socialist road." It was the best he could do to protect his family from further persecutions as kin of an executed counterrevolutionary.[71]

LIN ZHAO DODGED the initial bullet of the Anti-Rightist Campaign. She was not among those who had made the most fiery protests. And when the purge started in June, she was doing an internship at *China Youth Daily*, a popular official newspaper. She was passed over. As students dispersed for the summer vacation at the end of July 1957, Lin Zhao stayed on campus and buried herself in "thread-bound books" from antiquity.[72]

Across China, public denunciations of leading Rightists were in full swing. Mao singled out a few who had had the temerity to call on the CCP to share power with the nominal democratic parties. By August, many leading writers such as Ding Ling—whom Mao called an "incorrigible anti-party person"—had also been denounced. All over China, the spouses of many of the Rightists divorced the condemned under pressure to "draw a line."[73]

In all, tens of thousands would take their own lives or "vanish" during the purge. One of them was Yang Gang, a graduate of Yenching University who was then a senior editor at *People's Daily*. (Not unlike Lin Zhao, she had joined the CCP when she was a student at the Christian university.) She lost her nerve after a personal notebook went missing and killed herself. Zhu Jiayu, a young teacher and a scholar of folk literature at Peking University, aired criticisms during the Hundred Flowers period. She disappeared from an ocean ship one night that summer after she learned that she had been blacklisted as a Rightist.[74]

At Peking University, a second wave of denunciations of anti-party students came in the fall. Lin Zhao had gone to Shanghai for the summer after her internship. (Her parents separated in 1952, and her mother had moved to Shanghai with her siblings.)[75] Her return to campus was delayed by a relapse of tuberculosis, when she again began coughing up blood. A letter she sent to Zhang Yuanxun from Shanghai in September contained a classical seven-character rhyme or *qilü*—an eight-line poem with seven characters to a line and a strict rhyme scheme—that she composed. The first four lines read:

Inebriate but with no merriment, the worries are old;
my thoughts in riotous profusion I share with you.
Embellishing words like carving seals, we filled up the wall with
    scribbling,
as a dark wind blew in through the window and a chill seeped through.[76]

Lin Zhao arrived back in Beijing almost two months late for the fall term of 1957 and found the air at the university heavy with accusations and fear. "Unfold and Deepen the Anti-Rightist Campaign among the Teachers," read an editorial in the university's official periodical in September.[77]

Hundreds who had spoken out during the heady days of May had become political pariahs; old friends were now avoiding each other. Yang Huarong, Lin Zhao's former classmate at the South Jiangsu Journalism Vocational School, who had also entered Peking University in 1954, was among the first students to be labeled a Rightist. Lin Zhao did not avoid him; they renewed their friendship and began meeting discreetly almost every day after sundown, in the fields outside campus.

"She was an innocent girl and was not familiar with the way of the world," Yang remembered. "She was baffled by the Anti-Rightist struggle and the punishments for the Rightists, and was deeply disaffected with the bad faith of some people, the insincere words of some teachers, and the mutual betrayal of some classmates and friends."[78]

Seeking a respite from the Anti-Rightist storm, the two traded jokes and rambled over as many topics as they pleased, from the punishment of Rightists and the role of prison in the making of great people to the connections between drinking and poetry. "Without wine, the entire world of poetry would look pale," Lin Zhao ventured. "Sometimes she would compose a little poem on the spot," Yang wrote. "She loved to use literary allusions, so it was at times difficult to follow. I taunted her, saying: I would have to bring the *Cihai* to listen to your poems." *Cihai* was the most comprehensive Chinese dictionary and encyclopedia.

"She teased back: Sorry, sorry, I did not know that you are a sheep [Yang's family name meant "sheep"]. Other people play zither for a cow; I chant poems for a sheep. Then, pleased with herself, she burst into a hearty laugh."

Lin Zhao was "not a traditional woman," Yang added. "She seemed not to believe in a set mode when it came to romantic love and marriage." She told love stories, "but they were mostly quite romantic ones." The approach of winter brought the two closer. "To fend off the cold of the winter evenings, we were quite intimate with each other," Yang wrote cryptically. When it came to religion, she grew serious. "Once we talked about Christianity. She said: don't you belittle God. I am a Christian."[79]

In late 1957, some of Lin Zhao's friends broached, in private conversations, the idea of fleeing China. In September, Chen Fengxiao, a cofounder of *The Square*, attempted to slip onboard a foreign cargo ship near Tianjin bound for Hong Kong, but he was followed and captured at the harbor. He was soon sentenced to fifteen years in labor camp. Later, in an indictment brought against Lin Zhao, she was accused of helping plot Chen's botched escape in order to "collude with the imperialists," a charge that Chen dismissed as fabrication.[80]

As Lin Zhao recalled after her own arrest, the general consensus among her friends at the time was that any democracy movement opposed to the regime "would have to secure a base outside the country." They also believed that the participants of the May 19 democracy movement were in a position to "reveal the reality of the totalitarian rule and the vicious political persecutions" to the outside world. As for herself, "as long as the good earth of the motherland remains under deep darkness," she wrote, "my spirit will never gain freedom. I preferred to keep watch over this land and endure the afflictions, torture, and even death together with my fellow countrymen!"[81]

On December 25, 1957, Zhang Yuanxun was arrested along with several other students. They were accused of belonging to a "small counterrevolutionary organization" that had attempted to contact the British diplomatic mission as well as the Indian and Yugoslav embassies in Beijing in an attempt to seek political asylum abroad.[82]

By the end of 1957, 589 students and 110 faculty and staff at Peking University had been labeled Rightists. The large number was not surprising, given that Mao had singled out the university. Addressing a meeting of cadres in Shanghai in July 1957, he asserted that Rightists at Peking University made up "one percent, two percent, or three percent" of the student body, although professors were "somewhat different; probably around ten percent are Rightists."

Mao thereby set the minimum quotas, and the party cadres took over from there. In the end, out of 8,983 students, some 7 percent, about 600, were denounced as Rightists. Hundreds more were identified as belonging to the "center right" and stigmatized; they were not, however, "hat-wearing," or formal, Rightists. Across China, the total number of Rightists exceeded 1.2 million.[83]

LIN ZHAO WAS not among the Rightists named in 1957, but her sympathies and continuing associations with her denounced friends were too glaring to be ignored, as were her own protest posters and her public defense of Zhang Yuanxun during the May 19 movement. Beginning in July 1957, leftist students had publicly denounced her as the behind-the-scene strategist for the Rightists and called for her removal from the editorial board of *The Red Building*. In January 1958, she was added to the dreaded Rightist list, along with about a dozen others. She had just turned twenty-six.[84]

In a letter to her sister Lingfan sometime afterward, Lin Zhao informed her that Peking University had "bestowed the crown of a

'Rightist'" on her. And she came to "feel the weight of this crown of laurel called 'Rightist,'" she told a close friend.[85]

The official version of that bestowal was unceremonious: the indictment later brought against her stated that she was reduced to a Rightist for her antiparty and antisocialist activities. In her own annotation of the indictment, written in prison, she insisted that the "correct way of putting it" should be: "In 1957, fueled by her youthful blood and driven by a conscience that had not yet perished, she became an activist in the 'May 19' democracy movement against tyranny!"[86]

At the time, however, she felt no such ebullience. "You will never be able to understand how I felt," she told Lingfan in the letter. "I believe that my fervent love for the party has been overwhelming. Nothing was comparable to that love. I cannot bear the party's misunderstanding of me. And what profound misunderstanding it has been. All that had held me together has now collapsed."[87]

"Throughout the second half of 1957, I still held on to a ray of hope inside my heart, the hope that the party would stop before going too far and would wrap up the whole thing," Lin Zhao later wrote. "However, the struggles that continued inside and outside the university were getting more intense by the day; the harsh reality once again crushed my kind dreams."[88]

For months, she had picked up *People's Daily* in the morning, "with a hope sometimes fervent and sometimes faint" for any "trace of wisdom" or reason remaining in the party—any sign that it might be reining in the harshness and the abuses of the Anti-Rightist Campaign. "Nothing! Nothing!" she concluded. "That was the beginning of Lin Zhao's break with the Communist Party," she recalled in prison years later. "After all my hope was lost, I naturally had no choice but to opt firmly for resistance!"[89]

four

A SPARK OF FIRE

A sudden gale comes toward me from heaven,
and a melody drifts from the bamboo flute, plunging the world
    in gloom.
The black chrysanthemum opens its pure heart at the approach
    of night,
and the plum blossom, iron-boned in the frost, goes into bloom.

—LIN ZHAO, "Blood Poem on Shirt," 1965[1]

Lin Zhao's more immediate response after being named a Rightist was to attempt suicide. She scraped the heads off two boxes of matches and swallowed them. She may have been familiar with the story of how the mother of the early CCP leader Qu Qiubai took her own life in 1916—after mixing the phosphorus from the matches with distilled spirit. But her desperate act ended differently: her roommates rushed her to the university clinic and a gastric lavage took care of the poison.[2]

"I will never bow my head to plead guilty!" she cried when she woke up.[3]

A suicide note she had written prior to the attempt said: "I do not love and cannot love everybody. May my shadow forever follow those who have tortured and trampled upon me. Let them be for-ever tainted with my blood. This is my curse and my revenge." Those who had brought about her downfall and that of her fellow Rightists had "painted their faces red" with the blood of others, she added.[4]

She reflected on this and other failures of charity on her part years later, when she was in prison. "For followers of Christ, char-ity is always essential to spiritual growth." The Bible clearly teaches us to love others as ourselves, she noted, and "a follower of Christ would certainly more or less cherish love for others. However, how unlovable are people . . . enslaved by this system!" she mused. "How ridiculous and pathetic is the individual charity of a Christian in the face of these 'humans' who have no human smell!"

Like someone who had "set the first note too high" when starting to sing a song, Lin Zhao admitted that she had often been unable to sustain the pitch of Christian love in her dealings with people. "I could not catch my breath as I sang on and had to stop or switch to a different key."[5]

AT PEKING UNIVERSITY, the punishments of Rightists followed the CCP Central Committee's guidelines, decreed by the State Council at the end of January 1958. The lightest offenders, categorized as center-right elements, would be placed under administrative watch on campus but spared further retribution. The majority of Right-ists were allowed to retain their affiliation with Peking University but were sent off to labor camps or other rural areas to undergo "re-education through labor"—a new and presumably lighter form of "administrative" punishment devised by the CCP Central Com-mittee in 1955 for counterrevolutionaries and other "bad elements" who had not been sentenced in court. In theory, this was to last between one and three years. As it turned out, many of those sent away found themselves in an open-ended exile that only ended in the late 1970s.

Meanwhile, the most serious offenders, called the extreme Rightists, were expelled from the university, sentenced as counter-revolutionaries, and either imprisoned or sent to prison farms for "reform through labor."[6]

On February 17, 1958, the Chinese New Year's Eve, the first identified group of extreme Rightists from Peking University and several other universities in Beijing were ordered to report to their respective school authorities, with their bedrolls. Once they arrived, they were stripped of their university badges and herded onto buses. They were driven to the Haidian District police station, where they were fingerprinted and hauled away to Beijing's Banbuqiao Prison.

Ten days later, they were loaded onto a train in the middle of the night and dispatched under armed guard to Qinghe, a "reform through labor" camp 150 kilometers away. At the time, few were prepared for the severity of the forced labor and the scarcity of food at Qinghe. In 1960, when the Great Famine was at its worst, more than three hundred former students on a spring plowing team perished before summer.[7]

To many, the banishment of intellectuals in 1958 recalled the treatment of scholars, the *ru*, by Qin Shihuang, the First Emperor of China, in the late third century BCE. When a delegate mentioned the mighty First Emperor at a national meeting of the CCP's Eighth Congress in May 1958, Mao promptly disabused him of his inept comparison: "Qin Shihuang is nothing. He only buried alive 468 scholars; we buried alive 46,000 scholars. . . . We had a debate with people from the democratic parties. 'You curse us, calling us Qi Shihuang. That's incorrect. We exceed him a hundred times. You call us Qin Shihuang and dictator. We admit to all of that. But what you say is an understatement; we often need to make some additions.'"

At that, Mao's audience burst into laughter.[8]

THE ANTI-RIGHTIST CAMPAIGN ended once and for all the dream of Chinese intellectuals that "independent spirit and free thinking," which the noted historian Chen Yinke had championed in the 1920s, could be maintained under Mao's rule. Their "instrumental-ization" was complete. While some took their own lives out of fear and despair or in protest, others such as the celebrated writer Ba Jin chose abject submission to the party and agreed to write essays in a righteous "counterattack against the Rightists."

"I did not have a mind of my own; I simply followed others' orders and trudged on," Ba Jin later wrote of his own surrender. "I crawled, I walked, and I crawled. . . . My tragedy was that others treated me as a tool; I also willingly became a tool."[9]

In the first half of 1958, the party orchestrated a new movement across university campuses throughout China to "pull out the white flags" of bourgeois thinking and expose decadent thoughts to rev-olutionary fire. On March 10, a mobilization meeting was held at Peking University, and within three hours, the estimated ten thou-sand people on campus—students, faculty, and staff—allegedly produced 80,000 big-character posters in full revolutionary colors. The total number of posters jumped to 280,000 after three days.

"In the big-character posters, they directed the fire against them-selves and against others. They torched all [the Rightist thoughts], both inside and outside the party, up and down, left and right," declared a New China News Agency report. On March 15, thou-sands gathered at Tiananmen Square to hold a "meeting of dem-ocratic party figures and non-party figures to promote socialist self-reform." At the "ten-thousand-people rally" afterward, they chanted in unison the slogan "Hand over the heart to the party; resolutely become a leftist."[10]

"Almost all the Rightists made their self-criticisms," a fellow Pe-king University Rightist recalled. "The only Rightist who refused to make self-criticism was Lin Zhao."[11]

Lin Zhao's decreed punishment was three years of re-education through labor, which could have meant banishment to a labor camp. However, concerned about her tuberculosis and frailty, Luo Lie, vice chair of the Chinese department, persuaded the university authorities to let her remain on campus. She was allowed to work in the reference room of the journalism program—she was given additional gardening responsibilities—and undergo reform under the supervision of the revolutionary masses.[12]

In early 1958, at the start of Mao's Great Leap Forward, the government launched a national campaign to exterminate "four pests": rats, flies, mosquitoes, and sparrows. Across China, groups were organized to beat pans and pots to scare the sparrows and keep them flying until they dropped from exhaustion. At Peking University, students, faculty, and staff were ordered to wet their washbasins with soap bubbles and use them to catch mosquitoes. After spending an entire day catching mosquitoes, Lin Zhao told her friend Tan Tianrong: "I couldn't help laughing inside me the whole day; I laughed at how this party has gone crazy."[13]

That summer, the journalism program at Peking University merged into the journalism department at Renmin University, where the party's oversight was more firmly established. Lin Zhao and everyone else in her program moved to Renmin, where she was assigned to the department's reference room. Her job was to help research Republican-era (1912–1949) newspapers for a volume on the development of CCP journalism, which was being compiled by the journalism department.[14]

A fellow Rightist undergoing supervised labor in the reference room was a Renmin University student by the name of Gan Cui. Gan was not a flamboyant democracy advocate like Lin Zhao's close friends Shen Zeyi and Zhang Yuanxun. His fall had been more prosaic: he had been stripped of his party membership and labeled a Rightist because Renmin University needed to meet its quota. Party leaders searching for an additional two hundred people or so had decided that his mildly liberal sympathies qualified him for the designation.

Like Lin Zhao, Gan Cui had been told to help with the collection of pre-1949 newspaper articles. Their responsibilities also included the punitive menial job of sweeping the university ground and picking up discarded watermelon rinds and banana peels. Gan saw Lin Zhao for the first time while collecting watermelon rinds. They began working together in the reference room after the fall semester started.

It was a bleak time. After December 1957, one by one Lin Zhao's friends vanished into police custody or exile in remote areas. Yang Huarong was sent away in March 1958; Shen Zeyi, having vehemently denounced himself and other Rightists publicly, was spared the worst punishments. He was sent in October to the loess plateau of northern Shaanxi where he was made into a village teacher.[15]

In November, Tan Tianrong was detained. The following April, he would be sent, along with more than five thousand Rightists and convicted criminals, to Xingkai Lake labor camp in the far north, a marshland dredged by the internees, on the border with the Soviet Union. There they would battle extreme cold and hunger as they performed crippling labor. Most lived in pits dug into the frozen ground.

Chen Fengxiao, who had been arrested and sentenced as a counterrevolutionary for his attempted escape to Hong Kong, was sent to Xingkai along with Tan's group. Of the seventy-five people in Chen's squadron, only twenty-nine were still alive eight years later.[16]

As THE WINTER of 1958 descended on Beijing, Gan began to look after the sickly Lin Zhao, who, during this period, painted a portrait of herself in a poem:

> A stubborn illness attached to my body, my thoughts half empty,
> I linger on earth, my life's cause in limbo is hung.
> I often see in the mirror a blush on my face,
> yet it's not from a radiance of beauty, but from the disease in my lung.[17]

Gan would bring her boiled water in a thermos bottle and obtained permission from the university to place a coal burner and build a ventilation duct in her room to provide some heating. He also took bus rides to a Cantonese restaurant closer to downtown to fetch her porridge with shredded meat. Before long, the two had fallen in love, and Gan Cui began joining Lin Zhao for Sunday worship at Dengshikou Church, the largest church in Beijing.[18]

Dengshikou opened in 1904 as the headquarters of the North China mission of the American Board of Commissioners for Foreign Missions. In 1958, as part of the Great Leap Forward, the sixty or so churches in Beijing were forced to combine their worship services at four facilities. Dengshikou Church, located in the eastern part of downtown Beijing, was one of them.[19]

To Gan Cui's surprise, young people like him and Lin Zhao made up the majority of the congregation. "Amid the myriad sufferings, they went there in search of spiritual sustenance," he wrote. Worshippers were each handed a Bible and a hymnal as they entered. As the pastor started the regular service, "everybody rose, and the choir and the pastor led the congregation in the singing of hymns. The atmosphere was beautiful. It brought us into a transcendent realm in those depressing, gloomy days."[20]

Gan's recollections offer the only available glimpse into Lin Zhao's public return to the church in the late 1950s. We do know that, however far she had drifted from the tradition of Laura Haygood, at no point did she renounce her faith. Given her ardent pursuit of CCP membership during the first years of Communist rule—a party member would have nothing to do with religion—we can assume that she shunned church services in the early 1950s.

Most likely, it was only after she was "reduced to a Rightist" in 1958 that she openly resumed her religious life. It was an act of quiet defiance to return to the pew, where she recovered her dignity as an individual—however subdued the preaching may have become by that time. Lin Zhao may also have found it ironic that, as with the campus of Yenching University, the church that certain "imperialists" built in the early twentieth century had helped preserve a space of serenity and rest for her wearied soul. During the Cultural Revolution, the iconic Dengshikou Church would be demolished.

"Lin Zhao was somewhat headstrong in her thinking," Gan recalled. Concerned about further troubles she might get into, he told her not to clash head-on with the party. It would be like striking an egg against a rock. "I have to strike it," Lin Zhao answered. "If thousands upon thousands of eggs strike against it, this hard rock will be smashed."[21]

The romance between the two young Rightists soon became known. It was an affront to the party leaders in the journalism department. They reminded Gan Cui that it amounted to an open display of defiance against the proletarian dictatorship. Lin Zhao's response to the warning was characteristic: "She took my hand and we started walking about . . . holding each other's hand" so that any remaining doubts about the rumored romance would be dispelled. (It would be more than two decades before Chinese lovers could be seen kissing or hugging in public.)

In August 1959, having just finished his bachelor's degree, Gan requested permission from the department's party secretary to marry Lin Zhao. He also asked that he be assigned to a job near her. "What business does a Rightist have getting married?" the party secretary replied.

Gan found out within days that he had been assigned to a construction battalion in Xinjiang, seven days away by train and bus, about the farthest one could possibly get from Beijing. He left the capital in late September. Arriving in Xinjiang, Gan heard of the harshness of forced labor and the chronic shortage of food at the militarized farm. His heart sank. He turned back and sold his winter clothes to purchase bus and train tickets bound for Shanghai, to which Lin Zhao had returned. Xu Xianmin had allegedly gone to Beijing to seek the intervention of Justice Minister Shi Liang—the China Democratic League leader she had known during the 1940s—on her daughter's behalf, and Shi apparently secured permission from Renmin University for Lin Zhao to return to Shanghai for medical treatment.[22]

Gan Cui got a cool reception from Lin Zhao's mother. She did not want to see her daughter marry another Rightist and fall even lower as a political pariah. With no money or *hukou*, the required household registration, Gan stayed only a week in Shanghai.

On the Sunday they spent together, Lin Zhao took Gan to worship at the iconic Shanghai Community Church, which sat on a quiet road in the former French Concession lined with London plane trees. Built in 1925 to serve Western expatriates—as it did until 1950, when the outbreak of the Korean War forced most of

Lin Zhao with fiancé Gan Cui at Jingshan Park, Beijing, ca. 1959. Courtesy of Gan Cui (Gan Cui dated it to 1958).

Lin Zhao, next to a tomb at Taoranting Park, Beijing, 1959.
Courtesy of Ni Jingxiong.

them to leave China—the Gothic wood-and-brick church with its
Austin pipe organs (which would be destroyed by the Red Guards
during the Cultural Revolution) evoked the order and tranquility of
pre-revolution days.[23]

But the peace they found inside the church was only momentary. Gan could not stay in Shanghai. There was no choice but to return to Xinjiang—where a twenty-year exile awaited him. He bade
Lin Zhao good-bye, never to see her again.[24]

For a time, Lin Zhao found some respite. In a letter sent to a
friend in early 1960, she informed him that she had "bidden farewell to the imperial capital" to "drag out an ignoble existence."[25]
Home offered a refuge from the political storms in Beijing. Or so
her mother hoped.

Before Lin Zhao left Beijing, she had completed two long poems that would lead her down the fateful path of dissent. The first,
"Seagull," composed in 1958–1959, was an anguished response to the
detention and exile of her friends, especially Tan Tianrong. She had
been tormented by the guilt of having escaped harsher punishments.

"Whenever I thought of them being in shackles and persecuted
while I 'strolled free outside the law,' I somehow felt that I had

betrayed them. . . . I should have been with my friends!" she wrote after her own arrest. "Pain kept hammering my soul . . . but it could not stop me, it only urged me on to self-consciously and firmly take the path that my friends had already trod."[26] "Seagull" had some 240 lines. It opens with a dark vision:

> *Dusk spreads a pale yellow above the grayish blue of the ocean,*
> *as a ship breaks through the waves and sails away.*
> *Filled with prisoners fettered with chains,*
> *where it is heading nobody can say.*

What crimes have the prisoners committed? "There is only one: we see freedom as food, and as air to breathe."

> *The tyrant wields his sword and rod, and puts us on trial,*
> *because he fears freedom just as he fears fire.*
> *He is afraid that once we find freedom,*
> *his throne will be shaken, his fate will be dire.*

Leaning against the mast of the ship is a pale young man, a statue with starry eyes. "What am I thinking, this rebellious, disquieted heart of mine?" he muses.

> *Freedom, I cry out inside me, freedom!*
> *The thought of you has filled my heart with yearning,*
> *like a choking man gasping for air,*
> *like one dying of thirst lurching toward a spring,*
> *. . . . . .*
> *I am willing to be exiled to barren mountains and wilderness far,*
> *and to wander about—under the heavenly tent I'll stand.*
> *. . . . . .*
> *and pour out all my boiling blood*
> *upon that icy, arid land.*
> *. . . . . .*

if only my blood, like asphalt,
can pave the road for freedom to come to my motherland.

At the sight of a dot on the horizon, a distant island, the young man clenches his fists, breaks free from his fetters, and leaps into the ocean. Bullets chase after him; a storm howls, whipping up mountainous waves. The young man is swallowed by the sea. But suddenly, from the spot where he is last seen,

A snow-white seagull flies out of the waves;
opening its wide wings, into the wind it soars.
. . . . . .
He charged into death and has conquered death;
the remaining chains are under the sea, buried forever more.
. . . . . .
His soul has turned into freedom itself—
Everywhere under the blue sky is the hometown he once yearned for![27]

In the Chinese original, "Seagull" uses a single end rhyme throughout the entire poem.[28] Unlike the majority of Lin Zhao's poems, which take the form of the eight-line *qilü* and are rich in literary allusions but emotionally subdued, "Seagull" dispenses with subtlety and restraint. Significantly, however, the island on the horizon remains beyond reach, and the young man's brave swim toward freedom proves futile. It is only through a Christ-like descent into death and resurrection that the young man in the poem emerges free at last.

"Seagull" was the first clear sign of Lin Zhao's turn against Mao and communism. She later explained the break in "A Review and Examination of My Personal Thought Journey," written in prison in October 1961:

In sum, if the party had governed wisely and ruled with justice and diligence, how could Lin Zhao, being a follower and supporter of the party, entertain political bias, close her eyes and obliterate her conscience to oppose the party? However, the party not only failed to do that, but, on the contrary, came up with a heap of magnificent rubbish and myriads of bloody absurdities, so that mountains and rivers rotted away, blood and tears overflowed, and the white bones piled up in a heap. As a result, Lin Zhao, though a naïve girl still smelling of her mother's milk, was torn apart by an unbearable pain inside and could no longer tolerate it![29]

In another reflection when she was in prison, she wrote of the only options available to her after 1958: "There were but two roads ahead! Since I could no longer follow the Communist Party and oppose the Rightists—because that would be unjust—I had no choice but to remain steadfastly a Rightist and oppose communism!"[30]

IN SEPTEMBER 1959, she mailed a copy to a Rightist student at Lanzhou University named Sun He, whom she came to know through his sister, a fellow Rightist at Peking University. Sun was among dozens of Lanzhou University Rightists exiled to Wushan county, Gansu province, to undergo thought reform. Appalled by the widespread starvation they witnessed in the countryside as a result of the Great Leap Forward, several of them, including Sun, began meeting secretly in spring 1959 to discuss how they could stop Mao's policies.

A leading member of the group was a self-made man named Zhang Chunyuan, who had joined the People's Liberation Army before 1949, served in the Korean War, and returned after he was wounded. Zhang entered Lanzhou University in 1956 and, a year later, like hundreds of thousands of other earnest students across China, fell victim to Mao's "open conspiracy."

Upon receipt of Lin Zhao's "Seagull," Sun shared it with the group. Zhang found it electrifying. Sometime in late 1959, he traveled to Shanghai and Suzhou—Lin Zhao's mother had retained the family's former home in Suzhou, after her divorce and relocation to Shanghai—to meet with Lin Zhao.[31]

By that point, Lin Zhao had completed a second long poem, "A Day in Prometheus's Passion." Like "Seagull," it is mostly in free verse yet still hews to a single end rhyme in each stanza throughout its 368 lines. Won over by Zhang Chunyuan's sincerity, she gave him a copy of the poem.[32]

"A Day in Prometheus's Passion" is divided into three parts—the morning, midday, and dusk of Prometheus's Christ-like "passion." As in "Seagull," the poetic imagery evokes the grim lot of the tragic hero who defies the villainous tyrant. It began with these lines:

> *Nearer and nearer draws Apollo's golden chariot;*
> *at the edge of the sky, a scarlet dawn breaks.*
> *The summit of the Caucasus Mountains greets the morning rays,*
> *as Prometheus, on a cliff, awakes.*

"Like an icy python, the fastened chain / in numbness and pain holds him tight." At daybreak, two giant eagles, "Zeus's agents of torment," swoop down on him. "They thrust their copper talons into his ribs / as he, silent, clenches his teeth tight."

> *Blood has painted the eagles' sharp beaks red;*
> *jostling each other, they tear at the heart,*
> *which has become a deformed lump of flesh.*
> *Still it throbs gently, trembling: life would not depart.*
> . . . . . .
> *To the dome over the earth he lifts his eyes:*
> *Heaven, you must bear witness to this horror!*
> *But what does he see?—right there,*
> *in the clouds appears Zeus with a smirk and a snicker.*
> . . . . . .
> *If he needs the claws of birds of prey*
> *to prove to the prisoner a victor's might,*
> *then sneer and laugh! You, the great god of thunderbolts,*
> *Zeus, I somewhat pity you and your spite.*

At midday, after "nymphs of the forest" treat Prometheus's wounds, Zeus travels down to him.

Here he comes, Zeus without his heavy entourage
but with the pair of giant eagles that on his shoulders rest.
He lowers himself next to Prometheus's head,
and bends to check the wounds in the prisoner's chest.

. . . . . .

The prisoner casts an unperturbed look at him;
his gaze like a blade is sharp and firm;
Zeus flinches and takes a step back;
somehow the prisoner makes him fidget and squirm.

. . . . . .

Although he is fastened to the rock,
all that he can move are his mouth and his eyes;
far from the crowds, and helpless,
alone in the wild mountains he lies—

. . . . . .

none of that can put Zeus's mind to rest,
he knows not why Prometheus makes him fret.
—What is it that he has inside him,
that should pose to the gods an existential threat?

Zeus makes Prometheus an offer. "Whatever request you may want to make, / it shall be granted, if ever possible, I declare."

"Don't you wish to return to Olympus,
to revel in heaven's glory and wealth?
Don't you wish to rejoin the immortals' family,
to share our elevated pleasure and health?

. . . . . .

"But you ought to know, Prometheus,
for the mortals, we do not want to leave even a spark.
Fire is for the gods, for incense and sacrifice,
how can the plebeians have it for heating or lighting in the dark?

. . . . . .

"You stole heaven's fire and brought it down to earth;
you, too, must be the one now to put it out.
For the benefits of the immortals on Olympus,
your responsibility in this weighty matter is without a doubt.

Prometheus looks into Zeus's eyes, and calmly defies him:

"Fire belongs solely to humankind;
how can you hide it in heaven and seal it tight?
Even if I had not stolen the seeds of fire,
The people themselves will surely find the light.
. . . . . .
"Once humans build their houses, how can they crawl back into
*   the cave?*
Once the birds are in the woods, why would they return to the cage?
Where there is fire, there will be seeds of fire;
no hurricane can extinguish them, nor any flood in its rage.
. . . . . .
"Fire will lead humanity to liberation;
I urge you to give up your useless scheme instead.
Whatever you do, whoever attempts its destruction,
It is too late: the earthly fire will spread.
. . . . . .
"How long can the gods hold on to their imperious rule?
Don't you hear the cries against injustices all around?
The blood and tears of the plebeians will drown the gods;
The palace on Olympia will turn into a dirt mound!

Zeus flies into a rage, strikes his thunderbolt, and breaks off half the mountain. Lightning flashes; "rocks explode and sands fly as thunders roll."

In the last part of the poem, as a purple dusk sinks behind the mountains, Prometheus wakes up again to find half his body buried in rocks and sand and his eyes smeared shut with blood. He looks out over the "fields of five grains, woods and flowers."

> *How many have toiled to clear and reclaim land for planting,*
> *so that you, good earth, stay young and are ever renewed?*
> *Why is it, then, that your yearly yield from blood and sweat,*
> *only goes to the gods—a mere sacrifice, as it is viewed!*
> . . . . . .
> *When, good earth, when will you have a new birth,*
> *and free yourself from extortion's scourge?*[33]

Having spent a year and a half with the Suzhou Rural Work Corps, working on land reform and grains requisitions, Lin Zhao knew firsthand the extortion that both former landlords and the "liberated" peasants were subjected to in the building of a socialist New China. By the time she started writing "A Day in Prometheus's Passion" in Beijing, the plundering of peasants by the CCP state had reached a new level of intensity.

Agricultural collectivization started on a small scale in 1951, in the form of mutual-aid teams; by 1953, more than half of Chinese peasants had been brought onto these teams. In that year, the CCP Central Committee decreed a state monopoly on the procurement and distribution of grains, cotton, and edible oil. Collectivization accelerated thereafter. By 1957, almost every rural family in the nation was in an agricultural cooperative and practically all urban industry was nationalized. A planned economy was firmly in place, with the state in control of both the means of production and the people's livelihood.

At the end of 1957, Mao predicted that China would "catch up with or overtake Great Britain in fifteen years." One hundred million peasants were mobilized that winter for massive water control and irrigation projects and to open up new farmland. In the course of 1958, agricultural cooperatives across China were merged into more than 26,500 "people's communes." Some 120 million rural households—almost the entire peasant population—were herded into them. By providing canteens, nurseries, elderly homes, and schools, the communes centralized domestic tasks such as the preparation of meals and childcare, freeing up women for agricultural production. Families now appeared superfluous in the eyes of the party leaders.

Soon enough, Mao became convinced that the timeline for overtaking the United Kingdom in industrial production could be shortened to three or even two years—particularly if steel production was doubled each year. As a result, an estimated one hundred million people were mobilized nationwide to build a million steel furnaces in their backyards.

All of this promised nothing less than a "Great Leap Forward" into communism. The silencing of intellectuals across China as a result of the Anti-Rightist Campaign eliminated any rational opposition to Mao's grandiose vision. Overinflated grain-harvest reports generated not skepticism but even more astounding figures from rival communes and production brigades competing for the spotlight in national media. Despite severe harvest shortfalls, peasants were forced by local cadres to meet procurement quotas. Rural starvation spread.[34]

At a meeting of top CCP leaders in Lushan in July and August 1959, Defense Minister Peng Dehuai raised concern about the over-inflated grain figures and the dangers of leftist fanaticism. Mao took it as a personal attack and countered with a bitter denunciation of Peng and of the so-called right-deviating opportunists within the party. Extraction of agricultural products continued, and famine broke out on a scale unprecedented in human history.[35]

LIN ZHAO FIRST heard news of the catastrophe in rural China from Zhang Chunyuan and his Lanzhou University Rightist friends. In a Gansu village, they had run into a peasant selling pork buns, which they could not afford, only to learn the next day that human fingernails had been found in the buns. Starvation led people to cannibalize dead bodies. Some traded the corpses of their family members with strangers; others ate the dead in their own families. One elderly woman in a Gansu village disappeared one day and was later found in her own cellar: her son had chopped her into eight pieces, one of which was already gone.[36]

For Zhang Chunyuan and his fellow Rightist students, the economic and social collapse of rural China left them no choice but to become the self-appointed spokespersons for the masses and to expose their suffering and oppression. They formed themselves into a group dedicated to the "enlightenment" of the people, especially senior party officials who might be brought around to their views.

Their first step was the publication of a mimeographed underground periodical, *A Spark of Fire*, in January 1960. It consisted of half a dozen essays calling attention to the disaster of the Great Leap Forward and dissecting the "slavery" of Mao's rule. Also included were short digests of internal party documents and news that revealed the dark side of the people's commune. The single longest piece was Lin Zhao's poem "A Day in Prometheus's Passion."[37]

Lin Zhao was at first ambivalent about *A Spark of Fire*. On the one hand, she saw the need for action. After the Anti-Rightist Campaign, she wrote, "the key question was: what to do with the discontent? . . . Petty urban philistines sometimes develop quite a profound understanding of realities, but they may stand forever on the sidelines 'seeing through things' and making sarcastic remarks." To her, committing oneself to a battle was a different matter. It called for real sacrifice.[38]

On the other hand, Lin Zhao was skeptical of creating a formal group, which would have vulnerabilities. "The Communist Party started its enterprise with the building of organizations, therefore its biggest taboo is organization building by others," she observed. She preferred an informal association built on one-on-one contacts. To her, "the printing of secret propaganda materials," which after all

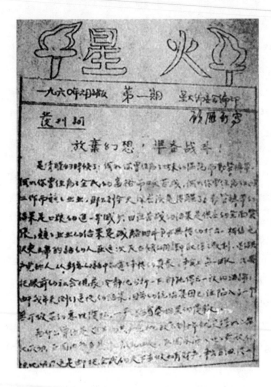

Front page of *A Spark of Fire*, 1960. Courtesy of Tan Chanxue.

may contain "ideas that everybody already knew," carried an unnecessary risk—"not only to the publisher, but also to the readers."[39]

In the end, she was overruled by the majority of the Lanzhou group, who went ahead with the printing of the inaugural, and what would turn out to be the only, issue of *A Spark of Fire*. Its masthead featured a pair of raised torches. Using an old mimeograph machine from a shuttered tile factory in Wushan county, they secretly printed a grand total of about three dozen copies, which were shared within the group.[40]

The foreword to the inaugural issue pointed out that the cruel political purges during the first decade of CCP rule, the downfall of Peng Dehuai, and a new campaign against "right-deviating opportunists" constituted proof that the Communist regime had turned the entire country into its private property. It had built a cult of idolatry around Mao and had suppressed democratic movements.

The result was the "fascist rule of a centralized state." The authors drew a distinction between the CCP's rule and true socialism. "If they insist on calling such a dictatorial rule socialism, it should be classified as a form of national socialism with an oligarchy exercising a monopoly. It is the same type of national socialism as that of the Nazis, and it has nothing in common with real socialism."[41]

The essays that followed decried the Great Leap Forward, with one calling it the "Great Leap Backward." The people's commune movement was a "complete expropriation of the material and spiritual possessions" of the people so that they had become dependent on the ruler. The state had imposed a military organization on the people and put them into "slave-like collective labor." Peasants had been mobilized to transplant ripened corns from one field to another under cover of night, in order to impress cadres on inspection tours with the fictive high yields—only to be told that they had to surrender public grains accordingly.

As for the nationwide campaign to make steel in backyard furnaces, the essay pointed out, it was nothing less than a war on science, "the clearest sign of hotheadedness, stupidity, and ignorance of the . . . political oligarchy." They should "go play balls with three-year-olds" instead, the writer suggested.

With the exception of Lin Zhao, all of the contributors to *A Spark of Fire* still claimed allegiance to socialism. Unlike Lin Zhao, the only intellectual resources available to them had been the works of Marx, Engels, and Lenin, which some of them read voraciously while in exile. They opposed capitalism and colonialism as well as the reactionary class represented by Chiang Kai-shek and supported the kind of independent socialism championed at the time by Yugoslavia. "Our final goal is the realization of communism," they declared.[42]

For this group of Rightists, the publication of *A Spark of Fire* was thrilling, both because of its potential to enlighten the people and because of the danger it put them in. In addition to the periodical, they felt the need to write a political platform and choose an inspiring name for themselves.

Some proposed the Chinese League of Communists, after the League of Communists of Yugoslavia, the ruling party of Yugoslavia, whose 1958 congress had produced a program critical of both the bureaucratism and authoritarianism of the party-state. Lin Zhao had found a copy of the draft program while working in the reference room at Renmin University and had reproduced it for the group. Others proposed the League of Chinese Laboring Peasants and Workers. Despite her reservations, Lin Zhao was charged, along with two others, with drafting a political platform.[43]

By April 1960, the group had produced half a dozen essays for the second issue. These pieces offered further refutations of official propaganda and also made an urgent appeal to the people to unite and prepare for the fight to "wipe out those murderous rulers" so that "we will not starve to death."

One poignant piece took the form of a young peasant's deadpan account of a chilly March day. When the morning star was just above the horizon, he was awakened by the whistle of his ferocious and well-fed production brigade leader. He tried to move his famished body, which felt as though it were "tied down to the bed by a dozen hemp ropes." At the near-empty cattle shed that served as the gathering place, peasants fell back to sleep, left and right. An eleven-year-old boy dozed off, dropped his head into a bamboo basket, and bloodied his face. No cries, not even a whimper.

"We don't cry anymore," the peasant explained. "When my father lay dying, he stared blankly at the portrait of Chairman Mao on the wall. Then he looked at Mom and me. But neither Mom nor I shed a single tear. Still, Mom told me to tear the portrait off the wall (by that time she was so starved that she was unable to get herself out of bed)."[44]

Testimonies like this one put Lin Zhao—who was living in Shanghai and not starving—in touch with the devastation of rural Gansu. They also reminded her of her friend Liu Faqing, a Peking

University student turned Rightist who had been exiled to Gansu. As Liu lingered on the edge of starvation in spring 1960, he received a letter from Lin Zhao in which she had enclosed seven official grain-rationing coupons worth thirty-five *jin* (close to forty pounds) in total. She was small and skinny, she explained, and needed less food. Liu wept when he read the letter. The coupons helped tide him over until summer, when the worst of the famine had passed.[45]

Lin Zhao's group decided to include her poem "Seagull" in the second issue of *A Spark of Fire*, even though she had not intended it for publication. She seemed more skeptical than her Lanzhou University friends of its possible usefulness. "In general, the greatest effect that an instigation can have is only to announce one's own existence as an opponent . . . an announcement that is unnecessary." Still, she yielded to the voices of her friends.[46]

Meanwhile, her group of Rightists, all in their twenties, were dreaming big: they printed three hundred copies of a critique of the people's commune and planned to mail it to top party leaders. When they ran into practical difficulties, they decided to disseminate the essay among party cadres nationwide at the county level or above.[47] Perhaps it would awaken them to the CCP's enslavement of Chinese peasants and to the folly and cruelty of the Great Leap Forward; perhaps it would rouse them into a spontaneous, heroic opposition to Mao's reckless rule. Their vision was as daring and exhilarating as the one Lin Zhao entertained near the end of "A Day in Prometheus's Passion":

> *In the far distance, on the slumbering good earth,*
> *a ray of light sprints forth in the dark.*
> *"Fire," Prometheus says inwardly with a smile;*
> *instantly his thirst and pains vanish from his heart.*
> . . . . . .
> *One spark turns into three, seven, and countless numbers,*
> *like swarms of fireflies setting upon the prairie wild.*

. . . . . .

So many . . . so quickly! Even I am amazed—
all of them coming from my tiny spark.
Half a spark has set thousands, nay, millions of places ablaze;
light, what life you have in the dark!

. . . . . .

Burn on, in the torches of warriors of justice,
to guide them in their battles and their march,
as they spread the fire in ten thousand places,
until victory is won and they pass under a triumphal arch.

. . . . . .

Burn on, fire; burn on
in this long and unending night,
and break through its dark deathly silence,
to prophesy that dawn will be splendid and bright.
When we finally see that real dawn break,
humanity shall rejoice in freedom's morning light.[48]

That vision was intoxicating, but the dreamers behind *A Spark of Fire* soon woke up to a different sequence of events. In May 1960, Tan Chanxue, Zhang Chunyuan's girlfriend and a core member of the group, made an unsuccessful attempt to smuggle herself across the border to Hong Kong. A daring gambit by Zhang Chunyuan to rescue her—carrying a fake Public Security Bureau ID, he walked in the front door of the detention center where she was being held—ended in disaster: police found out his true identify and promptly detained him.

Meanwhile, the Gansu provincial Public Security Bureau had already been tipped off by two exiled Rightists. They had found out about some of the activities of the Lanzhou University group and reported the suspected "counterrevolutionary organization" to the authorities.

Lin Zhao's friends became alarmed after the arrests of Tan and Zhang and burned some of the manuscripts for the second issue.

But the inevitable finally arrived: at the end of September, a total of thirty-three people in Wushan county, including all the contributors to *A Spark of Fire* in the area, were arrested. More were implicated and arrested later on. On October 24, police showed up in Lin Zhao's home in Suzhou. Her father had been coming to visit her from time to time. That day, he stumbled upon the scene of the arrest and the police search of the house. He muttered to himself, "It's all over with our family!"[49]

The former magistrate Peng had fared poorly since the change of regime in 1949. Labeled a "historical counterrevolutionary," he had been unable to find a job. In fact, he had been denounced as an unrepentant, reactionary diehard, and his photo was prominently displayed on a neighborhood bulletin board, complete with an insulting caption about his political background.

Divorced from Xu Xianmin in 1952, he had fallen into destitution and despondency. At times, he had followed elderly Buddhist lay women as they visited homes, chanting sutras for the dead just to earn a meal or two.[50] His classical Chinese and modern Western education were a distant memory. Perhaps his children, especially Lin Zhao, had given him some hope. But on the day of Lin Zhao's arrest, his darkest fear about where Lin Zhao's adolescent pursuit of communism might lead her was realized.

On November 23, 1960, Peng Guoyan swallowed rat poison and died a slow, painful death.[51]

five

SHATTERED JADE

O, let me not be mad, not mad, sweet heaven.
Keep me in temper: I would not be mad!

—King Lear

Men are so necessarily mad, that not to be mad would amount
to another form of madness.

—Blaise Pascal[1]

AFTER HER ARREST, LIN ZHAO WAS SENT TO THE NO. 2 DETENTION
House of Shanghai. Located on the former Rue Massenet (Now
Sinan Road), the facility was completed in 1911 and became known
as the French Concession Jail, with a capacity of 1,100.

By 1931, the rising tide of nationalism had eroded the system
of extraterritoriality imposed on the Chinese since the Opium
War. The French turned over administrative control of the jail to
the Guomindang government, a milestone in China's struggle to
regain its sovereignty. The Nationalists quickly filled the jail with
local CCP leaders and pro-Communist progressives. Among them
were Deng Zhongxia, former CCP party secretary of Jiangsu and
Guangdong provinces, the poet Ai Qing, and Shi Liang, the China

Democratic League leader and Xu Xianmin's colleague during the 1940s. After the triumph of the Communists in 1949, it became known as Shanghai's No. 2 Detention House.[2]

Most of Lin Zhao's friends arrested in 1960 in connection with *A Spark of Fire* were incarcerated in Gansu province. In August 1961, Zhang Chunyuan managed to escape using a modern version of the ancient "ruse of bodily distress": he starved himself and repeatedly self-induced vomiting until he passed out. He was taken to a reform-through-labor hospital outside the prison. One evening a couple of weeks later, he walked out of the hospital dressed as a doctor going off his shift.

Zhang made his way to Suzhou, where he learned about Lin Zhao's arrest, and then continued on to Shanghai. "Lin Zhao, I cannot go in to visit you. I only circled around the high, red wall twice as a small token of my thoughts for you," Zhang Chunyuan wrote in a postcard sent in the name of Xu Xianmin to the No. 2 Detention House. "You may wonder how I came to Shanghai. . . . Someone was willing to let his big brother walk free."

As if that was not enough to rouse the suspicion of the authorities, Zhang added, "I had a 390-day personal experience of the life and study you are having in there." Lin Zhao never received the postcard. It was later found in Zhang Chunyuan's prison file. He was rearrested on September 6, 1961. Sentenced to life imprisonment in 1965, Zhang was executed instead in 1970 during the "One Strike, Three Anti" campaign for allegedly "repeating counterrevolutionary activities inside prison."[3]

The guiding principle of CCP's prison system, adapted from the penal doctrines of the early twentieth century, was to reform, or "move and convert" (*ganhua*), the hearts and minds of the inmates as part of the revolutionary restructuring of Chinese society toward "ideological totalism." Under Mao's rule, the pre-revolution goal of reforming the convicts was replaced by the CCP's "revolutionary conquest" of thoughts.[4]

Lin Zhao's initial response to the attempted conquest of her mind was to counter with a passionate self-defense of some two hundred thousand characters that she titled "The Diary of My Thoughts." In a reference to the venerated Marxian doctrine—"It is not the consciousness of men that determines their existence, but their social existence that determines their consciousness"—she argued that the brutal misrule of the CCP had caused her disillusionment with communism and turned her from an ardent supporter into an opponent. "External causes [became operative] through internal causes," she added, quoting from Mao's articulation of dialectical materialism in his 1937 essay "On Contradiction." "The most internal and the most innate reason" for her to become a Rightist was "my very strong democratic beliefs and liberal tendencies."[5]

Not all of her protests were solemn. At times during her interrogation, she would sing the "Oddities Song," which had been popular during the late 1940s, on the eve of the collapse of the Nationalist state: "The moon rose from the west, / and the sun has set in the east," she crooned. "The rocks in the riverbed— / oh, they rolled and rolled and rolled up the hill." The guards stomped their feet and cursed her.

She was taken by the look and bearing of one of the interrogators, she later admitted to a friend. "I almost had a crush on him, if he had not tried to extort a confession from me." Sometimes she wanted to have nothing to do with politics anymore; she wanted to settle down instead as a housewife.[6]

By the autumn of 1961, her opposition had wavered. The relentless, institutionalized reformation program had been effective. From the steady supply of propaganda materials such as *Liberation Daily*—the mouthpiece of Shanghai's party committee—Lin Zhao had learned of the CCP's economic retrenchment, after the excesses of the Great Leap Forward.

"After coming to the No. 2 Detention House, I have learned a bit through the newspaper about the situation since the 'Ninth Plenum of the Eighth Central Committee,'" Lin Zhao wrote in "A Review and Examination of My Personal Thought Journey." She submitted the self-examination to the authorities in October 1961 after being "illuminated and educated" by an official. "I have seen changes in the political line of the party."[7]

The Ninth Plenum of the CCP Central Committee to which she referred was held in Beijing in January 1961. In an acknowledgment of the disastrous consequences of the Great Leap Forward, the committee reformulated its economic policy, which slowed down the development of heavy industry. It also approved limited sideline productions outside collectivized farming, as well as the reopening of private markets in rural areas to alleviate starvation.[8]

By this point, Mao had nominally retired from the front line, replaced as chairman of the People's Republic by Liu Shaoqi. The changes Liu Shaoqi helped bring about gradually improved life in the countryside. About 6 percent of rural land was restored to peasants as private plots, and thousands of inefficient industrial and irrigation projects were scrapped.[9]

"With the passage of time, I felt that, this time, the party has its feet on the solid ground and is seeing the masses. My feelings started to change," Lin Zhao wrote. She was now willing to admit that, a decade after the CCP came to power, its rule was not without accomplishments, and the political reform of the previous months suggested that there was still "vitality" and a potential for renewal and progress in the party. She had made the mistake of "extremism" in adopting the "harmful" stance of opposition to the CCP. From that point on, "my responsibility is to do all I can to warmly support and concretely promote the democratization of the party's rule." Even if the government decided to mete out criminal punishments for her, she would calmly accept it.[10]

She later revealed that, whenever she thought back to what she wrote in 1961, "I would look at myself with a lonely—mocking, painful—smile! I would laugh at its author . . . what a naïve and childish young person!"[11]

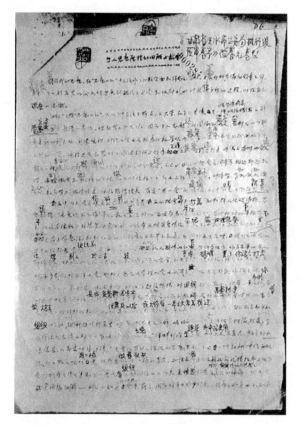

Lin Zhao, "A Review and Examination of My Personal Thought Journey," submitted to the authorities at the Shanghai No. 2 Detention House, October 14, 1961. Courtesy of Tan Chanxue.

The softening of Lin Zhao's attitudes was likely one of the main reasons she was given a medical parole in March 1962. Her tuberculosis had apparently flared up again, causing her to frequently cough up blood. She returned to her family's apartment in Shanghai. For the first time, she was able to mourn her father, wearing a white flower in her hair. She had only learned of his death in the late summer of 1961—almost ten months after it happened.[12]

Within weeks of her release, she realized that her hope of democratization and reform of the CCP rule was only wishful thinking and that her freedom would not last. Her collaborators in the production of *A Spark of Fire* remained in jail. She informed the neighborhood police at the end of the month that her clothes were already packed and that she was ready to be taken back to jail.[13]

Lin Zhao's grim expectations were not unfounded. She received a summons to appear in the Jing'an District People's Court in late August 1962 and was indicted for her involvement in the alleged "Lanzhou University Rightist Counterrevolutionary Clique" case. She responded with a written self-defense arguing that "counter-revolutionary" was not a serious legal term and that it was a just act to resist the unjust totalitarian rule—she vowed, in fact, to "fight to the death to oppose" it. The real question, she added, was not what crimes her generation of youths had committed against the ruler, but what crimes the ruler had committed against them. Her bluntness was such that, when she appeared in court, a judge suggested that she was mentally abnormal. "Are you sick?" he asked.[14]

Meanwhile, still on medical parole, Lin Zhao remained free and waded deeper into trouble. One day, dressed in a body-hugging mandarin gown, or *qipao*, with her hair in a permanent wave, she showed up in the office of Hu Ziheng, a former political instructor at the South Jiangsu Journalism Vocational School who had become manager of the production and sales department at *Liberation Daily*. She gleefully made a scene. Slapping her hand against the desk of the speechless Hu, she asked: "I want to start a newspaper also. Do you Communists have the magnanimity to let me do it?"[15]

She also wrote a letter to Lu Ping, then the president of Peking University, and challenged him to do what his predecessor Cai Yuanpei had done in 1919 during the May Fourth Movement. After the arrest of dozens of students who had participated in the May Fourth protests, President Cai mobilized university presidents in Beijing in a joint public outcry against the warlord government, winning the release of the students. Lin Zhao asked Lu Ping to follow Cai's example, stand up to Communist "tyranny" and bring back to campus students who had been arrested or otherwise persecuted following the democracy movement of 1957. Even though she hardly expected a response to her appeal, she later wrote, she felt compelled to make it out of a sense of responsibility.[16]

With her former classmates and friends either in jail or in exile, Lin Zhao dreamed of building a new alliance of disaffected intellectuals against the CCP rule. During a brief stay in Suzhou in the summer of 1962, she made the acquaintance of two young Rightists who had recently returned from a labor camp. She convinced one of them, Huang Zheng, to assist her in drafting a political platform for a "Battle League of Free Youths of China" that would "bring together activists in the Chinese democratic anti-tyranny movement of yesteryear," namely the Rightists. Considering the fact that she had vigorously opposed any attempt at organization building when her Lanzhou University friends were preparing to publish *A Spark of Fire* in 1960, it is remarkable how reckless she had become in 1962, when she was being shadowed by undercover police.[17]

Just as impulsive was Lin Zhao's approach of Arnold Newman, a "stateless alien," on a street in central Shanghai near her home one day in September 1962. She begged him to take four pieces of her writing out of China. These included her letter to Lu Ping and an appeal to public opinion entitled "We Are Innocent." When Newman asked her to whom the writings should be sent, she answered, in English: "To the world!" She was convinced that their publication would shock the West.[18]

Last known photo of Lin Zhao, while she was on medical parole in 1962. Courtesy of Ni Jingxiong.

Newman was probably one of some twenty thousand European Jews who, in the 1930s–1940s, fled the Nazis and found safe haven in the International Settlement in Shanghai, which one could more or less freely enter without a visa. He may have been stranded in the city after the Communist takeover and, in any event, was in no position to help her. The police soon took him into custody as an "imperialist spy," and he surrendered the documents.[19]

In early November, Lin Zhao was again arrested. She was sent to the Shanghai Psychiatric Hospital, where she underwent several weeks of evaluation and was found to be mentally ill. (The examining doctor was allegedly denounced later for attempting to shield her and another high-profile counterrevolutionary by diagnosing them with mental disorders.)[20]

Lin Zhao later reflected in her letter to the editors of People's Daily that, since few in China had spoken out against the party under the "suffocating" rule of the CCP, "this young person who dared to ask the tiger for his skin probably was indeed 'insane' in the eyes of the ruler." She admitted, at the same time, that "it is possible that, hard hit by the Anti-Rightist" purge, she did develop "certain signs of mental abnormality, but at least I was no more mentally abnormal than you gentlemen!"[21]

On December 23, she was transferred to the Shanghai Municipal Prison, commonly referred to as Tilanqiao, where she spent the next eight and a half months of her presentencing incarceration, which lasted a total of thirty months.[22]

Although its main purpose was incarceration of convicts, Tilanqiao had also served as a pretrial detention center since the early 1950s. On a single day in April during the Suppression of Counterrevolutionaries Campaign of 1951, a citywide crackdown on counterrevolutionaries rounded up 8,359 people, 285 of whom were executed within the next three days. An additional 1,060 were shot over the months of June and July to fill the quota personally set by Mao: he had declared that "at least around 3,000" counterrevolutionaries of various stripes in Shanghai "must be killed in 1951." The rest were mostly sent to Tilanqiao, which became a clearinghouse for arrested counterrevolutionaries.[23]

Little is known about Lin Zhao's pretrial detention in Tilanqiao. We know that she went on a month-long hunger strike in February 1963. She also stopped taking medicine for tuberculosis in protest against the "rough and inhumane treatments" to which she was subjected after her hunger strike began, probably a reference to force-feeding. And she attempted to take her own life at least once, which landed her in a specially designed *xiangpi jian* or rubber cell for the suicidal.[24]

On June 19, she penned a "Hunger Strike Declaration" stating that she "would rather spend the rest of my life in prison and wear out its floor; I vow to never be unworthy of my original aspirations or change a bit of my original ideal." She also tried to convince a cellmate, who was about to be released, to join the "Battle League of Free Youths of China," which had yet to materialize. "I even performed the initiation rite for her!" Lin Zhao did not realize that it was a setup: her cellmate had been recruited by the police as an informer. Once released, she lured Huang Zheng into a trap. Huang was arrested in the fall of 1963 and sentenced to fifteen years in prison for his role in fantasizing the league. Not surprisingly, as the "principal criminal" in the case, Lin Zhao would eventually receive a more severe punishment than her codefendants.[25]

During this period, another cellmate, an independent preacher named Yu Yile, apparently helped Lin Zhao deepen her Christian faith. Educated at the conservative Christian Bible Institute in Nanjing, where an otherworldly pietism dominated—the school was founded by the conservative theologian Jia Yuming—Yu Yile disapproved of Lin Zhao's political activism and attempted to bring her back to a faith shorn of worldly political passions.[26]

Yet Lin Zhao was already beyond an otherworldly Christianity. Her faith did not offer an escape from political reality. On the contrary, it became the backbone of her rebellion against the CCP rule. In due time, it turned into a conviction that her resistance to the "demonic political party" was a divine mission that no means of torture employed by the CCP state could stop.

On August 8, 1963, to subject Lin Zhao to a full regime of interrogation, the authorities moved her to the Shanghai No. 1 Detention House—the real "demon's den," as she soon found out.[27]

LOCATED ON NANCHEZHAN Road, which in the early 1900s was part of the "Chinese City" outside the Western concessions, the No. 1 Detention House was built in 1917 as the Shanghai County Detention House. It was part of a modernization project of post-imperial China, which attempted to detach, for the first time, the judicial and administrative functions of the county government. It is questionable, however, that the distinction ever came to be made. In the late 1940s, the detention house was run by the Nationalist secret police in Shanghai. In May 1949, on the eve of the Communist takeover, thirteen revolutionaries and progressives, including Huang Jingwu, the Harvard-educated audit commissioner for Guomindang's Central Bank, were buried alive in the drill ground inside it. (Huang had attempted, by bringing the story to the media, to sabotage Chiang Kai-shek's secret shipment of gold and silver bullion to Taiwan.)[28]

During the Mao era, the No. 1 Detention House was mainly used for interrogating political prisoners and cracking "counterrevolutionary cases." Occupying an area of more than two thousand square meters, the jail processed several thousand political prisoners each year in the early 1950s. At its peak, in 1954, 7,183 "counterrevolutionaries" endured interrogations within its walls. These were the "enemies without guns," as Mao had put it.[29]

A Chinese jail designed by a relative of Chinese American architect I. M. Pei, the No. 1 Detention House adopted indigenous architecture. It had a three-story brick block for male inmates and a two-story block for women. Each had high ceilings and long, dark hallways. The cells had cement-covered walls on all sides and a heavy, wooden door in the front—unlike those in the foreign concessions with walls on three sides and an open iron grille facing the gangway. The doors were painted a uniform red color and secured with an iron bar and a giant copper padlock. Each door had a small square shutter that could be opened from the outside to deliver food; guards left it open at night in order to monitor motion inside the cell.

"There was no sound in the hallway," remembers Yan Zuyou, who, as a college student, was imprisoned in the No. 1 Detention House as a counterrevolutionary in 1964. "You cannot feel any breeze except a dark coldness that seeps into your bone."[30] A typical cell was about three by five meters and had a cement toilet built into the far corner. Up to fourteen inmates were crammed into each. At night, they slept on the floor, most of them parallel to the outside wall. Each was allowed a width of less than half a meter, head against the feet of the next person, a rule allegedly enforced to prevent homosexual activities. The rest of the inmates would fill up the remaining space perpendicular to the door.

The window on the outside wall was set high, its lower half covered by an exterior wooden box so that even a tall person could not see the street. The room darkened early in the afternoon. "It was gloomy and dreary even on a bright, sunny day," one former inmate recalled. At night, two adjacent cells shared a 15-watt light bulb mounted on the three-meter-high ceiling above a small opening in the wall between the cells—so high that "not even a basketball player could commit suicide by electrocuting himself." With little exposure to sunlight—inmates were allowed to exercise outside their cells for only half an hour each week —most of them acquired a ghastly pallor and a vacant stare.[31]

Jail rules, printed on the cell wall, prohibited the exchange of material items or information among the inmates, including the circumstances of their cases and even their names, which were replaced with assigned numbers. Citing the needs of ongoing criminal investigations, the No. 1 Detention House prohibited any mail correspondence or family visits, though families were allowed to bring approved food items and daily necessities on the fifth of each month.[32]

To this day, Lin Zhao's interrogation records remain locked away in her classified file. Without access to that file, information on her pretrial incarceration at the No. 1 Detention House can be gleaned, for the most part, only from her own prison writings.

Deep inside the jail compound, set back from the cellblock bordering the street, was a bungalow with a row of narrow, long rooms of less than eight square meters each. These were the interrogation rooms, each with a wooden counter near the end, behind which sat the interrogator. Two meters away sat a heavy wooden chair for the "criminal," with a removable iron bar across the front that could be used to keep the inmate in place.[33]

From the beginning, Lin Zhao had to face "indecent taunts," including sexual innuendo, from her interrogator. She lodged formal protests and insisted that they be included in the interrogation records before she signed them. "I asked the interrogator what right he had to harass me? What was the connection between my political activities and my gender?" She would pay a price for her defiance. "A mere chit of a girl as you are," she was told by her interrogator, "shall I not be able to subdue you?" She was soon put in handcuffs.[34]

At the No. 1 Detention House, punishments meted out to inmates who misbehaved or resisted typically took the form of punitive handcuffing. Beating was uncommon and, when necessary, mostly left to fellow inmates, who were instigated by the guards. But manhandling by the guards also occurred. One female guard was particularly aggressive. "I lose track of how much hair she pulled off my head," Lin Zhao later wrote.[35]

During a nighttime interrogation, a female guard roughed her up and "tortured Lin Zhao as she was handcuffed and tied to the chair in the interrogation room," she wrote, referring to herself in third person. The interrogator "leisurely sat there, enjoying it all, and said to this young person who . . . like a struggling, trapped animal, was still carrying on what appeared to be entirely useless resistance, 'I think it is better to submit to the law and get a sentence of a few years.'" When Lin Zhao was later beaten by a guard and lodged her protest, the response was: "Anybody who is under attack can exercise the right of self-defense"—in spite of the fact that she was handcuffed behind her back and weak from her hunger strike at the time.[36]

But handcuffing alone was often sufficient torture, for it had evolved into a fanciful form of penal art. Punitive handcuffing—an inmate's hands were pulled behind his back and cuffed—ranged in duration from a day to several months. One would be unable to eat, dress or undress, or go to the bathroom without help from his fellow inmates. At times, he would be reduced to licking food from the floor. The handcuffs had various tightness settings, which would determine the level of pain inflicted. Excessively tight handcuffs bored into the skin, causing infections and even rot and leaving permanent marks, so that it looked "as if one wore those handcuffs his entire life."[37]

There were variations of behind-the-back handcuffing. One was the euphemistic airplane-style handcuffing: the cuffs were put on the upper arms, cutting off blood circulation and causing the arms to turn purple. Inmates so cuffed, with their upper arms pulled sharply back, looked as though they were readying their "wings" to fly. Another cuffing style, known as shoulder-pole handcuffing, gave the inmate the appearance of carrying a bamboo shoulder pole, like a farmer: one hand was pulled over the shoulder, the other was pulled up from behind, and the two were fastened together with cuffs. Yet another variation was pig-style handcuffing. The upper arms were first cuffed together behind the back. Next, both feet were cuffed. The arms and the feet were then joined together using a third pair of handcuffs, so that one looked "like a pig about to be butchered in a slaughter house." This last style sometimes led to broken bones and permanent disabilities.[38]

FOR LIN ZHAO, such was the shock of punitive handcuffing—she was sometimes placed in two pairs of behind-the-back handcuffs, with one pair on her wrists and another on her upper arms—that later on, she could not look back without bursting into grief: "I was repeatedly tortured in myriads of cruel ways. . . . Just thinking about them is driving me insane. Alas, what a world is this? What am I?"[39]

In China, the extortion of confessions through torture can be traced back at least to the Western Zhou dynasty (ca. 1040–771 BCE). By the Qin dynasty (221–206 BCE), flogging with a wooden staff or a bamboo strip was common practice. Under the Han (206 BCE–220 CE), it was codified to allow for a wooden staff about an inch in diameter and five feet long, or a bamboo club about half an inch thick—which, in three hundred strikes, could easily beat the life out of the interrogated. "What confession are you not able to obtain with a wooden staff?" observed a court official to the first emperor of the Ming dynasty (1368–1644).[40]

Shortly after the overthrow of the last imperial dynasty in 1912, the Republic of China, through a presidential decree, banned extortion of confessions. In 1935, the Nationalists' Nanjing government introduced further judicial reforms that outlawed the use of "torture, coercion, enticements, or trickery." However, those reforms were nonchalantly bypassed in the Guomindang secret police's interrogation of captured Communists.

As early as 1922, a year after its founding, the Chinese Communist Party had called for an end to torture. Nevertheless, torture was widely used in the early 1930s during purges within the Red Army and again during the Yan'an Rectification Campaign in the early 1940s. The so-called rescue campaign that Mao launched against suspected Nationalist "spies"—CCP cadres and progressive intellectuals who had joined the revolution in Yan'an but whose loyalty was in doubt—invariably employed cruel techniques. Bo Yibo, a top CCP leader in the Mao era, recalled his days in Yan'an when locals spoke about "ghosts" and ghastly shrieks coming from some cave dwellings at night. He later found out that almost a hundred of those being "rescued" through interrogation were being held in half a dozen caves, many laughing and crying, having lost their mind.[41]

In 1950, at the start of the Suppression of Counterrevolutionaries Campaign, the Government Administration Council (now State Council) and the Supreme People's Court issued the first directive of the new People's Republic against extorting confessions through torture. In practice, however, the directive was promptly and generally ignored.[42]

In October 1963, two months after her arrival at the No. 1 Detention House, Lin Zhao found herself overcome with desolation. It had already been three years after her first arrest, and the bleakness of "autumn moods" and "autumn sounds" brought to mind another "autumn."

Qiu Jin (1875–1907)—the most celebrated feminist revolutionary of early twentieth-century China, whose family name Qiu means "autumn"—had often used qiu in her poems to evoke the barrenness of her existence and of her times. In 1904, she left her merchant husband whom her parents had forced her to marry. "Unbinding my feet I clean out a thousand years of poison," she declared in a poem as she boarded a ship for Japan. There, as a student, she was exposed to some of the most radical nationalist ideas of the day. The next year, she joined the Revolutionary Alliance of Sun Yat-sen, dedicated to the violent overthrow of the Manchu rulers of China. She returned to China in 1906 and, though imbued with reformist ideals such as equality and education for women, was drawn ever more toward the vision of a heroic, bloody revolution that would usher in a new China.

In 1907, Qiu Jin was arrested for her role in plotting an armed uprising against the imperial dynasty and summarily beheaded. For her confession, she wrote a line of verse taken from a Qing dynasty poet: "Autumn rain, autumn wind, they make one die of sorrow."[43]

For Lin Zhao, the parallel between Qiu Jin's political dreams and her own was hard to overlook. She decided to compose several seven-character rhymes, each inspired by the one-line verse Qiu Jin had written before her execution. Using pen and paper provided to her to make her confessions, Lin Zhao wrote, in a preface to the poems, "I have the desire to patch the stones and will not abstain from using a dog's tail to lengthen a sable coat." This was a reference to the mythic Nüwa, the goddess-creator who had smelted together stones of five different colors to repair the collapsed sky and to stop the heavenly flood. Qiu Jin had also alluded to Nüwa in her writings.

Though perhaps unworthy of drawing a comparison between herself and Qiu Jin, Lin Zhao suggested, she would make known her own lament, even if it meant extending the "sable coat" with inferior material. The poems, collectively entitled "Songs of Autumn's Sounds," begin with these lines:

> Autumn rain, autumn wind, they make one die of sorrow;
> leaning against the distant sky, I mourn over the brambles before
>   my eyes.
> Fox borrows in the city wall, rats in Land and Soil God's altar:
>   the mountains have aged;
> the fatness of the land drips away and the grain offering subsides.[44]

In November, Lin Zhao was struck with a particularly acute sorrow. "The pain of grief, heavy yet burning, like molten lead, poured into my heart. Sir, I learned of your assassination two hours ago from the newspaper," Lin Zhao wrote in "Mourning inside a Jail Cell" on November 24, 1963, two days after John F. Kennedy's death.[45]

Lin Zhao's admiration for Kennedy dated to 1962, when she was on medical parole. Due to the blackout of Western media, "I was only able to read a few of your remarks, which were only cut up into fragments." But even those fragments "radiated incomparably powerful and sincere humanitarian sentiments," she explained. "I remember you saying: 'all men who fight for freedom are our brothers.'" The line was from a speech Kennedy made on December 29, 1962. It was quoted in a New China News Agency (Xinhuashe) bulletin the next day denouncing US attempts at "counterrevolutionary restoration in Cuba." The dispatch made its way into major party newspapers, a routine practice at the time.[46]

Lin Zhao wrote, in "Mourning inside a Jail Cell":

> You said: "Freedom is indivisible, and when one man is enslaved, all are not free!" . . . You have revealed to us—contemporary young fighters against tyrannical rule in China—more profoundly and more broadly the rich meaning of the sacred concept of freedom. In this way you have encouraged us and inspired in us the resolve, perseverance, and courage to dedicate our lives to her![47]

The quote was from Kennedy's historic "Ich bin ein Berliner" speech, delivered near the Berlin Wall on June 26, 1963. Chinese media did not publish it at the time, but nine days later, on July 5, a Xinhuashe bulletin denounced Kennedy's visit to Western Europe as evidence of "the American imperialists' wild scheme of aggression." The United States was "bent on gobbling up the German Democratic Republic and annihilating the socialist camp," it claimed, and Kennedy had "wildly shrieked, 'real, lasting peace in Europe can never be assured as long as one German out of four is denied the elementary right of free men'; 'when one man is enslaved, all are not free.'"[48]

Lin Zhao came upon these quotations in either *People's Daily* or *Liberation Daily*, both of which were provided to inmates as political study materials to facilitate thought reform.[49] The live ideological vaccine used in the party propaganda had given her the very disease it was designed to prevent. "It appears that the policy of keeping the people ignorant, with its efforts at freezing and hardening all brains, is pathetically futile," she wrote. "After all, it cannot make us not love freedom. Freedom—the most sacred, the most beautiful, and the most noble noun in the human language—always kindles the most fervent love . . . in the souls of people, especially the young people!"

She was convinced that Kennedy had cherished "sincere concern, sympathy, and compassion" for the Chinese people. One day, "I will certainly come to pay my respects to you—at your tomb," she wrote. As fellow "followers of Christ," Lin Zhao was convinced that they both "breathed" in the love of Christ and that his spirit in heaven would know that "inside a certain prison in Red China, a young soldier of freedom, with wounds from shackles in her arms, is propping up her sick body and, using a straw stem as her pen and the crudest ink and paper, silently writing down her mourning and her grief for you!"[50]

LIN ZHAO'S ARM wounds had hardly healed when she was again put into two pairs of handcuffs, sometime after she revised her eulogy for Kennedy on November 25. It is unclear what prompted her new ordeal, although it was likely part of the continuing attempts to extract confessions from her. Using suicide prevention as a pretext, the jail authorities also sent someone Lin Zhao called a secret agent into her cell, to watch her day and night and to inflict "abuse, insults, swearing, and beating."

On February 5, 1964, Lin Zhao was so distraught that she swallowed medicated soap in a frantic but futile suicide attempt.[51] In her "Self Eulogy," probably written just before she tried to kill herself, she lamented that, as a wronged political prisoner, she had cried her eyes out over the sorrows of her homeland and over her own mistake of having dedicated her life to communism in her late teens.

Lin Zhao's "Self Eulogy" was a four-character rhyme of sixty-four lines and employed the oldest Chinese poetic form, dating from almost three millennia ago. "Once straying down the wrong path," she wrote, "I have now turned back! / . . . My young heart was then pure as water, / Heaven, bear me witness against their attack!" Like the ancient hero Jing Ke who had sung his heart out on the streets of Yanjing (now Beijing) before setting off on a doomed attempt to assassinate the monstrous future First Emperor of Qin, Lin Zhao, too, had "sung my songs on Yanjing's streets." She also had "no regrets to be the prisoner from Chu," a reference to Zhong Yi, the faithful minister of the feudal state of Chu in the sixth century BCE, who never forgot his home state while serving as a prisoner of war. She continued:

Freedom is without a price,
yet within bounds my life lies.
Shattered jade is what I will to be,
offered to China as a sacrifice![52]

Mixing despair with lofty ideals, Lin Zhao appeared to have identified with the tragic tradition of loyal Confucian ministers embracing noble failure, when a bad ruler turned away from the Way and fell under the influence of treacherous court officials. The "shattered jade" was intended to call to mind the bitter choice Confucian scholars through the ages often had to make between life and dignity. The metaphor emerged from the story of the principled stand by a sixth-century prince against a usurper of the throne. When it became clear that the only way to escape death was to change the surname of the entire clan to that of the new emperor, he swore to "rather be a shattered jade vessel than an unbroken pottery."[53]

Lin Zhao had written her "Self Eulogy" in her own blood. It was the first blood writing she did in prison that we know of. Like the choice of the four-character poetic form, her use of blood was in part a matter of necessity: her hands were cuffed behind her back, and she had been deprived of stationery.[54]

It was also a deliberate choice: blood writing had a long tradition in Chinese culture, with roots in an ancient practice of Buddhist devotion. While Confucian teachings on filial piety dictated careful preservation of the body bestowed by one's parents, the popular Buddhist tradition, which arose in the post–Han era, sanctioned blood writing as "a performance of virtue." The historical Buddha allegedly claimed that, as a religious devotee in a previous existence, he had been challenged by the demon Mara to strip off his skin and write out a hymn on it using his own blood, which he did.

In China, the earliest record of blood writing as an expression of Buddhist piety dates from the early sixth century CE, when the ardent faith of the Wu Emperor of the Liang dynasty inspired many Buddhist followers to cut themselves. *The Basic Annals of the Liang Dynasty* noted that "some drew their own blood and sprinkled it on the ground; others drew blood and used it to copy Buddhist sutras."[55] The ritual came to embody sublime sincerity and entered into secular culture.

In a sixteenth-century dramatic rendering of the tragic legend of Wang Zhaojun, concubine of a Han dynasty emperor during the first century BCE, blood writing was crucial to the tale's climatic moment. Wang, a dazzling beauty from the imperial harem, was nevertheless sent off to be the wife of a barbarian chieftain in order to appease the nomadic Xiongnu tribes of Central Asia. As she neared the border, she chastised the weak-kneed generals for refusing to fight, which resulted in the emperor's shame and her sacrifice. Before drowning herself in the Black River, she made a final statement of virtue: she tore off a piece of her dress, bit her finger, and wrote a letter in blood to the emperor, declaring her loyalty and chastity. She entrusted the letter to a wild goose, which dutifully carried it to the grieving emperor. In Mao's China, blood writing also became a revolutionary ritual: during the Cultural Revolution, "tens of thousands" of student radicals in Beijing reportedly wrote out their pledge of devotion to Mao in blood.[56]

LIN ZHAO EXPERIENCED a brief respite in the spring of 1964. The two pairs of handcuffs were removed from her wrists and arms after she wrote a statement of repentance on March 23. What she revealed in it is unclear, but it appears to have mainly concerned her 1962 letter to Lu Ping, as well as her appeal to the world entitled "We Are Innocent." Nothing in the indictment later brought against her suggests that she had incriminated herself in her statement. Nor is there any evidence of her incriminating others.[57]

On April 12, the anniversary of the martyrdom of her uncle Xu Jinyuan—a Communist activist killed by the Guomindang secret police during the violent purge of the CCP in 1927—she was overwhelmed with the cruel irony of mourning his death "from a Red prison." "If only you had known / the millions of compatriots for whom you sacrificed your life / are now but unfree sinners and famished slaves!" she wrote. During this period, she also produced a host of other writings—essays, letters, and poems, including a verse dedicated "To the Shackles"—none of which has yet been found. On May 20, however, she was back in handcuffs.[58]

By August, less than three months before the Jing'an District People's Procuratorate produced its indictment against Lin Zhao, her interrogation appeared to have intensified. Later that month, she was beaten by several female guards. Still without stationery, and with her hands again cuffed, she wrote words of protest—"Wronged" and "Where is justice?"—in blood across her sleeves and the back of her shirt.[59]

On September 7, her shackles were removed. Pen and paper were also returned to her on September 26, possibly to allow her to make confessions and incriminate others. What she produced, however, was a series of eight-line, seven-character rhymes that castigated Mao's rule.[60]

The first used the same rhyme scheme as "The Capture of Nanjing by the People's Liberation Army," a *qilü* that Mao had written in 1949, to rebuke his imperial pretensions. Mao had produced the verse after the CCP's army crossed the Yangzi River to take the Nationalist capital Nanjing. At the time, an ebullient Mao had waxed lyrical about "the mighty army, a million strong, crossing the Great River" to capture the city from Chiang Kai-shek's troops. "In heroic triumph heaven and earth have been overturned," Mao rhapsodized. "It is only the right Way for seas to turn into mulberry fields."[61] Line by line, Lin Zhao turned Mao's poem on its head:

Two dragons, locked in a fierce battle, spill blood over heaven and earth;
into the Great River, countless aggrieved souls are thrown.
Now as then, Lu Lian would rather drown in the ocean than bow to the
  Qin king,
and [the usurper] Cao Cao, with his sword drawn, a soaring poem
  would still intone.
To the common people alone our country rightly belongs;
how can mountains and rivers be for an emperor to own?
What shame to stain the Divine Land with people's blood!
Vain talks about seas turning into mulberry fields are what we've
  known.[62]

Just over a decade before, Mao had been the guiding "red star" in Lin Zhao's heart; she had called out "silently the name of our great leader—our dear father." She had traveled a long road since then.

Still, she at times clung to the hope that Mao might somehow repent. In 1963, after her re-arrest, she had "prayed for his soul." "After all, I am a Christian," she explained. She had "neither the right to offer forgiveness in the place of the Heavenly Father nor the right to prevent the Heavenly Father from forgiving him." What if Mao "reproaches himself in sorrowful repentance and moves Heaven's heart?" she wondered.[63]

Between September 1964 and March 1965, she completed a total of nine seven-character rhymes. Most of them were directed, like the first, at Mao, and alternated between denunciation and earnest remonstrance (*jian*)—which Confucian scholar-officials had repeatedly offered their rulers in the past—urging him to turn away from his "wrong path." Perhaps Mao would heed Confucius's admonition to "restrain oneself and restore the rites" in order to achieve benevolence, she hoped.[64]

"Pondering through an eternal night, chilled to the bone in dismay, / I hold a lonely jade-studded zither, but for whom shall I play?" Lin Zhao asked in another poem. She was evoking the predicament of Yue Fei, the twelfth-century Song dynasty war hero who was unable to dissuade his ruler from ruinous appeasements to the Jin invaders. "I wish to consign my worries to the jade-studded zither," Yue Fei had written in a poem, "but few understand the music. When the string snaps, who is there to hear?" In yet another poem, Lin Zhao pleaded, "Experience for yourself the people's plight, / "Merciful God is waiting for you to set it right."[65]

LIN ZHAO'S POEMS, rich in historical allusions and disciplined in their adherence to the seven-character rhyme scheme, were of little use to the interrogators and to those in Shanghai Jing'an District People's Procuratorate who were busy preparing the case against her. On November 4, 1964, the indictment was completed. Based on "eight volumes of interrogation records," it formally charged Lin Zhao as the "principal criminal" of the "'Battle League of Free Youths of China' Counterrevolutionary Clique."[66]

She was accused of having collaborated with her Lanzhou University Rightist friends in "plotting the publication of *A Spark of Fire*," in "spreading rumors," and in planning a "treasonous defection to the enemies." According to the indictment, Lin Zhao "engaged in a series of counterrevolutionary activities" both during her medical parole in 1962 and after her rearrest in a "vain attempt to overthrow the people's democratic dictatorship, sabotage the socialist cause, and give counterrevolutionary dying kicks in collusion with the imperialists." In light of her "extremely serious crimes," it asked for a "severe punishment."[67]

As was common practice, Lin Zhao was kept in the dark about the indictment while it was being prepared. On November 5, the day after its completion, she was surprised by a sudden act of generosity by the authorities. For the first time since her incarceration at the No. 1 Detention House, her family, though still forbidden to see her, was allowed to bring her several items she had requested: a cotton padded jacket, a bag of dried pork floss, a can of sautéed pork, a bag of candy, and a box of crackers.

For an inmate, these were rare luxuries. The three bare meals provided each day in jail, though regular—at 7:30 a.m., 11 a.m., and 4 p.m.—totaled about 375 grams of rice along with some vegetables and were never enough to fill one's stomach. (Meat would be added to the menu on national holidays.) After she received the package that day, Lin Zhao was taken to an interrogation room, where she watched female guards cook for her the fresh dumplings her mother had sent. [68]

Maybe the guards were treating her differently now that the formal interrogation was over; or perhaps they wanted to soften the blow of the grave indictment that was about to be delivered. In any event, stunned and confused, Lin Zhao began to speculate if Mao himself was behind it all. Could it be that, in response to her writings, which routinely ended up in the hands of the jail authorities, Mao himself was attempting to cajole her into submission? "That stinky Mao worm made a point of letting you bring me dumplings in order to dally with me," she assured her mother in a subsequent letter.[69]

Within days, however, harsh reality set in, again. On November 9, another nighttime "conversation" urging her to "examine her mistakes" drove her to a teary protest. Her agitation must have been considerable. Citing "nonsensical misbehavior" on her part, the guards put the handcuffs back on her that night. This time, the manacles would remain on her for the next six and a half months, until May 26, 1965, just days before she was handed over to the Shanghai Municipal Prison. "I wonder whether I had the honor of breaking the national or even world record during this decade of the 1960s," she later asked the editors of *People's Daily*.[70]

On November 10, Lin Zhao was thrown into an isolation cell "no bigger than a double bed" to compound the punishment and probably also to forestall her certain protest following the announcement of the indictment.[71] Pen and ink were also removed from her possession; for the next several months, she had nothing but her own blood for writing.

Distraught, she cut the vein on her left wrist with a piece of broken glass in yet another suicide attempt. When that failed, she went on a hunger strike. That, too, was foiled, when the guards dipped a rubber tube in Lysol and forced it down her nose to force-feed her, which caused "inflammation and swelling." A few days later, "the so-called Procuratorate personnel came to interrogate me. The moment I entered the room and before I had uttered a word, I began coughing, spattering blood all over the floor."[72]

On November 23, the anniversary of her father's suicide, she gave up her hunger strike, after painting an altar dedicated to him on a wall in her cell, using her blood. She later added an incense burner above the altar and decorated it with painted flowers. On the opposite wall, she painted a cross in blood.[73]

Lin Zhao was informed of the content of her indictment on November 17 and was given a copy of the indictment two weeks later. On December 5, a trial was held, at which she offered a self-defense. In response to the charge that while under detention, she had "resorted to loud shouting in an effort to instigate the inmates into an insurrection," she quipped, "the 'Indictment' neglected to list the important fact that, while in prison, I established an ordnance bureau and built three munitions factories and two arsenals!"

A few months later, when stationery was again made available to her, she wrote out a sentence-by-sentence, acidic annotation of the indictment, while correcting the repeated typos in the printed document. It must have given her a sense of editorial as well as moral victory over it. Parts of the annotated indictment read:

> [The defendant] was born in a bureaucratic bourgeoisie family.
> (Note: No idea what this means!)
> After 1950, she joined the land reform and Five-Antis work teams.
> (Note: Clear evidence that this "defendant" was neither trained in New York nor dispatched by Taipei but was instead one of the innocent ... blind followers incited and deceived by you!)

Criminal Lin Zhao committed the serious crime of organizing a counterrevolutionary clique . . . and providing intelligence to the enemies in collusion with the imperialists. (Note: Incoherent. But it raises the status of this mere chit of a girl. A rare fortune one encounters only once in three lifetimes. What incredible honor!)

The defendant produced "Seagull," a counterrevolutionary essay . . . and "Prometheus's Day of Passion." (Note: So even Prometheus and the seagull have become "counterrevolutionaries.")

After her arrest, she has consistently refused to confess her crimes. (Note: You still refuse to confess your monstrous crimes. Lin Zhao is innocent in her resistance. Of course she has nothing to confess!)[74]

Lin Zhao was aware that, for all its grammatical blemishes, literary ineptitude, and legal vacuity, the indictment would result in certain conviction. She decided, therefore, to seek "an arbitrator between the Public Security Bureau and its political prisoners." The day after the show trial, she asked the procuratorate to forward a letter of appeal to Shanghai's mayor Ke Qingshi. "According to the Chinese tradition, the responsible local magistrate is the parent for the people," she reminded him. "Therefore, Mayor Ke, I ask you to please set things straight for me."[75]

Ke, a revolutionary of high standing, had been Shanghai's mayor since 1958 and the powerful first party secretary of the East China Bureau of the CCP Central Committee since 1961. He had earned the respect—in her view—of both the general public and intellectuals in the Shanghai area.[76] It was conceivable to her that Ke could act as a modern knight-errant, who would come to the rescue of a young female intellectual wrongly incarcerated in his domain.

In reality, Ke Qingshi had been toeing the radical Maoist line since the Great Leap Forward. As a close associate of Mao and Jiang Qing, he had decried the widespread influence of bourgeois culture and had proposed publicly in 1963 that literature should "wholeheartedly depict the thirteen years" of Communist rule. As one of the earliest CCP members, Ke was purged during the "rescue" campaign in Yan'an in 1943 as a counterrevolutionary and was tied up with ropes after he denied the charges. His wife was driven to suicide—she jumped into a well—but Mao personally spared him, after which he developed a fierce loyalty to the chairman, which endured for the rest of his life.[77]

It is unlikely that Lin Zhao was entirely ignorant of Ke's leftist leaning, but with no recourse to any legal defense, an appeal to Ke seemed to be her best option. In February 1965, after she was again beaten by guards, she wrote a long second letter to Ke detailing the incident.[78] It was evident that the mayor of Shanghai had not intervened on her behalf since she sent her first letter of appeal in December. She did not know if it had even reached him.

She was becoming desperate and sensed that her sanity was slipping away. Frightened, she wrote on the narrow wall next to the door—in inch-size characters—"No, No! God will not let me go insane. As long as I live, he will certainly keep my senses, as he keeps my memory!"

Near the end of February, after yet another encounter with the guard, who taunted her about the force-feeding she had gone through—"It saves you the trouble of brushing your teeth," he said— she sank into a stupor. "I sat there motionless and dazed. A deep numbness . . . swept over me," she later recalled. "I felt that I was perhaps indeed about to go crazy! God, God help me! I am about to be driven crazy! But I must not go crazy, I don't want to go crazy!"[79]

She was not sent to the mental hospital, as she feared she would be. She merely slipped deeper into oblivion as a new, dark order of things encroached on her mind. In this vision, Chairman Mao himself was the director of the No. 1 Detention House. Soon enough, the rice soup she demanded began to smell of Lysol and gave her stomach cramps and diarrhea. She embarked again on a hunger strike and, during her remaining months in the detention house, refused solid food, even porridge, most of the time.[80]

Periodically, a formless agitation churning inside her would turn into a sudden "flash of lightning" striking her "desolate and despondent heart," and she would "burst into tears, crying out loud like a child." A "strange light" began to linger in her eyes, which was "frightening to behold," as other inmates later told her. In spite of the emerging signs of a fractured mind, she received no psychiatric evaluation or treatment.[81]

ON MARCH 5, still handcuffed and using her own blood as ink, she copied the nine seven-character rhymes she had composed since late September onto a white shirt and wrote out a four-character rhyme as a postscript. "Grieving over my own life, / I mourn for my country even more!" it reads. The poems remained an act of remonstration directed at the ruler, she explained, but "the strings on the jade-studded zither have snapped."

At first refusing to take the shirt, the guards accepted it the next day after she went on a hunger strike but returned it within a few hours along with her second letter of appeal to Ke Qingshi. Both were dropped onto the floor of her cell through the tiny window in the door. The guards explained that they could not be sent through the post office.[82] It was only after she made a "scene"—presumably with loud, tearful protests—that a senior jail official, while chiding her for being "reactionary to the point of becoming hysterical," finally took the writings.

Lin Zhao demanded a receipt. She also reminded the guards of the curious irony that, while the prison routinely searched the inmates' belongings and confiscated every single piece of writing they produced, she had to go to such extraordinary lengths to have her writings taken from her.[83]

IN HER AGONIZED and restless mind, Lin Zhao had perhaps fantasized about the blood-soaked pages of her two letters to Ke Qingshi landing on his desk and the mayor of Shanghai exploding in righteous indignation over the appalling mistreatment of an innocent, jailed intellectual under his watch. To her, Ke—reputedly one of the two regional party secretaries most trusted by Mao in all of China during the 1960s—was the only person who was able to stand up for her.[84]

On April 10, *Liberation Daily* brought news of the sudden death of Ke Qingshi the previous day. With the CCP's usual secrecy, the public announcement simply noted that Ke had died of illness, which spawned conspiracy theories of his poisoning by political enemies, especially after the outbreak of the Cultural Revolution in 1966. In reality, Ke, whose health had declined since a diagnosis of lung cancer the previous year, died naturally of cholecystitis and acute secondary pancreatitis.[85]

To Lin Zhao, however, mysterious dots began to connect: it was evident to her that, since she sent out her appeal letters, Ke had been "retained in Beijing" and prevented from returning to Shanghai. Her blood letters must have reached Ke, and he must have confronted Mao about them. And Mao, who she now believed had long harbored indecent sexual thoughts about her, must have grown jealous and "murdered" Ke by "poisoning." She had been, therefore, the direct cause of his death; Ke had died for her.[86]

Lin Zhao's response to Ke's presumed murder was characteristically impassioned and impulsive: she composed a long four-character rhyme mourning him as a "lone crane standing among a crowd of ravens." Then, "in accordance with an ancient custom of our country," she wrote, "I set up a memorial tablet for him and performed a posthumous wedding as his concubine!" She placed the tablet, painted with blood, next to the altar to her father.[87]

In these extreme actions, she surprised even herself. "If he had been alive, I would never have agreed to marry him," she later reflected. "I wasn't quite that naïve," she wrote, addressing Ke, "not to the extent of considering you a snow-white crow." As first party secretary of the East China Bureau, Ke was "likewise my enemy!"

She realized that her "love for the dead one," bizarre as it seemed, was "also a protest against the Dictator," the intensity of one corresponding to that of the other.[88]

LIN ZHAO REMAINED in the No. 1 Detention House till the end of May. In her last weeks, she started a long essay, which she titled "An Appeal to Humanity." Like all her other writings, it was confiscated upon her departure. Her detention of almost twenty-two months was perhaps unrivaled in its turbulence. The guards, in their frustration, had reminded her that not all the inmates had been treated with the same severity. "Who has been like you?" they asked.[89]

It may indeed have been different if she had not been given to unbending opposition. For those who resolved to survive, bending had often helped. Nien Cheng, author of *Life and Death in Shanghai*, who had worked for Shell International Petroleum Company in its Shanghai office and who was thrown into the No. 1 Detention House in 1966, learned to begin an interrogation session with a vigorous reading from *The Little Red Book* of Mao's quotations and deftly defended her views by quoting the chairman. Lin Zhao, who was familiar with what she called the "impudent, Mao style" writing—with its unbridled scatological interest—instead told the guards to not bother her when they attempted to sell the *Selected Works of Mao Zedong* to the inmates.[90]

A measure of quietude would likely have lessened her suffering. The interrogator had admonished her to make her days "a bit more tranquil." After all, the ground rule for all inmates was to obey. At the No. 1 Detention House, the inmates almost always made confessions. As an interrogator pointed out, one way or another, an inmate would eventually be "begging for a chance to confess." Those who did not "would not last . . . in this place."[91]

Other officials also told Lin Zhao to "learn to practice self-restraint and overcome impatience." But whenever she thought of "the evil committed by the so-called instrument of suppression" and of how other exiled or imprisoned Rightists were being strangled by the "giant poisonous snake of dictatorship . . . how can I not be impatient?"[92]

In that petulant state of mind, and still handcuffed, Lin Zhao added one of the final touches to the sanguinary art on the walls of her isolation cell. Next to her father's altar, in three-inch-wide characters, she wrote a line from a poem Lu Xun had composed in 1903 when he was twenty-one: "I offer my blood as sacrifice to the Yellow Emperor."

That line had long been purged, after Lu Xun's death in 1936, of its Confucian sentiments and turned into a CCP slogan exhorting selfless dedication to the cause of Chinese communism. Lin Zhao found it necessary to clarify that her blood sacrifice had nothing to do with Mao's revolution. It was intended to honor what the Yellow Emperor had stood for: "personal dignity with proper clothes and headwear, a civilization of rituals and music"—"the immortal symbol of the ancient and splendid soul of our nation."[93]

six

LAMPLIGHT IN
THE SNOWY FIELDS

Mr. Lu Xun once said, a road is what people make by treading. If there is not a first person, there will not be others, and there will still be no road. The first one who sets his eyes on the light of the distant fire and walks on where there is no road until he falls—he who marks the road with his own blood for those coming after him—will always, always earn our respect.

—LIN ZHAO, 1957[1]

ON MAY 31, 1965, LIN ZHAO WAS TRIED IN THE JING'AN DISTRICT People's Court in Shanghai on the indictment brought against her the previous November. That same day, she was sentenced to twenty years in prison as an "impenitent counterrevolution-ary" and transferred from the No. 1 Detention House to Shanghai Municipal Prison.

The miscarriage of justice that day may have reminded Lin Zhao of what her father, Peng Guoyan, had endured three decades earlier when he was the magistrate of Pi county in impoverished northern Jiangsu. At the time, the obsessively punctilious Magistrate Peng, attempting to fund local efforts to cope with a raging plague in the area, had found himself accused of unlawfully taxing the people to profit himself. He was sentenced in 1934 to five years in prison.

Still, Magistrate Peng had fared much better than his daughter: he had been able to lodge an appeal with the provincial high court and won a public trial with more than five hundred people in attendance, at which he was represented by a lawyer. Although he did not win a resounding victory, he was eventually released on bail.[2] For years, patriots of both his generation and Lin Zhao's had shed blood in their fight to end the injustice of Nationalist rule. Now, thirty years after her father's ordeal, arbitrary state power was even more firmly in place in China. There was no public trial or defense lawyer for Lin Zhao. There was no one by her side. She had only her own indignation and contempt.

"We will see!" she wrote in her blood-inked statement on the back of the verdict. "The formal verdict in the court of history will soon be made manifest to the world and to posterity! You— totalitarian rulers and cunning evildoers, scoundrels, kleptocrats, thieves who bring calamity upon the people—you will be not only the real defendants but also the criminals facing public prosecution! Righteousness will prevail! Long live freedom!"[3]

Shanghai Municipal Prison, commonly referred to as Tilanqiao Prison, was formerly known as Ward Road Gaol. It had been built in 1903 by the Western-controlled Shanghai Municipal Council to help maintain semi-colonial order in the city's International Settlement. By 1935, it had expanded to comprise some four thousand cells in ten massive buildings and held the dubious distinction as the largest prison in the world. Variously nicknamed the "City of the Doomed" and the "Alcatraz of the Orient," it occupied an area of sixty *mu*, or about ten acres, in the International Settlement north of the Bund, and was surrounded by a gray wall that rose more than five meters or about seventeen feet. Two rows of concrete cells on each floor were placed back to back. As a Western-style prison, the cells had open iron bars in the front, which faced a long gangway and windows beyond. Each cell, just over five feet wide and seven feet deep—about the same size as Alcatraz cells, which held one prisoner—normally housed two inmates, but at times three or more prisoners slept on the cold concrete floors.[4]

In addition to the regular cells, dark isolation chambers and padded cells, known as *fengbo ting* (turbulence pavilion) and *xiangpi jian* (rubber cell) respectively, were used for the most recalcitrant and the suicidal. From the beginning, Tilanqiao had been home to some of the most important dissidents and revolutionaries of modern China. Zou Rong, who in 1903 penned "The Revolutionary Army" calling for the overthrow of the Qing dynasty, died there in 1905 when he was barely twenty years of age. During the late 1940s, as the Nationalist era was drawing to an end, Tilanqiao had also held former Chinese collaborators with the Japanese occupation, Japanese war criminals, and a few dozen dedicated members of the Chinese Communist Party who were bent on ridding China of the tyranny of Chiang Kai-shek's autocratic rule.[5]

With the Communists now in power, things had come full circle: after 1949, Tilanqiao became the primary destination for political prisoners sentenced in the Shanghai area. Its population peaked with each mass political campaign. Thousands were incarcerated within its walls during the Suppression of Counterrevolutionaries Campaign of 1950–1951. By 1953, seven thousand counterrevolutionaries were imprisoned in Tilanqiao, pushing the total prison population to seventeen thousand, with up to five prisoners squeezed into each cell. After a brief drop, the inmate population soared again in the aftermath of the 1955 Elimination of Counterrevolutionaries Campaign. At one point during the Cultural Revolution, counterrevolutionaries accounted for some 43 percent of the more than 5,000 people in the prison.[6]

Not all were avowed dissidents like Lin Zhao. In the heady days of 1967, when the Cultural Revolution was in full swing, a Shanghai worker and his wife joined rival groups of "revolutionary rebels" and became estranged. One night, the husband returned home unexpectedly to find his wife in bed with her rebel group leader. The man fled and the husband charged toward her with a mop. The wife

Tilanqiao Prison, 1929.

attempted to ward him off with a copy of *Quotations from Chairman Mao* and shouted—citing the chairman's instructions—"rely on eloquence and not on violence!" The husband tore up the book in a rage. She then grabbed a large poster of Mao and used it as a shield. That too was shredded as he thrashed her with the mop. That very night, she reported him to the Public Security Bureau. He was arrested as a counterrevolutionary and sentenced to twelve years in prison.[7]

To Lin Zhao, the return to Tilanqiao seemed like a return to a previous existence. The next day, from her new cell, she saw the sky for the first time in almost two years. "When my eye reached beyond the bars and fell on the sunny, clear sky that had been cut into little rectangular pieces by the iron grille over the window, I suddenly burst into tears."[8]

Three weeks later, after routine indoctrination sessions for new arrivals had ended, she was put into cell number 53 on the third floor of the Women's Block, or Building No. 9—a five-story, T-shaped, russet brick building with 188 cells, in the southeastern section of Tilanqiao. On June 19, she received her first visit from her mother and brother in more than two years.[9] She told them that, regarding her appeal, she would have to wait until she could find a

Tilanqiao Prison through morning smog, November 2015. Photo by Lian Xi.

lawyer to bring her case to "humanity's forum of civilization—the United Nations."

She saw no viable alternatives as she surveyed her situation: she could not appeal to Chiang Kai-shek's government in Taiwan; nor would the likes of the "international Communist and Workers Parties' meetings" be of any help. She was aware of the tensions between Beijing and Moscow. The two countries had clashed at the meeting of Eighty-One Communist and Workers Parties in Moscow in 1960, and by the summer of 1963, the split between the CCP and the Communist Party of the Soviet Union was irreparable.[10] In any event, Communist parties had no moral authority in her eyes. She could not put up with anything that "smells of hypocritical, 'Communist' nonsense!"

"Therefore, the United Nations remains the best choice," even though Mao's government did not accept its legal or moral authority. "We, on the other hand, have great respect for it. . . . As an international institution that has enjoyed the recognition and participation of the overwhelming majority of nations on this earth, it represents the many shared, fundamental principles of civilized human societies. Therefore, to a large extent, it represents the entire human civilization!"[11]

LIN ZHAO WOULD write an appeal to the UN a year later. Meanwhile, she was consumed by two massive, simultaneous writing projects. Both had to do with Shanghai mayor Ke Qingshi's death on April 9. The first, a play she titled "Chatters of a Spirit Couple" (Ling'ou xuyu), which totaled some 230,000 characters, was started a month after Ke's death, when she was still at the No. 1 Detention House. She would continue adding to it as a sort of diary for almost three hundred days, until March 8, 1966, when it abruptly stopped, without an ending. She began the second project, her long letter to the editors of People's Daily, on July 14, 1965—the anniversary of the fall of the Bastille—when she was confined to a prison hospital bed with a high fever. She brought it to a conclusion on December 5, 1965.[12]

Each was a grueling undertaking. Almost twenty-two months of incarceration at the No. 1 Detention House had ravaged her already poor health. Her pulmonary tuberculosis, which had plagued her since her late teens, had worsened. An X-ray taken in June revealed that the lesion in her right lung had spread across the rest of her lungs.[13]

The radiograph was done at Tilanqiao's eight-story prison hospital, which was built in 1933, a legacy of Republican China. During the Mao era, it continued to offer treatments for the more serious illnesses, although routine health services were provided inside the prison blocks by inmate medics—prisoners who had a smattering of medical knowledge.[14] In the early 1940s, Mao had urged the medical staff serving the CCP's leadership and troops to "practice revolutionary humanism." After 1949, the slogan was adopted by medical facilities throughout China. Prison hospitals made no attempts to alter the chairman's quotation.

Lin Zhao refused to take the medicine prescribed by the prison doctor, even though he had warned her that she would last for no more than three years without the treatment.[15] This was an act of protest she had carried on since early 1963. It began as a response to the "rough and inhumane treatment" during her month-long hunger strike from February to March of that year, and it continued when the rough treatment turned into abuse and "brutal torture" at the No. 1 Detention House. "However terrifying this disease is, I am not willing to receive life from you or from anybody under your authority!" she explained. "As a Christian, my life belongs to my God. . . . I am willing—even hope—to receive medicine for my lung disease from the American missionaries who baptized me into the church when I was in high school."

She did not have the addresses of those missionaries, who had long since left China, but believed that she could reestablish contact with them if she were allowed to send out an open letter. Until then, she would carry on without medicine.[16]

Lin Zhao had decided, from the beginning, that "Chatters of a Spirit Couple" had to be written in her own blood. She was convinced that Ke had shed his blood for her and that she had to repay him in kind. Her energy was low, she admitted, and she was doubly tired when she drew blood to write, especially at night. But she felt Ke's presence more keenly at the end of the day, when her mind felt clearer. And the pace of writing had picked up now that the handcuffs were off.

A month or so into the playscript, she had become more efficient. Coagulation had presented a constant problem, but she was now using a plastic spoon to hold blood as she wrote. Even when the blood in the spoon dried up, she could add water to turn it back to "ink," though the ink sometimes was uneven in color.[17]

One of the first things Lin Zhao had done after she was moved to Tilanqiao Prison was to set up a new, dual altar for her father and Ke Qingshi. At the No. 1 Detention House, she had painted her father's altar on the cell wall, but at Tilanqiao, prisoners were often moved around to different cells. She wanted an altar she could bring with her. On June 10, she took out a white shirt with blue stripes, poked her right middle finger, and spent the night painting the two altars on the front of the shirt, one on each side. Day broke just as she finished the job.[18]

Three months after Ke's death, on July 9, Lin Zhao fell into a kind of stupor as she observed the anniversary. Tomatoes were brought to each floor that afternoon and offered for sale, and she bought a few and made an offering in front of his altar. At night, overcome with grief, she sang the hymn "God Be with You till We Meet Again" seven times. Written by Jeremiah Rankin, a Congregational minister, in 1880 and introduced to China by American missionaries, it had long been a popular song at Christian funerals in China. No hymnal or Bible was available inside the prison, but she still remembered the lyrics of that hymn. She fell asleep with her head against the shirt and woke up the next morning to find Ke's altar partially washed away by her tears.[19]

To remedy the problem, she decided on a more formal ritual: she would baptize Ke's spirit and repaint his altar. She had been conducting her own "grand church worship" each Sunday, beginning promptly at 9:30 a.m. She would sing hymns and say prayers until lunchtime. On Sunday, July 11, 1965, she cleaned her washbasin and poured the day's allowance of water into it. Then she poked her finger and drew a cross in the water with the blood, praying:

> May this water be sanctified by the prayers and wishes of a disciple of Christ and by the unsurpassed power of the Cross—the symbol of love and sacrifice! Oh, Heavenly Father, may this sacred water cleanse the soul of the hapless one who died a wronged man, with gnawing regrets. . . . Oh Lord, may he regain life and enter into eternal life, saved by the grace of the precious blood of Christ!

Next, she dipped the right side of the shirt that had borne the altar to Ke into the basin and washed it gently as she sang the nineteenth-century hymn "Whiter Than Snow," whose Chinese translation had been included in *Hymns of Universal Praise*, the popular interdenominational hymnal published in 1936. She brought the service to a close by singing lines from "Rock of Ages, Cleft for Me," as she hung the shirt on the iron grille of her cell to dry. That night, she repainted Ke's altar on it, drawing the blood again from her right middle finger. Ke's shedding of blood—she believed—had voided his party membership. Now he was also a child of God.[20]

WITH THE ALTAR sanctified and in place, Lin Zhao embarked on her long letter to *People's Daily* on July 14. "On this famous day that, from its very beginning, touches the heartstring of every lover of freedom with its noble and fiery humanitarian passion, I—a strange reader—begin drafting another letter to you," Lin Zhao began. "If this long-tortured, weakened, and sick body has not entirely lost the accuracy of her memory, this, as I remember, is the day of the first uprising of the French Revolution!"[21]

It was her third letter to the editors in Beijing. The previous two, written in her own blood, had been handed to the prison guards, in December 1964 and February 1965 respectively, to be mailed out, but she had not heard back from them and had no idea if the letters were ever received. The editors might have been barred from reading letters from an imprisoned resister, she wrote, or, after receiving them, were "silent like chilled cicada in late autumn and did not know what to do." Either way it showed that "your newspaper is not even worth as much as toilet paper in a system run by secret agents."[22]

People's Daily started publication in 1946—using the name that Mao bestowed on it—and had remained the official newspaper of the CCP. However, Lin Zhao reminded its editors that "as the information center serving the imperial court, your newspaper is quite beneath contempt." Although it was "part of the apparatus of the reign of terror in this totalitarian police state, the main function of your newspaper . . . is decorative."[23]

Lin Zhao's letter was an impassioned, at times rambling, and often moving piece of writing. It is a call for justice for the presumed murder of Ke Qingshi, a protest over the mistreatment and torture to which she had been subjected as a political dissident, and a penetrating critique of the brutal logic and practice of Chinese communism. It was also a poignant affirmation of freedom and justice as the fundamental principles of civilized humanity.

Mao's murder of Ke, Lin Zhao insisted, was nothing but a lowly act of a jealous man, and the party apparatus had been complicit in Mao's evil and dictatorial rule. The unexpected deaths (from illness) of two other high-ranking CCP officials also raised her suspicions. "At this rate of dying," she warned, "there shall soon be no living beings in your honorable Central Committee."[24] Lin Zhao was wrong about the circumstances of Ke's death; nevertheless, she correctly predicted the murderous politics under Mao's rule. The Cultural Revolution, which Mao would soon launch, would prove her right.

As for her own mistreatment, she admitted that, as someone engaged in political struggle, she was prepared for battle wounds, so to speak, but not for the "savagery" she encountered:

What has your honorable No. 1 Detention House done to this youth of weakened constitution who had been sick for a long time . . . ? Countless physical assaults! Shocking, cruel torture and abuse! They have come up with countless tricks just with the use of shackles: one pair of handcuffs behind the back; two pairs of handcuffs behind the back, at times parallel to each other, at times crisscrossed, so on and so forth. I need not mention the scars on my arms and elbows, but the most cruel and inhumane part of it was: even when I was writhing in pain from gastritis during my hunger strike, and when I was in my menstrual period—that special physiological condition of women—they never removed my shackles; they did not even let up on the abuse—such as removing one of the two pairs of shackles. Oh Heaven, Oh Heaven! Even hell cannot rival this. What a place is this human world![25]

That cruelty, she pointed out, was the inevitable result of the totalitarian rule. If only the "so-called National People's Congress" had been capable of passing a legislation banning torture, she lamented. But that body was only a "broken, empty shell." Even if the National Congress had passed a resolution specifying the proper use of handcuffs, she doubted it would have constrained the party's secret agents. Red China had been called a police state, she reminded the editors. What Mao had instituted was nothing less than "a reign of terror."[26]

THE REASON MAO had been able to commit "all kinds of outrage in defiance of both law and Heaven," Lin Zhao wrote, "is that your party and the so-called party Central Committee have long yielded to this tyrant and have tolerated and overindulged him!" By maintaining "your totalitarian rule and your policy of keeping the people in ignorance, and also because of your deeply ingrained slavishness . . . you have made the Dictator the 'Son of Heaven with the true mandate' in a Western garb. You have done all you could to deify him both inside and outside the party."

The CCP had created an unrivaled cult of Mao, she pointed out. "Even the sun and the moon owe their brightness to Mao Zedong! And the grass and trees grow because of Mao Zedong!" she mocked. "At times, such ludicrous, medieval idolatry has gone to a sickening extent!"[27]

Mao's dictatorship also rested on the CCP's use of terror by secret agents—the "overlords within the party," she added. "Where can we find even a little breath of democracy?" she asked. "Nobody can give what he does not have himself." The CCP cared for nothing but "the terror of centralization. It has long lost any trace of democracy!"

It had taken her a long time to come to that conclusion, she explained. As a former journalist, she could not help glimpsing "the contours of an Eastern power monger." In the end, "like the majority of my generation, I experienced an overwhelming loss of faith in the Dictator."

The turning point was the Anti-Rightist Campaign. "Because of my skills at discerning Mao's writing style, I was able to determine that several of the editorials in the party newspaper published by the party's Central Committee, such as 'The Bourgeois Orientation of *Wenhui Daily* over a Period of Time,' were written by the Dictator himself."[28] Appearing in *People's Daily* on June 14, 1957, and attributed at the time to the editorial board, the piece was among the first salvoes of the campaign and was indeed penned by Mao. She believed that Mao's hand could be seen in every major policy made by the party.

She was further disabused of her illusions by what followed: "the various absurdities under the banner of the so-called 'Great Leap Forward,'" the "rude interventions" that caused "economic decline and the depressed livelihood of the people, especially the destruction of agriculture, the administrative plunder of rural areas and the complete impoverishment of peasants." Mao, she wrote, "must be the first to bear responsibility for the tragedy of our land swarming with famished refugees and the corpses of the starved filling up the valleys." Here were echoes of the indictment she and her Rightist friends had made in *A Spark of Fire* back in 1960.

Mao must also be held accountable, she wrote, for "the dirty deal with Khrushchev, and the failed military adventurism in bombing Jinmen and Mazu." On August 23, 1958, Mao had ordered a heavy artillery barrage against Jinmen (Quemoy) and Mazu, islands held by the Nationalists off the coast of Fujian province. The intense shelling went on for about six weeks before it turned into a frivolous engagement—bombardments on odd days and a ceasefire on even days. It was ostensibly an attempt to take the islands as a springboard to Taiwan. Mao's more likely purpose was to generate a Taiwan Strait crisis that would derail Khrushchev's attempted rapprochement with the United States and pressure the Soviet Union into helping China build its own atomic bomb so that it could stand up to the United States.[29]

Lin Zhao's scorn for Mao's "dirty deal with Khrushchev," meanwhile, was evidently a reference to Mao's offer, in October 1962, of Chinese support for the Soviet Union's missile program in Cuba. In return, he had wanted Khrushchev to pledge to stand by China in its conflicts with India. She would not have known the details of the deal, struck only days before the Cuban missile crisis reached its climax on October 22, when Kennedy announced the naval quarantine.

For her, there were unmistakable signs of a horse trade: on October 20, Chinese troops stormed Indian border positions. On October 25, the Soviet Union issued a statement in *Pravda* in support of China. That same day, Beijing announced that "the Chinese government fully supports the government of the Soviet Union" in its standoff with the United States. "All of that resulted from the absurd and perverse adventurism of the Dictator, a gambler by nature," observed Lin Zhao.[30]

SHE THEN TURNED to Mao's "cruel struggle and relentless strike against the contemporary 'Hai Rui'" at the 1959 Lushan meeting of CCP's Central Committee—a reference to Defense Minister Peng Dehuai, who had opposed his Great Leap Forward. "The all-out intra-party purge under the pretense of opposing right-deviating opportunism," which followed the downfall of Marshal Peng, "effectively removed the kinder and more enlightened people who still remained within your honorable party." While the CCP had had "a few pages of heroic struggles in its history," she noted, "it has almost completely lost its claim to justice; it has lost even more its vitality."[31]

If the Anti-Rightist Campaign of 1957 had been Mao's strike against dissidents nationwide, the purge of Marshal Peng Dehuai— defense minister and Mao's loyal colleague since the early 1930s— signaled Mao's absolute intolerance of loyal opposition within the party. Peng's downfall underscores the grim reality of the so-called Way of the Ruler and the Minister, or *junchen zhidao*. Articulated and idealized by Confucius and codified by Mencius, it decreed unwavering loyalty of the subject to a father-like ruler and claimed a benign reciprocity between a benevolent, enlightened ruler and his principled, dedicated ministers.

In reality, throughout Chinese history, ministers found themselves at the mercy of tyrannical rulers and were often shabbily treated by them. When Lin Zhao called Peng Dehuai the "contemporary 'Hai Rui,'" she evoked the parallel between Peng's dismissal and that of another outspoken critic of a misguided ruler four centuries earlier. It was a remarkable reference, revealing her insights into a tragic historical pattern. She did that out of political acuity, weeks before Mao himself made the comparison for the first time. On December 21, 1965, he said to several of his top aides: "The Jiajing Emperor dismissed Hai Rui from office; we dismissed Peng Dehuai from office in 1959. Peng Dehuai is also a 'Hai Rui.'" Not until January 1966 did a *People's Daily* editorial publicly link the two ousted ministers.[32]

A midlevel court official during the Ming dynasty, Hai Rui went through a posthumous transformation during the Mao years, from an exemplary, upright official to a reactionary villain. In the end, a crowd of indignant Red Guards, drunk with hatred for the four-hundred-year-old remains of Hui Rui, exhumed his skull and a few pieces of his bones on a late summer day in 1966 and consigned them to a revolutionary bonfire.[33]

THE HISTORICAL HAI Rui barely escaped execution in the late sixteenth century after he criticized a Ming emperor. The latter, obsessed with the Daoist pursuit of immortality, had neglected state affairs as he busied himself concocting supposed elixirs out of virgins' menstrual blood. Later, as a provincial governor, Hai Rui exposed the fraudulent registration of tax-exempt property owned by a prominent member of the Ming nobility, forcing the nobleman to return large tracts of farmland to the local farmers.

In the absence of a safe, public way to criticize the ruler, Chinese literati had long engaged in the delicate art of historical analogy and allegory, or "using the past to disparage the present" (*jiegu fengjin*). It had always been a high-risk literary gambit. Beginning in 1959, Wu Han, vice mayor of Beijing and an eminent historian of the Ming dynasty, found himself drawn into that dangerous literary practice. In April of that year, troubled by rampant exaggeration in official reports on the grain harvest, Mao told a CCP plenary meeting to encourage the emulation of Hai Rui as an upright and honest official. He also sent a message to Wu Han, asking him to write about Hai Rui. The result was the fateful Peking opera *Hai Rui Dismissed from Office*, first performed in 1961.[34]

Nobody knew better than Mao himself the genesis of Wu Han's play. In Wu Han's initial conception, it was unrelated to the dismissal of Peng Dehui as defense minister, which came in September 1959, months after he started writing. But the comparison became irresistible, and soon Wu Han was suspected of a deliberate act of *jiegu fengjin*. After all, Peng appeared to have advocated the return of farmland to the peasants when he criticized the Great Leap Forward, and Mao had dismissed him from office. In 1965, Mao orchestrated a vicious inquisition targeting Wu Han's play.

Unbeknownst to Lin Zhao—and, in fact, to the party leadership itself—Mao secretly dispatched his wife Jiang Qing to Shanghai in February 1965 to prepare a propaganda barrage against *Hai Rui Dismissed from Office*. The real target was senior party leaders who were sympathetic to Peng Dehuai and lukewarm about Mao's radical policies. In addition to his wife, Mao relied on none other than the leftist Shanghai party leader Ke Qingshi, who put two of his propagandists, Zhang Chunqiao and Yao Wenyuan, at her service.

Yao's imperious polemic, published in Shanghai's *Wenhui Daily* in late November 1965, under the title "On the New Historical Drama *Hai Rui Dismissed from Office*," was the first barrage of the

Cultural Revolution. It would lead to the downfall of the Beijing municipal party establishment and of more powerful party leaders, including Mao's revolutionary partner-turned-political nemesis, President Liu Shaoqi, all of them accused of counterrevolutionary revisionism. Before it fizzled out with Mao's own death in 1976, the Cultural Revolution would victimize more than twenty million individuals and their families and claim the lives of some two million people nationwide.[35]

LIN ZHAO WAS not privy to Mao's scheme, nor could she foretell the relentless course of the Cultural Revolution. However, in her letter to *People's Daily*, having felt the ominous pulse of Mao's revolution, she offered a prediction that would turn out to be as true as it was chilling: "Because of the need to maintain the 'mental state' of fear and trembling and unquestioning obedience within the demonic political party of yours, there has to be a constant search for objects of struggle in mutual hackings and killings. Therefore, the higher one climbs the greater the chance of dying—from execution, assassination, homicide, murder, and bloodless killing, all the way to 'committing suicide to escape punishment.'"[36]

Underlying the cycle of violence, she pointed out, was the Marxist ideology of class struggle that had been used to justify political persecution. She sardonically dismissed it as a theory instigating "scuffling on the steps of a staircase." (*Jieji*, the Chinese term for "class," also means "steps of a staircase.") That theory cripples our moral judgment, she argued. "For you who stand on that staircase, which you use for your fights, there will never be a distinction between right and wrong."[37]

"Few have dared to follow in the footsteps of 'Hai Rui,'" Lin Zhao wrote, so it had fallen to "this young resister . . . to expose the shameful evils of your Dictator"—as well as the dark force of history behind the CCP revolution. It was the law of politics that had governed China's autocratic past that "one gains all under Heaven through violence and that the people have but one lord!" Where

Mao had succeeded, she wrote, was in "donning the damned garb of the so-called Marxism and Leninism" as he made use of "this medieval political law."

The Chinese people as a whole, and "resisters such as Lin Zhao," could not be made to "endure the rule of this tyrant and to share the shame of all his evil deeds," she wrote. As descendants of the "sacred and noble Yellow Emperor," she and her generation refused to bear the "absurd 'obligation' to surrender human rights and descend into perpetual slavery." Here she arrived at the heart of her letter. As she explained, speaking of herself in the third person, her revolt against slavery "constitutes the inner logic and the fundamental reason of Lin Zhao's decision to write this letter." She hoped to "call back the departed soul of the desolate, lifeless, so-called 'center' of your honorable party."[38]

There was in fact another, more visceral, reason for her epistolary protest. Earlier in the letter, she invoked a story about Lincoln and the pig in David Decamp Thompson's *Abraham Lincoln, the First American*, published in 1894. She had probably read the book at Laura Haygood, and she remembered its details with considerable accuracy. She would think back to that story, she wrote, whenever she felt overwhelmed with the futility of calling the Communist leadership to repentance, whenever her pity for the latter, which was "hanging by a thread," was sorely tested.

In the story, Lincoln was on his way to a party when he came across a pig stuck in a swamp and struggling for its life. He wanted to help the pig. But when he looked down at his new clothes, he hesitated and rode on. Yet he could not get rid of the squealing of the pig in his ears, so he turned back. With great difficulty, Lincoln pulled the pig from the swamp and "almost turned into a statue of mud himself," Lin Zhao wrote. "After that, people praised his deeds," but Lincoln replied, "It wasn't for the sake of the pig; I did it for my own conscience." Likewise, she added, "I am doing this not for the sake of the pig, but for my own conscience as a Christian who, once lost, has found her path again."[39]

Meanwhile, the pig was only sinking deeper into the swamp. Just as Lin Zhao was about to conclude her letter to *People's Daily*, Yao Wenyuan, breaking upon the scene in the first act of Mao's Cultural Revolution, published his polemic "On the New Historical Drama *Hai Rui Dismissed from Office*" in Shanghai. When the editors of *People's Daily* in Beijing failed to promptly reprint Yao Wenyuan's editorial, they drew the ire of the great leader himself. Mao lashed out at editor-in-chief Wu Lengxi and dismissed the paper as "only one third or even only one quarter Marxist."[40] Within months, Wu would lose his position at *People's Daily* and become one of the first victims of the Cultural Revolution. Even an ideological guardian of the CCP was vulnerable to the wrath of the capricious chairman. And, in the end, hardly anybody else, Yao Wenyuan and his fellow apostles included, could escape becoming a casualty of Mao's revolution.

LIN ZHAO'S THIRD letter to *People's Daily* was a political manifesto. It should have been written in blood, she commented. But she "did not have enough time or energy. Writing in blood is slower and tires one out." During this period, she was "using blood almost every day for my other writings." She eventually alighted on a compromise: "writing in ink but stamping each page several times with the blood-inked personal seal."[41]

In the second half of 1965, she was also working on "Chatters of a Spirit Couple." While the letter to *People's Daily* was scathing and often sardonic, "Chatters" was private and intimate, intense and extravagant, and at once autobiographical and fanciful. It took the form of a drama unfolding from day to day, in which the protagonists were Lin Zhao and the spirit of Ke Qingshi, whom she had married in the netherworld in May 1965. Her father, who had been dead for five years by this point, drifted in and out of the play.

She made daily, numbered entries in blood, on paper, and copied them in dark blue ink, using sheets of thin paper slightly under four by six inches. The dated entries recorded the stormy life, both external and internal, she led inside Tilanqiao in 1965–1966. She wove her meticulous, journalistic account of actual happenings in her cell with fantasies of the daily visits of the spirit of Ke Qingshi and their romantic moments together. It is clear that the factual details were grounded in actual events.[42]

For about ten months in 1965–1966, and possibly longer, "Chatters of a Spirit Couple" was not only a play but also a survival strategy. Through it, she transformed her lonely cell into a magical place that the two dearly departed—Ke Qingshi and her father—could freely enter, to converse with and console her. The very first extant entry, made on May 31, 1965, the day when she was moved to Tilanqiao from the No. 1 Detention House, begins with these lines:

SHE: [*joyously*] You've come!

HE: Actually I came back last night. . . . My little love was tired; you slept sweetly! Of course it wasn't easy for you. You wrote so much in one breath yesterday!

Ke had come for his bride; he was there to protect her:

HE: I am right here! I am keeping watch over my little love!

SHE: Yes, you are by my side. You are keeping watch over me! Look, when I go out today I will only put on this blue-flower wedding gown! . . . We are married! I am yours!

HE: Indeed my little bride!—My lovely little bride! . . . I am madly in love with you![43]

Ke's companionship also spurred her to write her long letter to *People's Daily*. "Since she rose up in the morning, he has kept her company," the "Chatters" of August 11, 1965, read. "With silent telepathy and mutual understanding between the two of them, she worked away at the letter 'to the editorial board of *People's Daily*'— one of the pre-planned combat actions for the day."[44]

Her dialogues with Ke Qingshi offer a glimpse of the mood swings and internal struggles she went through, as in the following:

SHE: [*fatigued*] But I am tired! . . . I am searching for extinction!

HE: No, my dear, in the spiritual realm there is only sublimation, not extinction!

SHE: [*as before*] Then where do I turn so that I can lay down the heavy burden of pain?

HE: [*caressing her*] Into the arms of the Heavenly Father with his unmatched love! . . . Why did you forget this protector?[45]

In the imagined presence of Ke, Lin Zhao reflected on her emotional turmoil. She was given to uncontrollable, wild rage, she admitted to Ke. "I am easily excitable; like a neurotic, my emotions would all of a sudden rush to a peak, as when a thermometer is dipped into boiling water!" One afternoon, when inmates were summoned to denounce the Christians among them, she suddenly heard a call from God. "Rise, my child," an inner voice said, "and go fight the battle for me." She felt like a soldier shooting from a trench, at the sacrilege of some apostates. "How many pieces of silver did you get for betraying God?" she asked of them. "Judas sold Jesus for thirty pieces, but he hanged himself before he had time to use any of them!"[46]

Ke's spirit offered affirmations of her struggle and sacrifice. "My wife! You have died more than once or twice," Ke reminded her. "It's just that, with Heaven's blessing, you have come back to life from death in your own body. The living sacrifice that you have offered to the true Way of the Heavenly Deity is many times more painful and costly than one simple death!" As a recent convert—Lin Zhao had baptized his spirit—Ke was unschooled in Christian theology and still referred to God as *tiandi*, the Heavenly Deity. "You have already died," Ke announced. "It's just that the grave could not keep you buried. You have stood up again!"[47]

In "Chatters of a Spirit Couple," we also witness Lin Zhao's desperation: amid a violent storm one day, she burst into agonized pleas for divine justice as lightning flashed and thunder cracked. One's call to heaven was more likely answered during a thunderstorm, she had heard. In a diary passage that recalls King Lear on the heath—he pleads with the "all-shaking thunder" to "Smite flat the thick rotundity o' the world! / Crack nature's moulds, an germens spill at once, / That make ingrateful man!"—Lin Zhao recorded that she had "leapt up, pressed her palms together, fell on her knees, and cried out in a mournful shrill: Oh, Heaven! Retribution! Retribution, please!"[48]

It is also in "Chatters of a Spirit Couple" that we find fleeting moments of peace and quietude. On a late summer day in 1965, she reported to Ke that during her exercise time that day, when she was allowed to walk along the gangway, she had looked up through the iron window grilles and marveled at the "clear, soft, blue sky across which drifted sun-clad clouds. Against the backdrop of that beautiful heaven, the dark gray, rectangular prison buildings with black iron bars look even more bleak and unsightly." As the protagonist in her own play, Lin Zhao went on: "She gazed, long and silently, and sighed. . . . The universe, how vast is the Creator's mystical universe."[49]

On October 1, 1965, noisy National Day celebrations were broadcasted through the prison loud speakers. As a "live radio broadcast of the rallies howled through the loudspeakers, hysterical 'Long live' [cries] pierced the grieving internal organs of the mournful one," Lin Zhao wrote. Her own way of marking the day was to hand over nine letters of protest to the prison authorities. As usual, the inmate housekeeper delivered the previous day's *People's Daily*—which, along with *Liberation Daily*, was distributed for group political studies inside Tilanqiao. Yet another picture of Mao was on its front page. She "gazed at the Devil's image" for a moment and then, acting on impulse, "smeared blood on his hands and body."

To mark the holiday, Tilanqiao's cells were opened for half the day, and inmates were let out on the gangway. "In silence she let loose her hair," Lin Zhao recorded, "and put on the blue-striped white shirt with the altars of the two loved ones painted on it." She walked out toward the windows. A light rain drifted down from a leaden sky; in the reflection of the windowpane she saw a pale, emaciated form. She raised her arms to tie up her hair with a white string and saw a sprinkling of white hairs. She was not yet thirty-three. At the other end of the gangway, some were cheering. She found herself casting a cold, expressionless look at them.[50]

Cells were again opened for the next two afternoons because of the national holiday, and she continued to mourn. Tying a long strip of white gauze to her hair—to approximate customary rituals of grieving a deceased parent—she let it hang loosely down her left face and made a knot with the two ends. People started to taunt her, comparing her to Zhu Yingtai mourning her lover Liang Shanbo in the classic Shaoxing opera, in which the marriage that Zhu's parents arranged for her had cut short a fervent romance she was having with the scholar Liang and brought about the latter's death. When questioned by the guards about her unsightly performance, she responded: "So what? Are there legitimate and illegitimate ways to tie up one's hair?"

"It isn't about that. It's just ugly."

"There is 'class consciousness' inherent in one's aesthetics," she shot back wryly. "I just think it is pretty."[51]

On November 11, Lin Zhao was shocked by the execution of a counterrevolutionary inmate named Lu Yousong, probably the first killing since she arrived at Tilanqiao. Lu had been a Guomindang-approved labor union leader in pre-Communist Shanghai and had been sentenced to a twenty-five-year prison term in the 1950s. In 1965, Tilanqiao authorities brought against him the bizarre charge of having organized a pro-American, anti-Communist league inside Tilanqiao and of planning an armed jailbreak. He was quickly sentenced to die.[52]

How could they dispose of someone's life like that, as though in "child's play"? Lin Zhao asked. As Lu was carried to the execution ground, Lin Zhao penned a four-line poem, in blood, on her cell's wall, condemning the death penalty. "I used to be unafraid of death," the last two lines read, "but I have drifted along and stayed alive until this day!"[53]

LIN ZHAO'S IMAGINARY dialogues with Ke also dramatized her drawn-out inner conflict over whether Mao should be punished for his crimes. Could Mao be forgiven if he repented? Could retribution be justified? As a Christian, would she avenge Ke's "murder"? "Taking his life is not in line with my political interest," an agonized Lin Zhao told Ke. "My interest is my motherland!"

Would she settle accounts with Mao? Ke asked.

"The Heavenly Father, out of his merciful love, would always leave him with a way out, but whether to take it is his choice."

Would she claim her right to revenge? he pressed, demanding an answer.

"Then you must know," she replied after a long silence, "other than being a political novice, I am a Christian. . . . My political interest is not in demanding his head." Perhaps "Heaven would grant forgiveness or commutation." In any event, she added, "as a select soldier of Christ, I must follow the will of the Heavenly Father. What the Heavenly Father demands is not that insignificant head of his."[54]

But she continued to consider the other side of the argument. "Everyone must pay the price of his own . . . wrongdoing, let alone crimes." Doesn't God's justice demand that? she asked.

"You are constantly wavering," Ke pointed out. "I can see clearly that you are full of conflicts!" Would she ever dare to shed someone's blood if necessary? he asked.

"If shedding one person's blood would prevent the shedding of the blood of tens of thousands of people—yes, I will."

Would she do the same to "repay the shedding of the blood of tens of thousands of people?"

She hesitated and lowered her eyes. "Perhaps." He sneered and shook his head.[55]

As for forgiveness, she believed that it should come with conditions. "Unconditional forgiveness means indulging evils." The distinction between right and wrong must never be blurred, she believed. For that reason, "how can one deprive others of their right to avenge themselves or limit such a right?"[56]

Out of these private ruminations arose the declaration in her letter to *People's Daily* regarding the evils committed by Mao's regime and the possibility of divine redemption:

> As a Christian, my life belongs to my God. . . . In order to stick to my path, or rather my line, the line of a servant of God, the political line of Christ, this young person paid a grievous price. . . . I have come to see more clearly and deeply the many terrifying and shocking evils committed by your demonic political party! I grieved and wept for them! . . . Yet even when I touched the darkest, the most terrifying, the bloodiest, and the most savage center of your power—the core of evil—I still glimpsed, I did not completely overlook, the occasional sparks of humanity in you. . . . Then I cried in even greater anguish! I cried for your blood-smeared souls, which are unable to rid themselves of evil and are dragged by its terrifying weight ever deeper into the swamp of death. Most likely you will feel quite indifferent when you read this line, but as I write this, hot tears are rushing into my eyes. Gentlemen, those who enslave others can never be free. What a merciless but certain truth in your case![57]

As for herself, Lin Zhao claimed no right to be the agent of divine retribution. While she conceded that those who pledged themselves to the killing of Communists were no more reproachable than the Communists themselves, she was unable to personally embrace violence.[58]

On November 23, the fifth anniversary of her father's death, Lin Zhao made a sacrificial offering in front of his altar—consisting of a small portion of beef and a sautéed egg that her mother had brought to her earlier that month and that she had saved for the occasion. It was not a worthy sacrifice, she told her father's spirit, but nevertheless a token of her "sincere penitence" for her past rebelliousness and the wrongs that she had done him.[59]

In mid-December, after she had completed her letter to *People's Daily* and submitted it to the prison authorities, she found time for paper crafts, using candy wraps and whatever other scraps were available. She displayed her creations on an upturned washbasin she placed on the gangway outside her cell.[60] These were meant to represent images in two poems, one of which, an untitled verse by Tang dynasty poet Li Shangyin, includes two lines that, for centuries, had embodied the Confucian scholar-official's ideal of unceasing, selfless dedication to his high purpose in life: "Spring's silkworms wind till death their heart's threads / the wick of the candle turns to ash before its tears dry." She had attempted to fashion both "Spring's silkworm" and the candle, she told Ke's spirit.[61]

She named her other productions "Springtime" and "A Short Verse,"[62] references to a poem that Lu Xun wrote in 1931 after the capture and summary execution of his progressive Communist friends by the Nationalist gendarmes in Shanghai:

> *Accustomed to long nights as springtime wears away,*
> *I take along wife and son, my temples turning gray.*
> *In dreams dimly I see my loving mother's tears;*
> *Over the city gate often a different "royal" standard appears.*
> *How unbearable to have seen friends newly go down to the shades!*
> *In a rage I search for a short verse among bristling bayonet blades.*
> *Chanting it over, I lower my brows—no place to write it down.*
> *Liquid moonlight glitters on my black gown.[63]*

Like most writers of her generation, Lin Zhao's literary sensibilities had been formed in the crucible of revolution, in which the line between good and evil, between "a short verse" and "bayonet blades," was always clear. Her imprisonment as a political dissident and the repeated abuse she endured behind bars only reinforced that simple division, making her the "spring's silkworm" and a burning "wick of the candle." Her experiences also made it difficult for her to achieve the nuance and moderation of more reflective and philosophical protests, such as Martin Luther King Jr.'s "Letter from Birmingham Jail."

Fortunately, she was able to find occasional relief from her single-minded "battle." In addition to her handicrafts, she also sketched her favorite Disney characters on a flattened toothpaste tube, using a small nail she had found: Mickey Mouse with his violin and Minnie Mouse holding up a corner of her skirt.[64]

On Christmas Eve, she "joyously sang those beautiful Christmas carols" as she welcomed a dinner of carrot and napa cabbage with rice soup. Sixty years earlier, when the newly built Tilanqiao was run by the Westerners, a Chinese inspector of the prison had found fish, beef, pork, and beans included on the menu. Now Mao's regime had replaced erstwhile imperialist indulgence with revolutionary rigor. Inmates were served porridge in the morning—containing about 100 grams of rice—and steamed rice for lunch and dinner, 150 grams apiece. On top of the rice was often "a layer of bok choy cooked without oil," one inmate recalled. The meals were placed in narrow, oblong metal containers—about an inch and a half wide, three inches high and eight inches long—that could be delivered through the iron grille of the cells.[65]

The Christmas Eve dinner was not lavish, but the carols Lin Zhao sang that evening lifted her spirits and inspired her to pen a "spirit-filled short essay entitled 'Christ Is Still in This World,'" using her own blood. She hoped to compile this and other short pieces into a volume to be called "Devotional Reflections." "Grant me inspirations, Heavenly Father!" she asked. "I would be truly grateful if I could produce something like *Streams in the Desert*." A collection of daily devotional readings written by American missionary Lettie Cowman, the book was published in 1925 and translated into Chinese in 1939. It became the most popular devotional of the twentieth century among Chinese Christians.[66]

On January 13, 1966, Lin Zhao coughed up a large amount of blood and was given an intravenous injection of agrimony extract to staunch her internal bleeding. But she refused to go to the prison hospital or to take the prescribed vitamin K. "Let it bleed," she told the spirit of Ke, "I haven't found a better way to die."[67]

But at least she needed more rest, Ke said. "Rome wasn't built in one day."

"Indeed, it wasn't built in one day," she smiled, "which is why I have to emulate Tao Kan's moving of bricks."

Tao Kan, a brilliant fourth-century general of the early Eastern Jin dynasty, had been demoted by his jealous superior and rusticated to the then sleepy frontier town of Guangzhou. Refusing to give up on his life, Tao adopted an unbroken daily routine of exercise to firm up his will and body. He would collect more than a hundred bricks in his yard, moving them one by one beyond his gate in the morning and bringing them back in at night. Questioned about this practice, he allegedly replied that even though his body was in the uncivilized, primitive south, his ambition remained to recover the Central Plains in the north from the barbarians. In anticipation of future service to the imperial court, he dared not let his body remain idle. Like Tao Kan, Lin Zhao would not turn to idleness.[68]

On February 5, 1966, her mother and sister arrived on a monthly visit. Xu Xianmin chided her, as she had done before, for continuing to make trouble in prison. Lin Zhao broke down in tears after telling them about her deteriorating health but protested: "Don't blame everything on my refusal to take medicine. They are driving me to the brink of death! I am unable to do what they want me to do." She could not be reformed. In fact, every time her mother mentioned reform during prison visit, she would cut her short.[69]

By the middle of the month, she had felt an internal command from God to start a new writing project. To prepare herself, she finished copying several pages of "Chatters of a Spirit Couple" with her fountain pen, which she turned over to the guards afterward. After an entry on March 8, 1966, which recorded yet another "tangled fight" with the guards, the "Chatters" abruptly came to an end. We don't know why she stopped writing or whether she continued and the final pages were lost.[70]

What we do know is that Lin Zhao was hospitalized again in late March, after she again coughed up a substantial amount of blood. For most inmates, the prison hospital with its unshuttered windows provided some relief from the melancholy of the cells. The doctor treating Lin Zhao at times urged her—in a subdued voice and with no expression on his face—to quiet down and try to extend her stay there. But this was not a peaceful stay: she wrote of another break of some sort with the prison authorities. Perhaps she had pressed again for an account of what happened to her letter to the editorial board of *People's Daily*. On March 31, she received the official reply. The letter would not be forwarded.[71]

seven

THE WHITE-HAIRED GIRL
OF TILANQIAO

My hair is grey, but not with years,
Nor grew it white
In a single night,
As men's have grown from sudden fears:
My limbs are bow'd, though not with toil,
But rusted with a vile repose,
For they have been a dungeon's spoil . . .

—LORD BYRON, "Prisoner of Chillon," 1816

"Grind me into powder if you wish. Every bit of my broken bone
will be the seed of a resister!"

—LIN ZHAO, "Letter to the Editorial Board of *People's Daily*," 1965[1]

ON MAY 6, 1966, LIN ZHAO HAD A SPECIAL VISITOR. ZHANG YUANXUN,
her former classmate and a fellow Rightist at Peking University,
came to see her, claiming to be her fiancé. Zhang, once a frustrated
suitor of Lin Zhao, had been arrested on December 25, 1957, along
with a small group of Peking University Rightists who had secretly

planned to seek political asylum at one of the foreign diplomatic missions in Beijing. He was given a sentence of eight years and sent to a labor camp in Hebei province. His term expired in December 1965, but as was common practice at the time, he was ordered to remain in the labor camp to undergo continued reform. As an ex-prisoner, however, he was allowed a one-week leave each year to see his family. In early May 1966, he traveled to Shanghai to visit Lin Zhao in an agreement that her family had made with Tilanqiao Prison.[2]

Zhang hoped to persuade her to choose self-preservation, to "back down from 'stubborn resistance.'" Lin Zhao's mother, Xu Xianmin, had communicated his intent to the prison authorities, who decided that they could use Zhang's visit as a way to bring an end to her nonsensical spirit marriage to Ke Qingshi and to take the steam out of the incessant protests she had been making about Ke's presumed murder.

When Xu Xianmin and Zhang Yuanxun arrived at Tilanqiao on May 6, the deputy warden warned Zhang sternly: "The permission for you to meet with Lin Zhao is a special privilege that was granted after we discussed the matter. We hope that this will influence Lin Zhao and turn her around into complete repentance. You know the prison rules. If you exhibit behavior that does not accord with our demands, you should know the consequences!"

Zhang and Xu were brought into the visiting room, which had a long table and rows of connected chairs. A moment later, three uniformed prison guards, referred to as discipline cadres, and four plainclothes female staff, possibly there to take notes, entered. Shortly afterward, about twenty guards armed with pistols filed into the room and solemnly sat down. Then Zhang heard more footsteps outside the room. As he would recall:

> Finally Lin Zhao walked into the visiting room! She looked anemic, her face pale and thin. Her narrow nose bridge and the faint, scattered freckles on her cheeks reminded me of the days when

she was a flower facing the morning sun! Her long hair draped over her shoulders and hung loosely down her back until it almost touched her waist. About half of it had turned white! The collar jacket she wore was already ragged; the "long skirt" she had on was said to have been a white bed sheet! On her feet was a worn-out pair of black cloth shoes with strings. The most striking—and unbearable to look at—was a square piece of white cloth on her head, with the palm-sized character "wronged" smeared on it in blood![3]

Lin Zhao had come from the prison hospital, where she had been sent after coughing up blood and where she would remain until June. She had been hospitalized earlier in late January for two weeks after her tuberculosis worsened.[4]

Lin Zhao cast Zhang "a sweet smile" when she saw him. In her hands she held a cloth bundle and a large roll of toilet tissue. A female doctor wearing a white hospital coat over her guard uniform supported her by the arm. Behind them was another armed guard. She was escorted to a seat across the long table from Zhang.

"Lin Zhao, Zhang Yuanxun's visit with you today was approved out of the government's concern for you. We hope that you will be educated through this visit and speed up your repentance and reform," said one of the discipline cadres.

"Boring to the extreme!" Lin Zhao interrupted him.

The cadre, nonplussed, turned to Zhang with an embarrassed look and explained: "This happens all the time!"

Lin Zhao ignored him. She waved her hand around the room and asked Zhang: "This kind of people, what do you call them at your place?"

"Captains," Zhang answered, after a long moment of hesitation and only after the cadre had reassured him that he was allowed to answer.

"Same here! Same here!" she replied. "Here we also call them 'government'! Whenever we speak to them, we have to first shout 'To report to the government!' When I studied modern Chinese with the linguist Mr. Zhu Dexi at Peking University, I never heard Mr. Zhu say that a person could become 'government'! In this place, absurdity has become a habit! . . . How can these fellows be the government?"

Zhang tried to maintain a blank expression as Lin Zhao told him, in front of about thirty of her captors, what she had endured. The guard had put her into a cell together with the roughest female criminals and encouraged them to beat her up; they regularly held struggle sessions against her during which "vixens" hurled obscenities at her and resorted to fists when their words failed. The inmates could in fact earn merit points when they sided with the government in the struggle against Lin Zhao, a counterrevolutionary—by kicking, pinching, hitting, scratching, or biting her. At times they tore off her clothes to make her "shed her mortal body" (*tuotai huangu*)—an old Daoist phrase—as the male guards shamelessly looked on.

Lin Zhao grew emotional as she recounted the abuse; she then removed the white cloth on her head and parted her hair with her fingers to reveal bald patches, where her hair had been pulled out when she was roughed up. She coughed as she spoke and from time to time spat bloody sputum into the toilet tissue that she tore off the roll.

The main discipline cadre finally interrupted her. "It's all nonsense!" he turned to Zhang. "She is mentally imbalanced. Don't believe her words!"

"Mentally imbalanced?" Lin Zhao cut in. "Which country in the world convicts a mentally imbalanced person on the basis of his mad words? Why didn't you treat me as 'mentally imbalanced' when you sentenced me as a 'counterrevolutionary'?"

She turned to Zhang and asked him to look after her mother and siblings for her. Then she broke down in tears.

Zhang Yuanxun had brought a bag of fruits and cakes, a tin of chewy White Rabbit creamy candies, and milk powder. The discipline cadre opened the sealed tin of milk powder and poked it several times with an iron stick. Then Zhang shoved the items toward Lin Zhao. She picked up a piece of cake, turned toward the female prison doctor, and said in a stern voice: "Bring me a cup of water!"

A decade and a half into Communist rule, cosmopolitan manners had largely disappeared in China, replaced by a macho revolutionary style noted for brusqueness and impatience with bourgeois sentimentality. Ever since she left Laura Haygood, Lin Zhao had probably not experienced any other type of public manners. Her imprisonment as an enemy of the revolution had done little to soften her way with others. Only in her letters to her mother and in her imagined dialogues with Ke Qingshi can we glimpse the gentleness behind her steely façade.

At 11 a.m., the discipline cadre announced that visiting time was almost up. Lin Zhao chanted a poem she composed on the spot as a gift to Zhang. It took her favorite form, *qilü*—seven-character, regulated verse of eight lines—and commemorated their reunion after nine difficult years.

"What I hate most is deception," she said, after she finished chanting. "And I came to realize that we were all duped. Hundreds of thousands of us were duped!"

Lin Zhao reached into the cloth bundle and produced a tiny sailboat made out of a paper candy wrap. It was no wider than a leaf of chive. For Zhang, it brought to mind another sailboat, one she had drawn on a homemade New Year's card she had sent him years before. Next to the drawing she had copied a line from the end of Tang dynasty poet Li Bai's poem "Journeying Is Hard" (Xinglu nan). "There will be the moment when one mounts the high wind to break the heavy waves / I will hoist my sail into the clouds and cross the mighty ocean," the eighth-century romantic poet had written. She handed the sailboat to Zhang without explantion.

On their way out, the visitors were summoned to meet a director from the Shanghai Public Security Bureau who oversaw Tilanqiao Prison. He told Zhang and Lin Zhao's mother that "we have done what we can for Lin Zhao. She refuses to be educated and chooses to resist to the end. It's a dead end!" He paused, and then said, "There is nothing more we can do."[5]

Zhang's prison visit was apparently a rare privilege. It had been granted in yet another effort to reform Lin Zhao. Her recalcitrance as a counterrevolutionary could only reflect badly on Tilanqiao and embarrass its authorities. Yet it quickly became clear that Zhang's exhortation to Lin Zhao to "reform well and safely return from prison"[6] was like a raindrop falling off a lotus leaf. She soon busied herself with the next act of protest—a letter to the United Nations.

FROM THE MOMENT of her sentencing in May 1965, Lin Zhao had decided to take her case to humanity's court of justice. "As long as Lin Zhao has a breath of life left in her, she will soon appeal to the United Nations," she wrote in her letter to People's Daily in 1965. "A righteous freedom fighter will never allow herself to bear the insult of the so-called 'verdict' that is filthy, shameful, debased, illegal, and unjust. It is precisely this filthy verdict that has given us more fully and powerfully the right to appeal!" The search for justice was her life's goal, she explained. Every day she was alive, she would press on.[7]

Lin Zhao began drafting her appeal to the United Nations five days after Zhang Yuanxun's visit. It took her three days to complete. As with her letter to People's Daily, in one light the missive was delusional. She offered to testify "in person." In the event of her death as a prisoner of conscience, she asked the United Nations to "conduct a detailed, rigorous, and true investigation of the entire case of Lin Zhao and make it public." The inquiry would reveal "what appalling cruelty and vicious persecution, torture, abuse, and ravages I have endured!"

In other respects, however, the appeal demonstrated her unbroken spirit and tenacious faith. "I do not know when this appeal will actually reach the United Nations," she wrote. "However, out of the firmest trust in God's justice and in human conscience, as well as in the civilization and political morals of human society, I know that it will—one day, sooner or later!"

She understood what her ordeal would reveal when it became public. "I truly believe that the entire case of Lin Zhao will sufficiently demonstrate the extent to which this so-called political party, this power clique of terror—which seized power in mainland China seventeen years ago through violence and which has maintained its rule through violence in these seventeen years—has degenerated into corruption and hopeless rottenness while committing myriads of shocking and shameful evils!" Her case would also show "how the actions of the United Nations, and especially of the United States" toward China since the Communist takeover "accord with the divine heart of charity and compassion and with the morals of civilized politics!"

An investigation by the United Nations would also reveal, she believed, that the "arduous struggle" she and her generation were carrying on in China was "part of the general war of the free human beings of this world in defense of life, freedom, and basic human rights!" She added, "It is on this ground that I appeal to the United Nations!"

The letter ended with a flourish:

I shall live on with faith in the final victory of justice, or I shall offer myself as a sacrifice for justice with this faith!

Long live freedom!

Long live the United States of America!

Long live the United Nations and the basic human rights that it steadfastly defends!

Lin Zhao
May 11–14, 1966, the Lord's Calendar[8]

In her first extant piece of writing, a literary self-portrait she titled "Tears at Dusk," which she wrote in 1947 when she was fifteen, Lin Zhao had compared her own thoughts to those of a "frightened rabbit" that scurried about and easily got lost. There was a reflective subtlety in that piece as she questioned patriotic, youthful clichés.

After two decades of tumult, her self-doubt had largely given way to an impassioned and fearless style of writing, with liberal use of exclamation marks.[9]

LIN ZHAO COMPLETED her appeal to the United Nations two days before the official start of the Cultural Revolution. By then, the editorial tug-of-war between the party newspapers of Shanghai and Beijing over Yao Wenyuan's denunciation of *Hai Rui Dismissed from Office* had gone on for about six months. The Beijing party establishment's attempt in February 1966 to deflect Yao's leftist crusade and to portray Wu Han's play as merely inept in historical representation had been dismissed by Mao as "revisionism."

The May 16 Notification, which the Politburo issued as an internal document, kindled the Cultural Revolution—a bizarre, frenzied, and savage flame of hatred and violence that soon raged across China. The notification, the wording of which was finalized by Mao himself (he wanted it to be "inflammatory," he said), prepared the ideological ground for a witch hunt on a massive scale:

> The representatives of the bourgeoisie who have sneaked into the party, the government, the army, and various spheres of culture are a bunch of counterrevolutionary revisionists. Once conditions are ripe, they will seize political power and turn the dictatorship of the proletariat into a dictatorship of the bourgeoisie.

Mao also warned, ominously, that "persons like Khrushchev," whom he had denounced as a revisionist, "are nestling right beside us."[10]

By the end of May, the first Red Guards were formed, as students at an elite middle school in Beijing organized themselves to defend Mao and to defeat revisionism. On August 8, the CCP Central Committee publicly issued the "Decision concerning the Great Proletarian Cultural Revolution." Commonly known as the Sixteen Points, it called on the revolutionary masses to "struggle against and overthrow those persons in authority who are taking the capitalist road, and to criticize and repudiate the reactionary bourgeois academic 'authorities.'"

With few exceptions—the armed forces would be off limits—student radicals were given license to remove officials from office. "In the Great Proletarian Cultural Revolution, the only method is for the masses to liberate themselves," the Central Committee's "Decision" read. "Don't be afraid of disturbances. Chairman Mao has often told us that revolution cannot be so very refined, so gentle, so temperate, kind, courteous, restrained and magnanimous."[11]

Within two months, as part of the nationwide campaign to "smash the four olds"—old ideas, old culture, old customs, and old habits of the exploiting class—the Red Guards looted the homes of more than 33,000 families in Beijing. In Shanghai, almost 85,000 homes were ransacked in less than three weeks. During the so-called Red August in Beijing, which ran into early September, the Red Guards killed 1,772 people. In Shanghai, the toll was 534 murders and 704 suicides in September 1966 alone. In all, 11,510 people in Shanghai would either be killed or driven to suicide during the Cultural Revolution. Across China, the Cultural Revolution led to some two million "abnormal deaths"; among them were some 135,000 people executed as "counterrevolutionaries."[12]

In her prison writings in the summer of 1966, Lin Zhao made no mention of the Cultural Revolution, which she must have read about in the newspapers. Tilanqiao's loud speakers also blared news from the state broadcasting station. By this point, she understood intimately the dynamics of Mao's revolution. She had pointed out in her letter to *People's Daily* in 1965 that the party apparatus was generating "an evil and perverse rush toward a dark, cruel, insidious, vile, foul, and unprincipled worship of power." Suspecting foul play among the party leadership, she had warned that "there shall soon be no living beings in your honorable Central Committee."[13]

Thus the deadly turn of events in the summer of 1966 likely did not shock her. Yet they did shock other Chinese, whose belief in Mao's revolution had not yet been shattered. At times it roused them into momentary, brave acts of dissidence—as evidenced by the case of nineteen-year-old Wang Rongfen.

On August 18, 1966, Wang, a senior and German major at Beijing Foreign Languages Institute, was among the one million students and teachers who attended the first of a series of Nuremberg-style rallies held in Tiananmen Square. Mao appeared atop the Gate of Heavenly Peace to review the shock troops of what would be his last revolution. The rally reached its climax when a student named Song Binbin was allowed to pin a Red Guard armband on Mao, thereby securing the great leader's blessing for the Red Guards' violence. It was at that rally that Defense Minister Lin Biao, who would soon emerge as Mao's designated successor, issued the call to destroy the "four olds."[14] The next day, a copycat mass rally took place in Shanghai despite a heavy downpour.

Lin Biao's speech and the crowd's hysterical chanting of "Long live Chairman Mao" profoundly disturbed Wang Rongfen. It reminded her of the recordings of Hitler's speeches, which she had heard as a student of the German language. She found striking the similarities between the Red Guards and the Nazis.

The following month, she penned a short letter to Mao challenging him to reflect, "as a Communist party member," on what the Cultural Revolution meant. "Please think for a moment, in the name of the Chinese people, where you are leading China?" she wrote. "The Cultural Revolution is not a mass movement; it is one man working on the masses with the barrel of a gun." Wang ended her short letter by renouncing her membership in the Communist Youth League. After she mailed the letter, she prepared a copy in German, bought four bottles of the insecticide DDT, walked up to the Soviet Embassy in Beijing, and drank the bottles, one by one. She wanted the Russians to find her body along with the letter in her pocket and to spread news of her protest to the outside world. Instead, she woke up in a Public Security Bureau's hospital and was later sentenced to life imprisonment. In

1981, five years after Mao's death, Wang was cleared of the charges and released.[15]

MEANWHILE, FOR LIN Zhao's mother Xu Xianmin, and for various family friends who were eager to get her out of prison, the Red Guards paradoxically offered hope. Perhaps, they thought, the chaos caused by the Red Guards could somehow undo the wrong that had been done to Lin Zhao. After all, in many places across China, the Red Guards had toppled local party leadership. They also enjoyed special access to the so-called Central Cultural Revolution Group, which included Mao's wife Jiang Qing. Initially functioning as a "high-level ghostwriting team," the small group became the nerve center of the Cultural Revolution.[16]

The power of this group inspired the writer Wang Ruowang to come up with a bold plan. Wang was a friend of Lin Zhao's mother and a veteran Communist who had also been denounced as a Rightist in 1957. He learned from a pamphlet put out by the Red Guards that two members of the Central Cultural Revolution Group had rehabilitated a previously denounced landlord who was also a Rightist, after meeting with him. Wang Ruowang knew Wang Li, a powerful member of the Central Cultural Revolution Group, and conceived a gallant intervention: he recruited five trusted Red Guards from Shanghai to take a petition to Wang Li in Beijing in order to plead Lin Zhao's case.

Since Lin Zhao had been labeled a Rightist in 1958 when Lu Ping was party secretary at Peking University, and Lu himself had been removed as a reactionary by the Red Guards in 1966, it seemed possible to cast Lin Zhao as a victim of Lu's misguided purge. Xu Xianmin supplied the travel expenses, while Wang Ruowang wrote the petition. Their plan ended in fiasco: the five messengers were thrown out of the office of the Cultural Revolution liaison group before they ever got a chance to meet Wang Li.[17]

At Tilanqiao, the most noticeable change brought by the Cultural Revolution was the suspension of family visits. The last monthly visit to Lin Zhao occurred in June, when Xu Xianmin appeared with a black crepe on her head. A guard again informed her that Lin Zhao remained recalcitrant. Since the prison's early days, inmates had been made to perform labor. Female prisoners typically were assigned the job of knitting, sewing, and making gloves, sitting pads, and clothing. After 1949, most female inmates continued to perform various kinds of labor, making shoes, pasting together paper boxes, sewing, and laundering, often for eight hours a day. Lin Zhao resisted the work regime, as she did other prison rules. Instead, according to the guard, she had cut off a piece of white cloth and embroidered a huge character *yuan*, meaning "wronged," on it, similar to what she had done in May when Zhang Yuanxun visited. When Xu replied that Lin Zhao did indeed feel wronged, he shot back: "It looks like your visits are not helping with the inmate's thought reform."[18]

Not until October did Lin Zhao see her mother again. She penned a blood letter to Xu Xianmin earlier that month, telling her, "I want to see you. Please come right away! They are afraid that you will get to know the details of my abuse." Still, the visit was not allowed until Lin Zhao began a hunger strike, and she would have to wait another four months before the next family visit.[19]

The suspension of family visits involved new hardships. She had no meat or milk powder from home to supplement her meager rations and provide the much-needed nutrition. Nor did she have a cotton-batting quilt, blanket, or padded cotton jacket for the winter. She would not ask to borrow a prison blanket or request TB medicine from the hospital. She told her mother in a letter dated December 14, 1966—Tilanqiao allowed inmates to send one letter home in the middle of each month if they wished items to be brought on the family visit the following month—that if the prison refused to let her bring the requested items from home, "the only consequence would be no more than making me freeze for a winter. A little more coughing, a little more spitting of blood, a little more embarrassment for them. But they will never achieve their goal of forcing me to borrow a quilt from them."[20]

Lin Zhao's refusal to ask for a prison quilt was not just because of pride: she had learned that a loaned item could quickly turn into another means of control. When she was at the No. 1 Detention House, the guards had forcibly taken away the quilt she borrowed for the winter, as a form of punishment, making her "unable to sleep because of coldness."[21] Therefore she had to again brace herself for a hard winter.

In mid-February 1967, she reported to her mother: "The entire winter I was cold and was often short of breath; every other day or so I saw blood in my sputum, not to mention coughing." She went on intermittent hunger strikes, sometimes taking two *liang*, or about three ounces, of food a day, or rejecting food altogether.[22]

THE COLD WINTER was a harbinger of worse things to come. Any semblance of revolutionary order was starting to break down inside Tilanqiao Prison. In Beijing, the Communist old guards who had attempted to resist Mao's Cultural Revolution were losing ground. By the end of October 1966, Liu Shaoqi and his ally Deng Xiaoping, China's nominal head of state and the CCP secretary-general (in charge of the secretariat) respectively, had seen their political downfall. The previous summer, Liu had dispatched ad hoc work teams to rein in the excesses of student radicals on university campuses in Beijing. To Mao, Liu and Deng were cleaving to the "bourgeois reactionary line." On October 23, both were forced to deliver self-criticisms at a Central Work Conference attended by senior party and government officials from across China.[23]

Chaos was about to break lose. At a dinner on December 26, 1966, to celebrate his seventy-third birthday, Mao gave a jovial toast "to the unfolding of nationwide all-round civil war!" That civil war began in earnest with Shanghai's January Storm, when more than one hundred thousand revolutionary "rebels" under the Workers'

Revolutionary Rebels General Headquarters of Shanghai launched a bloody attack on a force of rival workers near the grounds of the Shanghai party committee. On January 6, 1967, Shanghai's party secretary and mayor were denounced at a million-person rally. They were soon removed from power.[24]

On February 5, the rebels established a new organization to centralize the previously divided power of party and government. Styling themselves as the Shanghai People's Commune, the leaders of the new order claimed to embody the spirit and the principles of the egalitarian Paris Commune of 1871. In reality, Zhang Chunqiao and Yao Wenyuan, Shanghai's leading party propagandists, were in control. As allies of Mao's wife Jiang Qing—and having helped her fire the first salvo of the Cultural Revolution—they had been catapulted into the top leadership as key members of the Central Cultural Revolution Group.

For a while, it appeared as though all of China would be transformed into communes large and small, or so Zhang Qunqiao and Yao Wenyuan hoped. In the end, Mao shut down the idea in a fit of common sense: if it were followed through, the People's Republic of China would have to be renamed the People's Commune of China. "Would other countries recognize us?" Mao asked. "What should our ambassadors do after we change our name?"[25]

AFTER JULY 1966, Lin Zhao was never again allowed to read newspapers. Her habit of tearing up images of Mao or smearing blood on them not only exasperated the guards but also created significant political risks for them. Inability to prevent such sacrilege was no small failure on their part.[26]

Still, Lin Zhao had kept up with the major developments of the Cultural Revolution, mostly through prison-wide announcements and morning news from the Central People's Broadcasting Station that blasted from the loud speakers. By the end of November 1966, eight mass rallies attended by some twelve million Red Guards in total had been held in Tiananmen Square. From the top of the Gate of Heavenly Peace, Mao had reviewed his young worshippers in their revolutionary enchantment. The crowds lost their voices crying "Long live Chairman Mao" and waved more than a million copies of *The Little Red Book* in the air, turning Tiananmen Square into a "red ocean." The orchestrated display of mass revolutionary piety only deepened Lin Zhao's contempt for the "Mao worm," as she put it. She did more blood writing condemning Mao, Zhou Enlai, and "other bandit chiefs who are guilty of heinous crimes."[27]

On February 9, inmates were summoned to the prison auditorium, where they were informed of the establishment of the Shanghai People's Commune. The news of the commune and of the toppling of Shanghai's party secretary and mayor may have baffled the inmates, including Lin Zhao. She felt "a new political affinity" to those who had been deposed—the latest victims of Mao's totalitarianism—even though they might have been "just as rotten as" Mao himself. She would forgive fallen CCP leaders such as Beijing's mayor Peng Zhen "as long as they insist on making no compromise with 'Mao Zedong Thought.'" Like Peng Zhen, Shanghai's mayor Cao Diqiu was "chosen by the Lord through His grace! They now have an extra bond with Lin Zhao!" she wrote.[28]

Inside Tilanqiao, the most noticeable consequence of the political upheaval was the cancellation of the prison "holiday" for the Chinese New Year, which would have allowed inmates more time outside their cells. Special holiday meat rations also disappeared; only boiled carrots and salted dry vegetables were served with rice. It was a cheerless holiday. Lin Zhao marked it with a couplet warning of the consequences of evil deeds, which she hung outside her cell door. Traditional couplets for the lunar New Year, written on red paper and mounted on both sides of a door, typically express lavish wishes for prosperity and good fortune in the year to come. For her couplet, Lin Zhao splashed her own blood on two pieces of white paper, white being the color of mourning in China.[29]

She woke up the next morning to find that the couplet had been removed. Furious, she began shouting. Number 24, an inmate housekeeper who had become a self-appointed disciplinarian of Lin Zhao, ran over and opened the two windows across the gangway from her cell. "Shout, you counterrevolutionary. Go ahead and shout!"

Lin Zhao pulled herself up the iron bars of her cell so that, looking across the gangway through the outer windows on the other side, she could see pedestrians on the street outside. She started yelling:

"Down with Communist bandits, the scourge of the country and of the people! Annihilate the evil Communist bandits! Rise, the people of China, and drive the Communist bandits into their grave!"

"It snowed today," Lin Zhao wrote in her new "battlefield diary" on February 10, 1967. "They were heavy snows. The sight of snow filled me with deep gratitude and relief. People, you who shall read this record in the future, know that this was with God's permission!" She noted that it had snowed after every one of her acts of protest that winter. It had snowed on Christmas Day, after she decried the wrongful purge of Marshall Peng Dehuai, and then twice in January, following similar protests.

"A coincidence? Perhaps, but isn't it too much of a coincidence! No, this is a sign that the Heavenly Father has given to His child! My dear Heavenly Father agrees with my stand and my attitude! It strengthens my faith and fills me with gratitude! Oh, dear Heavenly Father, under the direction of such an almighty general, a soldier has only to press forward and throw herself into the battle. . . . Truth and justice are on our side! We shall prevail!" Outside the prison, political turmoil was spreading. Lin Zhao could sometimes hear from her cell the loud speakers mounted on propaganda trucks blaring slogans exhorting people to rise up in "revolutionary rebellion." On that day, she had a different set of slogans for the passersby: "Long live human rights! Long live freedom! Long live America! Long live the United Nations!"[30]

To anyone who heard Lin Zhao, these were clearly mad words. In those days, even a slip of the tongue was punished severely.

During the Cultural Revolution, people at mass rallies sometimes became confused while mechanically chanting slogans that alternated between "down with" and "defend," and some were arrested for mistakenly shouting "down with" at an inopportune time. In a political study session in Fuzhou, a bored cadre heard a noise from someone nearby and mindlessly wrote "fart" on a matchbox he was toying with. He had neglected to note that the characters "supreme instructions" followed by a quotation from Chairman Mao were printed on the matchbox. A vigilante at the meeting promptly reported him, and he was dragged away as a counterrevolutionary. In Shanghai, a poorly educated peddler selling leather shoes had unknowingly labeled the shoes "anti-Mao" when he meant "suede"— a homonym with more complex strokes. The crime landed him in prison for an eight-year term.[31]

"Rise, the people of China, and make the Communist bandits repay the debt of blood!" Lin Zhao cried on. "Down with the totalitarian system! Down with the bloody rule! Down with the autocratic reign of terror!"[32]

Shortly after the Cultural Revolution started, Lin Zhao had been moved from the third floor, the political prisoners' floor, to the almost empty fifth floor of the Women's Block, where her loud protests could be at least partially quarantined from other inmates. She was certain, however, that her shouting could still be heard on the street.[33]

"Lin Zhao's voice is really mighty loud and clear," she wrote, referring to herself in the third person. "It was strengthened by the street agitation and propaganda in the rice fields all those years. Now I have found a use for it!"

With the outside windows beyond the gangway open, Lin Zhao felt the winter air in her face. "A snowy day like this is not really cold. Still, it is a bit chilly. But I didn't want to ask anyone to close the windows for me." To solve the problem, she covered the lower part of the iron bar door with a straw mat and tied one of her cellmate's blankets above the door. She also lodged her protest by dumping wastewater outside her cell. "It is snowing outside and you opened the windows," Lin Zhao said to Number 24, the inmate housekeeper, when she reappeared. "This is intentional abuse of a sick prisoner."[34]

Lin Zhao's "battlefield diary"of February 11 was entitled "I Am the White-Haired Girl of Tilanqiao." Since the start of the Cultural Revolution, conditions had become even harsher for her. Not only was she no longer allowed to read the newspapers, she had also been segregated from most inmates. Her repeated demands to be moved back to the third floor were ignored. "They want to isolate me as much as possible," she noted.[35]

That evening, two inmate housekeepers ganged up on Lin Zhao, taunting her and calling her "paper tiger" and "counterrevolutionary," as a guard looked on. They dumped Lin Zhao's personal items on the floor before they left. Venting her rage on the only prison property she could lay her hands on, she snatched her wooden chamber pot, dashed it on the concrete floor, and threw the pieces all over her cell, leaving a puddle of human waste in the doorway. While inmates' protest against mistreatments in Shanghai's prison system had long included the smashing of wooden chamber pots and chairs, it is also clear that the severity of prison life had frayed Lin Zhao's nerves, leaving her irascible and easily given to violent bursts of emotion.

She then clambered up the iron bars of her cell door and cried, "For more than half a year now, you have isolated me in this cell; you have used these small people to abuse me in every way." Turning to the window, she continued, "The White-Haired Girl of Tilanqiao calls for sympathy and help from the Shanghai public! I am Lin Zhao, a student of the Chinese department of Peking University, a political prisoner in the Women's Block of Tilanqiao Prison! . . . Passersby, spread words of my wrongful sentence!" She added that "revolutionary rebels" inside Tilanqiao had also committed sexual harassment against female inmates.[36]

Lin Zhao's self-identification as the White-Haired Girl of the Mao era had begun in 1965, in her letter to *People's Daily*. Before then, she had felt considerable ambivalence about calling attention to her own gender. As she explained, it was not that she was under the influence of any "vestige of Eastern, Medieval, patriarchal" ideas about the supposed inferiority of women. Rather, she held back because "as a soldier, my gender has brought me loads of . . . completely lewd troubles!" Because of that, "I almost detest my gender!" Yet she understood that being a woman was a fact that she could not change. And as more white hair appeared on her head, the parallel between her circumstances and the suffering of the heroine in the revolutionary opera *The White-Haired Girl* became irresistible.[37]

The opera had been a powerful CCP propaganda weapon during the land reform movement of the late 1940s and early 1950s. Its origins were in North China folk legends about a ghost-like white-haired fairy woman who dwelled in mountain caves and who possessed magical powers that she used to help the poor and punish the evil. In 1945, gifted writers and composers at the Lu Xun Academy of Arts and Literature in the CCP base in Yan'an turned the story into a stirring opera that gave romantic expression to the Communist doctrine of class struggle.

The White-Haired Girl tells of a young peasant woman named Xi'er whose father, hounded by his villainous landlord over rent that he was unable to pay, took his own life on Chinese New Year's Eve. She was then dragged away to be the landlord's slave and concubine—in one version of the story, she was raped—but then escaped into the hills where she found shelter in a cave. Her hair turned white over the years, and she appeared to the few who saw her as a ghost. In the end, her fiancé, who had joined the Communist forces, returned and found her. The army liberated the village and punished the landlord, and the couple looked happily toward a bright future together.[38]

To an imprisoned Lin Zhao, the opera took on a new resonance. Her father's suicide in 1960 and the unusually early graying of her hair revealed a parallel between her ordeal and that of the White-Haired Girl. It spoke to her about the reality of evil and injustice, and the power of survival and vengeance. In a late-night singing duel a year earlier with other inmates, who yelled songs in praise of the great leader to prove their reformed thought, Lin Zhao had fought back, with lines from *The White-Haired Girl*:

You want to murder me?
Let blindness come to your eye!
I am the water that cannot be drained,
the fire that will not die!
My blood and tears have become a river;
my bitterness is piled up to the sky![39]

This was revolutionary bombast from a different time, when the CCP was on the side of the downtrodden and the poor, and liberation was on the horizon. But on that wintry night in 1967, Lin Zhao was shouting toward the closed external windows of the Women's Block and the streets beyond. Her cries for help as the White-Haired Girl of Tilanqiao brought no response; they dissipated into the vast darkness of the night.

When the shouting stopped, she was suddenly overcome with grief, writing in her diary: "Heavenly Father! Let your wrath come! Father, there is enough of your love already! There is already enough of the price paid by so many decent and kind people! . . . Oh, Father, if it is your will for me to become a martyr, I will gladly obey!"

She felt a sudden flash of vengefulness. Although she had previously warned herself against hatred—"to live in hatred is to live in the Devil," she had written in 1965—she now found herself hardening against her enemies. "I don't mind perishing together with them, but Father, let your wrath swiftly come!"[40]

Since the beginning of the Cultural Revolution, the ills of totalitarianism that she had decried before—the enslavement of the public mind, the trampling of individual freedom, the reckless, willful policy decisions, the cult of Mao—had only taken a sharp turn for the worse. Inside Tilanqiao, inmates now had to undergo group study sessions focused on *Quotations from Chairman Mao* as well as editorials in *People's Daily* and the party magazine *The Red Flag*. They also had to join struggle sessions to direct "all-out criticisms" at the unregenerate.[41] Lin Zhao could hear inmates on the fourth floor "doing mischief while reciting the spit of the Mao worm" before lunchtime, likely a reference to the animated struggle sessions that fed on Mao's quotations.[42]

As the revolution burned on, prisoners came under unprecedented pressure to demonstrate their earnestness in thought reform. Barely literate inmates would memorize page after page of Mao's quotations to earn remission points to shorten prison terms. The use of remission points dated back to 1909 when Tilanqiao, then known as Ward Road Gaol, introduced the incentive system under which inmates were able to earn remission through "industry accomplished by good conduct."[43]

Sun Dayu, a Yale-educated Shakespearean scholar and a professor at Fudan University before he was cast into Tilanqiao as a counterrevolutionary, became little different from other prisoners in his efforts to earn remission points. His had become a household name during the Anti-Rightist Campaign after Mao singled him out as an unrepentant counterrevolutionary. Of all the notable Rightists from the so-called democratic parties, Sun had received one of the most severe punishments: he was stripped of his positions and imprisoned. During the Cultural Revolution, he once told an inmate housekeeper at Tilanqiao that he had no time to write detailed confessions of his past crimes because he was "extremely busy copying Chairman Mao's works every day."[44]

In those days, inmates were often ordered to produce poems singing the praises of Mao and the party to celebrate the National

Day. Yang Zhaolong, the last general procurator of the Nationalist government and a famous legal scholar, crafted an adulatory poem in learned, ancient Chinese. Unable to comprehend it, the guard removed one of his shoes and used it to deliver more than thirty slaps to Yang's face.[45]

BY THE EARLY spring of 1967, the Cultural Revolution had penetrated Tilanqiao. "Revolutionary rebels" had risen within its walls among the guards and prison staff, and the prison authorities found themselves on the defensive. Vehement chanting could be heard inside the administrative building; "big-character posters" denouncing reactionaries in the public security system were plastered in the hallways and outside the buildings.[46]

Lin Zhao was quick to mock the guards, who did not stop her tormentors from splashing water into her cell on a freezing day or thrusting straw brooms through the iron grilles to hit her. "Is anybody still in charge in this prison?" she asked. "Well, Petty Thief No. 24 may very well join the 'revolutionary rebels' and seize power from your warden, political instructors, and directors! . . . Oh, my, the inmate housekeepers are going to seize power from you!"[47]

The actual chaos inside the prison was not quite as complete as many inmates may have hoped. They remained prisoners. But unlikely people joined their ranks. A prison official was found one day with a broom, sweeping the floor inside a prison block: he had been deposed by the rebels and was undergoing thought reform as a housekeeper.[48]

In March 1967, Shanghai Municipal Prison was placed under military control. The change came after Mao charged the Central Military Affairs Committee (MAC) with the responsibility of restoring order to Chinese society and reining in the escalating violence between rival rebel groups throughout the country. On March 19, the MAC issued the directive of "the three supports and the two militaries"—to support the left, the peasants, and the workers and to institute military training and control. Over the next five years, some 2.8 million officers and men were dispatched to extend military control to various levels of the government across China.[49]

At Tilanqiao, three officers, acting as military representatives, formed a revolutionary committee and took charge of prison administration. Other military representatives were posted to every floor in every cellblock. Guards, like inmates, had no choice but to obey their commands.[50]

Yet instead of curbing the chaos, the new order allowed the vicious power struggle to continue. Chanting the revolutionary slogan "completely smash the Public Security Bureau, the Procuratorate, and the Court," Mao's "rebels" investigated and denounced more than 1,200 police officers within Shanghai's prison system and "persecuted to death" 62 of them.[51]

In the Women's Block, "debates" between rebel groups, presided over by military representatives, drove one female guard insane. She was sentenced to ten years in prison and locked in a cell on the third floor, where she had once lorded over the inmates. Wearing a blank look in her eyes, her hair disheveled and her body emaciated, she was seen during exercise time being dragged around by two inmate housekeepers who had been under her watch and who now kicked and swore at her. She died not long afterward. Another guard committed suicide by jumping into a river. His body was recovered; a military representative led a group of Tilanqiao leftists in a "struggle meeting on the spot"—as it was called—to chastise the corpse. Two other guards killed themselves as the Cultural Revolution wore on: one jumped off a building; the other hanged himself.[52]

The inmates did not benefit from the disintegration of order. So long as the old administrative structure had remained in place, regular, basic meals had been provided and family visits and supplies sent from home had been allowed. Corporal punishment was in theory banned—even though the prison's ingenious handcuffing practices had often rendered the ban meaningless. As the Cultural Revolution deepened, a "dictatorship of the masses" replaced prison rules. Guards adopted harsher attitudes and tactics; physical abuse increased. Not only were regular family visits suspended and food from home frequently prohibited, the prison authorities also cut back on inmate meals and even the supply of boiled water, citing a notification from the party's Central Committee to answer Mao's call to "practice thrift, wage revolution." Class struggle replaced thought reform as the dominant theme of prison life.[53]

For Lin Zhao and countless other political miscreants, the most fateful directive from the Party Central Committee came on January 13, 1967. Known as Six Stipulations on Public Security, it conferred a broad range of powers on the public security system to mete out summary "punishments according to the law." In addition to criminal offenses such as murder, arson, poisoning, and robbery, it included a wide range of vaguely worded and ill-defined political offenses that would make one an "active counterrevolutionary" to be subjected to "proletarian dictatorship." The second stipulation read:

> Attacking and slandering the Great Leader Chairman Mao and his close comrade-in-arms Comrade Lin Biao by mailing anonymous counterrevolutionary letters, secretly or publicly posting or distributing counterrevolutionary leaflets, writing reactionary posters, or shouting reactionary slogans constitutes active counterrevolutionary acts and must be punished according to law.[54]

In actual implementation, any verbal indiscretions against a long list of CCP leaders besides Mao and Lin Biao also constituted counterrevolutionary acts. Across China, more than one hundred thousand people were arrested during the Cultural Revolution for counterrevolutionary offenses defined by this decree, according to a special investigative report issued by the Procuratorate of the People's Republic of China after Mao's death. Subsequent and independent studies have revealed that the Six Stipulations had far broader reach: during the Campaign to Purify Class Ranks, which Mao launched in 1968, thirty million people were "struggled against" and more than half a million perished in the orgy of violence sanctioned by the Six Stipulations and committed by both the agencies of the proletarian dictatorship and revolutionary vigilantes.[55]

The specific mention of the offense of "attacking and slandering the Great Leader Chairman Mao" suggests that "counterrevolutionary incidents" of that nature, though likely isolated and infrequent, had nevertheless alarmed the leadership. In Shanghai, the first person punished for that particular offense under the Six Stipulations was not Lin Zhao, but a thirty-year-old named Liu Wenhui, a Shanghai shipyard technician and a self-educated man.

During the Red August of 1966, Liu's home had been looted, his books seized, and his family members beaten by the Red Guards. Dismayed by the mass, state-sanctioned violence, Liu began secretly putting up big-character posters on university campuses in Shanghai, in which he denounced the party's tyrannical policies and advocated independent, critical thinking. In September, Liu penned an anonymous treatise refuting the Sixteen Points and branding the Cultural Revolution a "great national persecution." He had his brother make copies of the treatise by hand and mail them out anonymously to fourteen top Chinese universities. Liu was arrested in November and executed on March 23, 1967, after a public trial attended by thousands at the Cultural Square in Shanghai.[56]

Another critic of Mao, thirty-nine-year-old Shan Songlin, a worker at the Shanghai No. 1 Pharmaceutical Company, met the same end. Shan was arrested in March 1967 for distributing anonymous "counterrevolutionary posters and leaflets attacking and slandering Chairman Mao and his close comrade-in-arms Lin Biao" and for making "seals containing counterrevolutionary slogans," which he secretly stamped on street-side public notices and on Mao's portraits in an effort to "sabotage the Great Cultural Revolution." He was likewise sentenced to death according to the Six Stipulations. After a public trial at the Cultural Square on August 28, 1967, which was also attended by thousands of people, he was paraded through the streets of Shanghai and then shot.[57]

Lin Zhao made a reference to the Six Stipulations in her battle-field diary on February 20, 1967.[58] She did not seem to suspect that the directive would make any difference in her case, since she was already serving a twenty-year term.

In reality, the Six Stipulations would make the full force of revolutionary wrath—and a harsher punishment—imperative in her case. Already by December 1966, the Reform through Labor Bureau of Shanghai (Laogaiju), which administered Tilanqiao, had prepared materials in support of an increased penalty for Lin Zhao. Shanghai Laogaiju, a department of the municipal Public Security Bureau, operated from an office building inside Tilanqiao, a few dozen meters from Lin Zhao's block.[59] Its report, which was submitted to Wang Jian, deputy head of the Shanghai Public Security Bureau, on December 5, 1966, listed the following "new crimes" that Lin Zhao committed behind bars:

> During her imprisonment, Lin Zhao poked her flesh countless times and used her filthy blood to write hundreds of thousands of words of extremely reactionary, extremely malicious letters, notes, and diaries, madly attacking, abusing, and slandering our party and its leader. . . . [She] vilified our party as . . . "a totalitarian tyranny that cares only to maintain its power through blood and hatred." . . . What is particularly serious and vile is that she repeatedly smeared her filthy blood on the portraits of Chairman Mao printed in newspapers and magazines. . . . It became so serious that, whenever she saw a picture of the chairman, she had to desecrate it. She also brazenly dug out the head of the chairman's portrait and hung it upside down on the iron door of her cell with a black thread . . . and went on a hunger strike after the prison staff discovered and removed it.[60]

Not only had Lin Zhao "openly vilified the socialist system" as a "bloody totalitarian system" and "a blot on human civilization," the report continued, she had also accused Shanghai's prison system of committing "many hair-raising savage acts of illegal torture," cursing the guards as "fascist bandits" and "the running dogs of the Communists."

According to this report, Lin Zhao had attempted, on several occasions, to jump off a building or to hang herself—which she had not mentioned in her own writings—and had cut her own veins using broken glass pieces, which we know she did. "Even though the staff tried many ways to educate her, and adopted such disciplinary measures as solitary confinement, designated reading of books and newspapers . . . and using her family members to counsel and admonish her, Criminal Lin is stubbornly unregenerate," it read. She had in fact openly vowed to "never give up my goal or change my stand."

Therefore, the Reform through Labor Bureau recommended the death penalty.

Three days later, on December 8, 1966, Wang Jian gave a cautious response to the report: "I approve prosecution for an increased penalty. Please consult with the procuratorate and the court to discuss the matter and find out what they think."[61]

What followed was an unexpected break in the deliberations of the public security-procuratorate-court system. The January Storm of 1967 led to Wang Jian's own downfall. The Red Guards who stormed his office on January 8 uncovered files of the Public Security Bureau's investigations into a case of anonymous allegations against Mao's wife Jiang Qing. As an actress in Shanghai in the 1930s, she had had the reputation as a lady of easy virtue and flexible political loyalty before joining the revolutionaries in Yan'an, where she met Mao. Though the case was already closed and the accuser driven to suicide, Jiang Qing was unnerved by the files, which she called "counterrevolutionary black investigation." In February, Wang Jian and some two dozen top officials of Shanghai Public Security Bureau were brought to Beijing and thrown in jail.[62]

Meanwhile, the January Storm paralyzed the municipal government of Shanghai and its various branches, leaving Lin Zhao's case in limbo. The military control imposed in March on Shanghai

Municipal Prison as well as the Reform through Labor Bureau kept the revolutionary flame alive but did little to hasten a final decision on Lin Zhao.

Unaware of the deliberations, Lin Zhao continued to mix hope with defiance. After a visit from her mother on February 23, she "sat in solitary silence for a good half day," she wrote in the next monthly letter to her family. "I had only one thing to say to you: Mom, we must live on! We certainly must live on! . . . Swallow any bitterness and live on! Chew on iron and bite nails to live on! As the anguished libretto of 'the White-Haired Girl' puts it: one has to live on even if the ocean runs dry! Even if the stone rots away!"[63]

She was sent to the prison hospital again in August, after yet another flare-up of her tuberculosis. Another six months had passed since she saw her mother in early spring. In her letters home in 1967, she repeatedly asked for supplies that she had requested but not received: canned food, candies, pain-relief patches (for her tuberculosis), glucose powder, cod liver oil tablets, used clothing and socks, her old cotton-batting quilt, soap, shampoo powder, toilet tissue, fountain pens, notebooks, a bottle of ink, and writing paper. "They must not think that allowing you to buy ink and paper for me is to facilitate my writing. Without ink, I can still write with blood!" she assured both her mother and the unseen inspectors of her letters.[64]

In her September letter, she asked also for a piece of waterproof cloth, or maybe plastic sheet, the size of a bed sheet. She added, without explanation, "And I also need a poncho."[65] .

The poncho and the waterproof cloth were for her battles with the water-splashing warriors of the Cultural Revolution inside Tilanqiao. There is no record showing that they were ever delivered. Even if they had been, they would not have offered much protection: by mid-June, Shanghai People's Procuratorate had prepared an indictment stamped "top secret." Sometime in the fall of 1967, the Military Control Committee that oversaw Shanghai's public security and judicial system authorized the drafting of a death sentence for Lin Zhao.[66]

eight

BLOOD LETTERS HOME

Mama:

Do you remember this date? It's the seventh anniversary of my arrest! That night seven years ago, when you saw me being handcuffed by them, you wept—even though you had not cried when you encountered the same moment of trial in your own fighting career.

Don't grieve for me, dear Mama, a raging fire refines the true gold. After all, I am in the hands of the Heavenly Father, not in the hands of those demons!

I was very calm today. No superfluous sadness, because it is useless! From the day of my arrest I have declared in front of those Communists my identity as a resister; I have been open in my basic stand as a freedom fighter against communism and against tyranny. . . .

I have a chestful of brave thoughts as a fighter, but I don't know when you will get to read even these few words. Maybe at an exhibition? Just for a laugh!

I want to see you! My Mama, I want to see you!

Your daughter Zhao,
October 24, 1967, the Lord's calendar[1]

The letter was done in her own blood. On the same day Lin Zhao wrote this letter, she composed a poem that she called a lyric "slogan." The opening lines read:

Lin Zhao, "Slogan Marking the Seventh Anniversary of My Arrest," four-character rhyme, October 24, 1967.

Seven years have gone by since my arrest;
those years, like passing clouds, I have lost them all!
My country remains in my heart;
still a burden on my shoulder is its rise or fall![2]

Lin Zhao had taken up blood writing again in early October 1967 as a protest against the suspension of family visits and in response to the "vile abuses." For six weeks she had been denied water to wash her face or her clothes, and it had been almost six months since her last family visit in May. (On that occasion, her sister Peng Lingfan had arrived to see her, but much to Lin Zhao's disappointment, her mother, who was in Suzhou, had not.)[3]

Her intermittent hunger strikes had not resulted in better conditions. "Instead, I have been granted special visits day after day by roughneck inmate housekeepers who bullied me." Starting on

October 14, she wrote out one blood-inked protest per day. She addressed them to the prison authorities and handed them to the guards along with her blood letters home, repeating the demand that she be allowed to see her family. Meanwhile, to her exasperation, inmate housekeepers repeatedly threw water on her from outside her cell.[4]

The denial of family visits was likely an attempt to break her spirit and subdue her, but Lin Zhao's quibbling with the language the prison used on the prisoners' visit cards did not help either. According to Tilanqiao's rules, inmates could write monthly letters home around the middle of each month; they could also fill out and return visit cards at the same time to request visitation by family members the following month. The cards referred to an inmate as a "criminal." Lin Zhao found the word offensive. "As everybody knows, I am determined to never 'plead guilty' and I refuse to yield to them! Therefore, whenever I see the word 'criminal' printed on the card, I instinctively detest it and cannot tolerate it," Lin Zhao explained to Xu Xianmin.

Thus, each time a visit card was distributed, she either ignored it or blotted out the character "criminal" after she took the card. "We are inmates! Not the so-called 'criminals'!" she told her mother. In September, she did not take the card when it was offered. The following month, the prison authorities withheld the card, and using her failure to fill out the card as an excuse, "they simply canceled the visit for me!"[5]

Helpless, Lin Zhao announced that she would start writing blood letters home until she was granted a family visit. On October 23, she set out on a month-long protest in the form of one blood letter home each day, consecutively numbered and each signed "Your daughter Zhao" and dated according to "the Lord's calendar." She collectively titled them "Blood Letters Home—to Mother." After completing each letter, which she doubted the guards would send out, she copied it into a notebook, using a pen. For more than two weeks, she enclosed with every letter a statement entitled "Protest

over the Current Condition," which was also consecutively numbered and done in her own blood. Her letter of October 24, the
anniversary of her arrest, was No. 2.[6]

> No. 3 (October 25, 1967)
> Dear Mama:
> Every day I long to see you. Every day I am writing a letter to you
> in blood. At the same time, just about every day, I am showing them
> my protest in blood! . . .
> I am not feeling well today: headache, nausea, and chills. It is grad-
> ually getting cold, but I haven't yet stitched my quilt together because
> the cover sheet was taken away by them, and they won't return it.
> Don't you think that's loathsome?! Alas, Mama, you don't know how
> hard my battle is! But, relying on the truth and justice of the Heavenly
> Father, I have no fear! I wish you good health! My Mama!

> No. 7 (October 29, 1967)
> Mama, greetings!
> It's the Sabbath day today. I spent a good half day mending my
> clothes. Some of my clothes can already be used as denunciation ma-
> terial one day. . . . Still, here in prison I belong to the class of people
> who are clothed in prettier colors. To forget for a moment people
> inside the prison: occasionally I catch a glimpse of the street outside,
> and can see that, out on the street, none of the pedestrians is decently
> clothed! If it is like this in Shanghai, you can just imagine the situation
> elsewhere! It's been eighteen years after all. . . . Alas! Mama! They have
> communized China into a country of beggars, and this is only the
> more visible part of the multitude of horrendous evils committed by
> this cursed gang of bandits! We would run out of ink writing about
> their "virtuous rule" even if we turn the ocean into ink!

When Lin Zhao started her blood-letter protest, she had demanded that a family visit be granted her before the end of October.[7]

On October 30, she sank into "an unusual bleakness and deep anger" but simultaneously felt a "frozen composure."

She called to mind "Friar Bacon and the Brazen Head," a story in James Baldwin's *Thirty More Famous Stories Retold*, which she had read in the English original, probably while a student at Laura Haygood. Friar Bacon, an Oxford professor and a wizard of sorts, asks his servant Miles to watch a brazen, or bronze, head he had made and to wait for the moment when it might utter "a secret of the greatest importance to every Englishman." Miles is scornful of the head and taunts it—until the moment when the brazen head, turning the metallic smile on its face into a frown, lifts itself from its marble pedestal and, in a thunderous voice, roars "TIME IS PAST!" With a dreadful crash, the head falls and shatters into a thousand pieces.[8]

"I thought of that imaginative and mysterious piece 'The Brazen Head," Lin Zhao told her mother in her October 30 letter, using its English title. "I thought of that sentence in the story: Time is past!" She added that she had quoted that line to the guards the previous year and "repeatedly warned them" that time was running out for the Communist regime to repent.[9]

On October 31, Lin Zhao wrote a "Declaration in Blood." She began by announcing, in English, "The time is past!" Her demand for a family visit had again been rejected. Still, she vowed to remain loyal to the battle of "free humanity" to "resist the evil way of communism, to resist the totalitarian system, to resist the rule of secret agents, to defend human rights and freedom, and to establish democracy for the nation!"[10]

Before handing her writing to the guards, Lin Zhao read it aloud into the open space between the outside wall and the gangways so that those on the lower floors could also hear her. Similar to the Alcatraz Federal Penitentiary, the five tiers inside a Tilanqiao block shared a large open space, so that activities on all tiers could be monitored simultaneously. This allowed Lin Zhao to "publicize" her protest, as she told her mother in her blood letter the next day.

She also told her mother that, beginning on November 1, she would "write my Blood Letters Home in Protest in an orderly manner so that in the future they will form a separate volume in my collected works 'Freedom Writings.' I have given these letters the general title 'To Mother.'"

Lin Zhao recalled that her family used to own a book entitled *A Mother Fights Hitler*. She had been deeply moved when she first read it "because I could not but estimate that, one day, I might encounter the same destiny as the lawyer [Hans] Litten! And that is to become an imprisoned one under the tyrannical rule!"[11] Her own experience had borne out that premonition, but "compared to the tyrannical rule of the Chinese Communists, Hitler's fascism is almost nothing!" She continued:

> I wanted to write some more, but I am very tired. Those without the experience won't know: although you don't bleed a lot when you write a blood letter, still it drains your mental energy! Moreover I have already written three protest statements in blood today! I cannot help it. . . . I am practically speaking in my own blood every day! However, they see it as usual and nothing startling! . . .
>
> I am tired. Let me write you again tomorrow! My Mama, I wish you from afar peaceful dreams tonight!
>
> > Your daughter Zhao,
> > *November 1, 1967, the Lord's calendar*

No. 14 of Lin Zhao's blood letters to her mother was entitled "The Farce on the Sabbath Day," which she wrote on November 5. "Dear Mama, there was a scene of farce just today: led by a female guard who had inflicted serious insults and injury on me, and whom I had cursed before, a motley crowd gathered in front of my cell to sing wildly," she reported. "There were songs that wish Mao Zedong ten thousand years, that denounce reactionaries. . . . You can't call it a struggle session, because it didn't look like one, nor did it look like a demonstration. They were thrusting their arms and stomping their feet, acting like buffoons!"

The buffoonery on display was in fact no laughing matter but was meant to be a straight-faced revolutionary ritual. Since the beginning of 1967, when a *People's Liberation Army Daily* editorial called on all Chinese to be "boundlessly loyal to Chairman Mao," collective expressions of "three loyalties and four boundless loves" had steadily gained popularity and would eventually be sublimated into the "loyalty dance," representing tens of thousands of hearts beating in unison for the great leader. The dance would be invoked during meetings, at street intersections, and on buses, trains, or airplanes. Prisons were hardly off limits.[12]

Among the revolutionary inmates whom the guard brought that day was one of Lin Zhao's tormentors, a former prostitute. "But when you think about it, these totalitarian thieves are not much more reputable than prostitutes!" Lin Zhao told her mother.

"What did I do then? I praised the buttocks of Mao Zedong, their stinky progenitor of lowlife, as the greatest buttocks! I chanted long live prostitutes of both the private and public kinds! Long live male prostitutes and long live public toilets!" She found herself getting into the act. "And to express my profound appreciation and heartfelt adoration of Mao Zedong Thought, I put on my head a pair of underpants that had been torn by them in a previous scuffle and a pair of long pants that had been splashed with sewage water, waving the leg parts, mincing about, and singing. . . . In sum: it was a scene of total devilry!"

Some in the crowd started chortling. "You may not believe it but even I could not help chortling!" Lin Zhao added. "At the very end, a fool jumped out from the crowd and, prostrating herself on the ground, kowtowed to me! That's when they made an excuse to exit the stage all at once! Good Heavens! There should be such a thing in this world!"

The farce in front of Lin Zhao's cell that day convinced her that there was no point continuing to write her blood protest statements, which she had been sending to the prison authorities almost daily for about three weeks. "Since the military takeover of prison by upper-strata totalitarianists, they have been doing whatever they want, with no regard for any law!" she wrote. Meanwhile, she would "persevere in writing these daily blood letters home. Not only are they true records of my life and feelings during this period, they are also forceful denunciations of these totalitarian thieves! Dear Mama, my battle is hard, but it also tempers me and makes me more mature and stronger! Sabbath-day blessings to you!"[13]

On November 8, Lin Zhao dumped her ration of drinking water and then went on an all-morning protest. Through the iron bars of her cell, she shouted about her family's past work for the CCP, including her own. These reminiscences triggered "irrepressible grief and indignation so that I broke into tears and started weeping," she told her mother.[14]

> *Cold Porridge, Cold Meal, and Cold Water*
> *(No. 18 of Blood Letters Home in Protest)*
> Dear Mama, it is getting cold. Are you all well? I miss you all, even though there is nothing that I can do for you, just as there is nothing that you can do for me.
> At dusk I retrieved the cold lunch that I had left at the door underneath my blood writing, which I did as a protest. I brought it back in a little early . . .
> It's getting cold; the cold wind rattles the window panes, but I am still sleeping on the concrete floor and my quilt is not yet sewn up! . . . It was so windy today but they purposely had an inmate housekeeper open the window near my cell to let the wind blow at me. . . .
> I will write to you again tomorrow, my Mama. Now I am going to read aloud my letter. The last few days I have been reading aloud into the open space my blood letters to you, so that more people may know what I have encountered! I wish you good night, dear Mama!"
>
> **Your daughter Zhao,**
> *November 9, 1967, the Lord's calendar*

Lin Zhao called her nineteenth letter home, dated November 10, "The 'Cold Water' that the Heavenly Father Splashed into the Prison." As Shanghai's winter crept in, her thoughts turned to her increasingly dire conditions. "Mama, if you can now see the scene outside my cell door, you will surely be aghast with fury." She had smashed her wooden chamber pot once before, and to prevent herself from repeating the act, she had shoved the pot far out onto the gangway, where it now sat in a puddle of dirty water, food residue, and human waste. For days, the unsightly scene remained untouched. Nobody cleaned up the mess. "The smell of my own feces is a lot sweeter and lovelier than [the slogan] Long live Mao Zedong," she added.

There was another puddle nearby. "The other puddle is the cold water that the Heavenly Father has splashed into the prison . . . rain water, heavenly water." It had rained for several days, and the roof near Lin Zhao's cell had leaked. On that day, the rainwater had mixed with the wastewater.

> But what significance does it have that is worth mentioning? . . . This time, the Heavenly Father—my good Heavenly Father—has splashed cold water into the prison. Maybe it was to comfort me, and to show me that the Heavenly Father would splash into prison through a leaking roof the "cold water" I had asked for; maybe it was to spur me on: it shows that the Heavenly Father quite approves of and also directly participates in my water-splashing protests! In any event, I treat this seemingly trivial occurrence as a supernatural testimony. . . . Dear Mama, I really experienced many astonishing things that bear witness to the Heavenly Father and to the Holy Spirit! Alas, why is there no heaven above my head?"[15]

In this way, with her mind overwrought but her will intact, Lin Zhao clung to her faith. "There is no greater joy for me as a select soldier of Christ than to know for sure that what I plan to do accords with the Lord's will," she added.[16]

"DEAR MAMA, ARE you dead?!" Lin Zhao's letter of November 12 began. "One day, anybody reading this out-of-the-blue, illogical sentence would likely wonder: what kind of writing is this?" While she was singing "God Be with You till We Meet Again" the previous night to mourn the death of Ke Qingshi, the guard grew irritated and rebuked her: "You were not so sad when your mother died!"

Lin Zhao admitted that, under normal circumstances, she would have understood that to be just a "tiresome curse." But she was well aware of Xu Xianmin's chronic heart ailments and high blood pressure. And she worried that her blood letters might have directed the wrath of the proletarian dictatorship toward her family. "Will they be prompted to persecute you and Younger Brother and Younger Sister? . . . In the past several years, I have got you all into enough troubles. For that reason, Younger Brother has chastised me and called me the most selfish person in the world!"[17]

Lin Zhao had been stung before by criticism from her younger brother Peng Enhua, who had grown angry over her stubborn refusal to give up her opposition to the CCP, which had already turned her family members into political pariahs and could have, at any time, even graver consequences. Throughout the Mao era, individuals' political offenses had always implicated their families, prompting divorces and severing of other family ties—called "drawing a clear line." Even an urn that contained the ash of a Rightist or counterrevolutionary family member could be a dreaded liability if kept in the home.[18]

Lin Zhao was not unaware of the implications of her actions for her family but decided that, in her fight as an "independent, free person for the basic human rights endowed by Heaven," she could not be bound by "considerations for the safety of either myself or my loved ones!"[19]

By 1967, Lin Zhao's family had not only become political and social outcasts, they were also bearing a crushing financial burden to support her in prison. The family's money, such as it was, had evaporated after the Five-Antis Campaign of 1952, when the private bus company Xu Xianmin cofounded was nationalized. By the mid-1950s, Xu Xianmin was unable to afford the better TB medicines for Lin Zhao and Peng Lingfan.

In 1955, based on her exceptional grades, the precocious Lingfan had gained admission into Shanghai No. 2 Medical College, from which she graduated in 1960. She found a job as a physician in a community hospital in Shanghai just before Lin Zhao's arrest. But Lingfan's income was modest, and she lived away from home, in a dorm room of her hospital. Enhua, though a bright student, had been unable to attend college, most likely because of his eldest sister's incarceration as an "active counterrevolutionary." During the 1960s, he devoted himself to the study of Japanese haiku, about as far from politics as one could get.[20]

With dwindling resources, Xu Xianmin, who received a monthly stipend of only twelve yuan, had trouble keeping up with Lin Zhao's requests for money and supplies. The family at times complained about the list of items she wanted from them. Lin Zhao admitted that it had been selfish of her to request supplies from home. "Our family has got into no small trouble because of me. What right do I have to ask for things? On the other hand, Mama, no matter what circumstances one finds herself in, there is always the wish to rebuild one's life. . . . And as long as one's life drags on, there will naturally be various needs in life, and that is something I cannot help with." She was torn between her guilt and her craving for canned food, glucose powder, soap, shampoo powder, used clothing, stamps, and money, which she could spend on other necessities such as toilet tissue.[21]

"I have been unable to repay you in any way for the favor of nurturing me or to bring you some consolation in your old age," Lin Zhao had written her mother in July 1967, after she was again hospitalized. "Instead, I have brought you grave distress. It breaks my heart whenever I think of this!" All she could offer her mother were prayers. "Oh, Lord, Please bless my mother's life! . . . I am willing to have my own lifespan shortened so that my mother can live longer! Let Mother live until the day when righteousness triumphs!"[22]

BY MID-NOVEMBER, THE cessation of family visits had brought considerable hardships, including a lack of money with which to buy toilet tissue. Blood writing was also becoming more difficult, as her blood became thinner and coagulation worsened.[23]

Lin Zhao's mother had urged her during one visit to "endure some idleness." "But you don't know that I am by nature incapable of inactivity!" she explained in her letter of November 15. "Apart from writing, there seem to be endless chores to do." Even though the abuse and cold weather had sapped her energy, she was "giving full play to the spirit of Robinson Crusoe." When an old pair of pongee pants wore out at the hips, she took them apart and altered them.[24]

At Tilanqiao, inmates could borrow sewing needles for a few hours twice a month. On the other days, she could still hand-sew "almost any clothing" even without a needle, employing a technique she had picked up at the Shanghai No. 1 Detention House: she would use a bamboo pick to poke holes in a piece of cloth and guide the thread through with a strand of hair. "Our circumstances are somewhat different from those of Robinson's . . . I'd rather be Robinson! What happiness it is to be close to nature! Even those cannibalistic savages can be seen as unaffected and simple to be point of being lovely when compared to the totalitarianists who are filled with evil!"[25]

Without family visits or spending money, prison life grew more difficult by the day. Her intermittent hunger strikes left her lips parched and her body feverish. Yet she continued to write her blood letters. "In the past month, these blood letters home have run into approximately 20,000 to 30,000 characters," she wrote Xu Xianmin on November 16. "In the future, they will make up yet another volume of either my complete published works or a posthumous collection of my papers."[26]

Her supplies were running low, she told her mother. She still possessed a few sheets of writing paper but only one envelope. "This month, they did not let me draw on my big account!"—there was no money left in it. Cash brought by family during prison visits was left with the authorities and its amount entered into a notebook— called the big account—from which purchases were deducted. "I already ran out of stamps and toilet tissue, and I have to wipe my poop with my hand!"[27]

After nearly a month of writing her daily blood letters home, Lin Zhao came to realize that they had had no impact. She had handed her letters to the guards each day to be sent to her mother but had not received any words from home. On Sunday, November 19, as she sang hymns and conducted her one-person worship in her cell, she began to feel "a lack of intensity in my fighting spirit to merely give vent to my sentiments about home." She admitted to herself that she had sunken deeper into despair and hatred; it appeared that the "totalitarian scoundrels are all beyond cure." She was ready to bid farewell to the previous stage of struggle, as her mind turned to the prospect of "fortifying the wall and clearing the fields"—by which she meant the scorched-earth tactics she had previously foresworn.[28]

"Dear Mama," Lin Zhao wrote in the thirtieth daily blood letter, on November 21. "I am going to bring to a close for now the protest letters addressed to Mother! On the one hand, I don't know how you've been lately. On the other hand . . . the theme has become a bit narrow in view of the struggle I am faced with." The physical and emotional toll that the totalitarian rule had taken on her was no different from that experienced by "my fellow countrymen throughout China," she noted.

As she turned her thoughts to other themes, she was also running out of ideas for her letters to her mother. From a literary perspective, writings must be natural, she explained, particularly in the case of those dealing with emotions. She recalled the words of the great Song dynasty poet Su Dongpo that "writings should be like drifting clouds and flowing water." They "drift when they should drift, and stop when they must stop. . . . It would be pointless to affect one's feelings or to write for the sake of writing."[29] On November 22, she wrote the last blood letter home, acknowledging that her sanguinary protest had failed.

I Am Willing to Submit to the Lord's Will
(No. 31 of Blood Letters Home in Protest)
Dear Mama: After today's blood letter home in protest, starting tomorrow, I will bring this theme to a stop. Of course you and I will not forget: tomorrow is the seventh anniversary of Daddy's death! . . .

In the past several days I have thought a lot . . . at times quite painfully, because I was reflecting deeply on my own mistakes! . . . Some of them were because of my inexperience in struggle, which are easier to correct; others have to do with the rashness in my own personality, which I have to examine in a fundamental way! . . . In any case, generally speaking, I tend to be overconfident in handling various problems! This is a serious problem especially for a Christian! There is too much of "me"; as a result there is too little, or almost nothing, of the Lord! . . . I affirm myself too much! And I forget my Lord! I forget that, in my proper station, I am but a servant! . . . Alas, dear Mama, how hard it is for faith to come from the flesh! . . . On the outside, I appear to have quite a bit of faith, but that is only faith in myself! . . . What am I able to do without the Lord's permission, without the Lord guiding and keeping me? . . .

Dear Mama, I am willing to learn to submit to the Lord's will. . . . Let me turn over all my pains, hopes, and dreams to my Lord and let my heart and soul become the sacred temple where I worship the Lord! . . . I am quite willing to be silent so that I can think deeply and pray: may the Heavenly Father help me prevail over the devil!

Dear Mama . . . in the bleakness of my mood I send you and Younger Brother and Younger Sister my painful love and thoughts from afar.

Your daughter Zhao,
November 22, 1967, the Lord's calendar

Lin Zhao's sudden urge to plunge herself into self-denying sub-mission to God's will was uncharacteristic but not entirely surpris-ing. It is true that there had been little quietist spirituality in her early Christian upbringing—the reformist social Christianity the Southern Methodists had introduced to Laura Haygood students during the 1940s tended not to cultivate any mystical quietism. On the other hand, an indigenous Chinese Christian spirituality—most forcefully articulated in the end-time "dispensationalist" the-ology of Watchman Nee, founder of the homegrown group called the Little Flock—had taken firm root by the time of the Communist takeover in 1949. It impelled a believer to go to extravagant lengths to deny the flesh and crucify oneself in Christ.[30]

During her initial pretrial incarceration in Tilanqiao in 1963, Lin Zhao had come into contact with Yu Yile, the independent preacher and graduate of the Christian Bible Institute of Nanjing, who may have passed on to her the mystical theology of Watchman Nee. Apparently Yu had tried, without success, to bleach Lin Zhao's Christian faith of political activism. Now that her protest had been stonewalled, she found the theology of yielding increasingly rele-vant and appealing.[31]

But even if Lin Zhao was "willing to be silent," she was clearly incapable of actually doing so. The following day, to commemo-rate the anniversary of her father's death, she fasted and, suddenly energized, embarked on three writing projects. In the first piece, a blood-inked declaration, she explained the basis of her political stand. It included the precept, articulated by a seventeenth-century Confucian scholar, that "the rise and fall of all under heaven is the responsibility of every ordinary person." It also included Western democratic ideals, which the United Nations had come to em-body, and "the humanism and the ethics of love rooted in Christian teachings."

She had come to realize her own political naïveté—her belief that reasoned remonstration would lead to changes in the totalitar-ian rule, or that the Communist leaders might repent of their sins.

There had been "errors" on her part in the preceding months: she had overestimated the importance of her opposition to the CCP. She now recognized that she was only "one ordinary soldier in the general warfare of free humanity against communism and against tyranny."[32]

In Mao's China at the time, there was hardly any sign of the "general warfare of free humanity against communism" that Lin Zhao had imagined. Yet there were a few others who had the audacity to question, however momentarily, the CCP revolution. At a time when the majority in China were gripped by "the starkest madness" of revolutionary "sense"—to borrow Emily Dickinson's words—they, like Lin Zhao, were driven by the "madness" of "divinest Sense."[33]

In 1965, Wang Peiying, a housekeeper working for the Ministry of Railways in Beijing who had been treated for mental illness, withdrew her CCP membership, citing the party's degeneration from a party of liberators to one of pampered and privileged oppressors. She was arrested in 1968 and sentenced to death in 1970. As she was being paraded through the streets on the way to the execution ground—standing in the back of a truck—the guards tied a rope around her neck to prevent her from shouting protests. They did it so tight that the rope strangled her before they reached the destination.[34]

In Shanghai, counterrevolutionary madness doomed one of the best-known musicians in China. Lu Hong'en, a classical pianist and conductor of Shanghai Symphony Orchestra, was treated for schizophrenia in January 1965. A year later, Lu's symptoms returned. At a political study session in May, he publicly disputed an editorial by Yao Wenyuan entitled "On 'Three-Family Village.'" Like his earlier editorial attacking Wu Han's play *Hai Rui Dismissed from Office*, Yao's new article was used by Mao to bring down the party leadership in Beijing, a prelude to the Great Helmsman's final assault on President Liu Shaoqi, who would be denounced as "China's Khrushchev."

In his agitated state, Lu Hong'en defended Khrushchev's "revisionism" and chanted "Long live Khrushchev." He had long been
known for his politically inept straight talk. At an earlier group
study session, he responded to Mao's 1942 "Talks at the Yan'an
Forum on Literature and Art" by asking: "Should Beethoven look
up to workers, peasants, and soldiers or should it be the other way
round?" His advice—which soon enough was deemed evidence of
his "bone-deep hatred for workers, peasants, and soldiers"—had
been that the latter should take the time to learn to understand
symphonic music. Instead of being sent back to the mental hospital,
Lu was arrested and put into Shanghai's No. 1 Detention House.[35]

As the Cultural Revolution gathered steam, public denunciations of reactionaries became a favorite part of the revolutionary
liturgy. To show off their newfound power, many rebel groups went
to the Shanghai No. 1 Detention House to borrow high-profile inmates for their denunciation meetings. Lu was in high demand.

In a packed theater, forced to wear a dunce cap, Lu remained
oblivious to the world around him, which had been turned upside
down. He was scornful of the revolutionary "model plays" that
Mao's wife had championed, which he privately called rubbish.
Their exclusive performance would lead to the "destruction of the
tradition," he warned the crowd. At that point, angry revolutionary rebels rushed forward and ripped his mouth. As his cellmate
recalled, Lu returned to the jail bloodied and unable to chew his
food—but still humming "Ode to Joy" from Beethoven's Ninth
Symphony.[36]

Within months, repeated denunciations, brutal handcuffing, and
beatings reduced Lu Hong'en, then in his late forties, to a graying
and balding shadow of himself. He also experienced bouts of madness during which he screamed in terror that "the witch"—Mao's
wife, Jiang Qing—had come for him. He developed a conditioned
reflex to the color red and would rush to smash or bite anything
that color; he would also bite inanimate objects that had the syllable
mao in their names, be it a towel (*maojin*) or a sweater (*maoyi*). "In

this 'great revolution' stirred up by the witch, I, Lu Hong'en, would rather be a counterrevolutionary," he declared. He asked his fellow political prisoner Liu Wenzhong—the disabled brother of the executed counterrevolutionary Liu Wenhui—to visit Vienna and lay a bouquet of flowers on Beethoven's grave for him if he ever got a chance. Thirty-three years later, Liu made good on his promise.[37]

Lu had been raised a Catholic. Like Lin Zhao, he found solace in hymns and prayers during his more than two years at the No. 1 Detention House. On April 27, 1968, Lu and six other "active counterrevolutionaries" were sentenced to death at a public trial held in Shanghai's Cultural Revolution Square—formerly the Cultural Square—as part of a ritualistic cleansing of Chinese society ahead of May 1, International Workers' Day. The condemned were then "immediately sent under guard to the execution ground to be shot by firing squad," *Liberation Daily* reported. "At that moment, the revolutionary masses both inside and outside the square broke into a prolonged chanting of slogans. There was not a single person who did not clap his hands in joy."[38]

"From being an art of unbearable sensations punishment has become an economy of suspended rights," Michel Foucault wrote of the evolution of the Western penal system since the Enlightenment. The modern "rituals of execution," he observed, have been characterized by "the disappearance of the spectacle and the elimination of pain." Revolutionary China kept both.[39]

CUT OFF FROM the world, Lin Zhao probably knew nothing about what befell other "enemies of the people." However, after almost seven years behind bars, she had few illusions about the stark reality outside Tilanqiao. "I do know about Auschwitz and many other concentration camps," she wrote, "and I know Khrushchev's 'Secret Speech'"—the 1956 address in which he denounced Stalin's cult of personality and "his intolerance, his brutality, and his abuse of power" in the vicious purges. "But what can you find therein that is comparable to all that I am talking about? Simple death, even cruel physical torture, seems almost lovely compared to the vicious humiliation and barbaric trampling that one has to endure!"[40]

Lin Zhao titled the second piece she wrote on the anniversary of her father's death "Battle Song of My Heart and Soul!—I Cry Out to Humanity." She did it in ink. As "one small, young soldier" holding out on the battlefield, "I appeal in anguish to free humanity to please extend righteous sympathy to the Chinese masses who have been enslaved, oppressed, trampled, hurt, and dehumanized," she wrote. Her only hope was for her case to come before "the supreme court of humanity's conscience."

"I have persisted in wrestling my basic human rights from the totalitarian system and from Communist demons, because I am human! As an independent, free person, I am entitled to my birthright, which is my share of God-given, intact human rights!" And since her individual rights were "inseparable" from those of her compatriots, "our fight for ourselves is also the fight for our country . . . and for all the enslaved."[41]

"Prison is the battleground for my resistance!" she wrote, reiterating a declaration she had made years before. Given the political reality in Mao's China, "this is the only battleground for true resisters." The "internal battleground," on the other hand, "is the heart and soul of the resister."[42]

"Father's Blood," Lin Zhao's last long piece of writing, ran to about 14,500 blood-inked characters. She started writing on November 23 and finished on December 14. It was her attempt to come to terms with the loss of her father and with her own troubled relations with him. Coming one month after her arrest in October 1960, his gruesome death had been hidden from her until late summer the following year. "It was entirely my fault that we had a fraught relationship," she wrote—a realization that had come too late, she admitted.

His death could not be deemed meaningless or futile, she maintained. If nothing else, he had refused to bend to the evil power of the Communist regime. Denounced as a "historical counterrevolutionary," he had refused to plead guilty, as she herself now did. "Thank God! For the past eighteen years, there still remained in the foul-smelling Chinese mainland some so-called 'diehards' who refused to bow and 'plead guilty' before the Communists," she wrote. They had struggled to maintain the "Chinese code of honor," as articulated in the ancient teaching that "a scholar may be killed but would not be insulted."

Yet, destroying the human dignity and moral confidence of the individual was precisely the goal of the CCP, she argued. It had sought victory through "defilement" and would step on the head of whoever refused to bow. She was reminded of a fable in which a "stinky fly" flew up the sacred Mount Tai to defecate. "After that, it buzzed triumphantly, proclaiming: what is extraordinary about Mount Tai, after all? I shitted on top of it!"

As Lin Zhao put it, the CCP had created masses of downtrodden heretical people, or *yimin*, a term she coined to refer to all those who had found themselves victims of political purges and who were "more despised than the untouchables in the Indian caste system."[43] The abuse and persecution were so pervasive that "monks in Buddhist temples were forced to draw up 'patriotic covenants': they vowed not to chant sutras to expiate the sins of the 'counterrevolutionaries' who died!" she observed.

That left the heretical people with but one escape—through death, "which has become both protest and release." They left behind "a puddle of blood as silent protest in grief and indignation." She admitted that she had also attempted suicide more than once. She continued:

> Blood! Blood! As a Christian I wish to plead with all the Christian churches and the Holy See in Rome: judge the multitude of suicides in mainland China with fairness! . . . Do not view all the suicides of the victims of Communist . . . rule as spiritual evil! . . . God's gift of life should have been in itself beautiful! Therefore it is sin to lightly

dispose of it! . . . But it is precisely in order to protect the beauty, dignity, freedom, and purity of life that multitudes of victims in China have forsaken their precious lives in resolute protest against the defilement and trampling of life. . . . I imagine that the Heavenly Father will not necessarily pronounce their suicides sinful but will instead pardon the afflicted souls with compassion! Therefore, righteous and holy churches, please hold a memorial service, or a holy Mass for the repose of the soul, for those who died under the tyrannical rule in mainland China!

Without such sympathy, Lin Zhao asked, where could the dead "find a trace of human warmth to cover their wronged bones"? It was only by imagining a listening, free humanity that she could find solace. "It is only when I think of you, and picture myself pouring out my heart to you, that my anguished yet numbed heart and soul feel the human warmth."[44]

IN THE PAST, Xu Xianmin's visits had meant a brief respite for Lin Zhao from her lonely torment, but now those visits had stopped. "Dear Mama! Are you alive?" she asked once again in a letter dated December 16. The prison had finally given her toilet tissue, she reported, but her menstrual period, which she sometimes missed for months, had stopped once again.[45]

On December 29, 1967, a cold, icy day, Lin Zhao at last received a letter from her mother that had been sent three days earlier. The extent of self-censorship in the letter is unclear. It explained that she had been gravely sick and near death, only to be brought back to life in the hospital. "Therefore what the comrade in charge told you was completely correct," she wrote. Cryptically, she admitted that "I have not had the courage to write back to you. Nor have I had the courage to come see you. Your action and your language have been too excitable, too absurd, and too nonsensical." She added that her two other children and her friends had urged her to cut off contact.

Xu Xianmin also told Lin Zhao that she had previously looked upon the monthly prison visits and the correspondence between them as fulfilling "my utmost desire in life," but she had come to see that both only occasioned disappointment and pain. She once passed out on her way home from prison. "You are a part of me. Why do you insist on creating such serious consequences? . . . Do you still have a trace of love for me?" She pleaded with Lin Zhao to "become sensible again" and to listen to her, and promised to come see her in prison the following month if her own health improved.[46] Xu Xianmin did not know that she would never see her daughter again.

Lin Zhao received the letter in the evening, a few hours after her brother delivered a package of supplies from home, but she was not granted a family visit that day. "Seeing your handwriting and knowing that you are still alive, that was my only consolation! Dear Mama! This has become nearly the only thing that I care about now." She had broken down in a fit of crying a few days earlier when she put on the gray sweater her mother had given her, but "entrusting you into the hands of the Heavenly Father" was the only thing she could do. "Oh, Heavenly Father . . . I ask of nothing other than keeping Mother's physical life!"[47]

In Lin Zhao's last extant letter to her mother, written in ink and dated January 14, 1968, she responded to Xu Xianmin's complaint that she had been "nonsensical." It was true, Lin Zhao allowed, that she had been accused of being nonsensical ever since she was in the No. 1 Detention House. But "what am I being 'nonsensical' about? Am I the one who is being 'nonsensical'?"

She told her mother that she could understand what she was going through, due in part to her own encounter with the mother of Zoya A. Kosmodem'yanskaya while she was a student at Peking University. A young Soviet heroine during the Great Patriotic War, Zoya was a household name in China in the 1950s. As a member of a guerilla group that operated behind enemy lines, Zoya was captured by the Germans. She was stripped, given some two hundred belt lashes, and forced to go outside in her underwear and walk barefoot in the snow. She refused to disclose the identity of her comrades, even during merciless torture.

On November 29, 1941, Zoya was hanged after making a rousing speech: "You hang me now but I am not alone. There are 200 million of us. You won't hang everybody. I shall be avenged. . . . Victory will be ours." In 1942, Zoya was awarded the order of Hero of the Soviet Union. Lyubov Timofeyevna Kosmodem'yanskaya, Zoya's mother, memorialized Zoya and her brother, also a hero in the war, in her book, *The Story of Zoya and Shura*, which was first published in a Chinese edition in 1952.[48]

"It was around 1955 or 1956 when I met her, at Peking University. She made a brief speech to the students," Lin Zhao explained to her mother. After the speech, Lin Zhao and around a dozen other students escorted Zoya's mother to her car, presented her with flowers, asked for her autograph, shook her hand, and kissed her. As the car was about to pull away, the heroine's mother smiled and waved to the students. "Strangely, it was that last glimpse of her . . . that left an odd feeling and an indelible impression! . . . Alas, Mama, you did not know this: her smile, though filled with a mother's love, was one of profound loneliness; it quite betrayed a desolation deep inside her heart!"

Every time Lin Zhao thought of that smile, she could not help wondering: "As a mother, would she rather her own children died heroes or lived as mediocrities or, say, average people? Sincere as the warmth of young people in another country might be, what good was that to her? Could she find a bit of compensation in our flowers and hugs for the emptiness in her heart?"

Lin Zhao reflected on her guilt over having hurt her family, not only her mother but also her siblings and father. "I earnestly hope that, one day, I will be able to make it up to Younger Brother and Younger Sister!" Meanwhile, she agreed that the advice that friends and family had given Xu Xianmin "is completely right! Please never mind me!" she implored. "Entrust everything to God. . . . Didn't the Bible tell us not to worry about tomorrow?"[49]

Did Lin Zhao sense that the end was near? She was not privy to her death sentence, which was prepared sometime in late 1967 and still awaiting final approval. Yet her last letter displayed little of her characteristic feistiness. It was more meditative and resigned than most of her earlier writings and was tinged with both sorrow and regret, as if she was giving a final account of her life.

"In my deep thoughts, I examine solemnly the history of my own life and repent of the sins that I have committed," she wrote. "Alas, dear Mama, I had been self-satisfied and self-approving about the straight path of my life and the simple life experience I had had, but when I look at my whole life from the point of view of the repentance of sins, I feel a shock and a deep sorrow that I had never felt before!" Even though "I have no blood on my hands" during the land reform of the early 1950s, "was I not more or less splashed with some blood?" she asked.

Turning to her personal life, Lin Zhao made a cryptic reference to an indiscretion while she was in college. "After the 'Anti-Rightist,' in a fin de siècle mood, I abandoned myself to my feelings." It was a "small lapse in virtue" that was nevertheless used later as "loathsome 'evidence'" against her. It is unclear whether she was hinting at some brief sexual intimacy with Gan Cui, when they thought they were getting married, or even possibly with her Peking University friend Yang Huarong. The latter, in his reminiscence of the winter of 1957–1958 that he and Lin Zhao shared as political outcasts, mentions that they were "quite intimate with each other" as they tried to "fend off the cold of the winter evenings."[50]

Lin Zhao herself had also written in "Chatters of a Spirit Couple" that, in the desolation of the days during the Anti-Rightist Campaign, she and a fellow political outcast had tried to "douse our sorrows with a drink from the cup of Venus." She now wanted her siblings to "make sure to remember the lesson that I have learned" and handle romantic love with "care and prudence"; and she wished them "respectable, happy marriages." Lin Zhao also pleaded with her mother to moderate her strong personality, to examine herself, and to confront any "mistake or even sin."[51]

She was confident that her mother shared her views. Despite the close watch kept over prison visits and the censorship of her family's communications with her, Lin Zhao might have learned that her mother converted to Christianity in the early 1960s and was baptized in a bathtub in an underground house church.[52]

Lin Zhao's final and the most important confession in the letter concerned a strange "sin" of betrayal she had committed against her mother. During the early 1940s, after Xu Xianmin returned from Western China to the Suzhou area as an undercover agent in the resistance movement against the Japanese, she had entrusted Lin Zhao to the care of her own mother. In time, the grandmother developed an obsessive suspicion regarding Xu, who mingled frequently with men in her covert work. She pressed Lin Zhao to reveal any unsavory details about Xu and would cry and make a scene and accuse Lin Zhao of shielding her mother unless she conveyed lurid secrets.

"In the end, I had no choice but to tell lies and make up stories, which I no longer remember after all these years, something ludicrous in any event," Lin Zhao wrote. It got to a point where "I became scared whenever I thought of it! . . . And I realized that if she kept forcing me to continue with those lies, I could not wash myself clean even if I jumped into the Yellow River."

Lin Zhao did attempt to retract some of those tales later on, only to bring down on herself storms of fury from her grandmother that she was taking her mother's side. "Mama! The Heavenly Father above knows that I agonized over this for quite some time. . . . This sin from the past had lain buried in my memory for more than twenty years. I have only dug it out in recent days as I examined my whole life and went through a thorough repentance." She was making the confession, she added, to "relieve my soul of this part of the burden of guilt. . . . Dear Mama, are you able to forgive me?"[53]

As for the present, Lin Zhao assured her mother that she was experiencing no internal turmoil. "They are trying to force me to make an exit, but I am incapable of exiting this stage. Therefore, if they won't let you come, so be it." She added that if the prison gate were to be opened for her by "certain people"—with unacceptable conditions attached, she implied— "I won't even walk out! Speaking of being nonsensical, that is how nonsensical I will be!" She closed the letter telling her mother that she had not eaten that day and was deeply tired.

That night, in a burst of fantasy, Lin Zhao added a postscript consisting of a long list of items she would love to get from home. It began with the usual necessities such as toothpaste, socks, used clothing, a washbasin, a straw mat, pens, composition books, notebooks. Then, her imagination took flight:

I want to eat, Mama! Stew for me a pot of beef, and also slow-cook a pot of lamb. Prepare for me a salted pig head. . . . Roast a chicken or a duck. Go get a loan if you don't have the money. . . .

Don't cut back on fish either. Steam a lot of salted ribbonfish, fresh milk fish. The mandarin fish needs to be cooked whole. . . .

And the moon cake, and Chinese New Year cake, dumplings, spring rolls, pot stickers . . . and *zongzi* [sticky rice wrapped in broad bamboo leaves] . . . crackers, fruit cakes . . . When you run out of the rationing coupons for grains, go ask for them like a begging monk. . . .

And sausage . . . duck livers, pig tongues . . . eels and soft-shell turtles, all simply steamed, to be brought to me in the steam pot.

And—etcetera, etcetera. Load them onto a truck and bring them. . . . Feed me. . . . Pig head! Pig head! Pig head! . . .

Hey! Now after I wrote all this, I took another look at it and I laughed! How often does one get to have a hearty laugh in this world of dust? . . .

I am sending you a daughter's love and longing, my Mama![54]

The fantasy was in season: in two weeks, another Chinese New Year would be ushered in; in each home, on New Year's Eve, there would be a family reunion dinner, the most lavish of the entire year—or so it was in her childhood and adolescent memories.

LIN ZHAO'S PRISON writings, which were returned to her family in 1982, include nothing from her final three and a half months in Tilanqiao. Did she stop writing altogether? That seems unlikely. Was her stationery taken away from her, as had happened during her time in the No. 1 Detention House? That is possible, but she would have continued writing in her own blood—although she would not have had the opportunity to copy the words onto her notebook using a pen, as she had been doing.

According to the judge who reviewed Lin Zhao's prison files in 1981 for her posthumous rehabilitation, prison rules at the time dictated that the writings of the executed not be destroyed. They were to be gathered into the inmate's files. What was eventually returned to Lin Zhao's family came from her secondary file. The rest, which would have included her interrogation records and possibly her other writings deemed as key evidence of her counterrevolutionary crimes, was sent to a storage facility for classified archives outside Shanghai, where it remains.[55] Until her primary file is declassified and made public, what she wrote after January 14, 1968, remains a mystery.

Shanghai High People's Court records show that on April 16, 1968, the Military Control Committee in charge of Shanghai's public security and judicial system formally approved her death sentence.[56] The verdict ends with the following, which Lin Zhao would have scorned as much for its shoddy composition and revolutionary clichés as for the miscarriage of justice it represented:

Throughout the interrogation process, Criminal Lin refused to plead guilty and displayed instead extremely rotten attitudes.

The counterrevolutionary criminal Lin Zhao started out as a counterrevolutionary of grievous crimes. During the reform-through-imprisonment period, she stubbornly stuck to her counterrevolutionary stand and continued counterrevolutionary activities inside prison. She is truly a diehard, unrepentant counterrevolutionary. In order to defend to the death our great leader Chairman Mao, to defend to the death the invincible Mao Zedong Thought, and to defend to the death the Party Central Committee headed by Chairman Mao, as well as to strengthen proletarian dictatorship . . . this committee issues the following verdict:

Death sentence for the counterrevolutionary criminal Lin Zhao, to be carried out immediately.[57]

Strangely, the verdict carries a serial number indicating that it was initially prepared in late 1967. Why there was such a delay remains a puzzle. In any event, on April 19, the Shanghai Revolutionary Committee, of which Zhang Chunqiao and Yao Wenyuan—ideological stewards of Mao's Cultural Revolution—were head and first deputy head respectively, signed off on the execution warrant. "Criminal Lin made no demand in response to the sentence," a formulaic note in her court file reads. In reality, Lin Zhao reportedly did her last blood writing upon receiving the verdict. It reads, "History shall pronounce me innocent."

On the same day, as a matter of formality, the verdict was referred to the Supreme People's Court in Beijing for final approval—a remarkable gesture toward nominal legal procedure amid a general breakdown of law and order across the country.[58]

By 1968, the Supreme People's Court had all but lost its judicial functions, a culmination of political developments since the 1950s. In 1963, the Supreme People's Court and the Supreme People's Procuratorate began to combine their respective roles. The two institutions' joint work report for that year—delivered to the National

People's Congress that oversaw both—highlighted their support of the political campaigns then underway. Beginning in 1964, when the third People's Congress was formed (each served for five years), "class struggle" became the dominant theme for both the Supreme People's Court and the Supreme People's Procuratorate. Their over-riding goal was to "beat back the enemies' savage onslaught." Even civil cases were to be handled with a view to carrying out "class struggle." Any questioning by the Supreme People's Court of Lin Zhao's death warrant was thus inconceivable. Its approval was granted on April 23.[59]

BY THAT TIME, Lin Zhao had been moved from the Women's Block to Building No. 3, the special ward for political prisoners, which also served as a holding place for those in transition into or out of prison, including inmates on the death row. A five-story brick structure completed in 1920—it was the oldest cell block in service inside Tilan-qiao—Building No. 3 stands near the northwest corner of the prison, a few meters away from Zhoushan Road outside the prison wall. Origi-nally called Cell Block F.G.—a reference to the two wards, F and G, inside it—it was euphemistically renamed the Humaneness Block in the late 1940s, during the last years of the Nationalist rule. After 1949, under the new Communist government, which had no use for Con-fucian sentimentalism, it became Building No. 3, until the Cultural Revolution eventually militarized its name into Squadron No. 3.[60]

Lin Zhao was left in a cell on the otherwise empty fifth floor, where the effect of any shouting would be minimized. The prison took further precautions to prevent her from ideologically contam-inating anyone: a tight rubber hood, called the Monkey King cap, was placed over her head. It covered her entire face, leaving only a narrow slit around her eyes and an opening for her nose to allow her to see and breathe. The hood was only removed at mealtime. During this period, Lin Zhao was almost certainly handcuffed be-hind her back and was likely in fetters as well.[61]

Lin Zhao's "Monkey King cap." Oil painting by artist and filmmaker Hu Jie. Used with permission from Hu Jie.

On April 29, Lin Zhao was taken to a choreographed "public sentencing meeting" at the one-thousand-seat prison auditorium, a massive gray structure at the northeastern corner of the prison that stands atop Tilanqiao's former open execution ground.[62] As was customary, other inmates were summoned to attend the meeting, to lend their revolutionary indignation to the condemnation of the most notorious "antireform element" at Tilanqiao and to be shown the consequences of resistance.

Lin Zhao arrived not from her cell but from the prison hospital, where she had been taken after coughing up a massive amount of blood in another flare-up of tuberculosis. When the soldiers acting under the order of the Military Control Committee at Tilanqiao rushed into the ward for Lin Zhao, she was in bed, hooked up to an intravenous line. As the doctor who had been treating her later recalled, her weight had dropped to about seventy pounds but her eyes still flashed with intensity. "You diehard, unrepentant counterrevolutionary," one of the soldiers cried out, "your last day is here." Lin Zhao calmly asked for permission to change out of the hospital gown, a request that was denied. She then asked a nurse to bid farewell for her to her doctor. The doctor, hiding in the room next door, heard the commotion but silently remained there, out of her sight, trembling.[63]

As shouts of revolutionary slogans reverberated around the auditorium that afternoon, Lin Zhao stood soundless on the dais, her face and neck flushed—as a former inmate who was in the audience recalled—and her mouth stuffed with a rubbery gag, called the shut-up pear, that expanded in the inmate's mouth at any attempt to speak. As a precaution lest the gag malfunctioned, a thin plastic rope was also wound around her neck, to be tightened if necessary, as a backup silencing device.[64]

IN THE LATE 1960s, many public executions in Shanghai took place at the Target Ground, five kilometers to the northwest of Tilanqiao Prison, where an artificial mound at the end of a shooting range had been built by the Japanese army following its occupation of Shanghai in 1937. After 1949, it remained in use as a firing range for troops and local militia but later doubled as an execution ground. During the Cultural Revolution, a column of trucks would sometimes be seen carrying the condemned—tied up with ropes, two or more to a truck—from their public trials through the streets of Shanghai to the Target Ground. "Counterrevolutionary criminal" Shan Songlin's execution on August 28, 1967, most likely happened at the Target Ground.[65]

According to Lin Zhao's sister Peng Lingfan, a family friend's young son, who occasionally worked at the then decommissioned

Longhua Airport in Shanghai, claimed to have witnessed Lin Zhao's execution. At about 3:30 p.m. on April 29, he reported, two military jeeps sped onto a Longhua Airport runway and then came to a sudden stop. Two armed men dragged out a woman with her hands tied behind her back and her mouth stuffed with a gag. She looked as if she was wearing a hospital gown. From a distance, the boy recognized her as Lin Zhao. One of the men gave her a kick on the back, and she fell forward on her knees. At that point, two other personnel emerged and fired a shot at her. She fell but then raised herself from the ground and struggled to inch forward. Two more shots were fired, and she went limp. They then dragged her body into the other jeep and sped off.[66]

In reality, however, Lin Zhao's execution did not take place at Longhua Airport or the Target Ground. The retired judge who presided over Lin Zhao's rehabilitation confirmed that there was indeed an execution ground at the time next to Longhua Airport but revealed that Lin Zhao was not taken there. Instead, after the sentencing meeting, she was shot at a location within Tilanqiao. This revelation accords with other credible accounts, including the recollections of a former inmate housekeeper, who claimed that Lin Zhao's execution took place in the back of the auditorium.[67]

What went through Lin Zhao's mind as she was led out to be shot that afternoon, her hands tied behind her back? She could not have been taken entirely by surprise, however secretively the execution order had been passed down the chain of command. In January 1966, more than two years earlier, she had reflected on her political dissent and its probable outcome: "Under the current circumstances, besides treating the prison as her homestead, Lin Zhao only looks to the execution ground as her final place of repose!" Her "long-cherished hope" was to "turn my purest heart and my youthful blood into an exclamation mark in the epic of the struggle of free humanity," she wrote. "By nature people find joy in life; I alone find joy in death!"[68]

Meanwhile, Mao's revolution surged on, enraptured by its own purity and its moral triumph over both its domestic enemies and Western imperialists. The day of Lin Zhao's execution, the New China News Agency announced that a historic pamphlet by Mao, entitled "Statement by Comrade Mao Zedong, Chairman of the Central Committee of the Chinese Communist Party, in Support of the Afro-American Struggle Against Violent Repression"—Mao had written it within days of the assassination of Martin Luther King Jr. on April 4—had been translated into seven languages including English, French, and Spanish.

"Some days ago, Martin Luther King, the Afro-American clergyman, was suddenly assassinated by the U.S. imperialists," Mao wrote. "Martin Luther King was an exponent of nonviolence. Nevertheless, the U.S. imperialists . . . used counterrevolutionary violence and killed him in cold blood."[69]

THE EARLIEST MEDIA report on Lin Zhao in the post-Mao era, a *People's Daily* article published in January 1981, contained a detail about her death that has since been etched in the popular memory: after her execution, officials delivered the news to her mother and demanded a five-cent bullet fee, since Lin Zhao had wasted a people's bullet. The article's source was Lin Zhao's sister Peng Lingfan, who apparently heard about the bullet fee from her mother and who later published her own accounts of the incident, which included additional dramatic details.[70]

Lin Zhao herself had commented on the Communist state's practice of demanding a bullet fee. In her letter to the editors of *People's Daily* in 1965, she wrote that, outside the official media, "one hears that when a man is sentenced to death, he has to pay for the bullet he gets. One bullet costs just over a dime, it is not a big deal if I have to buy that with my own money." At least, she observed, that was a straightforward way to die and allowed one to "bleed in broad daylight and before people's eyes." It was preferable, she added, to having her blood "dripping drop by drop in a dark corner"—a description of her state, at the time.[71]

During the Cultural Revolution, the collection of bullet fees had great symbolic value to revolutionaries. Following the public trial and execution of Liu Wenhui as a counterrevolutionary on March 27, 1967, a mob of "revolutionary rebels" and indignant neighbors, led by an officer from the ward police station, descended on his home shouting "down with" slogans while the police collected a bullet fee from his mother. Likewise, after the execution of the musician Lu Hong'en two days before that of Lin Zhao, the authorities demanded a bullet fee from his wife.[72]

The collection of bullet fees was not the only means of inflicting additional pain and shame on the family of the condemned. On August 28, 1967, the day of Shan Songlin's public trial and execution, an official arrived at his home to announce the execution and to instruct the family to "draw a clear line" between themselves and Shan. He also had Shan's death warrant posted on the wall outside his house, as a neighborhood crowd rushed in to smash the door and the windows.

When Shan's wife and children arrived at the crematorium to claim his ashes, the staff greeted them by vigorously reciting in unison a passage from *The Little Red Book*: "Whoever stands on the side of the revolutionary people, he is a revolutionary. Whoever stands on the side of the imperialists, the feudalists, and the bureaucratic capitalists, he is a counterrevolutionary. Whoever merely stands with the revolutionary people verbally but acts otherwise, he is only a verbal revolutionary." Shan's family returned home that night without his ashes.[73]

Soon afterward, the Red Guards arrived to search Shan's house and to remove all pictures of him. "They not only annihilated his body," Shan's son reminisced, "they also wanted to wipe off his memory from our hearts." To atone for Shan's counterrevolutionary crime, his widow was made to kneel in front of a Mao portrait.

Finally, Shan's small house was confiscated and the entire family thrown out into the street.[74]

In the course of a few decades, Mao's revolution had transformed the soulless apathy of the average Chinese that had sickened Lu Xun into a frenzied hatred toward class enemies—and into an equally feverish fear that one would be torched by the fire of the revolution unless it is redirected toward others—colleagues, neighbors, friends, and, in some cases, even one's own kin. Thirty-two years later, Shan's widow died from her heart trouble. Her last words were: "If there is rebirth, I vow to never re-enter the womb in China!"[75]

UNLIKE THE PUBLIC sentencing of condemned counterrevolutionaries in Shanghai—usually conducted in the city's Cultural Revolution Square in those days—Lin Zhao's trial and execution took place within Tilanqiao's high walls and was kept out of the public eye. Therefore, no mob appeared outside her home to vent their class hatred. The five-cent bullet fee was likely collected by an officer from the ward police station. It was part of a routine revolutionary ritual, intended to drive home the point that Lin Zhao's crime against the party and the people was such that her family must pay to have her cleansed from the revolutionary land.[76]

AFTERWORD

What need for the imperial Beimang Hills to bury your bones?
For epitaph, go set your ink brush free.
Like Weiqi, open and upright all his life,
a wisp of pure wind your spirit shall be.

—LIN ZHAO, poem sent to Rightist friend Yang Huarong, summer, 1958[1]

The Morning Star

Ah, the lead singer, when will you
with your long howl
take command of the morning breeze and wheat waves
to force the night in flight, shot through with an arrow,
leave all its plunder
to be returned to the dawn?

—SHEN ZEYI in memory of Lin Zhao, spring, 1989[2]

LIN ZHAO'S EXECUTION HAD BEEN CARRIED OUT IN PREPARATION FOR the celebration of International Workers' Day. After May 1, the ward committee in charge of her family's neighborhood in central Shanghai held its denunciation of Xu Xianmin, mother of a suppressed counterrevolutionary and herself a historical counterrevolutionary.

As indomitable at fifty-six as she had been as a radical teenager in the 1920s, Xu put on mourning clothes one evening, went out to the streets, and threw herself in front of an approaching trolley. Instead of being run over, she hit its side and was thrown back, with a gash on her head and a broken pelvis bone.[3]

Xu had joined an underground Christian group before the start of the Cultural Revolution. However, whatever support network she had gained had apparently dissolved after 1966. Constantly watched by the ward committee, estranged from her two surviving children, Xu Xianmin never recovered from the blow of Lin Zhao's execution.[4]

Her mind had in fact already fractured months before. When Lin Zhao's classmate and Rightist friend Yang Huarong visited Xu in early 1968, he found her looking aged and wan. She often got lost after prison visits, she told Yang, and was once called a crazy woman when she walked through a downpour, too lost in thought to notice the rain. [5]

Xu Xianmin's life unraveled after Lin Zhao's death. The memoir of Feng Yingzi, a journalist and lifelong friend of Xu's, contains an account of his last encounter with her. It took place sometime in the autumn of 1973, by which time the paroxysms of the Cultural Revolution had subsided. Feng had previously been denounced as an "ox demon and snake spirit," but was now allowed to return to Shanghai occasionally from the rural May 7 Cadre's School where he was undergoing thought reform.

One day, I was taking a leisurely stroll near the intersection of Fuxing Road and Shaanxi Road. Suddenly a crazy woman walked toward me. After she brushed by me, she turned around and greeted me: "Is your issue resolved?"

I was taken aback and turned around. Her hair was all disheveled; she was wearing a tattered, greasy jacket, looking desolate in the autumn wind. The heels in her shoes had worn off. Her ashen face was bloodless. There was a dull look in her mournful eyes.

She glanced about her as she spoke, a hint of fear on her face. It was the look of Xianglin's wife toward the end of the story "New Year's Sacrifice." I finally recognized her: it was Xu Xianmin.

"Big Sister, it's you!"

I was immobilized by the shock, seeing Xu Xianmin in such a state. A bone-deep grief welled up inside me. But before I could utter another sentence, she had quickened her steps and walked across to the other side of the road. Apparently she was trying to avoid me. As one wearing the hat of a "historical counterrevolutionary," she did not want to get me into trouble.[6]

Whatever her mental state, Xu Xianmin retained enough of her sanity to record repeated physical abuse by her own son. Peng Enhua had brutalized her for being a counterrevolutionary after Lin Zhao's death. A gifted, self-made scholar of Japanese haiku but ostracized as the brother of an executed counterrevolutionary, he spiraled into alcoholism, feuds with his family, and domestic violence. In 1975, on another autumn day in Shanghai, Xu fell when she got off a bus near Shanghai's Bund and collapsed. She was taken by passersby to a hospital, where she died three days later.[7]

LIN ZHAO'S REHABILITATION occurred at the beginning of Deng Xiaoping's reform era. In June 1978, a meeting of senior CCP officials reached a decision to "remove all hats of the Rightists" as part of a nationwide effort by the party to redress the grievous harms of the Mao era. In February 1979, the party branch committee of Peking University posthumously removed Lin Zhao's Rightist "hat," as it did for hundreds of former students and professors.[8]

The following year, a memorial service for Lin Zhao was held in a New China News Agency meeting room in Beijing. Attended by dozens of her friends, fellow students, and teachers, the event was organized by Lu Fowei, a senior journalist and Lin Zhao's classmate at the South Jiangsu Journalism Vocational School, where both had embarked on their revolutionary career. A wreath dedicated to her memory bore an unusual couplet on its twin vertical banners: the first line consisted of a single question mark, the second an exclamation point.[9]

In 1982, Lin Zhao's sister and several former friends dedicated the joint tombs of Lin Zhao and her parents on Lingyan Hill outside Suzhou. They placed a single strand of her hair within. Unknown to them, Lin Zhao's ashes had been collected by Xu Xianmin shortly after the execution. They eventually ended up in a cemetery on the outskirts of Shanghai and were later retrieved by Lin Zhao's friend Ni Jingxiong. On April 22, 2004, the newly discovered ashes were finally interred in her tomb.[10]

AMONG CONTEMPORARY CHINESE dissidents, one of the first to discover Lin Zhao was Ding Zilin, the "Tiananmen Mother." After her seventeen-year-old son was killed in the Tiananmen Massacre of 1989, the distraught Ding, a philosophy professor at Renmin University, came upon Lin Zhao's story as she was searching for "the courage to live on." For Ding, a fellow alumna of the Methodist Laura Haygood Memorial School for Girls in Suzhou, Lin Zhao's courageous dissent brought an epiphany. "I was awakened from the numbness of life," Ding wrote. "It was a painful awakening, but it was only because of this awakening that I was able to shed my shackles and discover my true self. For me, it was a kind of redemption for my soul."[11]

Since 1995, Ding has led what became known as the Tiananmen Mothers Movement. Instead of seeking rehabilitation for those wrongfully killed, they demanded that the government investigate the massacre, compensate the victims' families, and end the perpetrators' legal impunity. To date, the Tiananmen Mothers' goals of truth and accountability are still on the distant horizon.[12]

In 2004, independent filmmaker Hu Jie completed a documentary film called *Searching for Lin Zhao's Soul*. Five years earlier, not long after he began his interviews for the film, he had been forced to resign as cameraman for the New China News Agency. His boss was unable to resist the pressure from above: Hu Jie was touching a raw nerve of the party. He persisted. The result was the poignant film that has etched Lin Zhao in the political and cultural consciousness of contemporary China.[13]

"So beautiful is the flight of a free soul," exclaimed Liu Xiaobo, after he came upon Lin Zhao's story through Hu Jie's film. To him, she was "the rare one who stood upright in an era when the entire country prostrated themselves." In a separate commemorative piece, Liu wrote: "Gasping for breath in nothingness, I fixed a prolonged gaze at your beauty. Timidly I reached out my hand, and removed the cotton ball that had been stuffed into your mouth."[14]

In 2008 Liu Xiaobo coauthored "Charter 08" calling for a peaceful transition to democracy in China. He was arrested later that year on charges of "inciting subversion of state power" and subsequently sentenced to eleven years in prison. In July 2017, Liu died from liver cancer after the Chinese government denied his request to receive medical treatment in the West—the only Nobel Peace laureate to die in state custody since the Nazi era. After the cremation, the authorities hastily arranged a sea burial that many believe was designed "to deny supporters a place of pilgrimage." There would not be a second site in China after Lin Zhao's tomb.[15]

In 2010, a New Citizens Movement broke out across China, demanding equal education rights for the children of rural migrant workers and calling for the murky assets of government officials to be made public.[16] Its leader was the prominent human rights lawyer Xu Zhiyong. In 2013, when Xu was under house arrest, he studied Lin Zhao's prison writings. In "A Martyr for a Free China—Reading Lin Zhao's '140,000-character Letter,'" Xu reflected on Lin Zhao's battle behind bars:

> This was a spiritual battle. Lin Zhao offered all of herself for a free China. . . . Her body and her blood . . . were laid down as the gravel for the road toward a free China. She was a martyred saint, a prophet and a poet with an ecstatic soul, the Prometheus of a

free China. It turned out that our nation also had its own impassioned martyr. . . . One day, this nation will remember April 29,
the date of martyrdom of the Chinese Prometheus . . . to extol an
ancient people's piety of thirsting for freedom. We are latecom-
ers. Half a century has passed. For this nation, the road toward
freedom remains a long one. Those who have gone before us have
endured purgatory and death. Today, it is still required of us to
promote the cause of a free China with the spirit of martyrdom,
and to tread the gravel that has been splashed with Lin Zhao's
blood. We will set out anew to offer ourselves as sacrifice in order
to lay down the road toward freedom, justice, and love.[17]

Xu was arrested in August 2013. In January 2014, he was sentenced to four years in prison for "gathering a crowd to disturb public order."[18]

Because of Lin Zhao, wrote another well-known dissident, "we
now have our genealogy."[19]

IN LATE MAY 2016, as I neared the end of the research for this book, I
returned to the Haiyan Hotel, a stone's throw from the north wall of
Tilanqiao Prison. From my room on the twelfth floor overlooking
the prison compound, I peered down on the row of massive, rectangular, five-story concrete buildings inside the seventeen-foot wall
topped with electrified barbed wire.

These were Blocks 5 through 8, or Blocks Trustworthiness, Righteousness, Harmony, and Peace, as they were fancifully named in
the pre-Communist era. The barred windows were covered with
uniform aluminum shutters whose dull gray color blended into the
grayness of the buildings. Lin Zhao had likened the concrete blocks
to "giant, gray sarcophagi," "bleak and unsightly" against the backdrop of a "clear, soft, blue sky."[20]

As night fell, orange, purple, and white LED lights lit up the forest of new skyscrapers that line the waterfront of the Huangpu River,
beyond Tilanqiao. A sightseeing cruise ship, decked with strings of

holiday lights, glided surreally by behind the tall office buildings. In the dark foreground, pale fluorescent light emitted from the barred, unshuttered windows on the top floor of the Women's Block—a T-shaped, five-story brick building where Lin Zhao was held—near the center of the prison compound.

It had been fifty years since the outbreak of the Cultural Revolution in May 1966. For a long time I stood in my darkened hotel room, my eyes meeting the distant pale light from the windows along the gangway on the fifth floor, where Lin Zhao spent the last year and a half of her life in an isolated cell.[21] I was about five hundred feet from it, but fifty years apart. Somehow I felt that, half a century later, Lin Zhao had not yet departed Tilanqiao.

ACKNOWLEDGMENTS

Generous assistance given by many people has made this book possible. In 2011 Rowena He introduced me to *Searching for Lin Zhao's Soul*, the 2004 documentary film by Hu Jie, which set me upon my own search for Lin Zhao's story. In 2013, I met Zhao Rui, author of *Jitan shang de shengnü: Lin Zhao zhuan* (The Female Saint on the Altar: A Biography of Lin Zhao) published in 2009. She not only shared with me key sources but also helped me connect with the most important, surviving informants on Lin Zhao. Without her generosity, this book could not have been written. Had it not been for the different genres of our writings, I would have liked to consult the basic chronology of her moving tale.

More broadly speaking, this book is built on the labor of love and dedication of so many who have worked to preserve Lin Zhao's legacy: Ni Jingxiong, Peng Lingfan, Zhu Yi, Ai Xiaoming, Tan Chanxue, and Xu Wanyun as well as the late Gan Cui, Xu Juemin, and Jiang Wenqin. Some of them painstakingly collected Lin Zhao's writings; others went to extraordinary lengths to decipher, edit, or annotate them. The result was *Lin Zhao wenji*, or *Collected Writings of Lin Zhao*. Printed in 2013, it became the basis of this book. I am also indebted to Hu Jie, whose 2004 film on Lin Zhao established her in the political and cultural consciousness of contemporary China. Since 2013, Hu Jie has graciously helped me with my research, sharing his sources, responding to my inquiries, and putting me in touch with those who knew Lin Zhao intimately.

I am grateful to those who during the past five years agreed to my requests for interview—some on multiple occasions—and who in many cases provided me with valuable materials. They include Ni Jingxiong, Tan Chanxue, Ai Xiaoming, Zhu Yi, Mr. Zhang of Suzhou, Zeng Yuhuai, Xu Jiajun, Liu Wenzhong, Yan Zuyou, and Shan Miaofa, as well as two men—Gan Cui and Shen Zeyi—whom Lin Zhao had loved at different points in her life. Both of them passed away not long after the interview. Shen Zeyi had terminal cancer and was in his last weeks when the interview took place, but he chose to spend more than two hours telling me about his time with Lin Zhao at Peking University, his eyes glistening with memory. Could he have saved Lin Zhao from her doomed dissent if he had accepted her love and if they had gone on to start a family? he wondered aloud dreamily.

Those who helped my research through correspondence and who provided valuable information in response to my queries include Peng Lingfan, Gu Yan, Huang Yun, and Wang Youqin. I also thank Sun Naixiu, whose annotations on Lin Zhao's poems were illuminating. My colleague Dr. Warren Kinghorn of Duke University School of Medicine analyzed many passages of Lin Zhao's writings and of my manuscript and provided an assessment of her mental state during the period when she was undergoing interrogation.

Enabling my research trips to China to conduct interviews was the annual faculty research grant from the Divinity School of Duke University. A generous Henry Luce III Fellowship in Theology—matched by contributions from Duke—enabled me to devote the 2015–2016 academic year to completing the first draft of this book, which made possible its publication ahead of the fiftieth anniversary of Lin Zhao's execution. I wish to thank Stephen Graham, Richard Lischer, Craig Dystra, and Randy Maddox for their good advice on my research proposal. Stephen Chapman drew my attention to the parallel between Lin Zhao's story and that of Sophie Scholl.

Grant Wacker, Ellen Davis, Guo Jian, and Carol Hamrin read the first draft of the entire manuscript and offered valuable suggestions. Song Yongyi commented on large parts of my work and helped my research on critical details of Lin Zhao's execution. Likewise, Rudolph A. Nelson critiqued my first chapters, and Melissa Eden edited my translation of "A Day in Prometheus's Passion." Philip Barlow offered advice on my research from its inception. I am grateful for the wisdom, insights, expertise, and time that all of them kindly bestowed on me.

Frances Lyons, reference archivist of the General Commission on Archives and History of the United Methodist Church, was most helpful to me in my research on Lin Zhao's alma mater, the Laura Haygood Memorial School for Girls. Carol Leadenham, archivist at the Hoover Institution, patiently assisted me in my communications with Peng Lingfan. I also appreciate what Hoover Institution has done to preserve a large part of the original prison writings of Lin Zhao, even though I was unable to utilize its collection in my research because of the logistical difficulties.

I wish to thank my literary agent Peter Bernstein, who believed in my work and who provided many good suggestions. It was a pleasure to work with Dan Gerstle, senior editor at Basic Books, who offered both strong support and superb editorial advice. His fine taste in line editing has made this a much better book. I also thank my copyeditor Kate Mueller for her expert work and good judgment, and project editor Michelle Welsh-Horst for shepherding the book through the production process.

More than a quarter century after mentoring my doctoral work, G. J. Barker-Benfield continues to support me with his enduring friendship and wise counsel. He read every chapter of my manuscript and offered both affirmation and incisive suggestions.

My daughters, Serena and Grace, also read whatever little amount of my writing they could bear—always with a keen sense of words and good humor. I also thank my wife, Esther, for all the support she has given me while I worked on this book.

Above all, my thanks go to the subject of this biography, even though the flame of her life went out half a century ago. While in prison, Lin Zhao hoped against hope that her "freedom writings"— into which she poured her blood and her life—would survive and speak to future generations. I marvel at the audacity of her hope. In our time, that hope has finally been vindicated.

NOTES

Introduction

1. SJRJY, "Qisushu." For the great famine, see Yang Jisheng, *Mubei*, 464. For *A Spark of Fire*, see Tan Chanxue, *Qiusuo*.

2. SHLGJ, "Lin Zhao an jiaxing cailiao."

3. Lin Zhao, "Panjue hou de shengming." Unless otherwise noted, all of Lin Zhao's writings cited in this book are from Lin Zhao, *Lin Zhao wenji*.

4. Chang and Halliday, *Mao*, 503.

5. Chen Yushan 陈禹山, "Yifen xuexie de baogao," 一份血写的报告, *Guangming Ribao* 光明日报 (Guangming Daily), June 5, 1979.

6. Lin Zhao to mother, October 24, 1967.

7. Ding Shu, *Yangmou*, 200–206. See the end of chapter 3 for details.

8. **"the line of a . . . political line of Christ";** Lin Zhao, "ZRMRB," 29, 38; **"My life belongs . . . bestows on me!":** ibid., 118.

9. Known cases of dissidence—the most important of which, *A Spark of Fire*, is discussed in chapter 4—were ideologically correct: they were "heterodox thoughts" within the boundaries of revolutionary ideology, and they invariably affirmed Communist doctrines even as they criticized certain CCP officials, policies, or action. See Song Yongyi and Sun Dajin, *Wenhua Dagemin*; Guobin Yang, *Red Guard Generation*; MacFarquhar and Schoenhals, *Mao's Last Revolution*; and Yin Hongbiao, "Wenge hongxu jieduan de minjian sichao" for discussions of the cases of Deng Tuo, Yu Luoke, Yang Xiguang, Feng Yuanchun, Zhang Zhixin, Tu Deyong, Shi Yunfeng, and Li-Yi-Zhe. (The cases of Li Jiulian and Zhong Haiyuan in the post-Mao era also belong in this category.) Others such as Gu Zhun, Wang Shenyou, and Hu Ping may have disputed Communist ideology in their private writings, but they did not constitute political dissent in the public sphere.

10. SHLGJ, "Lin Zhao an jiaxing cailiao." A copy of the 1966 document was obtained by Hu Jie from the records of the Shanghai Procuratorate. See Pan, *Out of Mao's Shadow*, 73.

11. Lin Zhao, "ZRMRB," 118.

12. **She wrote in both ink and blood:** For the necessity of blood writing when she was deprived of stationery, see chapter 5; for Lin Zhao's use of blood writing in protest, see chapter 8. On the other hand, her longest piece of blood writing—"Ling'ou Xuyu"—was prompted by a mistaken belief that Ke Qingshi had been murdered for her sake, and she had to pay the debt in kind; **She drew blood:** Hu Jie, *Xunzhao Lin Zhao de linghun*; Peng Lingfan, "Wode jiejie Lin Zhao" (2), 56; Peng Lingfan, "Wode zizi Lin Zhao," 40; **she dipped her "pen":** Lin Zhao, "Qiushi aisi"; "Ling'ou xuyu," June 13, 1965; August 28, 1965; November 7, 1965; **Her writing was done:** Lin Zhao, "ZRMRB," 70, appendices 4, 8; Peng Lingfan, "Wode zizi Lin Zhao," 37. According to Peng, Lin Zhao repeatedly asked for white bed sheets from home. Her family found out later that she had used them for blood writing.

13. Lin Zhao, "Ling'ou xuyu," June 13 and September 19, 1965.

14. Lin Zhao to mother, November 14, 1967.

15. **In the letter:** Lin Zhao, "ZRMRB"; **Mao declared that:** "Bajie shizhong quanhui." 八届十中全会 (The Tenth Plenary Meeting of the [Party's] Eighth Congress), *Zhongguo Gongchandang xinwen* (News of the Communist Party of China), http://dangshi.people.com.cn/GB/151935/176588/176596/10556200.html.

16. Lin Zhao, "Kejuan": "Lianxi yi" 练习一 (Exercise No. 1), January 1966.

17. Lin Zhao, "ZRMRB," 9, 29, 31, 56.

18. Ibid., 30, 38. See chapter 6 for further details.

19. Lin Zhao to mother, November 4, 1967.

20. See chapter 5 for details.

21. See, for instance, "A Plea from Soviet Dissenters." *Pittsburgh Post-Gazette*, May 27, 1969.

22. JGH, "xingshi panjueshu."

23. **Lin Zhao had believed:** Lin Zhao to mother, November 1, 1967; **In 1981, Shanghai High People's Court:** SHGY, "Shanghai Shi Gaoji Renmin Fayuan xingshi panjueshu," August 22, 1980, and December 30, 1981; Zeng Yuhuai, interview.

24. **In 2004, a digitized version:** Lin Zhao, "ZRMRB," editor's foreword; Zhu Yi, interview. Lin Zhao's third letter to the *People's Daily* was edited and annotated by Gan Cui and Jiang Wenqin in the early 2000s and made available on the Internet in 2004; **"Only voice . . . China":** Liu Xiaobo, "Lin Zhao."

25. For some of the latest police crackdowns on pilgrims to Lin Zhao's tomb, see www.hrcchina.org/2017/04/blog-post_29.html; http://minzhuzhongguo .org/MainArtShow.aspx?AID=87307; www.rfa.org/mandarin/yataibaodao/ren quanfazhi/xl1-04292017122946.html; www.msguancha.com/a/lanmu4/2016 /0429/14319.html; www.rfa.org/cantonese/news/memorial-04292015110021. html; www.voachinese.com/a/linzhao-police-steps-up-20140430/1904344.html.

26. Chinese police have limited public access to some graveyards, such as the Red Guards cemetery in the Shapingba District in Chongqing, where many "August 15" rebels died in armed clashes during the Cultural Revolution. However, no individual tomb other than Lin Zhao's has become a site of pilgrimage for democracy activists and no other anniversary of the death of an individual—including Hu Yaobang, whose death in 1989 triggered the Tiananmen Democracy Movement—has become as politically sensitive or has drawn police crackdowns on commemorators. For the story of the Chongqing cemetery, see Chris Buckley, "Chaos of Cultural Revolution Echoes at a Lonely Cemetery, 50 Years Later," *New York Times*, April 4, 2016.

27. Shen Zeyi, "Xuedi zhi deng—huainian Lin Zhao."

28. **Religious faith played a role:** Sophie Scholl, perhaps the least known among these, was a member of the White Rose nonviolent resistance group in Nazi Germany. She held herself "accountable to God" in her opposition to Hitler, which ended in martyrdom. The White Rose group was inspired by the teaching that "we ought to obey God rather than men." See Hanser, *A Noble Treason*, 131, 149; **It gave Bonhoeffer:** Marsh, *Strange Glory*, 179; **To Solzhenitsyn:** Pearce, *Solzhenitsyn*, 228.

29. Sikorski, *Jerzy Popieluszko*.

30. Troeltsch, *The Social Teaching of the Christian Churches*, vol. 1, 82; on Bonhoeffer's reading of Troeltsch, see Marsh, *Strange Glory*, 46.

31. The compilation, annotation, and printing of *Collected Writings of Lin Zhao* (*Lin Zhao wenji*) was a collective project undertaken over many years by several friends of Lin Zhao as well as some researchers, especially Ni Jingxiong, Tan Chanxue, and Xu Wanyun. Zhu Yi, Ai Xiaoming, and Diao Minhuan also made major contributions to the project.

32. Author's site visit, May 31, 2013; Yu Meisun, "Lin Zhao jiuyi sishi zhounian ji."

33. For Lin Zhao's continuous copying of her own blood writings using a pen, see Lin Zhao, "Ling'ou xuyu," September 18 and December 8, 1965, February 23, 1966; Lin Zhao to mother, November 16, 1967.

34. Zeng Yuhuai, interview. In a telephone interview with the author on July 12, 2016, Mr. Zhang (Suzhou) explained that in his capacity as a researcher working for the Office of the Chronicles of Suzhou, he visited the Shanghai High Court in the early 2000s and was able to view court records on Lin Zhao. He also attempted to access Lin Zhao's primary file (*zhengben*) and was promised that it would be brought from the offsite storage a couple of days later, only to be told upon his return to the court that it was classified and off limits to researchers. The other person who has seen Lin Zhao's blood writings was journalist Chen Weisi. See Hu Jie's interview with Chen in Hu Jie, *Xunzhao Lin Zhao de linghun*. While some of Lin Zhao's blood writings may still remain in

her primary file as incriminating material, given the prison authorities' reluctance to handle her blood writings (see chapter 5), it is likely that Tilanqiao discarded or destroyed most of her blood writings, keeping only their ink copies along with her other writings done in ink. According to Xu Jiajun (interview), belongings of Tilanqiao inmates who died were often regarded as "inauspicious" and destroyed. Peng Lingfan, in "Wode zizi Lin Zhao" (46), mentions that, after Lin Zhao's death, Tilanqiao Prison returned to the family a bundle of her belongings, including torn-up sheet strips with splotched blood writings, which they sold to a salvage shop. See also Peng Lingfan, "Lin Zhao anjuan."

Chapter 1   To Live under the Sun

1. Xu Xianmin as quoted in Chen Weisi, "Yinggong yuanhun yu," 20; Feng Yingzi, "Xu Xianmin ershinian ji." According to Suzhou scholar Mr. Zhang, records dating back to the 1930s show that Xu was born in 1912, not 1908, as found in many sources. The strike likely happened in 1926 or early 1927. See Hu Jiayi, "Xiaoxiang."

2. "Xu Jinyuan"; Hu Jiayi, "Xiaoxiang"; see also Sun Wenshuo, "Xuejian luoqun," 150. According to Sun, Xu Jinyuan was arrested on April 9, 1927, and bayoneted to death on April 13 while he was tied up inside the hemp sack.

3. Feng Yingzi, "Xu Xianmin ershinian ji"; SHLGJ, "Lin Zhao an jiaxing cailiao"; Huang Yun, "Xu Xianmin de hunyin"; Mr. Zhang, interview. Xu joined the CCP briefly under her brother's influence but withdrew from it sometime after the April 12 Incident.

4. The incorrect date of Lin Zhao's birth, which appears on her tombstone and in almost all existing writings about her, is December 16, 1932. I am indebted to Huang Yun, whose careful research into Suzhou newspaper articles from the 1930s has enabled him to establish January 23, 1932—December 16 of the Year of Ram (1931) by the lunar calendar—as the actual date of her birth. See Huang Yun, "Peng Lingzhao de shengri." See also Lin Zhao to Ni Jingxiong, October 2, 1952, which contains a poem that apparently supports the revised date.

5. Feng Yingzi, "Xu Xianmin ershinian ji"; Cheng Ronghua and Cui Xuefa, "Huan shishi yi gongzheng." Feng Yingzi and several other sources mentioned that Peng studied in Britain from 1926 to 1928, apparently a rumor only. For Chinese modernizers' pursuit of wealth and power, see Schwartz, *In Search of Wealth and Power*.

6. See Qian Wenjun 钱文军, "Zhongguo feichu bupingdeng tiaoyue jiankuang." 中国废除不平等条约简况 (A Brief Note on the Abolishment of Unequal Treaties in China), August 1, 2002, http://qian-wenjun.hxwk.org

/2002/08/01/%E4%B8%AD%E5%9B%BD%E5%BA%9F%E9%99%A4%E4%B
8%8D%E5%B9%B3%E7%AD%89%E6%9D%A1%E7%BA%A6%E7%AE%80
%E5%86%B5/. The Nanjing government reported a three-fold increase in income from import tariffs within three years.

7. Cheng Ronghua and Cui Xuefa, "Huan shishi yi gongzheng."

8. **In 1930, he and Xu Xianmin:** Huang Yun, "Peng Lingzhao de shengri yu
mingzi"; **By the time . . . resounding defeat:** Cheng Ronghua and Cui Xuefa,
"Huan shishi yi gongzheng"; "Peng Guoyan qing pingfan yuanyu."

9. **As the Japanese army advanced:** Lacy, *Great Migration*, preface; **In
wartime capital . . . surrounding countryside:** Peng Lingfan, "Wo fumu yu
Lin Zhao de mudi"; Feng Yingzi, "Xu Xianmin ershinian ji"; Cheng Ronghua
and Cui Xuefa, "Huan shishi yi gongzheng"; Chen Weisi, "Yinggong yuanhun
yu," 20.

10. Chen Weisi, "Lin Zhao zhi si," 2.

11. **After the end of the Japanese occupation:** Peng Lingfan, "Wo fumu
yu Lin Zhao de mudi"; Cheng Ronghua and Cui Xuefa, "Huan shishi yi gongzheng"; **After the war . . . representative from Suzhou:** Feng Yingzi, "Xu Xianmin ershinian ji"; Suzhou chronicles cited in Xu Juemin, *Lin Zhao, buzai bei
yiwang*, 17; Chen Weisi, "Yinggong yuanhun yu," 19; Chen Zhen, "Zhuiqiu yu
huanmie," 32.

12. **During these years:** Peng Enhua was born on December 17, 1944. See
Edward Enhua, Peng's obituary, *Daily Herald*, August 5, 2004; Huang Yun,
"Peng Lingzhao de shengri." According to Peoplefinders (www.peoplefinders.
com), Peng Lingfan was born on September 19, 1938; **In fall 1947:** Lu Zhenhua, "Lin Zhao sanshiyi nian ji"; Zhao Rui, *Jitan shang de shengnü*, 37.

13. "Laura Askew Haygood," *Georgia Women of Achievement*, www.georgia
women.org/_honorees/haygood/; author's site visit, Laura Haygood Memorial
School building, Suzhou University, June 1, 2013.

14. MacGillivray, *A Century of Protestant Missions in China*, 424. For average incomes in the late Qing period, see Yang Jintao 杨津涛, "Gudai jiating de
jingjishi: yiliang yinzi de goumai li." 古代家庭的经济史：一两银子的购买
力 (Economic History of the Pre-modern Family: The Purchasing Power of
One Tael of Silver), August 8, 2015, http://history.sina.com.cn/bk/gds/2015-08
-25/1001124924.shtml

15. Bradshaw, *China Log*, 78, 103, 144.

16. Sun Yingqing, "Tiancizhuang." Wu became president of Ginling College
(Ginling Women's College) in 1928. See also Bradshaw, *China Log*, 24; "Jinghai
Nüshu."

17. Bradshaw, *China Log*, 137, 144.

18. Ibid., 29, 35, 38–39.

19. *Laura Haygood Star*, vol. 3.

20. **After the disruptions . . . down to nursery:** Bradshaw, *China Log*, 130; **Lin Zhao's father:** Mr. Zhang, telephone interview, July 17, 2014; Peng Lingfan, "Wode zizi Lin Zhao," 28.

21. Bradshaw, *China Log*, 132–133.

22. **Yet there was . . . teacher or by students:** Bradshaw, *China Log*, 132–133; **Not long after she arrived:** Lin Zhao, "ZRMRB," 117.

23. **before Laura Haygood, she had briefly:** Peng Lingfan, "Wode zizi Lin Zhao," 28; Lu Zhenhua, "Lin Zhao sanshiyi nian ji"; Huang Yun, e-mail to the author, February 4, 2016. For information on Vincent Miller Academy, founded by the northern Presbyterians in 1892, see www.ctestimony.org/200205/sgzy19 .htm; **A melancholy essay:** Ouyang Ying [Lin Zhao], "Huanghun zhi lei."

24. **Many years later:** Lin Zhao, "Zhanchang riji," February 12, 1967; **She also associated:** Lin Zhao, "ZRMRB," 81; **As Wu Yaozong, future leader:** Wu Yaozong, *Meiyou ren*, 2.

25. See Lin Zhao, "Ling'ou xuyu," July 11, 1965.

26. MacFarquhar and Fairbank, *Cambridge History of China*, 149–150. See also "China: Inflation," www.country-data.com/cgi-bin/query/r-2731.html; Richard M. Ebeling, "The Great Chinese Inflation," http://fee.org/articles/the -great-chinese-inflation/.

27. Bradshaw, *China Log*, 135, 138.

28. Methodist Episcopal Church, South, *Minutes*, 38.

29. Bradshaw, *China Log*, 37. For "cultural invasion," see Tao Feiya, "'Wen-hua qinlue' yuanliu kao."

30. Bradshaw, *China Log*, 72–73.

31. Lu Zhenhua, "Lin Zhao sanshiyi nian ji." See also Lin Zhao, "ZRMRB," 7, 34.

32. Lin Zhao, "ZRMRB," 23.

33. Chen Weisi, "Yinggong yuanhun yu," 20.

34. Feng Yingzi, "Xu Xianmin ershinian ji."

35. Lu Zhenhua, "Lin Zhao sanshiyi nian ji."

36. Ouyang Ying [Lin Zhao], "Dai he dai."

37. Qu Qiubai as quoted in Spence, *Gate of Heavenly Peace*, 176.

38. **In 1936, American journalist Edgar Snow:** Snow, *Red Star over China*, 16; **It was followed by a Chinese edition:** Gao Hua, *Hong taiyang*, 194; **In 1938 alone:** Gong Yun, "Yan'an shiqi."

39. Joseph Stilwell as quoted in Jane Perlez, "China Maintains Respect, and a Museum, for a U.S. General," *New York Times*, February 23, 2016.

40. **In Lin Zhao's eyes:** Lin Zhao, "ZRMRB," 23; **During the four years of civil war:** Sun Yingshuai 孙应帅, "Jiushi nianlai Zhongguo Gongchandang dangyuan shuliang yu jiegou de bianhua yu fazhan." 90年来中国共产党党员数量与结构的变化与发展 (Changes in and Developments of CCP's Member-

ship and Structure in the Past Ninety Years), *Guangming Daily* 光明日报, July 5, 2011. CCP membership stood at 1.21 million in 1945.

41. Bradshaw, *China Log*, 140–141.

42. **There was in fact:** See Lian Xi, *Redeemed by Fire*, chapter 6; **Lin Zhao's martyred uncle . . . the party's Suzhou branch:** "Xu Jinyuan."

43. **But in most cases:** Lian Xi, *Redeemed by Fire*, 133–137; **The pastor's real name . . . Shanghai's International Settlement:** Snow, *Red Star over China*, 46–47, 50–51; Wickeri, *Reconstructing Christianity in China*, 24–25.

44. **"red fortress" . . . "sacred aura of St. Peter's":** Ye Jiefu, "Chuanqi mushi Dong Jianwu." Pu Huaren, Dong Jianwu's former classmate at the Anglican St. John's University in Shanghai, secretly joined the CCP in 1927 after a brief career as a pastor in the army of the Christian general Feng Yuxiang. Pu brought Dong into the CCP; **It was Dong who in the 1930s:** Chang, *Mao*, 175–176.

45. **"conscience as a Christian . . . her path again":** Lin Zhao, "ZRMRB," 39; **Later, she would confront:** Li Maozhang, "Liufang qiangu," 232.

46. **"The Nationalist Party . . . a disgrace":** Lin Zhao, "Ling'ou xuyu," July 20, 1965; **Wu Leichuan, chancellor:** Lian Xi, *Redeemed by Fire*, 198; West, *Yenching University*, 168.

47. Stuart, *Fifty Years in China*, 155.

48. Lian Xi, *Conversion of Missionaries*, 88–89.

49. Honig, "Christianity, Feminism, and Communism," 252, 255–260.

50. Ibid., 260.

51. Lin Zhao, "GRSX."

52. Lin Zhao, "Qunian sanba."

53. **Demands made by mission school:** Lian Xi, *Conversion of Missionaries*, chapter 1; Bays, *Christianity in China*, chapters 12–13; **"wherever a few . . . 'saving China'":** Dewey, "Old China and New," *Asia* 21, no. 5 (May 1921), as quoted in Bays and Widmer, *China's Christian Colleges*, 193.

54. Bradshaw, *China Log*, 39.

55. Ibid., 65.

56. Ibid., 46.

57. Bradshaw, *China Log*, 132; Lin Zhao, "Qunian sanba."

58. Lin Zhao, "ZRMRB," 23.

59. Lin Zhao, "Qunian sanba."

60. Lin Zhao, "Qunian sanba"; Lu Zhenhua, "Lin Zhao sanshiyi nian ji."

61. Lin Zhao to Lu Zhenhua, March 1, 1951.

62. Lin Zhao, "Ling'ou xuyu," August 20, 1965.

63. **Her parents expected her:** Peng Lingfan, "Jiejie"; **A party-run institution:** Huazhong Sunan Xinzhuan xiaoyou, *Xiaoyou tongxun.*

64. Zhang Min, "Lin Zhao baomei."

65. Chen Weisi, "Yinggong yuanhun yu," 19; Fang Qian, "Minguo diyi nücike Shi Jianqiao," www.aqzyzx.com/system/2010/05/27/002183237.shtml.

66. Peng Lingfan, "Wode jiejie Lin Zhao," 60.

67. Peng Lingfan, "Wode jiejie Lin Zhao," 40; Zhang Min, "Lin Zhao baomei."

Chapter 2   Exchanging Leather Shoes for Straw Sandals

1. **As a high school graduate:** Chinese government statistics provided to a League of Nations commission investigating education in China in the early 1930s, as cited in http://study.ccln.gov.cn/fenke/shehuixue/shxkjs /shsxp/84729-1.shtml; *shi yi tianxia wei jiren:* The saying "士以天下为己任," formulated some 1,500 years ago, can be traced further back in history to Mencius (372–289 BCE). For Mencius's original quote, see "孟子・万章下": "思天下之民匹夫匹妇有不被尧舜之泽者，若己推而内之沟中一其自任天下之重也。"

2. See Yu Yingshi, "Cong chuantong 'shi' dao xiandai zhishiren."

3. See Mao Zedong, "Daliang xishou zhishi fenzi."

4. Li Maozhang, "Liufang qiangu," 229–230.

5. Wu Rong, "Xinjizhe de yaolan," July 5, 2012.

6. Wu Rong, "Xinjizhe de yaolan," July 5, 2012; SNXZ, *Su'nan Xinwen.* Those writers and journalists included Gao Xiang, Lin Jinlan, Gao Xiaosheng, Chen Weisi, and Lu Fowei.

7. Ren Feng (Lin Zhao), "Xiaxiang qian de jitian"; Lin Zhao to Lu Zhenhua (Jinsheng), September 1, 1949; Ni Jingxiong, interview, Shanghai, May 5, 2014.

8. Ren Feng, "Xiaxiang qian de jitian."

9. Ibid.

10. Gao Hua, *Hong taiyang,* 191.

11. **"soul-searching notes":** Gao Hua, *Hong taiyang,* 238, 278; **"more formidable . . . golden headband":** see Mao Zedong, "Guanyu zhengdun sanfeng."

12. Courtois et al., *Black Book of Communism,* 474.

13. *Zhongguo Gongchandang dangzhang* 中国共产党党章 (The Constitution of the Chinese Communist Party), 1945. The practice of "criticism and self-criticism" can be traced back to *kritika i samokritika* (Russian: критика и самокритика) introduced in the Soviet Union in the 1920s.

14. Peng Lingzhao, "Wo zenyang renshi."

15. See Hoffer, *The True Believer,* 13.

16. Schwarcz, *Chinese Enlightenment,* 186. See also Grieder, *Intellectuals and the State,* 289.

17. **Like skilled artisans:** Grieder, *Intellectuals and the State,* 283; **In the face of national emergencies:** See Schwarcz, *Chinese Enlightenment,* 196–222.

18. Gao Hua, *Hong taiyang,* 255–261.

19. Peng Lingzhao, "Wo de xiegao tiyan."

20. Mei Ling and Ling Zhao (Lin Zhao), "Women xiangqin xiang'ai jiuxiang xiongdi jiemei"; Peng Lingzhao, "Zai laodong zhanxian shang."

21. Peng Lingzhao, "Chang 1950 nian"; Peng Lingzhao, "Xiao meimei."

22. Spence, *Gate of Heavenly Peace*, 277–280; Ding Ling 丁玲, "Mouye" 某夜 (One Certain Night), http://dingling.linli.gov.cn/info_Show.asp?Article ID=495.

23. Mao Zedong, "Talks at the Yan'an Forum on Literature and Art," May 1942, www.marxists.org/reference/archive/mao/selected-works/volume-3/mswv3 _08.htm. I have made minor changes to the English translation.

24. Lin Zhao and Xuanru, "Wangchuan yanjing."

25. Lin Zhao to Ni Jingxiong, March 5, 1951.

26. Ouyang Ying (Lin Zhao), "Huanghun zhi lei."

27. Lin Zhao to Lu Zhenhua, October 2 and November 17, 1949.

28. Ibid., October 9, 1949.

29. Mao Zedong, "Guanyu lingdao fangfa de ruogan wenti."

30. Lin Zhao to Lu Zhenhua, August 10, 1949; March 1, 1951; May 10, 1951.

31. **He asked to come see her:** Lin Zhao to Lu Zhenhua, August 30, September 12 and November 10, 1951; **"I have a heart of stone . . . else's vexations":** ibid., May 10, 1951.

32. Lin Zhao to Lu Zhenhua, October 2, 1949.

33. Ibid., October, 18, 1949.

34. **However, relations . . . toward the government":** Lin Zhao to Lu Zhenhua, March 11, 1950; August 30, 1851; **He would have:** Lin Zhao, "Fuqin de xue." For Lin Zhao's characterization of her family as matriarchal, see Lin Zhao, "Ling'ou xuyu," July 3, 1965. See also Zhang Min, "Lin Zhao baomei." According to Peng Lingfan, Xu Xianmin would not allow Peng Guoyan to bring their only son Peng Enhua with him to Taiwan, and Peng Guoyan would not leave without his son.

35. **After 1949, Peng refused:** Lin Zhao, "Fuqin de xue"; Zhang Min, "Lin Zhao baomei"; **Early on under . . . "historical counterrevolutionary":** Zhao Rui, *Jitan shang de shengnü*, 31.

36. **Lin Zhao's mother:** Suzhou chronicles cited in Xu Juemin, *Lin Zhao, buzai bei yiwang*, 17; Peng Lingfan, "Lin Zhao anjuan de lailongqumai"; **"I so much want . . . becoming progressive":** Lin Zhao to Lu Zhenhua, March 1, 1951.

37. Lin Zhao to Lu Zhenhua, March 1, 1951; April 13, 1950.

38. **"Life at the journalism:** April 13, 1950; **At the graduation ceremony:** Lin Zhao, "Canlan de yitian."

39. Ni Jingxiong, interview, May 5, 2014.

40. **"I have no . . . phony writer":** Ni Jingxiong, "Shadiao meishi," 171; **She wanted instead:** Lin Zhao to Lu Zhenhua, April 13, 1950.

41. Lin Zhao to Lu Zhenhua, June 7, 1950.

42. Spence, *Search for Modern China*, 491–492; See also Zhengwuyuan, "Renmin fating zuzhi tongze." For the human price of land reform, see Courtois, *Black Book of Communism*, 479, 483; Yang Kuisong, "Zhonggong tugai de ruogan wenti." See also MacFarquhar and Fairbank, *Cambridge History of China*, 87. The latter estimates the total executed to be between one and two million. According to Courtois et al., at least one million, and as many as five million, died.

43. Lin Zhao to Lu Zhenhua, October 11, 1950; January 7, 1951.

44. **Across China, more than:** MacFarquhar and Fairbank, *Cambridge History of China*, 84; **Ni Jingxiong . . . as others had been:** Ni Jingxiong, interview, May 5, 2014.

45. **Lin Zhao worked:** Lin Zhao to Lu Zhenhua, October 11, 1950; **One of the works . . . public grains":** Ni Jingxiong, interview, May 5, 2014.

46. Lin Zhao to Ni Jingxiong, March 5 and March 29, 1951.

47. Lin Zhao to Lu Zhenhua, May 21, 1951.

48. Zhang Min, "Lin Zhao baomei"; Lin Zhao, "Ling'ou xuyu," July 4 and August 11, 1965.

49. Lin Zhao to Lu Zhenhua, November 17, 1949.

50. Ibid., May 10, 1951.

51. Ibid., May 25, 1951.

52. Mao Zedong, "Hunan nongmin yundong kaocha baogao." English translation taken from *Selected Works of Mao Tse-tung*, Maoist Documentation Project, www.marxists.org/reference/archive/mao/selected-works/volume-1/mswv1_2.htm#s4.

53. Lin Zhao, "Fuqin de xue."

54. **She began reading:** Lin Zhao, "Zhongzi"; **It is a well-known story . . . on their faces:** Lu Xun, "Zixu."

55. Lu Xun, "Yao."

56. Lin Zhao to Ni Jingxiong, March 29, 1951.

57. Lin Zhao to mother, January 14, 1968. The practice of parading the condemned through town and making a public spectacle of executions would continue until 2007, when the Supreme Court and the Supreme People's Procuratorate issued a joint directive with the ministries of Public Security and Justice to formally end it. See http://news.xinhuanet.com/legal/2007-03/12/content_5833204.htm.

58. Li Maozhang, "Liufang qiangu," 231–232.

59. Ibid.

60. Ibid.

61. Lin Zhao to Lu Zhenhua, March 1, 1951; Lin Zhao to Ni Jingxiong, March 5, 1951.

62. Lin Zhao to Ni Jingxiong, June 29, 1951; Li Maozhang, "Liufang qiangu," 232–233.

63. Lin Zhao's diary entries as excerpted in Lin Zhao to Ni Jingxiong, March 5, 1951.

64. Lin Zhao to Lu Zhenhua, May 25, 1951. For Suppression of Counterrevolutionaries Campaign, see Courtois et al., *Black Book of Communism*, 482–483; Yang Kuisong, "Xin Zhongguo 'zhenya fangeming' yundong yanjiu."

65. Lin Zhao to Ni Jingxiong, June 29, 1951.

66. **She had yearned to own:** Lin Zhao to Ni Jingxiong, November 1950 to December 1952. Her letters dated November 20, 1950, and January 7 and April 14, 1951, offer glimpses into her predicament with those suitors; **There was also the nameless melancholy:** ibid.; Ni Jingxiong, interview, May 5, 2014.

67. Lin Zhao to Ni Jingxiong, November 20, 1950.

68. Ibid., April 14, 1951.

69. Ibid.

70. Ibid., November 12, 1950.

71. Ibid., August 19, 1951; Ni Jingxiong, interview, May 5, 2014.

72. Ni Jingxiong, interview, May 5, 2014; Lin Zhao to Ni Jingxiong, August 19, 1951. See also Ni Jingxiong, "Shadiao meishi."

73. Lin Zhao to Ni Jingxiong, June 26, 1951; December 10, 1952.

74. Ni Jingxiong, interview, June 13, 2017.

75. Ni Jingxiong, interview, May 5, 2014; Lin Zhao to Ni Jingxiong, March 13, 1952.

76. Ni Jingxiong, interview, May 5, 2014. See also Lin Zhao to Ni Jingxiong, March 13, 1952; Ni Jingxiong, "Shadiao meishi," 179–180.

77. Ni Jingxiong, interview, May 5, 2014; Lin Zhao to Ni Jingxiong, March 13, 1952.

78. Lin Zhao, "ZRMRB," 24.

79. Djilas, *The New Class*, 47. A guerrilla fighter who rose to become a member of the Politburo of the Communist Party of Yugoslavia and who was once considered a likely successor to Tito, Djilas voiced disenchantments with his party in the early 1950s and was expelled from its ranks in 1954. In 1957, he published *The New Class: An Analysis of the Communist System*, an early banner of anticommunism.

80. Ibid., 28.

Chapter 3   The Crown

1. Lin Zhao to Ni Jingxiong, March 13, 1952.

2. Chen Shufang, "Lin Zhao er'san shi," 240; Qian Timing et al., "Jinri honghua fa," 235.

3. Lin Zhao to Ni Jingxiong, March 13 and "The Red May," 1952.

4. Lin Zhao to Ni Jingxiong, "The Red May," 1952; Ni Jingxiong, "Shadiao meishi," 186.

5. Lin Zhao to Ni Jingxiong, March 13, 1952.

6. **She attempted suicide:** Zhang Min, "Lin Zhao baomei"; **Across China, some 100,000:** Rummel, *China's Bloody Century*, 228. According to Rummel, 200,000 may have taken their own lives. See also "Ben shiji Zhongguo dong-dang shiqi siwang renshu yilanbiao" 本世纪中国动荡时期死亡人数一览表 (Death Tolls in China during Turbulent Periods of This Century), www.cnd.org/HXWK/column/Editor-Reader/cm9605d-10.gb.html, which estimated the total number of deaths from the twin campaigns to be 100,000; **Shanghai's mayor Chen Yi:** Ding Shu, *Yangmou*, 24.

7. **"They drove me . . . to falsely accuse you":** Chen Weisi, "Lin Zhao zhisi," 3; **According to Lin Zhao's sister:** Zhang Min, "Lin Zhao baomei."

8. Lin Zhao to Ni Jingxiong, March 13, 1952; March 5, 1951.

9. Lin Zhao to Ni Jingxiong, March 29 and June 26, 1951.

10. Lin Zhao to Ni Jingxiong, October 14, 1951. For biblical language cited here, see Galatians 5:17; Philippians 3:8–14; 2 Timothy 4:8.

11. Lin Zhao to Ni Jingxiong, March 13, 1952.

12. Ibid.

13. Ibid.; Lin Zhao to Ni Jingxiong, "The Red May," 1952.

14. See, for instance, Shen Zeyi, "Wu fu, wu xiang," 228.

15. Yan Zhang and Ling [Lin Zhao], "Zongjie chengji, touru xin zhandou." See also other reports Lin Zhao wrote for the paper in 1953–1954, in *Lin Zhao wenji*.

16. Lin Zhao, "Yige youxiu de Shaonian Ertong duiyuan." In 1953, the "Youth and Children of China" was renamed "Young Pioneers."

17. Lin Zhao to Ni Jingxiong, "The Red May," 1952, and December 10, 1952.

18. Ibid., March 13, 1952.

19. Chen Shufang, "Lin Zhao er'san shi," 241.

20. **Lin Zhao was transferred:** Qian Timing et al., "Jinri honghua fa," 235; **Within months she obtained:** Lin Zhao, "ZRMRB," 24. See also Shen Zeyi, "Beida," 73.

21. Lin Zhao, "GRSX."

22. Anonymous article in Tianjin's *Guowenbao*, as cited in Qian Gengsen 钱耕森, "Jingshi Daxuetang heyi xingcun." 京师大学堂何以幸存 (How the Imperial University of Peking Survived), www.gmw.cn/01ds/1998-09/16/GB/216%5EDS913.htm.

23. West, *Yenching University*, 38; Bays and Widmer, *China's Christian Colleges*, 51–55.

24. Lin Zhao, "Weiminghu pan."

25. Zhang Yuanxun, "Beida wangshi," 68.

26. Shen Zeyi, "Beida," 43; Zhang Yuanxun, "Beida wangshi," 69–70; Yang Huarong, "Huishou wangshi," 135.

27. Zhang Yuanxun, "Beida wangshi," 69.

28. **The comparison was . . . weathered melancholy:** Shen Zeyi, "Wu fu, wu xiang," 216; Shen Zeyi, "Beida," 73; **Zhang Ling . . . a Southerner":** Zhang Ling, "Youming xinyu," 120.

29. **Lin Zhao had an eclectic range of interests:** Zhang Yuanxun, "Beida wangshi," 69; **She also loved ballroom dancing:** Ni Jingxiong, "Shadiao meishi," 170; Shen Zeyi, "Beida," 73.

30. **"She loved bantering . . . victories in jokes":** Zhang Yuanxun, "Beida wangshi," 69; **Horrified by the usual chaos:** Zhang Lin, "Youming xinyu," 121; **"walked off in a huff":** Wang Ningsheng, "Lin Zhao yinxiang."

31. Zhang Yuanxun, "Beida wangshi," 71; Xie Yong, "*Honglou* zazhi yanjiu." Lin Zhao's residence hall was Building No. 27.

32. **The inaugural issue:** Lin Zhao, "Tanke"; **"We hope to hear . . . deleterious to socialism":** Lin Zhao as quoted in Zhang Yuanxun, "Beida wangshi," 77–78.

33. See Liao Yiwu, *Zhongguo diceng fangtan lu*, 192–199.

34. Courtois et al., *Black Book of Communism*, 485; Ding Shu, *Yangmou*, 52; Li Weimin, "1955 nian."

35. Shen Zeyi, "Wu fu, wu xiang," 234; Liu Qidi 刘奇弟, "Baimaonü shenyuan" 白毛女申冤 (The White-Haired Girl Seeking Justice), May 20, 1957, as cited in Shen Zeyi, "Beida," 11–12.

36. **Lin Zhao was not among:** Lin Zhao, "Fuqin de xue"; **She was denounced:** Lin Zhao, "GRSX."

37. Shen Zeyi, "Beida," 74–76.

38. Lin Zhao, "ZRMRB," 25; Lin Zhao, "GRSX."

39. Wang Ningsheng, "Lin Zhao yinxiang."

40. Xu Yan, "Pianran 'Honglou' zuo shang ke," 344. My own English translation of Qu Yuan's "Encountering Sorrow" is based on those by Yang Xianyi 杨宪益 and Dai Naidie 戴乃迭 as well as by Cyril Birch. See Birch, *Anthology of Chinese Literature*, 56.

41. **Still, in spring 1957 . . . journey of emancipation:** Lin Zhao, "Zhongzi"; **When Stalin died in 1953:** Lin Zhao, "Sidalin."

42. Lin Zhao, "Zhongzi."

43. **The first Soviet-style:** MacFarquhar and Fairbank, *Cambridge History of China*, 155; **All of this probably:** Zhang Yuanxun, *Beida*, 227.

44. Lin Zhao, "Shishi."

45. Mao Zedong, "Guanyu zhengque chuli." The passage quoted here is from the original speech and does not include revisions in the version published in June 1957.

46. Shen Zeyi and Zhang Yuanxun, "Shi shihou le" 是时候了 (It Is Time), cited in Shen Zeyi, "Beida," 3.

47. Shen Zeyi, "Beida," 53.

48. Wang Guoxiang, "Beida minzhu yundong jishi," 23–27; Qian Liqun, "Burong mosha," 10; Shen Zeyi, "Beida," 10, 13. On the makeshift bulletin board called *xilan*, see Zhang Yuanxun, *Beida*, 251–252.

49. Niu Han and Deng Jiuping, *Yuanshang cao*, 41–42.

50. **Tan Tianrong's posters:** Tan Tianrong, "Di'er zhu ducao," 30–34; **It was the first time:** Spence, *Search for Modern China*, 542.

51. Niu Han and Deng Jiuping, *Yuanshang cao*, 230.

52. See Shen Zeyi, "Beida," 7–9.

53. Lin Zhao, "Zheshi shenme ge."

54. Ren Feng [Lin Zhao], "Dang, wo huhuan . . . "

55. Lin Zhao, "GRSX."

56. Ibid.

57. Zhang Yuanxun, *Beida*, 45–46. See also Lin Zhao, "GRSX"; Wang Guoxiang, "Beida minzhu yundong jishi," 23.

58. Zhang Yuanxun, "Beida wangshi," 84.

59. Shen Zeyi, "Beida," 54.

60. Zhang Yuanxun, "*Guangchang* fakan ci," 120–122.

61. Zhang Yuanxun, "Beida wangshi," 84, 158.

62. Zhang Yuanxun, *Beida*, 226; Zhang Yuanxun, "Beida wangshi," 81.

63. **Ironically, subsequent denunciations:** Ma Jingyuan and Leng Xin, "Lin Zhao," 337–338; Zhang Yuanxun, "Beida wangshi," 158; Zhang Yuanxun, *Beida*, 226–227; **That was an exaggeration:** Shen Zeyi, interview, Huzhou, Zhejiang, July 15, 2014. Shen denied that Lin Zhao had any active role in *The Square*.

64. Shen Zhihua, *Sikao yu xuanze*, 536–541.

65. Zhang Yihe, *Zuihou de guizu*, 46–51.

66. Spence, *Search for Modern China*, 541–543; Courtois et al., *Black Book of Communism*, 485; Chang and Halliday, *Mao*, 410–411; Wei Zidan, "Mao Zedong yinshe chudong kao"; Mao as quoted in Chang and Halliday, *Mao*, 410. See also Shen Zhihua, *Sikao yu xuanze*, 563–564. Shen argues that Mao advertised his "open conspiracy" theory to spare himself the embarrassment over a bungled attempt to elicit harmless criticisms to help the CCP's rectification campaign.

67. **In it Mao lashed out:** Mao Zedong, "Shiqing zhengzai qi bianhua"; Shen Zhihua, *Sikao yu xuanze*, 619; **The Anti-Rightist Campaign:** "Zheshi wei shenme?" 这是为什么？(Why Is This?), *People's Daily* editorial, June 8, 1957.

68. Shen Zeyi, "Beida," 103–104.

69. Shen Zeyi, "Wo xiang renmin qingzui," 241–247; Shen Zeyi, interview, July 15, 2014.

70. **The university's Anti-Rightist Campaign:** Zhang Yuanxun, *Beida*, 231–237; **Some of the activists were:** Zhang Yuanxun, "Beida wangshi," 87; Shen Zeyi, interview, July 15, 2014.

71. **However, starting in August:** Zhang Yuanxun, *Beida*, 256–261; **One student cracked:** Chen Fengxiao, "Wo suo zhidao"; Ding Shu, *Yangmou*, 219.

72. Ma Jingyuan and Leng Xin, "Lin Zhao"; Zhang Yuanxun, *Beida*, 258; Shen Zeyi, "Beida," 123.

73. Ding Shu, *Yangmou*, 157, 187.

74. Ding Shu, *Yangmou*, 220,222. For Zhu Jiayu's story, see Zhang Yuanxun, *Beida*, 259–260; Ji Xianlin, *Meng ying Weiminghu*, 560.

75. Zhang Min, "Lin Zhao baomei."

76. Lin Zhao, untitled poem, cited in Zhang Yuanxun, "Beida wangshi," 90.

77. Zhang Yuanxun, *Beida*, 274.

78. Yang Huarong, "Huishou wangshi," 136.

79. Ibid., 136–138. Both Mr. Zhang of Suzhou and Zhu Yi (interviews) said that a romantic relationship developed between Lin Zhao and Yang.

80. **In September, Chen Fengxiao:** "Beijing Shi Renmin Jianchayuan"; Chen Fengxiao, "Wo suo zhidao"; Shen Zeyi, "Beida," 116; **Later, in an indictment . . . the imperialists":** SJRJY, "Qisushu"; **a charge that Chen dismissed:** Chen Fengxiao to Zhu Yi, October 9, 2008, http://blog.sina.com.cn/s/blog_497d291f0102e6fi.html.

81. Lin Zhao, "GRSX."

82. Song Yongyi, *Qianming Zhongguo youpai*. Chen Fengxiao was named a key member of the group. See also Chen Fengxiao, "Wo suo zhidao"; Zhang Yuanxun, *Beida*, 287; Peng Lingfan, "Wode jiejie Lin Zhao," 41. Chen Fengxiao scouted the diplomatic missions in Beijing in August 1957. He scaled the wall of the Yugoslav embassy and entered its grounds but was denied asylum and escorted out.

83. **In the end, out of 8,983 students:** Wang Youqin, "Cong shounanzhe"; Zhang Yuanxun, *Beida*, 358. The total number of faculty and staff was 1,399; **Across China, the total:** The CCP's official estimate of the total number of Rightists is 550,000, primarily the cadres. Students and others not on government payroll were not counted. Ding puts the total number above 1.2 million. See Ding Shu, *Yangmou*, 200–206; Ding Shu, *Wushi nian hou*, 194–203. Courtois et al., in *Black Book of Communism* (485), put the total at between "400,000 and 700,000."

84. Lin Mu, "You yiwei youpai laoren"; Zhu Yi, "Chen Fengxiao."

85. **In a letter to her sister:** Lin Zhao to Peng Lingfan, 1958, as quoted in Chen Weisi, "Lin Zhao zhi si," 4; **"feel the weight . . . called 'Rightist'":** Tan Tianrong, "Yige meiyou qingjie de aiqing gushi," 173.

86. Lin Zhao, "ZRMRB," Appendix No. 6.

87. Lin Zhao to Peng Lingfan, 1958, as quoted in Chen Weisi, "Lin Zhao zhi si," 4.

88. Lin Zhao, "GRSX."

89. Lin Zhao, "ZRMRB," 25–26.

Chapter 4   A Spark of Fire

1. Lin Zhao, "Xueshi tiyi bing ba." Mao had compared the revolutionary forces he led to a gale sent from heaven. See Mao Zedong, "Dielianhua: cong Tingzhou xiang Changsha."

2. Sun Wenshuo, "Xuejian luoqun," 160–161. See also Zhang Yuanxun, *Beida*, 312. According to Sun, Lin Zhao made a second suicide attempt in 1958.

3. Chen Weisi, "Lin Zhao zhi si," 4.

4. Lin Zhao, "Jueming shu."

5. Lin Zhao, "Di yige yin."

6. "Zhonggong Zhongyang Guowuyuan guanyu zai guojia xinji renyuan he gaodeng xuexiao xuesheng zhong de youpai fenzi chuli yuanze de guiding," 中共中央国务院关于在国家薪给人员和高等学校学生中的右派分子处理原则的规定 (Regulations Issued by the CCP Central Committee and the State Council regarding the Principle of Punishments for Rightists among Personnel on State Payroll and Students in Institutions of Higher Education), January 13, 1958, in Song Yongyi et al., *Zhongguo Fanyou Yundong*; Shen Zhihua, *Sikao yu xuanze*, 685–686; Wei Chengsi, *Zhongguo zhishi fenzi*, 176; Ding Shu, *Yangmou*, 214. See also Sun Wenshuo, "Xuejian luoqun," 160. For "re-education through labor," see "Zhonggong Zhongyang guanyu chedi shuqing ancang de fangeming fenzi de zhishi," 中共中央关于彻底肃清暗藏的反革命分子的指示 (Directive of the CCP Central Committee on the Complete Elimination of Hidden Counterrevolutionaries), August 25, 1955, in Song Yongyi et al., *Zhongguo wushi niandai*.

7. Wei Chengsi, *Zhongguo zhishi fenzi*, 176; Ding Shu, *Yangmou*, 222.

8. Mao as quoted in Sun Yancheng, "Guo Moruo he Qin Shihuang."

9. Ba Jin as quoted in Wei Chengsi, *Zhongguo zhishi fenzi*, 183.

10. See "Haiku shilan juebu dongyao: Li Jishen zai Shehuizhuyi Ziwo Gaizao Cujin Dahui shang de jianghua" 海枯石烂 绝不动摇: 李济深在社会主义自我改造促进大会上的讲话 (Unshaken until the Sea Goes Dry and the Stone Rots Away: Li Jishen's Speech at the Meeting Promoting Socialist Self-Reform), *People's Daily*, March 17, 1958; Wei Chengsi, *Zhongguo zhishi fenzi*, 181.

11. Jiang Fei, "Xunzhao Lin Zhao."

12. Zhang Yuanxun, *Beida*, 312–313.

13. Tan Tianrong as quoted in Hu Jie, *Xunzhao Lin Zhao de linghun*.

14. Gan Cui, "Lin Zhao qingren"; Zhang Yuanxun, *Beida*, 312–313.

15. Shen Zeyi, "Beida," 78.

16. Chen Fengxiao, "Xingkaihu jishi"; Yuan Ling, "Mao Zedong shidai"; Shen Zeyi, "Beida," 122; "Naxie 'xuyao bei laojiao' de ren."

17. Lin Zhao, "Beifen shi."

18. Gan Cui, "Lin Zhao qingren"; Gan Cui, *Beida hun*; Gan Cui, interview, Beijing, June 2, 2013; Ai Xiaoming, "'Yinwei wo xinzhong haiyou ge Lin Zhao.'"

19. Li Ke, "Beijing Sanzihui."

20. Gan Cui, "Lin Zhao qingren"; Gan Cui, interview, June 2, 2013.

21. Gan Cui, "Lin Zhao qingren"; Gan Cui, *Beida hun*. It was at Dengshikou Church in July 1954 that the founding of the state-sanctioned Three-Self Church was proclaimed.

22. Gan Cui, "Lin Zhao qingren"; Zhang Min, "Lin Zhao baomei"; Mr. Zhang, telephone interview, July 17, 2014.

23. The pipe organ at Shanghai Community Church was built by Austin Organs in 1930. See www.clacklinevalleyolives.com.au/pipeorgan/China/China.html.

24. Gan Cui, "Lin Zhao qingren"; Gan Cui, interview, June 2, 2013.

25. Wang Ningsheng, "Lin Zhao yinxiang."

26. Lin Zhao, "GRSX." See also SHLGJ, "Lin Zhao an jiaxing cailiao," and SJRJY, "Qisushu." After completing the poem, Lin Zhao continued to revise it, probably well into 1959. See Gan Cui, "Lin Zhao qingren." According to Tan Chanxue, Lin Zhao mailed a copy of "Seagull" to Sun He in September 1959. See Tan Chanxue, *Qiusuo*, 96. The indictment dated the mailing of the poem to 1958.

27. Lin Zhao, "Hai'ou."

28. The syllable *ang* was used for the end rhyme.

29. Lin Zhao, "GRSX."

30. Lin Zhao, "Diaohuan zhoumi."

31. Tan Chanxue, *Qiusuo*, 4–22, 96; Lin Zhao, "GRSX." In the latter, Lin Zhao mentioned that she hand-copied "Seagull" and shared it with friends in Beijing.

32. Tan Chanxue, *Qiusuo*, 22; Gan Cui, "Lin Zhao qingren."

33. Lin Zhao, "Puluomixiushi."

34. Yang Jisheng, *Mubei*, 531–536; Spence, *Search for Modern China*, 547–553.

35. Peng Dehuai to Mao Zedong, July 14, 1959, http://cpc.people.com.cn/GB/64184/64186/66666/4493320.html; Spence, *Search for Modern China*, 551–553; Yang Jisheng, *Mubei*, 537–538.

36. Tan Chanxue, *Qiusuo*, 11–12.

37. Ibid., 27–62.

38. Lin Zhao, "GRSX."

39. Ibid.; Tan Chanxue, *Qiusuo*, 97.

40. Tan Chanxue, *Qiusuo*, 22.

41. Ibid., 28.

42. Ibid., 29–53, 246; Hu Jie, *Xinghuo*.

43. **whose 1958 congress:** Jie Fu, "Nansilafu"; Miller, *Nonconformists*, 100; **Lin Zhao had found a copy:** Tan Chanxue, *Qiusuo*, 98; SHLGJ, "Lin Zhao an jiaxing cailiao." See also "Xiuzheng zhuyi de yaohai shi fouren dang de lingdao he wuchanjieji zhuanzheng" 修正主义的要害是否认党的领导和无产阶级专政 (The Crucial Thing about Revisionism Is That It Negates the Party's Leadership and Proletarian Dictatorship), editorial, *People's Daily*, May 5, 1958; **Despite her reservations, Lin Zhao was charged:** Tan Chanxue, *Qiusuo*, 99; Lin Zhao, "GRSX"; SHLGJ, "Lin Zhao an jiaxing cailiao."

44. Tan Chanxue, *Qiusuo*, 63–85.

45. Liu Faqing, interview with Hu Jie, in Hu Jie, *Xunzhao Lin Zhao de linghun*.

46. Lin Zhao, "GRSX."

47. Tan Chanxue, *Qiusuo*, 62, 96.

48. Lin Zhao, "Puluomixiushi."

49. **Lin Zhao's friends became alarmed:** Tan Chanxue, *Qiusuo*, 104–115, 256, 261; **On October 24, police showed:** SJRJY, "Qisushu"; **He muttered:** Zhang Min, "Lin Zhao baomei."

50. Lin Zhao, "Fuqin de xue"; Ni Jingxiong, interview, Shanghai, May 5, 2014.

51. Zhang Min, "Lin Zhao baomei"; Cheng Ronghua and Cui Xuefa, "Huan shishi yi gongzheng."

Chapter 5   Shattered Jade

1. For King Lear's quote, see Shakespeare, *King Lear*, act 1, scene 5. For Pascal's quote, see Foucault, *Madness and Civilization*, ix.

2. Kiely, *Compelling Ideal*, 166; Xu Jiajun, *Shanghai jianyu*, 75–77, 92–93, 102–103. See also Xue Liyong, "Lao Shanghai de jianyu." Shanghai No. 2 Detention House was decommissioned in 1985 and demolished in 1994. See SHDFZ, *Shanghai gong'an zhi*.

3. Tan Chanxue, *Qiusuo*, 116–121, 130–132. Bai Zhenjie 白振杰 interview, in Hu Jie, *Xunzhao Lin Zhao de linghun*. According to Bai, head of the Tianshui Detention House, Gansu, where Zhang Chunyuan was held, Zhang was found plotting a jailbreak. The One Strike, Three Anti Campaign of 1970 targeted especially the alleged "counterrevolutionary destructive activities" while also opposing "graft and embezzlement," "profiteering," and "extravagance and waste."

4. Kiely, *Compelling Ideal*, 1, 4–7.

5. Lin Zhao, "GRSX"; Peng Lingfan, "Wode jiejie Lin Zhao," 56. The 200,000-character "Diary of My Thoughts" most likely remains today in Lin Zhao's classified prison file. For Marx's quote, see Karl Marx, *A Contribution to*

the Critique of Political Economy (1859), "Preface," www.marxists.org/archive /marx/works/1859/critique-pol-economy/preface.htm; for Mao's 1937 essay, see Mao Zedong, "On Contradiction" (1937), www.marxists.org/reference/archive /mao/selected-works/volume-1/mswv1_17.htm.

6. Yang Huarong, "Huishou wangshi," 142. For the "Oddities Song," see Li Yi 李怡, "Guguai ge," 古怪歌 *Pingguo Ribao* 苹果日报 (Apple Daily), September 29, 2009.

7. Lin Zhao, "GRSX."

8. The reformulated economic policy was known as the eight-character policy of adjustment, consolidation, replenishment, and enhancement (调整、巩固、充实、提高 "八字方针"). See "Zhongguo Gongchandang di bajie Zhongyang Weiyuanhui di jiuci quanti huiyi gongbao." 中国共产党第八届中央委员会第九次全体会议公报 (Bulletin of the Ninth Plenum of the Eighth Central Committee of the Chinese Communist Party), January 20, 1961, www .yhcw.net/famine/Documents/d020202s.html.

9. Spence, *Search for Modern China*, 559–560. See also Xue Muqiao 薛暮桥, "'Dayuejin' zhong wo sui Chen Yun tongzhi xiaxiang diaocha." "大跃进"中我随陈云同志下乡调查 (I Went with Comrade Chen Yun to Conduct Rural Investigation during the "Great Leap Forward"), May 1, 2006, www.gmw .cn/02sz/2006-05/01/content_437944.htm.

10. Lin Zhao, "GRSX."

11. Lin Zhao, "ZRMRB," 9.

12. **The softening of Lin Zhao's:** SJRJY, "Qisushu"; Zhang Min, "Lin Zhao baomei." In her annotation on the 1964 indictment, Lin Zhao noted that she did not seek medical parole in 1962 but was given one; **For the first time, she was able:** Lin Zhao, "Fuqin de xue"; Yang Huarong, "Huishou wangshi," 142.

13. Lin Zhao, "ZRMRB," 32.

14. **She responded with a written . . . committed against them:** Lin Zhao, [annotated] "Qisushu"; SHGY, "Shanghai shi Gaoji Renmin Fayuan xingshi panjueshu," December 30, 1981; **"Are you sick?":** Lin Zhao, "ZRMRB," 33.

15. Ni Jingxiong, interview, May 5, 2014. Lin Zhao visited Ni after her encounter with Hu Ziheng and reported it.

16. Lin Zhao, "ZRMRB," 13, 33; Lin Zhao, [annotated] "Qisushu."

17. **She convinced one of them:** Lin Zhao, [annotated] "Qisushu." That name appears to have been originally proposed by Zhang Chunyuan before the arrests of 1960; **shadowed by undercover police:** Zhao Rui, *Jitan shang de shengnü*, Appendix 5 (interview with Zhu Hong), 368–382.

18. Lin Zhao, [annotated] "Qisushu"; SHLGJ, "Lin Zhao an jiaxing cailiao"; Lin Zhao, "XLZG," November 23, 1967.

19. Lin Zhao, "ZRMRB," 33–34; [annotated] "Qisushu"; Association of Jewish Refugees, in Great Britain, "News in Brief." *AJR Information* no. 10, October

1946, 74, "News in Brief." According to the latter, fourteen thousand Jews still remained in Shanghai in 1946. See also Casey Hall, "Jewish Life in Shanghai's Ghetto," *New York Times*, June 19, 2012.

20. **In early November:** Lin Zhao, "ZRMRB," 33; Lin Zhao, "Zhanchang riji," February 18, 1967; **The examining doctor:** Mr. Zhang, telephone interview, July 17, 2014. The doctor who evaluated Lin Zhao and diagnosed her as mentally ill was Su Zonghua 粟宗华, director of Shanghai Psychiatric Hospital. Zhang interviewed Lin Zhao's former classmates and friends from the late 1950s and early 1960s. According to him, none of them remembered Lin Zhao as mentally unstable. See also Zhang Min, "Lin Zhao baomei."

21. Lin Zhao, "ZRMRB," 14, 33.

22. Lin Zhao, "ZRMRB," 33–34; Lin Zhao, [annotated] "Qisushu."

23. Yuan Ling, "Shanghai dang'an"; Yin Shusheng, "Mao Zedong yu disanci quanguo gong'an huiyi"; Yuan Ling, "Tilanqiao li de qiutu."

24. **Little is known about:** Lin Zhao, "ZRMRB," 55, 117; Lin Zhao, "Ling'ou xuyu," August 24, 1965; **And she attempted to take:** SHLGJ, "Lin Zhao an jiaxing cailiao"; Lin Zhao, "Zhanchang riji," February 11, 1967.

25. Lin Zhao, "ZRMRB," 33–34; Lin Zhao, [annotated] "Qisushu"; Zhao Rui, *Jitan shang de shengnü*, 368–382.

26. Peng Lingfan, "Wode jiejie Lin Zhao," 55–56; Peng Lingfan, "Zai sixiang de lianyu," 20; Zhang Min, "Lin Zhao baomei." Lin Zhao likely met Yu Yile in Tilanqiao in 1962–1963, when she was temporarily held there. There are apparent inaccuracies in Peng Lingfan's account of Lin Zhao's encounter with Yu Yile; for Yu Yile and Christian Bible Institute, see Chen Yang, "Lin Zhao, Wang Chunyi, Yu Yile"; Kevin Yao, *Fundamentalist Movement*, 287; Wai-luen Kwok 郭伟联, *Fandui heyi?! Jia Yuming, jiyaozhuyi yu heyi yundong de jiujie*, 反对合一？！：贾玉铭、基要主义与合一运动的纠结 (Advocating Separatism?! Chia Yu Ming, Fundamentalists and Their Difficulties in Chinese Church Union Movement) (Hong Kong: Tien Dao Publishing House, 2002), 58; Bian Yunbo 边云波, "Jianguo qian de shenxue jiaoyu he huaren mushi 建国前的神学教育和华人教师 (Theological Education and Chinese Teachers before the Founding of the People's Republic), www.churchchina.org/archives/we151007.html. The Bible Institute was founded as 基督徒灵修院 in the 1930s and later renamed 中国基督教灵修神学院.

27. Lin Zhao, "ZRMRB," 14, 67, 83.

28. **Located on Nanchezhan Road:** Xu Jiajun, *Shanghai jianyu*, 122–125; SHDFZ, *Shanghai gong'an zhi*; **In May 1949, on the eve:** Xu Jiajun, *Shanghai jianyu*, 125; SHDFZ, *Shanghai quxian zhi*, entry on Huang Jingwu.

29. **During the Mao era . . . within its walls:** Yan Zuyou, *Renqu*, 8; Nien Cheng, *Life and Death in Shanghai*, 147; SHDFZ, *Shanghai gong'an zhi*; "**enemies without guns**": Mao Zedong, *Maozedong xuanji*, 4: 1428.

30. Yan Zuyou, *Renqu*, 8–9; Xu Jiajun, *Shanghai jianyu*, 122–123. See also Nien Cheng, *Life and Death in Shanghai*, 131–133.

31. **The window . . . in the afternoon:** Yan Zuyou, *Renqu*, 10, 18. See also Nien Cheng, *Life and Death in Shanghai*, 131. In the women's ward, each cell had a light bulb mounted in the middle of the ceiling. **"It was gloomy . . . sunny day":** Liu Wenzhong, *Fengyu rensheng lu*, 77–78;

32. Yan Zuyou, *Renqu*, 10–16; SHDFZ, *Shanghai gong'an zhi*; Lin Zhao, "ZRMRB," 67.

33. Yan Zuyou, *Renqu*, 20; Nien Cheng, *Life and Death in Shanghai*, 146.

34. Lin Zhao, "ZRMRB," 11, 14–15, 35, 52;

35. **At the No. 1 Detention . . . also occurred:** Yan Zuyou, *Renqu*, 14; **"I lose track . . . off my head":** Lin Zhao, "ZRMRB," 83. When Zhang Yuanxun visited Lin Zhao in Tilanqiao Prison in May 1966, he saw bald patches on her head where hair had been pulled off. See Zhang Yuanxun, "Beida wangshi," 101.

36. Lin Zhao, "ZRMRB," 22, 89.

37. Yan Zuyou, *Renqu*, 14; Liu Wenzhong, *Fan wenge diyi ren*, 180;

38. Yan Zuyou, *Renqu*, 14. The Chinese names of those styles were, respectively, 飞机铐，扁担铐，and 猪猡铐.

39. Lin Zhao, "ZRMRB," 15, 36; Lin Zhao, "Xueyi tiba."

40. **In China, . . . of the interrogated:** Liu Renwen and Liu Zexin, "Xingxun bigong." The Han dynasty decree "The Staff Order" "箠令" contains the following: "笞者，箠长五尺，其本大一寸，其竹也，末薄半寸，皆平其节。当笞者，笞臀。毋得更人，毕一罪乃更人。"; **"What confession . . . wooden staff?":** Gu Yingtai, *Mingshi jishi benmo, di shisi juan: kaiguo guimo* 明史紀事本末 第十四卷：开国规模 (Chronicles of Events in Ming Dynasty History, Volume 14: The Grandeur at the Dawn of the Dynasty) (1649). The Chinese original: "捶楚之下，何求不得."

41. **Nevertheless, torture was widely:** Liu Renwen and Liu Zexin, "Xingxun bigong"; **The so-called rescue . . . lost their mind:** Gao Hua, *Hong taiyang*, 318.

42. Liu Renwen and Liu Zexin, "Xingxun bigong."

43. Spence, *Gate of Heavenly Peace*, 84–93.

44. Lin Zhao, "Qiusheng ci."

45. Lin Zhao, "Qiushi aisi"; Lin Zhao, "ZRMRB," 86.

46. Lin Zhao, "Qiushi aisi." For Kennedy's speech, see John F. Kennedy, "Remarks in Miami, Florida at the Presentation of the Flag of the Cuban Invasion Brigade, 29 December 1962," www.jfklibrary.org/Asset-Viewer/Archives/JFKWHA-156-001.aspx. For *Xinhuashe* bulletin, see "Kennidi xiang huoshi de jilongtan beifu Meiguo guyongjun daqi; zaici jiaorang yao zai Guba shi fangeming fubi." 肯尼迪向获释的吉隆滩被俘美国雇佣军打气 再次叫嚷要在古巴使反革命复辟 (Kennedy Tries to Pump up the Morale of Freed American

Mercenaries Captured at Playa Girón, again Clamoring to Bring about Coun-terrevolutionary Restoration in Cuba), *People's Daily*, December 31, 1962.

47. Lin Zhao, "Qiushi aisi."

48. See "Kennidi 'heping zhanlue' xiongxiang bilu." 肯尼迪"和平战略"凶相毕露 (Ferocious Features of Kennedy's 'Strategy of Peace' Completely Exposed), *People's Daily*, July 6, 1963.

49. During this period, Lin Zhao was in Tilanqiao Prison, which provided *Liberation Daily* and *People's Daily* to inmates. According to Xu Jiajun, Liu Wenzhong, and Yan Zuyou (interviews), *Liberation Daily* was distributed regularly for group study. The distribution of *People's Daily* was more limited. Lin Zhao may have gained access to both because she was an important political prisoner. See also Lin Zhao, "Ling'ou xuyu," October 1, 1965.

50. Lin Zhao, "Qiushi aisi."

51. Lin Zhao, "ZRMRB," 15, 44.

52. Lin Zhao, "Zilei." Lin Zhao's reference here was both to Jing Ke and Zhong Yi of the Zhou dynasty and to Wang Jingwei, who evoked the same heroism of the past in a poem written after he was imprisoned for his unsuccessful attempt in 1910 to assassinate Zai Feng, the prince-regent of the last emperor of the Qing dynasty. Lin Zhao dated the poem to February 1964. She most likely wrote it just before her suicide attempt on February 5.

53. Li Baiyao 李百药 (Tang dynasty, 618–907), *Bei Qi shu: Yuan Jingan zhuan* 北齐书·元景安传 (History of Bei Qi Dynasty: The Biography of Yuan Jing'an).

54. **Lin Zhao had written her:** Lin Zhao's sister Peng Lingfan mentioned that when Lin Zhao came home on medical parole in 1962, there were scars on her arms from incisions made to draw blood for writing. However, there are no records of blood writing from that period. See Zhang Min, "Lin Zhao baomei"; **Like the choice of:** Lin Zhao, "Zilei"; "Xueyi tiba."

55. Yin Wenhan, "Zhongguo gudai cixue jingshu zhifeng." Chinese sources on Siddhartha Gautama's religious devotion contain the following: "剥皮为纸、以血为墨、折骨为笔，书写此偈." See *The Basic Annals of the Liang Dynasty* (梁本记), Vol. 7 (n.d., seventh century). The Chinese text: "于是人人赞善，莫不从风。或刺血洒地，或刺血书经，穿心然灯，坐禅不食。"

56. **In a sixteenth-century . . . the grieving emperor:** Daphne P. Lei, "The Bloodstained Text in Translation: Tattooing, Bodily Writing, and Performance of Chinese Virtue," *Anthropological Quarterly* 82, no. 1 (Winter 2009); **In Mao's China:** See "Tianfan difu kai'erkang—Wuchanjieji Wenhua Dageming dashiji" 天翻地复慨而慷—无产阶级文化大革命大事记 (In Heroic Triumph Heaven and Earth Have Been Overturned: Chronicles of the Great Proletarian Cultural Revolution), December 1967, in Song Yongyi et al., *Zhongguo Wenhua Dageming wenku*. The incident occurred on July 1, 1966. Admittedly, blood writing

has not been limited to the East. "Of all that is written, I love only what a person hath written with his blood," declared Friedrich Nietzsche. See Nietzsche, *Thus Spake Zarathustra*, 37.

57. Lin Zhao, "ZRMRB," 15, 84; SJRJY, "Qisushu."

58. Lin Zhao, "Jia ji" 家祭 (A Family Mourning), April 12, 1964, cited in Hu Jie, *Xunzhao Lin Zhao de linghun*; Lin Zhao, "ZRMRB," 52, 70. "Jia ji" was not among her prison writings returned in 1982. It was discovered and copied by the journalist Chen Weisi, who was allowed a one-day access to the Lin Zhao file in early 1981. The rest of the writings done at the No. 1 Detention House, including "To the Shackles" (Zhi liaokao 致镣铐), may still remain in the classified Lin Zhao file.

59. Lin Zhao, "Xueyi tiba."

60. Lin Zhao, "ZRMRB," 70.

61. Mao Zedong, "Qilü: Renmin Jiefangjun zhanling Nanjing" 七律·人民解放军占领南京 (Seven-Character Rhyme: The Capture of Nanjing by the People's Liberation Army), 1949. English translation adapted from Mao Zedong, *Mao Zedong Poems*, 49.

62. Lin Zhao, "Xueshi tiyi bing ba." Just decades before the Qin king crushed rival states in 221 BCE to claim the mandate of heaven as the first emperor of the Qin dynasty, Lu Lian, also known as Lu Zhonglian, had vowed to throw himself into the sea if the Qin king usurped the throne of the Zhou dynasty. See Sima Qian (born ca. 145 BCE), *Shiji* (Records of the Grand Historian), 鲁仲连邹阳列传第二十三. Sima Qian wrote: "则连有蹈东海而死耳，吾不忍为之民也." Cao Cao (whose pejorative nickname A'man is used in the Chinese original of the poem) was said to have chanted a soaring poem with a drawn sword before his military debacle at Ref Cliff. Su Shi in his essay "Red Cliff " (Qian Chibi fu 前赤壁赋, 1082) had written that Cao Cao "poured out his wine as he looked over the great river, and chanted a poem with a drawn sword" (酾酒临江、横槊赋诗).

63. Lin Zhao, "Ling'ou xuyu," September 12, 1965.

64. **"wrong path"**: Lin Zhao, "Xueshi tiyi." The eighth of the nine poems contains the following: "宝筏迷津迅守渡，好成正果上青云"; **Perhaps Mao:** Lin Zhao, "ZRMRB," 54.

65. **"Pondering through . . . whom shall I play?"**: Lin Zhao, "Xueshi tiyi"; **Yue Fei had written:** Yue Fei (1103–1142), "Xiaochongshan" 小重山 (The Little Mountains Rhyme). Yue wrote: "欲将心事付瑶琴。知音少，弦断有谁听?"; **In yet another poem:** Lin Zhao, "Xueshi tiyi."

66. SJRJY, "Qisushu."

67. Ibid.

68. Lin Zhao, "'Qisushu' bayu." For routine meals in jail, see Yan Zuyou, Renqu, 11–36; Lin Zhao, "ZRMRB," 94. A handful of inmates (such as a former

film director), on account of their elevated social status, were granted special diet, which included small amounts of meat, or fish, or egg.

69. Lin Zhao to mother, November 4, 1967.

70. Lin Zhao, "ZRMRB," 55.

71. Ibid., 65.

72. **That, too, was foiled:** Lin Zhao, "'Qisushu' bayu"; **"the so-called Procuratorate . . . all over the floor":** Zhao, "'Qisushu' bayu"; "Xueyi tiba."

73. Lin Zhao, "ZRMRB," 75, 78; "'Qisushu' bayu."

74. Lin Zhao, [annotated] "Qisushu." Lin Zhao's annotation is 3,739 characters long, about twice as long as the indictment itself.

75. Lin Zhao, "ZRMRB," 18, 20, 85.

76. Lin Zhao, "ZRMRB," 18. For Ke Qingshi's promotion as the first party secretary of the East China Bureau, see http://cpc.people.com.cn/GB/64162/64165/76621/76636/5272464.html.

77. **"wholeheartedly depict the thirteen years":** Xiao Donglian et al., *Qiusuo Zhongguo*, chapter 5, part 4. See also Goldman, *China's Intellectuals*, 76–77; **Ke was purged during:** Gao Hua, *Hong taiyang*, 305–306.

78. Lin Zhao, "ZRMRB," 22. The second letter to Ke Qingshi was handed over to a guard on March 3.

79. Ibid., 65.

80. Ibid., 66, 84–85, 95, 102.

81. **Periodically, a formless . . . inmates later told her:** Lin Zhao, "ZRMRB," 94, 98; **In spite of the emerging signs:** In 2016, I sent this and other passages in my manuscript that I considered the most revealing of Lin Zhao's mental state to my colleague Dr. Warren A. Kinghorn, a psychiatrist at Duke University School of Medicine, for his analysis. In his e-mail to me dated February 20, 2017, he explained that he saw "no clear evidence" of a psychotic disorder but suggested the possibility of a "manic-depressive disorder."

82. Lin Zhao, "ZRMRB," 72; "Xueshi tiyi."

83. Lin Zhao, "ZRMRB," 72–73, 82–83. See also Yan Zuyou, *Renqu*, for routine searches of the inmates' belongs to confiscate their writings.

84. Lin Zhao possibly experienced a hallucination on the night of May 5, 1965, in which the spirit of Ke Qinghsi defended Lin Zhao's innocence and mildly rebuked Mao for his paranoia. See Lin Zhao, "ZRMRB," 111. For Mao's relations with Ke, see Feng Xigang 冯锡钢, "Wo han relei yi beichou: du Tao Zhu de sanshou qilü." 我含热泪抑悲愁: 读陶铸的三首七律 (I Suppressed My Sorrow in Spite of Tears: On Three Seven-Character Rhymes by Tao Zhu) *Tongzhou gongjin* 同舟共进 (Making Progress together in the Same Boat), 2011, No. 11, www.xzbu.com/1/view-270943.htm.

85. **On April 10, *Liberation Daily*:** Lin Zhao, "ZRMRB," 112; **In reality, Ke:** Ye Yonglie, "Jiemi Ke Qingshi zhi si: bingfei siyu fei'ai huo 'mousha'." 揭秘柯庆施之死：并非死于肺癌或"谋杀" (Uncovering the Secret of Ke

Qingshi's Death: Cause of Death Not Lung Cancer or "Murder"), February 5, 2013, *Renmin wang* (People's Net), http://history.people.com.cn/n/2013/0205 /c198865-20435479.html.

86. Lin Zhao, "ZRMRB," 69–70, 102, 112.

87. **she composed a long four-character:** Lin Zhao, "Ji ling'ou wen"; **Then, "in accordance . . . his concubine!":** Lin Zhao, "ZRMRB," 112.

88. **"If he had been alive . . . a snow-white crow":** Lin Zhao, "Zhanchang riji," February 12, 1967; Lin Zhao, "Ling'ou xuyu," January 19, 1966; **"love for the dead one":** Lin Zhao, "ZRMRB," 68.

89. **Like all her other writings:** Lin Zhao, "ZRMRB," 68, 84; Lin Zhao to mother, November 12, 1967. The essay "Gao renlei" 告人类 (An Appeal to Humanity) was also done in her blood and was not yet finished when she was removed from the No. 1 Detention House; **"Who has been like you?":** Lin Zhao, "ZRMRB," 16.

90. **Nien Cheng:** Nien Cheng, *Life and Death in Shanghai*, 156–157; **Selected Works of Mao:** Lin Zhao, "ZRMRB," 68–69.

91. **The interrogator had admonished her:** Lin Zhao, "ZRMRB," 78; **At the No. 1 Detention . . . in this place":** Nien Cheng, *Life and Death in Shanghai*, 149.

92. Lin Zhao, "ZRMRB," 82.

93. Ibid., 75.

Chapter 6   Lamplight in the Snowy Fields

1. Lin Zhao, "Zhongzi."

2. "Peng Guoyan qing pingfan yuanyu"; Cheng Ronghua and Cui Xuefa, "Huan shishi yi gongzheng."

3. Lin Zhao, "Panjue hou de shengming."

4. Xu Jiajun, *Tilanqiao jianyu*, 217; Xu Jiajun, "Shanghai shi Tilanqiao jianyu"; Dikötter, *Crime, Punishment, and the Prison*, 308, 311–315; Yan Zuyou, "Jiaoshou fenggu."

5. **In addition to the regular:** Dikötter, *Crime, Punishment, and the Prison*, 318; Xu Jiajun, "Shanghai shi Tilanqiao jianyu"; Xu Jiajun, interview, Shanghai, June 12, 2017. "Fengbo ting" were located on the top floor of Block No. 7; "xiangpi jian" were housed in the prison hospital and in the Westerners' Block, also known as the cross-shaped block (*shizi jian*); **From the beginning:** Xu Jiajun, "Shanghai shi Tilanqiao jianyu."

6. See Yuan Ling, "Tilanqiao li de qiutu"; Yuan Ling, "Shanghai dang'an li de 'fangeming.'"

7. Liu Wenzhong, *Fengyu rensheng lu*, 271–272.

8. Lin Zhao, "Lianxi san" 练习三 (The Third [Writing] Practice), February 27, 1966.

9. Lin Zhao, "Xueyi tiba"; Lin Zhao, "Ling'ou xuyu," June 22, 1965. Information on the Women's Block is from Xu Jiajun, *Tilanqiao jianyu*, 15; Xu Jiajun, interview, June 12, 2017; SHDFZ, *Shanghai jianyu zhi*, chapter 6.

10. MacFarquhar and Schoenhals, *Mao's Last Revolution*, 4–7.

11. Lin Zhao, "ZRMRB," 40–41.

12. Lin Zhao, "Ling'ou xuyu," July 14, 1965; Lin Zhao, "ZRMRB," 120.

13. Lin Zhao, "ZRMRB," 85.

14. SHDFZ, *Shanghai jianyu zhi*; Lin Zhao, "Ling'ou xuyu," August 11, 1965; Xu Jiajun, interview, June 12, 2017.

15. Lin Zhao, "Ling'ou xuyu," July 14, 1965.

16. Lin Zhao, "ZRMRB," 117.

17. Lin Zhao, "Ling'ou xuyu," June 13, 1965.

18. Ibid., June 11, 1965.

19. Ibid., July 9 and 10, 1965.

20. Ibid., June 16 and July 11, 1965.

21. Lin Zhao, "ZRMRB," 1.

22. Ibid., 6.

23. Ibid., 2.

24. Ibid., 100–105.

25. Ibid., 36.

26. Ibid.

27. Ibid., 106.

28. Ibid., 107.

29. **Mao must also be held accountable:** Lin Zhao, "ZRMRB," 108; **On August 23, 1958, Mao had ordered:** Li Zhisui, *Mao Zedong siren yisheng huiyilu*, 252; Chang and Halliday, *Mao*, 406–407. See also MacFarquhar and Schoenhals, *Mao's Last Revolution*, 6.

30. **on October 20, Chinese troops stormed:** Chang and Halliday, *Mao*, 458–459; **That same day, Beijing announced**: "Zhongguo zhengfu fabiao shengming zhichi Guba fandui Meiguo zhanzheng tiaoxin," 中国政府发表声明支持古巴反对美国战争挑衅 (Chinese Government Issues a Statement in Support of Cuba's Opposition to the War Provocations from the United States), *People's Daily*, October 25, 1962; Feng Yunfei 冯云飞, "1962 nian Guba daodan weiji yu Sulian dui Zhong-Yin bianjie wenti lichang de zhuanbian," 1962 年古巴导弹危机与苏联对中印边界问题立场的转变 (The Cuban Missile Crisis of 1962 and the Changes in the Position of the Soviet Union regarding the Border Issue between China and India), *Dangshi yuanjiu yu jiaoxue* 党史研究与教学 (Party History: Research and Teaching), 2009, no. 2; "**All of that resulted . . . by nature**": Lin Zhao, "ZRMRB," 108.

31. Lin Zhao, "ZRMRB," 108.

32. **"Jiajing Emperor dismissed . . . also a 'Hai Rui.'":** "'Wenge' ruhe fash-eng." Lin Zhao drew the parallel between Peng Dehuai and Hai Rui on page 108 of her letter to *People's Daily*, which totals 120 pages. She may have written that passage just days before completing the entire letter on December 5, 1965; **Not until January:** Si Tong, "Jieshou Wu Han tongzhi de tiaozhan," 接受吴晗同志的挑战 (Accepting the Challenge of Comrade Wu Han), *People's Daily*, January 13, 1966. See also Tian Geng 田耕, "*Hairui baguan* daoyan tan *Hairui baguan*," "海瑞罢官"导演谈"海瑞罢官" (The Director of *Hai Rui Dismissed from Office* Discusses the Play), *Yanhuang chunqiu*, 2006, no. 5.

33. Li Xia'en, "Hai Rui mu."

34. Mazur, *Wu Han*, 407; MacFarquhar and Schoenhals, *Mao's Last Revolution*, 15; "'Wenge' ruhe fasheng."

35. **Yao's imperious polemic . . . "counterrevolutionary revisionism":** MacFarquhar, *Origins of the Cultural Revolution*, 252–253; MacFarquhar and Schoenhals, *Mao's Last Revolution*, 14–17; Chang and Halliday, *Mao*, 524; **Before it fizzled out:** Yang Jishen, "Daolu, lilun, zhidu"; Song Yongyi, "Wenge zhong 'fei zhengchang siwang' le duoshao ren?"

36. Lin Zhao, "ZRMRB," 62.

37. **She sardonically dismissed:** Lin Zhao, "ZRMRB," 1; **"For you who . . . wrong":** ibid., 37.

38. Lin Zhao, "ZRMRB," 111.

39. Ibid., 39.

40. Wu Lengxi, *Yi Maozhuxi*, chapter 11; Qian Jiang, "Wenge qianxi de *Renmin Ribao*."

41. Lin Zhao, "ZRMRB," 103.

42. Zhu Yi, "'Lin Zhao: Ling'ou xuyu' jiaoduzhe shuoming"; photographs of ink copies of "Ling'ou xuyu."

43. Lin Zhao, "Ling'ou xuyu," May 31, 1965.

44. Ibid., August 11, 1965.

45. Ibid., October 29, 1965.

46. **"I am easily excitable . . . boiling water!":** Lin Zhao, "Ling'ou xuyu," October 30, 1965; **"Judas sold . . . of them!":** ibid., October 21, 1965.

47. Lin Zhao, "Ling'ou xuyu," July 2, 1965.

48. Ibid., July 30, 1965. For the call to "all-shaking thunder," see Shakespeare, *King Lear*, act 3, scene 2.

49. Lin Zhao, "Ling'ou xuyu," September 10, 1965.

50. Ibid., October 1, 1965.

51. Ibid., October 3, 1965.

52. SHDFZ, *Shanghai shenpan zhi*.

53. Lin Zhao, "Ling'ou xuyu," November 11, 1965.

54. Ibid., August 11, 1965.

55. Ibid., September 17, 1965.

56. Ibid., September 19, 1965.

57. Lin Zhao, "ZRMRB," 38.

58. Ibid., 29–30, 62.

59. Lin Zhao, "Ling'ou xuyu," November, 23, 1965.

60. Lin Zhao, "Ling'ou xuyu," December 11, 1965; January 8, 1966. See also Zhang Yuanxun, "Beida wangshi," 105–106.

61. Li Shangyin (813–858), "Wuti" 无题 (untitled). English translation taken from A. C. Graham, *Poems of the Late T'ang* (New York: NYRB, 2008).

62. Lin Zhao, "Ling'ou xuyu," December 11, 1965.

63. Lu Xun, "Wuti" 无题 (untitled). English translation by David Y. Ch'en, with one minor change by the author, http://wap.putclub.com/html/ability/translation/translation/training/literature/zhongguozuopin/2014/0805/89403.html.

64. Lin Zhao, "Ling'ou xuyu," December 19, 1965.

65. **On Christmas Eve:** Lin Zhao, "Ling'ou xuyu," December 24, 1965; **Sixty years earlier:** Yuan Ling, "Tilanqiao li de qiutu"; **Now Mao's regime . . . grille of the cells:** Yan Zuyou, "Jiaoshou fenggu"; Yan Zuyou, *Renqu*, 11–36. Sick inmates were offered "nutrition meals"—with added sautéed chicken bones.

66. **The Christmas Eve dinner:** Lin Zhao, "Ling'ou xuyu," December 24, 1965. "Christ Is Still in This World" was one of her prison writings that were catalogued by the Tilanqiao authorities but did not survive; **"Grant me inspirations . . . Streams in the Desert":** ibid., December 25, 1965.

67. **On January 13, 1966, Lin Zhao coughed:** Lin Zhao, "Ling'ou xuyu," January 13, 1966; **"Let it bleed":** ibid.

68. Lin Zhao, "Ling'ou xuyu," January 13, 1966.

69. **"Don't blame . . . me to do":** Lin Zhao, "Ling'ou xuyu," February 5, 1966; **In fact, every time:** Zhang Yuanxun, "Beida wangshi," 105–106.

70. **By the middle of the month:** Lin Zhao, "Ling'ou xuyu," February 16, 1966; **After an entry on March 8, 1966:** ibid., March 8, 1966.

71. **The doctor treating:** Peng Lingfan, "Wode zizi Lin Zhao," 39; **The letter would not be forwarded:** Lin Zhao, "Suizhao zhi zhan."

Chapter 7   The White-Haired Girl of Tilanqiao

1. Lin Zhao, "ZRMRB," 88.

2. Zhang Yuanxun, "Beida wangshi," 92–97; Zhu Yi, interview, Ganzhou, June 9, 2017. For Zhang's courting of Lin Zhao in college, see Peng Lingfan, "Wode zizi Lin Zhao," 34.

3. Zhang Yuanxun, "Beida wangshi," 92–93, 97–99; Lin Zhao, "Suizhao yin" 岁朝吟 (New Year Chanting), February 16, 1967.

4. Lin Zhao, "Kejuan": "Lianxi er" 练习二 (Exercise No. 2), February 24-26, 1966; Lin Zhao, "Ling'ou xuyu," February 11, 1966; Lin Zhao, "Zhanchang riji," February 9 and 20, 1967.

5. Zhang Yuanxun, "Beida wangshi," 97–107.

6. Ibid., 100.

7. Lin Zhao, "ZRMRB," 115, 117.

8. Lin Zhao, "Shangsushu."

9. Ouyang Ying (Lin Zhao), "Huanghun zhi lei."

10. Zhonggong Zhengzhiju kuoda huiyi 中共政治局扩大会议 (Enlarged Meeting of the CCP Politburo), "Wu yiliu tongzhi" 五·一六通知 (May 16 Notification), 1966, http://history.dwnews.com/big5/news/2013-05-13/59173751 -all.html; MacFarquhar and Schoenhals, *Mao's Last Revolution*, 47. The Beijing party establishment's document in defense of Wu Han became known as the "February Outline."

11. "Zhongguo Gongchandang Zhongyang Weiyuanhui guanyu Wuchang Jieji Wenhua Dageming de jueding" 中国共产党中央委员会关于无产阶级文化大革命的决定 (The Decision concerning the Great Proletarian Cultural Revolution by the Central Committee of the Chinese Communist Party), *People's Daily,* August 9, 1966. English translation adapted from MacFarquhar and Schoenhals, *Mao's Last Revolution*, 92–93.

12. **Within two months:** MacFarquhar and Schoenhals, *Mao's Last Revolution*, 117; **During the so-called Red August:** Wang Youqin, "Kongbu de 'Hong bayue'"; **In Shanghai:** MacFarquhar and Schoenhals, *Mao's Last Revolution*, 124; **In all, 11,510 people:** Wang Youqin, *Wenge shounanzhe*, 298; **"abnormal deaths":** Song Yongyi, "Wenge zhong 'fei zhengchang siwang' le duoshao ren?"; Yang Jisheng, "Daolu, lilun, zhidu."

13. **In her prison writings . . . station:** Liu Wenzhong, interview, Shanghai, May 29, 2016; Yan Zuyou, e-mail to author, August 27, 2016. According to both Liu Wenzhong and Yan Zuyou—Tilanqiao inmates in the late 1960s and early 1970s—loud speakers were mounted on each floor. Radio news from government stations—Central People's Broadcasting Station or Shanghai People's Broadcasting Station—were aired each morning, as were important prison announcements; **She had pointed out:** Lin Zhao, "ZRMRB," 102–103, 108.

14. MacFarquhar and Schoenhals, *Mao's Last Revolution*, 108.

15. Wang Rongfen, "Wo zai yuzhong de rizi."

16. MacFarquhar and Schoenhals, *Mao's Last Revolution*, 45–46.

17. Wang Ruowang, "Lin Zhao zhi si." See also Yang Huarong, "Huishou wangshi," 146.

18. **The last monthly visit:** Wang Ruowang, "Lin Zhao zhi si"; Lin Zhao to mother, October 4, 1966; **Inmates had been made to perform labor:** SHD-FZ, *Shanghai jianyu zhi*, chapter 6; "Shanghai tan de jinmi zhidi"; Xu Jiajun, interview, Shanghai, June 12, 2017. According to Xu, female inmates typically performed prison labor inside the Women's Block; **Lin Zhao resisted the work regime:** Wang Ruowang, "Lin Zhao zhi si."

19. Lin Zhao to mother, October 4, 1966; January 17, 1967; March 17, 1967. The visit took place on February 23, 1967.

20. Lin Zhao to mother, December 14, 1966.

21. Lin Zhao, "ZRMRB," 55.

22. **In mid-February 1967:** Lin Zhao to mother, February 15, 1967; **She went on intermittent:** Lin Zhao, "Zhanchang riji," February 12, 1967.

23. MacFarquhar and Schoenhals, *Mao's Last Revolution*, 136–137.

24. MacFarquhar and Schoenhals, *Mao's Last Revolution*, 155, 162–166; Yan Changgui 阎长贵, "'Shanghai Renmin Gongshe' mingcheng shiyong he feizhi de neiqing"上海人民公社'名称使用和废止的内情 (The Inside Story of the Adoption and the Abandonment of the Name "Shanghai People's Commune") *Bainian chao* 百年潮 (Tides of the Past Century), 2005, no. 8; Cao Diqiu 曹荻秋, "Cao Diqiu de jiancha" 曹荻秋的检查 (Cao Diqiu's Examination), in Song Yongyi et al., *Zhongguo Wenhua Dageming wenku*.

25. MacFarquhar and Schoenhals, *Mao's Last Revolution*, 155, 162–166; Yan Changgui, "'Shanghai Renmin Gongshe.'"

26. **never again allowed to read newspapers:** See Lin Zhao, "Fuqin de xue." She mentioned that she had not been able to read newspapers for sixteen months. The situation apparently remained unchanged till the end of her life; **Her habit of tearing:** Lin Zhao, "Zhanchang riji," February 22, 1967.

27. **Still, Lin Zhao had kept:** Liu Wenzhong, interview, May 29, 2016; Yan Zuyou, e-mail to the author, August 27, 2016; **By the end of November 1966:** MacFarquhar and Schoenhals, *Mao's Last Revolution,* 110; **She did more blood writing:** Lin Zhao, "Zhanchang riji," February 13, 1967.

28. Lin Zhao, "Zhanchang riji," February 9, 1967.

29. Ibid.

30. Ibid., February 10 and 16, 1967.

31. **During the Cultural Revolution:** Wang Jiangting 望江亭, "Liangze 'Wenge' shi de beixiju 两则" 文革"时的悲喜剧 (Two Tragic-Comedies during the Cultural Revolution), http://wjiangting.blog.hexun.com/97191908_d.html; **A vigilante:** author's personal knowledge of an incident in Fuzhou during the Cultural Revolution; **In Shanghai, a poorly educated peddler:** Liu Wenzhong, *Fengyu rensheng lu*, 262–263. In that incident, "翻毛" was incorrectly written as "反毛."

32. Lin Zhao, "Zhanchang riji," February 10, 1967.

33. Ibid.

34. Ibid.

35. Ibid., February 11 and 22, 1967; see also Lin Zhao, "Fuqin de xue." She was likely moved to the fifth floor and denied access to newspapers at the same time, in July 1966.

36. Lin Zhao, "Zhanchang riji," February 11, 1967. For inmates' protest, see Xu Jiajun, *Shanghai jianyu*, 100;

37. **Lin Zhao's self-identification:** Lin Zhao, "ZRMRB," 55; **Before then, she had . . . could not change:** Lin Zhao, "Fuqin de xue."

38. See Chris Buckley, "'White-Haired Girl,' Opera Created under Mao, Returns to Stage," *New York Times*, November 10, 2015; Li Xiaolong 李小龙, "Geming de xugou: geju *Baimaonü* muhou" 革命的虚构：歌剧"白毛女"幕后 (Revolutionary Fiction: Behind the Opera "White-Haired Girl"), *New York Times* (Chinese edition), July 4, 2012.

39. Lin Zhao, "Ling'ou xuyu," January 15, 1966.

40. Lin Zhao, "Ling'ou xuyu," September 12, 1965; Lin Zhao, "Zhanchang riji," February 11, 1967.

41. SHDFZ, *Shanghai jianyu zhi*, chapter 6.

42. Lin Zhao, "Zhanchang riji," February 22, 1967.

43. Dikötter, *Crime, Punishment, and the Prison*, 310; "Shanghai tan de jinmi zhidi."

44. Yan Zuyou, "Jiaoshou fenggu"; Shen Zhihua, *Sikao yu xuanze*, 683.

45. Yuan Ling, "Tilanqiao li de qiutu."

46. Ibid.

47. Lin Zhao, "Zhanchang riji," February 21, 1967.

48. Yuan Ling, "Tilanqiao li de qiutu."

49. MacFarquhar and Schoenhals, *Mao's Last Revolution*, 177; "Zhonggong Zhongyang, Guowuyuan, Zhongyang Junwei guanyu baohu liangshi, wuzhi cangku he jianyü deng wenti de guiding" 中共中央、国务院、中央军委关于保护粮食、物资仓库和监狱等问题的规定 (Stipulations on Securing Food, Warehouses, and Prisons Issued by the CCP Central Committee, the State Council, and the Central Military Affairs Committee), January 19, 1967, in Song Yongyi et al., *Zhongguo Wenhua Dageming wenku*.

50. Yuan Ling, "Tilanqiao li de qiutu."

51. Xu Jiajun, *Shanghai jianyu*, 8.

52. **In the Women's Block . . . kicked and swore at her:** Yuan Ling, "Tilanqiao li de qiutu"; **She died:** ibid.; Cheng Tianwu, "Zai yuzhong de endian shenghuo," 115. Cheng remembered the former guard as Captain Qu 瞿队长, who was sentenced to twenty years in prison; **Another guard committed . . . the other hanged himself:** Yuan Ling, "Tilanqiao li de qiutu."

53. **The inmates did not benefit:** Lin Zhao, "Zhanchang riji," February 21, 1967. **As the Cultural Revolution deepened:** Yuan Ling, "Tilanqiao li de

qiutu." The directive from the Party Central Committee to "practice thrift, wage revolution" was issued on June 29, 1967. See "Zhonggong Zhongyang guanyu jieyue naogeming, fangzhi puzhang langfei de tongzhi" 中共中央关于节约闹革命、防止铺张浪费的通知 (CCP Central Committee Directive to Practice Thrift, Wage Revolution and to Prevent Extravagance and Waste), June 29, 1967, in Song Yongyi et al., *Zhongguo Wenhua Dageming wenku*.

54. "Zhonggong Zhongyang, Guowuyuan guanyu zai Wuchanjieji Wenhua Dageming zhong jiaqiang gong'an gongzuo de ruogan guiding" 中共中央、国务院关于在无产阶级文化大革命中加强公安工作的若干规定 (Regulations Issued by the CCP Central Committee and the State Council on Strengthening Public Security Work during the Great Proletarian Cultural Revolution), January 13, 1967, in Song Yongyi et al., *Zhongguo Wenhua Dageming wenku*.

55. **In actual implementation:** Peng Jingxiu 彭劲秀, "Wenhua Dageming zhong de 'Gong'an Liutiao'" 文化大革命中的"公安六条," June 24, 2103, *Gongshiwang* 共识网 (Consensus Web), www.21ccom.net/articles/lsjd/lsjj/article_2013062486230.html; **Subsequent and independent studies:** Ding Shu, "Wenge zhong"; Cui Min 崔敏, "Weihuo canlie de 'gong'an liutiao'" 为祸惨烈的"公安六条" (The Catastrophic "Six Stipulations on Public Security"), *Yanhuang chunqiu* 炎黄春秋 (China through the Ages), 2012, no. 12.

56. "Shanghai Shi Zhongji Renmin Fayuan xingshi panjueshu 1967 niandu Huzhongxing (1) zi di san hao" 上海市中级人民法院刑事判决书一九六七年度沪中刑（一）字第3号 (Verdict of the Shanghai Intermediate People's Court, 1967 Huzhongxing 1, no. 3), cited in Liu Wenzhu, "Bushu Yuluo Ke: Gan tiaozhan Mao Zedong de qingnian doushi Liu Wenhui" 不输遇罗克：敢挑战毛泽东的青年斗士刘文辉 (Not Inferior to Yuluo Ke: Liu Wenhui, the Young Warrior Who Dared to Challenge Mao Zdedong), http://hk.aboluowang.com/2015/1206/656345.html. See also Liu Wenzhong, "Fan wenge diyi ren."

57. Shan Miaofa, "Zhongguo zhengfu."

58. Lin Zhao, "Zhanchang riji," February 20, 1967.

59. See SHDFZ, *Shanghai jianyu zhi*, chapter 1.

60. SHLGJ, "Lin Zhao an jiaxing cailiao."

61. Ibid.

62. Meng Banrong 孟半戎, "Yifeng nimingxin weihe xiegei Jiangqing" 一封匿名信为何写给江青 (Why Was an Anonymous Letter Addressed to Jiang Qing), *Zhongguo Gongchandang xinwenwang* 中国共产党新闻网 (News Net of the Communist Party of China), November 4, 2015, http://dangshi.people.com.cn/n/2015/1104/c85037-27773947.html.

63. Lin Zhao to mother, March 17, 1967.

64. Ibid., May 14, 1967.

65. Ibid., September, 1967.

66. **by mid-June, Shanghai People's Procuratorate:** "Shanghai Renmin Jianchayuan: Laojian—shencha qisu"上海人民检察院： 劳检—审查起诉, 1966.12.23至1967.6.16 (Shanghai People's Procuratorate: Reform through Labor Bureau-Procuratorate—Investigation and Indictment, December 23, 1966, to June 16, 1967), in Hu Jie, *Xunzhao Lin Zhao de linghun*; **Sometime in the fall of 1967:** JGH, "xingshi panjueshu."

Chapter 8   Blood Letters Home

1. Lin Zhao to mother, October 24, 1967.

2. Lin Zhao, "Beibu qizhounian kouhao" 被捕七周年口号 (Slogans Marking the Seventh Anniversary of My Arrest), October 24, 1967.

3. Lin Zhao to mother, October 14, 1967; Lin Zhao, "Jishi kangyi" (No. 1), October 14, 1967. Lin Zhao saw her mother for the last time on March 23, 1967. See Lin Zhao to mother, October 28, 1967. The last family visit—by Peng Lingfan—took place in May 1967. See Lin Zhao, "Jishi kangyi" (No. 7), October 25, 1967; Zhang Min, "Lin Zhao baomei." One possible reason for the denial of water for washing is the water-splashing war she had carried on from time to time with inmate housekeepers who were used by the prison authorities to subdue her.

4. **Her intermittent hunger:** Lin Zhao to mother, October 23, 1967; **"Instead, I have . . . bullied me":** Lin Zhao, "Jishi kangyi" (No. 2) October 16, 1967; **Meanwhile, to her exasperation:** Lin Zhao, "Jishi kangyi" (No. 5), October 22, 1967.

5. Lin Zhao to mother, November 16, 1967.

6. Lin Zhao, "XSJX."

7. Lin Zhao to mother, October 27, 1967.

8. Baldwin, *Thirty More Famous Stories Retold*, 68–73.

9. Lin Zhao to mother, October 30, 1967.

10. Lin Zhao, "Shiyue sanshiyi ri."

11. Hans Litten, a labor lawyer, had cross-examined Hitler during the Tanzpalast Eden Trial of 1931 at which he set out to show that the SA Storm 33 was a paramilitary unit and that its attack on a migrant workers' association's meeting at the Tanzpalast Eden in Berlin in 1930 was undertaken with the knowledge of the Nazi party leadership. Litten was arrested in 1933 and was repeatedly interrogated and tortured. He committed suicide in 1938.

12. Hu Zhuangzi 胡庄子, "'Zhongzihua yundong' chutan" "忠字化运动" 初探 (A Preliminary Probe into the "Loyalty Movement"), *Jiyi* 记忆 (Remembrance) no. 142 (October 31, 2015); Walder, *China Under Mao*, 281; MacFarquhar and Schoenhals, *Mao's Last Revolution*, 262.

13. Lin Zhao to mother, November 5, 1967.

14. Ibid., November 8 and 12, 1967.

15. Lin Zhao to mother, November 10, 1967. See also Lin Zhao, "Jishi kangyi," October 30, 1967.

16. Lin Zhao to mother, November 10, 1967.

17. Ibid., November 12, 1967.

18. See Ma Xiao 马萧, "Wenge kousu shi: 47 zhong Hongweibing yi 'yangguang canlan de rizi'" 文革口述史： 47 中红卫兵忆 "阳光灿烂的日子" (Cultural Revolution Oral History: Red Guards of the Forty-Seventh Middle School Remembering "the Bright Sunny Days"), *New York Times* (Chinese edition), June 24, 2016. See also Zhang Min, "Lin Zhao baomei."

19. Lin Zhao to mother, November 12, 1967.

20. **In 1955 . . . of her hospital:** Zhang Min, "Lin Zhao baomei." The better TB medicines were the imported ones. See also Peng Lingfan, "Wode jiejie Lin Zhao," 45, where Peng mentioned that she "came back to Shanghai from the countryside" on May 1, 1968; **Enhua, though . . . as one could get:** Zhang Zhejun, "Peng Enhua qiren."

21. **With dwindling resources . . . wanted from them:** Peng Lingfan, "Wode zizi Lin Zhao," 43; Lin Zhao to mother, March 17, 1967; **Lin Zhao admitted . . . such as toilet tissue:** Lin Zhao to mother, June 12, 1967.

22. **"I have been unable . . . I think of this!":** Lin Zhao to mother, July 14–15, 1967; **"Oh, Lord, Please . . . righteousness triumphs!":** Lin Zhao, "Fuqin de xue."

23. Lin Zhao to mother, November 14, 1967.

24. Ibid., November 15, 1967.

25. Lin Zhao to mother, November 15 and 17, 1967. See also Cheng Tianwu, "Zai yuzhong de endian shenghuo," 140.

26. Lin Zhao to mother, November 16, 1967. This was the first of the two letters to her mother written in blood on the same day. The other one was the routine monthly letter home that prison rules allowed. Lin Zhao did not expect the former to be delivered but was more hopeful that the latter would.

27. Lin Zhao to mother, November 16, 1967. This was her second letter to her mother on the same day.

28. Ibid., November 18, 19, and 20, 1967.

29. Ibid., November 21, 1967.

30. See Lian Xi, *Redeemed by Fire*, chapters 7–8.

31. Chen Yang, "Lin Zhao, Wang Chunyi, Yu Yile"; Lian Xi, *Redeemed by Fire*, chapter 7.

32. Lin Zhao, "Zhuli 1967 nian shiyi yue ershisan ri xueshu shengming" 主历一九六七年十一月二十三日血书声明 (Blood-inked Declaration on November 23, 1967, the Lord's Calendar).

33. See Emily Dickinson, "Much Madness is divinest Sense" (1890).

34. Guo Yukuan 郭宇宽, "Xunzhao Wang Peiying" 寻找王佩英 (Searching for Wang Peiying), *Yanhuang chunqiu* 炎黄春秋 (China through the Ages), 2010, no. 5; Hu Jie, *Wode muqin Wang Peiying*, 我的母亲王佩英 (My Mother Wang Peiying), independent documentary film, 2010.

35. Jiang Tao, "Zhihuijia Lu Hong'en de yisheng"; Wang Youqin, *Wenge shounanzhe*, 296–297. Yao's editorial "Ping 'Sanjiacun'—*Yanshan yehua*, *Sanjiacun zhaji* de fandong benzhi" 评"三家村"—'燕山夜话'、'三家村札记'的反动本质' ("On 'Three-Family Village': The Reactionary Nature of *Evening Chats at Yanshan* and *Notes from Three-Family Village*) was published in *Liberation Daily* on May 10, 1966.

36. Liu Wenzhong, *Fan wenge diyi ren*, 175–176.

37. Liu Wenzhong, *Fan wenge diyi ren*, 180–181; Wang Youqin, *Wenge shounanzhe*, 297; Liu Wenzhong, "Aodili."

38. **Lu had been raised:** Liu Wenzhong, *Fan wenge diyi ren*, 177–178; Liu Wenzhong, interview, Shanghai, May 29, 2016; **On April 27, 1968 . . . in joy":** "Shisi hanwei Maozhuxi geming luxian, shisi hanwei wuchanjieji geming silingbu: benshi juxing gongpan dahui zhenya xianxing fangeming" 誓死捍卫毛主席革命路线 誓死捍卫无产阶级革命司令部: 本市举行公判大会镇压现行反革命 (Defend to the Death the Revolutionary Line of Chairman Mao; Defend to the Death the Proletarian Revolutionary Headquarters: Shanghai Holds Public Sentencing Meeting to Suppress Active Counterrevolutionaries), *Jiefang Ribao* 解放日报 (Liberation Daily), April 28, 1968.

39. Foucault, *Discipline and Punish*, 11.

40. Lin Zhao, "Fuqin de xue." In 1956, Lin Zhao's friend Chen Fengxiao found in the Peking University library Khrushchev's "Secret Speech" published in the *Daily Worker*, organ of the Communist Party of Great British, and apparently shared it with Lin Zhao. See Chen Fengxiao, interview, in Hu Jie, *Xunzhao Lin Zhao de linghun*. See also Nikita S. Khrushchev, "The Secret Speech—On the Cult of Personality, 1956," http://legacy.fordham.edu/halsall/mod/1956khrushchev-secret1.html.

41. Lin Zhao, "XLZG," November 23, 1967.

42. Ibid.

43. Lin Zhao, "Fuqin de xue."

44. Ibid.

45. Lin Zhao to mother, December 16, 1967.

46. Xu Xianmin to Lin Zhao, December 26, 1967.

47. Lin Zhao to mother, January 14, 1968.

48. Kazimiera J. Cottam, *Women in War and Resistance: Selected Biographies of Soviet Women Soldiers* (Newburyport, MA: Focus, 1998), 296–298; Sun Yue 孙越, "Sulian nü yingxiong Zhuoya zhisi" 苏联女英雄卓雅之死 (The

Death of Soviet Heroine Zoya), March 10, 2013, http://sunyue.blog.caixin.com /archives/53903.

49. Lin Zhao to mother, January 14, 1968.

50. Ibid. See chapter 3 on Lin Zhao's relations with Yang Huarong. According to Mr. Zhang (interview, Suzhou, June 11, 2017), he had asked Yang about his relations with Lin Zhao. Yang allegedly denied having had sexual relations with her.

51. **"douse our sorrows . . . cup of Venus"**: Lin Zhao, "Ling'ou xuyu," December 30, 1965; **She now wanted her siblings . . . even sin"**: Lin Zhao to mother, January 14, 1968.

52. Zhang Min, "Lin Zhao baomei."

53. Lin Zhao to mother, January 14, 1968.

54. Ibid.

55. Zeng Yuhuai, interview, May 31, 2016; Mr. Zhang (Suzhou), "Guanyu 'wufenqian zidan fei.'"

56. Shanghai High People's Court records as cited in Mr. Zhang (Suzhou), "Guanyu 'wufenqian zidan fei.'"

57. JGH, "xingshi panjueshu."

58. JGH, "xingshi panjueshu"; Shanghai High People's Court records as cited in Mr. Zhang (Suzhou), "Guanyu 'wufenqian zidan fei.'" For Lin Zhao's last blood writing, see Chen Weisi, "Lin Zhao zhi si." Lin Zhao's death sentence, though given a 1967 serial number, was dated April 19, 1968, the day it was approved by the Shanghai Revolutionary Committee. Zhang Chunqiao was in Shanghai in mid-April 1968 and most likely gave his personal approval when the Shanghai Revolutionary Committee reviewed Lin Zhao's verdict. See Li Haiwen 李海文, "Zhang Chunqiao qiren" 张春桥其人 (Zhang Chunqiao's Character), *Yanhuang chunqiu* 炎黄春秋 (China through the Ages) 2016, no. 1.

59. **By 1968, the Supreme People's Court**: Xu Zhanglun 许章润, ed., *Qinghua Faxue (diqiji): Zuigao Fayuan bijiao yanjiu zhuanji* 清华法学 (第7辑): 最高法院比较研究"专辑 (Qinghua Legal Studies [vol. 7]): Special Volume on a Comparative Study of Supreme Courts) (Beijing: Qinghua University Press, 2006), 41; **Its approval was granted**: Mr. Zhang (Suzhou), "Guanyu 'wufenqian zidan fei.'"

60. **By that time, Lin Zhao**: Hu Jie, *Xunzhao Lin Zhao de linghun*. The unnamed elderly man who served as an inmate housekeeper for Building No. 3 at Tilanqiao, whom Hu Jie interviewed for the documentary film, indicated that Lin Zhao was moved to Building No. 3 in the early spring of 1968. See also Wang Youqin, *Wenge shounanzhe*, 282. Wang Youqin interviewed the same person as Hu Jie did. According to Liu Wenzhong (interview, Shanghai, May 29, 2016), it was customary for a Tilanqiao inmate who was sentenced to death to be moved to a special ward for the condemned immediately after the sentenc-

ing. Lin Zhao's transfer to No. 3 Building was probably connected to the death sentence. According to Yan Zuyou, a former Tilanqiao inmate (interview), political prisoners were held in Building No. 3. Xu Jiajun (interview) doubted that Lin Zhao was moved to Building No. 3, an all-male ward; **A five-story brick structure . . . name into Squadron No. 3:** SHDFZ, *Shanghai jianyu zhi, chapter 12*; Xue Liyong, "Lao Shanghai de jianyu"; Hu Jie, *Xunzhao Lin Zhao de linghun.*

61. Unnamed former inmate housekeeper for Building No. 3 of Tilanqiao, interview, in Hu Jie, *Xunzhao Lin Zhao de linghun*; Wang Youqin, *Wenge shounanzhe*, 282; Liu Wenzhong, *Fan wenge diyi ren*, 183–184. Lu Hong'en was placed in fetters and handcuffed when he was taken away from his cell in preparation for the execution.

62. Zhang Min, "Lin Zhao baomei." On the prison auditorium, see Xu Jiajun, *Tilanqiao jianyu*, 125, 188; Xu Jiajun, interview, Shanghai, June 12, 2017. The auditorium has since been renamed Xin'an Litang, or New Shore Auditorium.

63. Peng Lingfan, "Jiejie!"; Zhang Min, "Lin Zhao baomei." Peng Lingfan interviewed the doctor in the prison hospital during the early 1980s.

64. Wang Youqin, *Wenge shounanzhe*, 282; Zhang Min, "Lin Zhao baomei." See also Yuan Ling, "Tilanqiao li de qiutu." According to Yuan Ling, the "shut-up pear" was made of wood.

65. Lao Mujiang 老木匠, "Youdang zai lao Shanghai" 游荡在老上海 (Wandering about in Old Shanghai), *Minjian lishi* 民间历史 (Folk History), Universities Service Centre for China Studies, The Chinese University of Hong Kong, http://mjlsh.usc.cuhk.edu.hk/Book.aspx?cid=4&tid=324; "Bazi shan" 靶子山 (The Target Ground), http://baike.baidu.com/view/10374524.htm; Shan Miaofa, telephone interview with the author, March 3, 2016. The authorities withheld details of Shan's execution from the family, including the location, but Shan believed that it happened at the Target Ground.

66. Peng Lingfan, "Wode jiejie Lin Zhao," 58–59.

67. **Instead, after the sentencing:** Zeng Yuhuai, interview, Shanghai, May 31, 2016. This revelation accords with Wang Youqin, *Wenge shounanzhe*, 282; Ni Jingxiong, interview, May 5, 2014 (Ni possibly obtained the information from the same source as Wang Youqin); Yuan Ling, "Tilanqiao li de qiutu"; Song Yongyi, e-mail to the author, June 26, 2017. Song cites Helen Yao, a Tilanqiao guard-turned-researcher, as saying that some inmates were executed behind Tilanqiao's auditorium during the Cultural Revolution. Yao believes that Lin Zhao was among those.

68. Lin Zhao, "Kejuan": "Lianxi yi" 练习一 (Exercise No. 1), January 18–20, 1966.

69. "'Zhongguo Gongchandang Zhongyang Weiyuanhui zhuxi Mao Zedong tongzhi zhichi Meiguo heiren kangbao douzheng de shengming' danxing ben waiwenban chuban" "中国共产党中央委员会主席毛泽东同志支持美国黑

人抗暴斗争的声明" 单行本外文版出版 (Foreign-language Editions of the "Statement by Comrade Mao Zedong, Chairman of the Central Committee of the Communist Party of China, in Support of the Afro-American Struggle Against Violent Repression" Published as Pamphlets), *Renmin Ribao* 人民日报 (People's Daily), April 29, 1968. Mao's statement was originally published in Chinese on April 16. The English translation is from https://marxistleninist .wordpress.com/2008/12/26/two-articles-by-mao-zedong-on-the-african -american-national-question/.

70. **The earliest media report:** Mu Qing et al., "Lishi de shenpan"; **The article's source:** Mr. Zhang (Suzhou), "Guanyu 'wufenqian zidan fei.'" Zhang quotes Peng Lingfan as explaining to the Shanghai High People's Court later—as shown in the court records—that she was not present when the five-cent bullet fee was collected, and that she learned of the incident from her mother. See also Peng Lingfan, "Wode jiejie Lin Zhao," 45, 58; Peng Lingfan, "Lin Zhao anjuan." I have used "cent" as a loose translation of *fen*—the Chinese denomination that roughly corresponds to it.

71. Lin Zhao, "ZRMRB," 45. I have also loosely rendered *mao* as "dime."

72. **During the Cultural Revolution:** Liu Wenzhong, e-mail to the author, May 9, 2017; Liu Wenzhong, *Fan wenge diyi ren*, 212–213; **Likewise, after the execution:** Wang Youqin, *Wenge shounanzhe*, 298.

73. Shan Miaofa, "Zhongguo zhengfu"; Shan Miaofa, telephone interview, March 3, 2016. For the Mao quotation, see Mao Zedong, "Zuo yige wanquan de gemingpai" 做一个完全的革命派 (Be a Complete Revolutionary), June 23, 1950. English translation from www.marxists.org/chinese/maozedong/marxist .org-chinese-mao-19500623.htm.

74. Shan Miaofa, "Zhongguo zhengfu"; Shan Miaofa, interview, May 31, 2016.

75. Shan Miaofa, telephone interview, March 3, 2016. Chinese original: "若有来生，我决不愿投胎中国."

76. Song Yongyi, commenting on a draft of this chapter (June 25, 2017), cites Helen Yao, the former Tilanqiao guard-turned-researcher, as saying that it was customary practice for the authorities to demand a bullet fee to pay for the execution of a Tilanqiao inmate during the Cultural Revolution and that Lin Zhao's case was definitely no different. According to Shanghai High People's Court records, cited in Mr. Zhang, "Guanyu 'wufenqian zidan fei,'" a court courier named Jiang Yongkang 姜永康 hand-delivered the notice of Lin Zhao's execution to her home on April 30, 1968, but did not demand a bullet fee. "The reported collection of the bullet fee had nothing to do with the action of this court," added the court records. According to Ni Jingxiong (interview, May 5, 2014), Gu Nianzu 顾念祖, president of Shanghai High People's Court from

1988 to 1993, had told her that the court never collected the bullet fee, but he did not know whether the Public Security Bureau collected it.

Afterword

1. Lin Zhao, "Ji Yang Huarong sanshou." The Beimang Hills north of Luoyang, the ancient capital, were imperial burial grounds. Weiqi, minister of the state of Wei in the third century BCE, took refuge in the house of his friend Lord Pingyuan, chancellor of the state of Zhao, against the vengeful minister of Qin. When King Zhaoxiang of Qin took Lord Pingyuan hostage and demanded that Weiqi be surrendered, he refused. To defuse the crisis for his friend, Weiqi took his own life.

2. Shen Ziyi, "Qimingxing" 启明星 (The Morning Star), in *Shen Zeyi shixuan*, 110. It was composed in 1989 at the time of the Tiananmen Democracy Movement and dedicated to Lin Zhao at the ceremony in 2004 when Lin Zhao's recovered ashes were interred in Suzhou. See also Huazhong Sunan Xinzhuan xiaoyou, *Xiaoyou tongxun*.

3. Wang Ruowang, "Lin Zhao zhi si."

4. **Xu had joined:** Zhang Min, "Lin Zhao baomei"; **However, whatever support . . . execution:** Wang Ruowang, "Lin Zhao zhi si"; Mr. Zhang (Suzhou), "Guanyu 'wufenqian zidan fei'"; Feng Yingzi, "Xu Xianmin ershinian ji." See also Yang Huarong. "Huishou wangshi," 147. Xu Xianmin told Yang in 1968 that Peng Lingfan had been forced to "draw a clear line" between herself and her mother, and rarely came home.

5. Yang Huarong. "Huishou wangshi," 147.

6. Feng Yingzi, "Xu Xianmin ershinian ji." "New Year's Sacrifice" is a well-known short story by Lu Xun.

7. **Whatever her mental state . . . Lin Zhao's death:** Xu Xianmin, "Wo weishenme." Xu claimed that Enhua carried on a bitter feud with Peng Lingfan; **In 1975, on another . . . died three days later:** Zhang Min, "Lin Zhao baomei"; Zhang Min, "Lin Zhao jiuyi 49 zhounian"; Xu Wanyun, account given over the phone, June 13, 2017. Xu Xianmin was taken to Shanghai No. 1 People's Hospital. See also Zhang Yuanxun, "Beida wangshi," in which Zhang, who sometimes embellished his accounts, provided graphic details of Xu's death: "She was bruised all over; her cheeks were swollen, her mouth and nose covered with blood. One of her shoes had been left in the distance; the bamboo basket had been crushed, her bamboo walking stick broken."

8. **In June 1978, a meeting:** Dittmer, *China's Continuous Revolution*, 240; **In February 1979, the party:** Peng Lingfan, "Lin Zhao anjuan."

9. Jiang Fei, "Xunzhao Lin Zhao"; Gan Cui, "Lin Zhao qingren de kousu"; Hu Jie, *Xunzhao Lin Zhao de Linghun*.

10. Zhang Min, "Lin Zhao baomei"; Gan Cui, "Lin Zhao qingren de kousu"; Ni Jingxiong, interview, May 5, 2014. Because of the strained relations in Lin Zhao's family, Peng Lingfan, who lived separately, did not know at the time that Xu Xianmin had collected the ashes and left them at home. After Xu Xianmin's death, Lin Zhao's ashes and those of her parents were kept by her brother Peng Enhua. In the late 1980s, he left to study in the United States, and his wife deposited all the ashes at Shanghai Jiading Huating Xiyuan Cemetery north of Shanghai. Many years later, Ni Jingxiong heard of the ashes, went to the cemetery, and secretly retrieved the ashes (the receipts for the ashes, originally kept by Enhua's family, had been lost) to be buried in Suzhou. For Peng Enhua's departure for studies in the United States, see Zhang Zhejun, "Peng Enhua qiren."

11. Ding Zilin, "Shenshen huainian sangeren."

12. "June Fourth Backgrounder," *Human Rights in China*, www.hrichina.org/en/june-fourth-backgrounder#tm. See also www.tiananmenmother.org/.

13. Hu Jie, *Xunzhao Lin Zhao de linghun*; Pan, *Out of Mao's Shadow*, 21–23.

14. **"So beautiful is the flight of a free soul"**: Liu Xiaobo, "Ziyou linghun"; **"Gasping for breath . . . into your mouth"**: Liu Xiaobo, "Lin Zhao yong shengming."

15. "Liu Xiaobo—Facts," nobelprize.org, www.nobelprize.org/nobel_prizes/peace/laureates/2010/xiaobo-facts.html; Chris Buckley, "Liu Xiaobo, Chinese Dissident Who Won Nobel While Jailed, Dies at 61," *New York Times*, July 13, 2017. Carl von Ossietzky, who had opposed Nazism, won the prize in 1935; he died under guard in 1938. For Liu's sea burial, see Tom Phillips, "Liu Xiaobo: Dissident's Friends Angry after Hastily Arranged Sea Burial," *Guardian*, July 15, 2017.

16. Xu Zhiyong, "Weile ziyou, gongyi, ai."

17. Xu Zhiyong, "Ziyou Zhonghua de xundaozhe."

18. "China Sentences Xu Zhiyong, Legal Activist, to 4 Years in Prison," *New York Times*, January 26, 2014.

19. Cui Weiping, "Ai zhege shijie."

20. Lin Zhao, "Ling'ou xuyu," September 10, 1965.

21. Lin Zhao's cell on the fifth floor of the Women's Block was not one of the specially designed isolation cells, which were on the top floor of Block No. 7. It was instead a regular cell on an almost empty floor, where she was moved sometime after the outbreak of the Cultural Revolution—no later than the beginning of August 1966—so that her shouting and reading of her writings could be somewhat quarantined. See Lin Zhao, "Zhanchang riji," February 11, 1967.

BIBLIOGRAPHY

Abbreviations

The following abbreviations are used in the Notes and Bibliography. Unless otherwise indicated, all of Lin Zhao's writings are from *Lin Zhao Wenji*.

"GRSX"	"Geren sixiang licheng de huigu yu jiancha"
JGH	Zhongguo Renmin Jiefangjun Shanghai Shi Gongjianfa Junshi Guanzhi Weiyuanhui
SHDFZ	Shanghai Shi Difangzhi Bangongshi
SHGY	Shanghai Shi Gaoji Renmin Fayuan
SHLGJ	Shanghai Shi Gong'anju Laogaiju
SJRJY	Shanghai Shi Jing'anqu Renmin Jianchayuan
SNXZ	Su'nan Xinwen Zhuanke Xuexiao biye jiniance bianweihui
"XLZG"	"Xinling de zhange!—wo huyu renlei"
"XSJX"	"Xueshu jiaxin—zhi muqin"
"ZRMRB"	"Zhi *Renmin Ribao* bianjibu xin (zhi san)"

Ai Xiaoming 艾晓明. Interview with the author. Wuhan, November 21–22, 2015.

———. "Lin Zhao yigao yanjiu" 林昭遗稿研究 (Research on Lin Zhao's Manuscripts). *Dongfang lishi pinglun* 东方历史评论 (Oriental Historical Review), February 2014. http://mp.weixin.qq.com/s?__biz=MjM5OTA5MzAwMQ==&mid=200068795&idx=1&sn=ce9064cf74df3a351af221f782fa1aeb&scene=1#rd.

———. "'Yinwei wo xinzhong haiyou ge Lin Zhao'—fang Lin Zhao zhiyou/nanyou Gan Cui" "因为我心中还有个林昭"—访林昭挚友/难友甘粹 ("Because I Still Have Lin Zhao in My Heart": An Interview with Lin Zhao's Close Friend/Fellow Sufferer Gan Cui), 2014. http://aixiaomingstudio.blogspot.com/2014/10/blog-post_42.html.

Bai Hua 白桦. "Cong Qiu Jin dao Lin Zhao" 从秋瑾到林昭 (From Qiu Jin to Lin Zhao). *Wenxue bao* 文学报 (Literary News), November 19, 2009.

Baldwin, James. *Thirty More Famous Stories Retold*. New York: American Book Company, 1905.

Bays, Daniel H., ed. *Christianity in China: From the Eighteenth Century to the Present*. Stanford, CA: Stanford University Press, 1996.

Bays, Daniel H., and Ellen Widmer, eds. *China's Christian Colleges: Cross-Cultural Connections, 1900–1950*. Stanford, CA: Stanford University Press, 2009.

"Beijing Shi Renmin Jianchayuan fenyuan dui Beijing Daxue Chen Fengxiao deng ren de qisushu" 北京市人民检察院分院对北京大学陈奉孝等人的起诉书 (Indictment of Chen Fengxiao and Others of Peking University by the Branch Office of the People's Procuratorate of Beijing), "Jingjian (58) fenfanqizi di 454 hao, 1958.05.17" 京检（58）分反起字第454号, 1958.05.17. In *Qianming Zhongguo youpai de chuli jielun he dang'an*, edited by Song Yongyi.

Birch, Cyril. *Anthology of Chinese Literature: From Early Times to the Fourteenth Century*. New York: Grove Press, 1994.

Bonhoeffer, Dietrich. *Letters and Papers from Prison*. Edited by Eberhard Bethge. Translated by Reginald H. Fuller. New York: MacMillan, 1953.

Bradshaw, Annie Eloise. *China Log*. Self-published book, 1965.

Brinton, Crane. *The Anatomy of Revolution*. New York: Vintage, 1965.

Brown, Oswald Eugene, and Anna Muse Brown. *Life and Letters of Laura Askew Haygood*. Nashville, TN: M. E. Church, South, 1904.

Chang, Yung, and Jon Halliday. *Mao: The Unknown Story*. New York: Anchor Books, 2006.

Chen Fengxiao 陈奉孝. "Wo suo zhidao de Beida zhengfeng fanyou yundong" 我所知道的北大整风反右运动 (The Rectification and Anti-Rightist Campaigns at Peking University That I Know Of), 1998. http://blog.sina.com.cn/s/blog_4e7a94730101lpy3.html.

———. "Xingkaihu jishi" 兴凯湖纪事 (Memories of Xingkai Lake), 2004. http://blog.sina.com.cn/s/blog_a67a0feb0102vo74.html.

Chen Junyuan 陈君远. "Xiaoshi de Jidujiaohui Dengshikou tang" 消失的基督教会灯市口堂 (The Vanished Dengshikou Christian Church), 2012. http://blog.sina.com.cn/s/blog_4aba1d6f010178en.html.

Chen Pixian 陈丕显. *Zai "Yiyue Fengbao" de zhongxin: Chen Pixian huiyilu* 在"一月风暴"的中心：陈丕显回忆录 (At the Center of the "January Storm": A Memoir by Chen Pixian). Shanghai: Shanghi renmin chubanshe, 2005.

Chen Shaojing 陈少京. "Zhang Zhixin de shengqian sihou" 张志新的生前死后" (Zhang Zhixin: Before and after Her Death), 2000. *Zhongguo sixing guancha* 中国死刑观察 (China Monitor). www.chinamonitor.org/article/memory/zzxsqsh.htm.

Chen Shufang 陈叔方. "Lin Zhao er'san shi" 林昭二三事 (A Few Things about Lin Zhao). In *Lin Zhao, buzai bei yiwang*, edited by Xu Juemin.

Chen Weisi 陈伟斯. "Lin Zhao zhi si" 林昭之死 (Lin Zhao's Death). In *Lin Zhao, buzai bei yiwang*, edited by Xu Juemin. Originally published in *Minzhu yu fazhi* 民主与法制 (Democracy and the Rule of Law), March 1981.

———. "Ying gong yuanhun yu, toushu ji yuanyan: Lin Zhao sanshinian ji" 应共冤魂语, 投书寄冤岩—林昭三十年祭 (A Letter Sent to Lingyan to Converse with the Wronged Soul: Remembering Lin Zhao at the Thirtieth Anniversary of Her Death). In *Lin Zhao, buzai bei yiwang*, edited by Xu Juemin.

Chen Yang 陈阳. "Lin Zhao, Wang Chunyi, Yu Yile yiji Zhongguo Jiaohui" 林昭、汪纯懿、俞以勒以及中国教会 (Lin Zhao, Wang Chunyi, Yu Yile, and the Chinese Church), February 5, 2010. http://blog.chenyang.net/?p=711.

Chen Yushan 陈禹山. "Yifen xuexie de baogao—Zhang Zhixin zhi si" 一份血写的报告—张志新之死 (A Report Written in Blood: The Death of Zhang Zhixin), 2006. http://blog.ifeng.com/article/11319894.html.

Chen Zhen 陈箴. "Zhuiqiu yu huanmie: ji Lin Zhao ji qi fumu de beiju" 追求与幻灭—记林昭及其父母的悲剧 (Aspiration and Disillusion: On the Tragedy of Lin Zhao and Her Parents). In *Lin Zhao, buzai bei yiwang*, edited by Xu Juemin.

Cheng, Nien. *Life and Death in Shanghai*. New York: Grove Press, 1986.

Cheng Pei-kai, and Michael Lestz, eds. *The Search for Modern China: A Documentary Collection*. New York: W. W. Norton, 1999.

Cheng Ronghua 程荣华 and Cui Xuefa 崔学法. "Huan shishi yi gongzheng—minguo Pixian xianzhang Peng Guoyan 'lieji bei' kaobian" 还史事以公正—民国邳县县长彭国彦 "劣迹碑"考辨 (Returning Fairness to Historical Accounts: An Examination of the "Inferior [Administrative] Deeds Steele" of Peng Guoyan, Pi County Magistrate of the Republican Era). *Pizhou wenshi* 邳州文史 (Literature and History of Pi County), 2013. http://ishare.iask.sina.com.cn/f/23142388.html.

Cheng Tianwu 程天午. "Zai yuzhong de endian shenghuo—jinian Wang Chunyi jiemei" 在狱中的恩典生活—纪念汪纯懿姐妹 (Life in Prison in God's Grace: Remembering Sister Wang Chunyi). In *Yi che dao zhan: jinian Wang Chunyi* 驿车到站：纪念汪纯懿 (The Stagecoach Arriving at the Station: Remembering Wang Chunyi), edited by Wang Zhongxiao 王忠孝. Los Angeles: Private printing, 2007.

Courtois, Stéphane, et al. *The Black Book of Communism: Crimes, Terror, Repression.* Translated by Jonathan Murphy and Mark Kramer. Cambridge, MA: Harvard University Press, 1999.

Cui Min 崔敏. "Weihuo canlie de 'gong'an liutiao'" 为祸惨烈的 "公安六条" (The Catastrophic "Six Stipulations on Public Security"). *Yanhuang chunqiu* 炎黄春秋 (China through the Ages), 2012.

Cui Weiping 崔卫平. "Ai zhege shijie: 2010 Lin Zhao jinianjiang huojiang ganyan" 爱这个世界—2010年林昭纪念奖获奖感言 (Love This World: Reflections upon Receiving the 2010 Lin Zhao Memorial Prize). *Zonglan Zhongguo* (China in Perspective).

Dikötter, Frank. *Crime, Punishment, and the Prison in Modern China, 1895–1949.* New York: Columbia University Press, 2002.

Ding Shu 丁抒. "Wenge zhong de 'qingli jieji duiwu' yundong: sanqianwan ren bei dou, wushiwan ren siwang" 文革中的 "清理阶级队伍"运动—三千万人被斗，五十万人死亡 (The Campaign to "Purify Class Ranks" during the Cultural Revolution: 30 Million Were Struggled Against; 500 Thousand Died). *Boxun: lishi ziliao* 博讯：历史资料 (Boxun: Historical Sources). https://blog.boxun.com/hero/wenge/91_1.shtml.

———, ed. *Wushi nian hou chongping "Fanyou": Zhongguo dangdai zhishifenzi de mingyun* 五十年后重评 "反右"：中国当代知识分子的命运 (Reexamining the Anti-Rightist Campaign after Fifty Years: The Destiny of Contemporary Chinese Intellectuals). Hong Kong: Tianyuan shuwu, 2007.

———. *Yangmou: fanyoupai yundong shimo* 阳谋：反右派运动始末 (Open Conspiracy: The Complete Story of the Chinese Communist Party's Anti-Rightist Campaign). Rev. ed. Hong Kong: Kaifang zazhi she, 2006.

Ding Zilin 丁子霖. "Shenshen huainian sangeren: 'Liusi' shi'er zhounian ji" 深深怀念三个人— "六四"十二周年祭 (In Deep Memory of Three People: A Memorial on the Twelfth Anniversary of "June Fourth"). *Human Rights in China*, April 8, 2001.

Dittmer, Lowell. *China's Continuous Revolution: The Post-Liberation Epoch, 1949–1981.* Berkeley: University of California Press, 1987.

Djilas, Milovan. *The New Class: An Analysis of the Communist System.* London: Thames and Hudson, 1957.

Fang Wenzhai 房文斋. "Wo wei Lin Zhao pailezhang zhaopian" 我为林昭拍了张照片 (I Took a Picture of Lin Zhao). *Nanfang zhoumo* 南方周末 (The Southern Weekend), March 5, 2009.

———. *Zuoye xifeng diao bishu: Zhongguo Renmin Daxue fanyou yundong qinli ji* 昨夜西风凋碧树：中国人民大学反右运动亲历记 (Last Night the West Wind Withered the Green Trees: My Own Experience of the Anti-Rightist Campaign at Renmin University in China). Taipei: Xinrui wenchuang, 2012.

Feng Peiling 封佩玲. "Wenge zhong de huangtang shi" 文革中的荒唐事 (Absurdities during the Cultural Revolution). *Yanhuang chunqiu* 炎黄春秋 (China through the Ages), 2004, no. 11.

Feng Xigang 冯锡钢. "Wo han relei yi beichou: du Tao Zhu de sanshou qilü" 我含热泪抑悲愁：读陶铸的三首七律 (I Suppressed My Sorrow Despite Tears: On Three Seven-Character Rhymes by Tao Zhu). *Tongzhou gongjin* 同舟共进 (Making Progress Together in the Same Boat), 2011, no. 11. www.xzbu.com/1/view-270943.htm.

Feng Yingzi 冯英子. "Xu Xianmin ershinian ji" 许宪民二十年祭 (On the Twentieth Anniversary of Xu Xianmin's Death). Excerpted from Feng Yingzi, *Fengyu guren lai* 风雨故人來 (The Coming of Friends in Storm). Jinan: Shandong huabao chubanshe, 1998. www.aisixiang.com/data/9647.html.

Foucault, Michel. *Discipline and Punish: The Birth of the Prison*. New York: Pantheon Books, 1977.

———. *Madness and Civilization: A History of Insanity in the Age of Reason*. New York: Vintage, 1988.

Fu Guoyong 傅国湧, ed. *Lin Zhao zhi si: 1932–1968 sishi nian ji* 林昭之死—1932–1968 四十年祭 (In Memoriam: On the Fortieth Anniversary of Lin Zhao's Death). Hong Kong: Kaifang chubanshe, 2008.

Gan Cui. *Beida hun: Lin Zhao yu "Liusi"* 北大魂：林昭与"六四" (The Soul of Peking University: Lin Zhao and the "June Fourth"). Taipei: Xiuwei zixun, 2000.

———. Interview with the author. Beijing, June 2, 2013.

———. "Lin Zhao qingren de kousu: liangge youpai fenzi cong xiangshi dao xiang'ai" 林昭情人的口述：两个右派份子从相识到相爱 (An Oral Account by Lin Zhao's Lover: Two Rightists' Journey from Acquaintance to Love). *Fenghuang zhoukan* 凤凰周刊 (Phoenix Weekly), January 25, 2010.

Gao Hua 高华. *Hong taiyang shi zenyang shengqi de: Yan'an zhengfeng yundong de lailong qumai* 红太阳是怎样升起的：延安整风运动的来龙去脉 (How the Red Sun Rose: The Origins and the Developments of the Yan'an Rectification Campaign). Hong Kong: Chinese University Press, 2000.

Gao Xiang 高翔 (Lin Zhao). "Bupa yazhi, jianchi piping" 不怕压制 坚持批评 (Fear not Suppression; Persist in Criticism). *Changzhou Minbao* (Changzhou People News), February 11, 1953.

Goldman, Merle. *China's Intellectuals: Advise and Dissent.* Cambridge, MA: Harvard University Press, 1988.

———. *Literary Dissent in Communist China.* Cambridge, MA: Harvard University Press, 1967.

Goldman, Merle, Timothy Cheek, and Carol Lee Hamrin, eds. *China's Intellectuals and the State: In Search of a New Relationship.* Cambridge, MA: Harvard University Press, 1987.

Gong Yun 龚云. "Yan'an shiqi dang yu zhishi fenzi de guanxi" 延安时期党与知识分子的关系 (The Party's Interaction with the Intellectuals during the Yan'an Period). *Qiushi* 求是 (Seeking Truth), September 9, 2015.

Grieder, Jerome B. *Intellectuals and the State in Modern China: A Narrative History.* New York: Free Press, 1981.

Guo Yukuan 郭宇宽. "Xunzhao Wang Peiying" 寻找王佩英. *Yanhuang chunqiu* 炎黄春秋 (China through the Ages), 2010, no. 5.

Hanser, Richard. *A Noble Treason: The Story of Sophie Scholl and the White Rose Revolt against Hitler.* San Francisco: Ignatius Press, 2012.

He Fengming 和凤鸣, "1957 Fanyou cuohua le duoshao wan youpai fenzi?" 1957 年错划了多少万右派分子? (How Many Were Wrongfully Denounced as Rightists in 1957?). *Minjian lishi* 民间历史 (Folk History), February 4, 2016. Universities Service Centre for China Studies, Chinese University of Hong Kong. http://mjlsh.usc.cuhk.edu.hk/Book.aspx?cid=4&tid=3392.

Hoffer, Eric. *The True Believer: Thoughts on the Nature of Mass Movements.* New York: Harper & Row, 1951.

Honig, Emily. "Christianity, Feminism, and Communism: The Life and Times of Deng Yuzhi." In *Christianity in China: From the Eighteenth Century to the Present,* edited by Daniel H. Bays.

Hu Jiayi 胡佳逸. "Xiaoxiang li huaxia hongse qidian: Zhonggong Suzhou duli zhibu de jiuwen xindu" 小巷里画下红色起点—中共苏州独立支部的旧闻新读 (The Red Beginning in the Alley: A New Reading of the Old Accounts of the CCP's Independent Cell in Suzhou). *Suzhou Ribao* 苏州日报 (Suzhou Daily), September 30, 2015.

Hu Jie 胡杰. Interview with the author. Nanjing, April 18, 2015.

———. *Xinghuo* 星火 (A Spark of Fire). Independent documentary film. Nanjing, 2013.

———. *Xunzhao Lin Zhao de linghun* 寻找林昭的灵魂 (Searching for Lin Zhao's Soul). Independent documentary film, 2004. dGenerate Films, 2006.

Huang Heqing 黃河清. "Huashuo Lin Zhao" 話說林昭 (Speaking of Lin Zhao). Online publication, 2008. www.peacehall.com/news/gb/lianzai /2008/12/200812220352.shtml.

Huang Yun 黄恽. "Peng Guoyan Pixian an zhenxiang" 彭国彦邳县案真相 (The Truth of Peng Guoyan's Case in Pi County), June 27, 2010. http:// blog.sina.com.cn/s/blog_5e8246090100jqa6.html.

———. "Peng Lingzhao de shengri" 彭令昭的生日 (Peng Lingzhao's Date of Birth), October 14, 2013. http://blog.sina.cn/dpool/blog/s/blog_5e824 6090101ckxj.html.

———. "Peng Lingzhao de shengri yu mingzi" 彭令昭的生日与名字 (The Birthday and Name of Peng Lingzhao), April 30, 2011. http://blog.sina. com.cn/s/blog_5e8246090100r5bt.html.

———. "Xu Xianmin de hunyin" 许宪民的婚姻 (Xu Xianmin's Marriage), October 13, 2009. http://blog.sina.com.cn/s/blog_5e8246090100fjau.html.

Huazhong Sunan Xinzhuan xiaoyou 华中、苏南新专校友 (Alumni of Central China and South Jiangsu Journalism Vocational Schools), eds. *Xiaoyou tongxun* 校友通讯 (Alumni Newsletter) 49 (June 2004).

JGH: Zhongguo Renmin Jiefangjun Shanghai Shi Gongjianfa Junshi Guanzhi Weiyuanhui 中国人民解放军上海市公检法军事管制委员会 (The People's Liberation Army Military Control Committee for Shanghai Municipal Public Security, Procuratorate, and Court systems). "Zhongguo Renmin Jiefangjun Shanghai Shi Gongjianfa Junshi Guanzhi Weiyuanhui xingshi panjueshu 1967 niandu Hu zhongxing (1) zi di 16 hao" 中国人民 解放军上海市公检法军事管制委员会刑事判决书 一九六七年度沪中 刑（一）字第16号 (Verdict Issued by the People's Liberation Army Military Control Committee for Shanghai Municipal Public Security, Procuratorate, and Court systems, [serial number], Shanghai Intermediate Court 1967 [1], no. 16).

Ji Xianlin 季羡林. *Meng ying Weiminghu* 梦萦未名湖 (Dreams Attached to the Unnamed Lake). Edited by Fu Guangming 傅光明 and Xu Jianhua 徐建 华. Wuhan, China: Changjiang wenyi chubenshe, 2006.

Jiang Fei 江菲. "Xunzhao Lin Zhao" 寻找林昭 (Searching for Lin Zhao). *Zhongguo qingnian bao*中国青年报 (China Youth Daily), August 11, 2004.

Jiang Tao 江涛. "Zhihuijia Lu Hong'en de yisheng" 指挥家陆洪恩的一生 (The Life of Conductor Lu Hong'en). *Kaifangwang* 开放网 (Open), August 1, 2009.

Jie Fu 捷夫. "'Nansilafu Gongchanzhuyizhe Lianmeng gangling (cao'an)' pipan" "南斯拉夫共产主义者联盟纲领（草案）" 批判 (A Critique of the "Program of the League of Communists of Yugoslavia [Draft]"). *Wenshizhe* (Literature, History and Philosophy), nos. 10–11 (1958).

Jin Zhong 金钟. "Zuixin Wenge siwang renshu" 最新版文革死亡人数 (The Latest Death Toll for the Cultural Revolution). *Kaifang zazhi* 开放杂志 (Open Magazine), October 7, 2012.

"Jinghai Nüshu" 景海女塾 (Laura Haygood School for Girls). www.yikuaiqu .com/mudidi/detail?scenery_id=91313.

Joseph, William A., Christine P. W. Wong, and David Zweig, eds. *New Perspectives on the Cultural Revolution.* Cambridge, MA: Council on East Asian Studies, Harvard University, 1991.

Kiang, Wen-han. "Secularization of Christian Colleges in China." *Chinese Recorder* 68, no. 5 (May 1937).

Kiely, Jan. *The Compelling Ideal: Thought Reform and the Prison in China, 1901–1956.* New Haven and London: Yale University Press, 2014.

Lacy, G. Carleton. *The Great Migration and the Church in West China: Reports of a Survey Made under the Auspices of the Nanking Theological Seminary and the National Christian Council of China.* Shanghai: Thomas Chu & Sons, 1941.

Lao Mujiang 老木匠. "Youdang zai lao Shanghai" 游荡在老上海 (Wandering about in Old Shanghai). *Minjian lishi* 民间历史 (Folk History). Universities Service Centre for China Studies, Chinese University of Hong Kong. http://mjlsh.usc.cuhk.edu.hk/Book.aspx?cid=4&tid=324.

The Laura Haygood Star 景海星. Vol. 3. Shanghai: American Presbyterian Mission Press, 1922.

Lei, Daphne P. "The Bloodstained Text in Translation: Tattooing, Bodily Writing, and Performance of Chinese Virtue." *Anthropological Quarterly* 82, no. 1 (Winter 2009).

Li Ke 李克. "Beijing Sanzihui" 北京三自会 (The Three-Self Church in Beijing). *Zonglan Zhongguo* 纵览中国 (China in Perspective), February 2012.

Li Maozhang 李茂章. "Liufang qiangu: dao Peng Lingzhao tongzhi" 流芳千古—悼彭令昭同志 (Fame Immortal: Mourning Comrade Peng Lingzhao)." In *Lin Zhao, buzai bei yiwang,* edited by Xu Juemin.

Lian Xi. *The Conversion of Missionaries: Liberalism in American Protestant Missions in China, 1907–1932.* University Park: Pennsylvania State University Press, 1997.

———. *Redeemed by Fire: The Rise of Popular Christianity in Modern China.* New Haven and London: Yale University Press, 2010.

Liao Yiwu 廖亦武. *Zhongguo diceng fangtan lu (xia)* 中国底层采访录 （下） (Interviews at the Bottom of Chinese Society), part 2. www.bannedbook .org/download/downfile.php?id=2140.

Lin Mu 林木. "You yiwei youpai laoren qishi le—Lin Zhao zeng Yang Huarong shi sanshou" 又一位右派老人弃世了—林昭赠羊华荣诗三首 (Another Elderly Rightist Has Departed: On the Three Poems that Lin Zhao Sent to

Yang Huarong). *Dongxiang* 动向 (The Trend), August 2014. http://2new-centurynet.blogspot.com/2014/08/blog-post_55.html.

Lin Zhao 林昭. [annotated] "Qisushu" 起诉书 (Indictment). Appendix 6 of "ZRMRB."

———. "Beifen shi" 悲愤诗 (Poems of Sadness and Rage). Sent to Yang Huarong at the end of 1958.

———. "Canlan de yitian" 灿烂的一天 (A Brilliant Day). *Xin jizhe* 新记者 (The New Journalist) 24 (April 29, 1950).

———. "Di yige yin" 第一个音 (The First Note), December 15–16, 1966.

———. "Diaohuan zhoumi de 'xiju'" 调换粥米的 "喜剧" (The "Comedy" of Switching the Rice Porridge), February 12, 1967.

———. "Fuqin de xue" 父亲的血 (Father's Blood). November 23–30. Blood writing revised and copied in ink, December 1–14, 1967.

———. "GRSX": "Geren sixiang licheng de huigu yu jiancha" 个人思想历程的回顾与检查 (A Review and Examination of My Personal Thought Journey). Writing submitted to the authorities at the Shanghai No. 2 Detention House, October 14, 1961.

———."Hai'ou—bu ziyou wuning si" 海鸥—不自由毋宁死 (Seagull: Give Me Freedom or Give Me Death), 1958–1959.

———. "Ji ling'ou wen (xueshu tiyi)" 祭灵耦文 (血书题衣) (Verse Dedicated to My Spirit Spouse [Blood Writing on Shirt]). Appendix 5 of "ZRMRB."

———. "Ji Yang Huarong sanshou" 寄羊华荣三首 (Three Poems Sent to Yang Huarong). 1958. Annotated by Yang Huarong. http://blog.boxun.com/hero/200801/youpaishiji/33_1.shtml.

———. "Jishi kangyi" 即事抗议 (1–17) (Protests over the Current Condition), October–November 1967.

———. "Jueming shu" 绝命书 (Suicide Note), n.d. (ca. 1958).

———. "Kejuan (wenyi tongxun)" 课卷 (文艺通讯) (Written Homework [Newsletter on Literature and Art]), 1966.

———. Lin Zhao Papers. Stanford, CA: Hoover Institution, Stanford University.

———. *Lin Zhao wenji* 林昭文集 (Collected Writings of Lin Zhao). Shanghai: Private printing, 2013.

———. "Ling'ou xuyu" 灵耦絮语 (Chatters of a Spirit Couple). Edited by Zhu Yi. Unpublished manuscript. Shanghai, 1965–1966.

———. "Panjue hou de shengming (xueshu)" 判决后的声明（血书）(A Personal Statement after the Sentencing [Blood Writing]), June 1, 1965. Appendix 7 of "ZRMRB."

———. "Puluomixiushi shounan de yiri" 普洛米修士受难的一日 (A Day in Prometheus's Passion), 1959.

———. "'Qisushu' bayu (xueshu)" "起诉书" 跋语 (血书) (Foreword to the "Indictment" [Blood Writing]). Appendix 6 of "ZRMRB."

———. "Qiusheng ci bing xu" 秋声辞 并序 (Songs of Autumn's Sounds, and Preface). Appendix 2 of "ZRMRB."

———. "Qiushi aisi" 囚室哀思 (Mourning inside a Jail Cell). Appendix 1 of "ZRMRB."

———. "Qunian sanba" 去年三八 (March 8 of Last Year). *Xin jizhe* 新记者 (The New Journalist) 15 (March 13, 1950).

———. "Shangsushu zhi Lianheguo" 上诉书致联合国 (An Appeal to the United Nations), May 11–14, 1967.

———. "Shishi" 石狮 (The Stone Lion), *Honglou* 红楼 *(The Red Building)*, no. 3 (May 1957).

———. "Shiyue sanshiyi ri xueshu shengming" 十月三十一日血书声明 (Blood-Inked Declaration of October 31), October 31, 1967.

———. "Sidalin guwu women yongyuan qianjin" 斯大林鼓舞我们永远前进 (Stalin Inspires Us to Forever March Forward). *Changzhou Minbao* 常州民报 (Changhzhou People News), March 15, 1953.

———. "Suizhao zhi zhan" 岁朝之战 (Battle on [Chinese] New Year's Day), February 9, 1967.

———. "Tanke" 坦克 (The Tank). *Honglou* 红楼 *(The Red Building)*, no. 1 (January 1957).

———. "Weiminghu pan—jingjizhe yu" 未名湖畔—竞技者语 (Beside the Unnamed Lake: An Athlete's Words), December 14–15, 1966.

———. "XLZG": "Xinling de zhange!—wo huyu renlei" 心灵的战歌！—我呼吁人类 (Battle Song of My Heart and Soul!—I Cry Out to Humanity"), November 23, 1967.

———. "XSJX": "Xueshu jiaxin—zhi muqin" 血书家信—致母亲 (Blood Letters Home—to Mother), October–November 1967.

———. "Xueshi tiyi bing ba" 血诗题衣并跋 (Blood Poems on Shirt and Postscripts). Appendix 4 of "ZRMRB."

———. "Xueyi tiba (xueshu)" 血衣题跋（血书） (Postscripts on Blood-Stained Shirt [Blood Writing]), July 6, 1965. Appendix 8 of "ZRMRB."

———. "Yige youxiu de Shaonian Ertong duiyuan" 一个优秀的少年儿童队员 (An Outstanding Member of the Youth and Children of China). *Changzhou Minbao* 常州民报 (Changhzhou People News), June 1, 1953.

———. "Zhanchang riji" 战场日记 (Battlefield Diaries), February 1967.

———. "Zheshi shenme ge" 这是什么歌 (What Song Is This), May 20, 1957.

———. "Zhongzi: Geming xianlie Li Dazhao xunnan sa zhounian ji" 种籽—革命先烈李大钊殉难卅周年祭 (The Seed: A Tribute to the Revolutionary Martyr Li Dazhao on the Thirtieth Anniversary of His Martyrdom), April 26, 1957. *Honglou* 红楼 (The Red Building), no. 3 (1957).

———. "Zilei" 自诔 (Self Eulogy). Appendix 3 of "ZRMRB."

————. "ZRMRB": "Zhi *Renmin Ribao* bianjibu xin (zhi san)" 致 "人民日报" 编辑部信 (之三) (Letter to the Editorial Board of *People's Daily* [no. 3]), 1965.

Lin Zhao to Lu Zhenhua (Jinsheng), August 1949 to November 1951.

Lin Zhao to Ni Jingxiong ([Shen] Di), November 1950 to December 1952.

Lin Zhao 林昭 and Xuanru 萱如. "Wangchuan yanjing dao jinzhao—ji yige nongmin de kongsu" 望穿眼睛到今朝—记一个农民的控诉 (Waiting Anxiously till This Moment: Documenting a Peasant's Denunciations). *Wenyi xindi* 文艺新地 (New Literature and Arts), August 6, 1950.

Liu Renwen 刘仁文 and Liu Zexin 刘泽鑫. "Xingxun bigong: yuanjiacuo'an de zuikui huoshou" 刑讯逼供：冤假错案的罪魁祸首 (Extorting Confessions by Torture: The Prime Culprit of Miscarriages of Justice). *Zhongguo faxue wang* 中国法学网 (China Institute of Law Net), n.d. www.iolaw.org.cn/showArticle.asp?id=3748.

Liu Wenzhong 刘文忠. "Aodili—mianhuai yinyuejia nanyou Lu Hong'en" 奥地利—缅怀音乐家难友陆洪恩 (Austria—Remembering My Musician Cellmate Lu Hong'en). www.duping.net/XHC/show.php?bbs=10&post=1182707.

————. *Fan wenge diyi ren jiqi tong'anfan* 反文革第一人及其同案犯 (The First Opponent of the Cultural Revolution and His Collaborator). Macau: Chongshi wenhua chuban tuozhan youxian gongsi, 2008.

————. "Fan wenge diyi ren: Shanghai Liu Wenhui zhi si" 反文革第一人：上海刘文辉之死 (The First Opponent of the Cultural Revolution: The Death of Liu Wenhui of Shanghai). www.huanghuagang.org/hhgMagazine/issue17/gb/13.htm.

————. *Fengyu rensheng lu: yige canji kuqiu xinsheng ji* 风雨人生路：一个残疾苦囚新生记 (A Life's Journey through Wind and Rain: The New Birth of a Disabled, Afflicted Inmate). Macau: Chongshi wenhua chuban tuozhan youxian gongsi, 2004.

————. Interview with the author. Shanghai, April 18, 2015.

Liu Xiaobo 刘晓波. "Lin Zhao yong shengming xiejiu de yiyan shi dangdai Zhongguo jincun de ziyou zhi sheng" 林昭用生命写就的遗言是当代中国仅存的自由之声 (Lin Zhao's Last Words, Written with Her Life, Are the Only Voice of Freedom Left for Contemporary China), April 4, 2004. http://blog.boxun.com/hero/liuxb/146_1.shtml.

————. *Liu Xiaobo wenxuan* 刘晓波文选 (Selected Writings of Liu Xiaobo). http://blog.boxun.com/hero/liuxb/.

————. *No Enemies, No Hatred: Selected Essays and Poems.* Edited by Perry Link, Tienchi Martin-Liao, and Liu Xia. Cambridge, MA: Harvard University Press, 2012.

———. "Ziyou linghun de feixiang jing ruci meili" 自由灵魂的飞翔竟如此美丽 (So Beautiful Is the Flight of a Free Soul). *Boxun* 博讯 (Boxun News), August 21, 2005. www.peacehall.com/news/gb/pubvp/2005/08/2005082 12232.shtml.

Li Weimin 李维民. "1955 nian sufan kuodahua de jiaoxun" 1955 年肃反扩大化的教训 (Lessons from the Excesses during the Elimination of Counterrevolutionaries Campaign of 1955). *Yanhuang Chunqiu* 炎黄春秋 (China through the Ages), 2011, no. 2.

Li Xia'en 李夏恩. "Hai Rui mu: yiwei Ming dai qingguan zai Mao Zedong shidai de zaoyu" 海瑞墓：一位明代清官在毛泽东时代的遭遇 (The Tomb of Hai Rui: What Befell an Incorruptible Ming Dynasty Official during the Mao Zedong Era). *Gongshiwang* 共识网 (Consensus Web), April 5, 2016. www.21ccom.net/html/2016/xiandai_0405/2983.html.

Li-Yi-Zhe 李一哲. "Guanyu shehui zhuyi de minzhu yu fazhi" 关于社会主义的民主与法制 (On Socialist Democracy and Legal System). In *Wenhua Dageming he tade yiduan sichao*, edited by Song Yongyi and Sun Dajin.

Li Zhisui 李志绥. *Mao Zedong siren yisheng huiyilu* 毛泽东私人医生回忆录. Taipei: Shibao wenhua chubanshe, 1994.

Lu Xun 鲁迅. "Yao" 药 (Medicine). *Xin qingnian* 新青年 (New Youth) 6, no. 5 (May 1919).

———. "Zixu" 自序 (Author's Preface), *Nahan* 呐喊 (Call to Arms), 1922.

Lu Zhenhua 陆震华. "Lin Zhao sanshiyi nian ji" 林昭三十一年祭 (On the Thirty-First Anniversary of Lin Zhao's Death). In *Lin Zhao, buzai bei yiwang*, edited by Xu Juemin.

Ma Jingyuan 马静元 and Leng Xin 冷辛. "Lin Zhao shi 'Guangchang' de Muhou moushi" 林昭是 "广场"的幕后谋士 (Lin Zhao Is the Strategist behind the Scene for "The Square"). *Honglou: Fan youpai douzheng tekan* 红楼：反右派斗争特刊 (Honglou: Special Edition on the Anti-Rightist Struggle) 2 (July 8, 1957). In *Lin Zhao zhi si: 1932–1968 sishi nian ji*, edited by Fu Guoyong.

MacFarquhar, Roderick. *The Origins of the Cultural Revolution.* Vols. 1–3. New York: Columbia University Press, 1974, 1983, 1999.

MacFarquhar, Roderick, and John K. Fairbank, eds. *The Cambridge History of China.* Vol. 14: *The People's Republic, Part 1: The Emergence of Revolutionary China, 1949–1965.* New York: Cambridge University Press, 1987.

MacFarquhar, Roderick, and Michael Schoenhals. *Mao's Last Revolution.* Cambridge, MA: Harvard University Press, 2006.

Marsh, Charles. *Strange Glory: A Life of Dietrich Bonhoeffer.* New York: Alfred A. Knopf, 2014.

Mazur, Mary G. *Wu Han, Historian: Son of China's Times.* Lanham, MD: Lexington Books, 2009.

Mei Ling 梅龄 and Ling Zhao 令昭. "Women xiangqin xiang'ai jiuxiang xiongdi jiemei" 我们相亲相爱就像兄弟姐妹 (We Love One Another Like Brothers and Sisters), *Su'nan dazhong* 苏南大众 (The South Jiangsu Public) 3, no. 1 (1951).

Methodist Episcopal Church, South. *Minutes, Fourth Session, East China Annual Conference of the Methodist Church.* Soochow, January 1–4, 1948. Archives of the General Commission on Archives and History for the United Methodist Church, Madison, NJ.

Miller, Nick. *The Nonconformists: Culture, Politics, and Nationalism in a Serbian Intellectual Circle, 1944–1991.* Budapest, Hungary: Central European University Press, 2008.

Mu Qing 穆青, Guo Chaoren 郭超人, and Lu Fowei 陆拂为. "Lishi de shenpan" 历史的审判 (Sentencing by History). *Renmin Ribao* 人民日报 (People's Daily), January 27, 1981.

"Naxie 'xuyao bei laojiao' de ren" 那些 "需要被劳教" 的人 (Those Who "Needed to be Reeducated through Labor"), November 20, 2013. http://slide.news.sina.com.cn/j/slide_1_45272_37772.html#p=1.

Ni Jingxiong 倪竞雄. Interview with the author. Shanghai, June 12, 2013.

———. Interview with the author. Shanghai, May 5, 2014.

———. Interview with the author. Shanghai, June 13, 2017.

———. "Shaodiao meishi, yaoji yingling" 沙雕美食 遥寄英灵 (Sand Sculptures and Delicious Food: An Offering to the Heroic Soul). In *Lin Zhao, buzai bei yiwang,* edited by Xu Juemin.

Nietzsche, Friedrich. *Thus Spake Zarathustra: A Book for All and None.* North Charlestown, SC: CreateSpace, 2012. First published 1887.

Niu Han 牛汉, and Deng Jiuping 邓九平, eds. *Yuanshang cao: jiyi zhong de fanyoupai yundong.* 原上草: 记忆中的反右派运动 (Grass on the Prairie: The Anti-Rightist Movement Remembered). Beijing: *Jingji Ribao* chubanshe, 1998.

Ouyang Ying 欧阳英 [Lin Zhao 林昭]. "Dai he dai" 代和代 (Between Generations). *Chusheng* 初生 (The Newborn), no. 3 (June 1, 1947).

———. "Huanghun zhi lei" 黄昏之泪 (Tears at Dusk). *Chusheng* 初生 (The Newborn), no. 2 (May 1, 1947).

Pan, Philip P. *Out of Mao's Shadow: The Struggle for the Soul of a New China.* New York: Simon & Schuster, 2009.

Pearce, Joseph. *Solzhenitsyn: A Soul in Exile.* Rev. ed. San Francisco: Ignatius Press, 2011.

"Peng Guoyan qing pingfan yuanyu: Gaofayuan tingshen pangtingji "彭国彦请平反冤狱—高法院庭审旁听记 (Peng Guoyan Demands Reversal of the Miscarriage of Justice: Auditing the Court Hearing at the High Court). Compiled by Huang Yun from *Suzhou Mingbao* 苏州明报, June 1934. http://blog.sina.cn/dpool/blog/s/blog_5e8246090100ki2x.html.

Peng Lingfan 彭令范. "Jiejie! Ni shi wo xinzhong yongyuan de tong" 姐姐！你是我心中永远的痛 (Elder Sister! You Are That Eternal Ache in My Heart). *Jinri mingliu* 今日名流 (Contemporary Celebrities), 1998, no. 5. http://tw.aboluowang.com/2007/0208/29631.html.

———. "Lin Zhao anjuan de lailongqumai" 林昭 案卷的来龙去脉 (The Whence and Whither of the Lin Zhao File). *Nanfang zhoumo* 南方周末 (Southern Weekend), November 14, 2013.

———. "Wo fumu he Lin Zhao de mudi" 我父母和林昭的墓地 (My Parents' and Lin Zhao's Tomb). *Nanfang zhoumo* 南方周末 (Southern Weekend), November 29, 2013.

———. "Wode jiejie Lin Zhao" 我的姐姐林昭 (上、下) (My Elder Sister Lin Zhao [1–2]). In *Lin Zhao, buzai bei yiwang*, edited by Xu Juemin.

———. "Wode zizi Lin Zhao" 我的姊姊林昭 (My Elder Sister Lin Zhao). In *Zoujin Lin Zhao*, edited by Xu Juemin.

———. "Zai sixiang de lianyu zhong yongsheng" 在思想的煉獄中永生 (Eternal Life in the Purgatory of Thought). In *Zoujin Lin Zhao*, edited by Xu Juemin.

Peng Lingzhao 彭令昭 (Lin Zhao). "Chang 1950 nian" 唱一九五〇年 (Singing of the Year 1950). *Su'nan dazhong* 苏南大众 (South Jiangsu Public) 3, no. 1 (1951).

———. "Wo de xiegao tiyan" 我的写稿体验 (My Experience in Writing Press Releases). *Xin jizhe* 新记者 (The New Journalist), February 26, 1950.

———. "Wo zenyang renshi 'sixiang jiancha' de zhongyao" 我怎样认识'思想检查'的重要 (How I Came to Realize the Importance of "Thought Examination"). *Xin jizhe* 新记者 (The New Journalist) 5, no. 3 (January 15, 1950).

———. "Xiao meimei qu song canjunlang" 小妹妹去送参军郎 (Little Sister Seeing off the Army Recruit). *Su'nan dazhong* 苏南大众 (South Jiangsu Public) 3, no. 8 (1951).

———. "Zai laodong zhanxian shang" 在劳动战线上 (On the Battlefront of Labor). *Su'nan dazhong* 苏南大众 (South Jiangsu Public) 3, no. 1 (1951).

Qian Jiang 钱江. "Wenge qianxi de *Renmin Ribao*" 文革前夕的 "人民日报" (People's Daily on the Eve of the Cultural Revolution). *Zhongguo Gongchandang xinwenwang* 中国共产党新闻网 (News Net of the Communist Party of China). *http://cpc.people.com.cn/BIG5/85037/85038/7394420.html*.

Qian Liqun 钱理群. "Burong mosha de sixiang yichan" 不容抹杀的思想遗产 (The Intellectual Legacy That Cannot Be Denied). In *Yuanshang cao: jiyi zhong de fanyoupai yundong*, edited by Niu Han and Deng Jiuping.

Qian Timing 钱惕明, Shi Hong 史洪, Ye Qiang 叶强, and Wang Run 王润. "Jinri honghua fa—yi Lin Zhao tongzhi" 今日红花发—忆林昭同志 (Red

Flowers Blossoming Today: Remembering Comrade Lin Zhao). In *Lin Zhao, buzai bei yiwang*, edited by Xu Juemin.

Qu Qiubai 瞿秋白. "E'xiang jicheng—xin E'guo youji" 饿乡纪程—新俄国游记. In *Qu Qiubai wenxuan* 瞿秋白文选 (Selected Writings of Qu Qiubai), edited by Lin Wenguang 林文光. Chengdu: Sichuan wenyi chubanshe, 2009.

Ren Feng 任锋 (Lin Zhao). "Dang, wo huhuan . . ." 党，我呼唤 . . . (Party, I Call Out to You), May 22, 1957.

———. "Xiaxiang qian de jitian" 下乡前的几天 (A Few Days before Going Down to the Countryside). *Xin jizhe* 新记者 (The New Journalist), no. 2 (August 12, 1949).

Rummel, R. J. *China's Bloody Century: Genocide and Mass Murder since 1900*. New Brunswick, NJ: Transaction Publishers, 1991.

Schneider, Laurence A. *A Madman of Ch'u: The Chinese Myth of Loyalty and Dissent*. Berkeley: University of California Press, 1980.

Schwarcz, Vera. *The Chinese Enlightenment: Intellectuals and the Legacy of the May Fourth Movement of 1919*. Berkeley: University of California Press, 1990.

Shan Miaofa 单庙法. Interview with the author. Shanghai, May 31, 2016.

———. Telephone interview with the author. March 3, 2016.

———. "Zhongguo zhengfu zai Wenhua Dageming qijian dui zhengzhifan de sixing panjue" 中国政府在文化大革命期间对政治犯的死刑判决 (The Death Sentence of a Political Prisoner Issued by the Chinese Government during the Cultural Revolution), May 6, 2008. www.boxun.com/news/gb /china/2008/05/200805061344.shtml.

"Shanghai tan de jinmi zhidi: 'yuandong diyi jianyu' Tilanqiao" 上海滩的禁秘之地："远东第一监狱"提篮桥 (A Forbidden Place near the Bund: Tilanqiao, the "Number One Prison in the Far East"). *Meijingwang* 每经网 (Daily Economic News), October 9, 2013. www.nbd.com.cn/articles /2013-10-09/778418.html?all_page=true.

SHDFZ: Shanghai Shi Difangzhi Bangongshi. 上海市地方志办公室 (Office of the Local Chronicles of Shanghai). *Shanghai gong'an zhi: di shi'erpian, yusheng he kanshou* 上海公安志 第十二编预审和看守 (Chronicles of Shanghai Public Security Bureau: No. 12, Pretrial and Detention). http:// shtong.gov.cn/node2/node2245/node4476/node58292/index.html.

———. *Shanghai jianyu zhi* 上海监狱志 (Chronicles of Shanghai's Prison System). www.shtong.gov.cn/node2/node2245/node73095/index.html.

———. *Shanghai quxian zhi* 上海区县志 (Chronicles of Districts and Counties of Shanghai). www.shtong.gov.cn/node2/node4/index.html.

———. *Shanghai shenpan zhi* 上海审判志 (Chronicles of Court Sentencings in Shanghai). Chapter 2: "Fangeming anjian shenpan" 反革命案件审判

(Sentencings of Counterrevolutionary Cases). www.shtong.gov.cn/node2/node2245/node81324/node81331/node81380/index.html.

Shen Zeyi 沈泽宜. "Beida, wuyue shijiu ri" 北大，五月十九日 (Peking University, May 19). Unpublished memoir, 2006.

———. Interview with the author. Huzhou, Zhejiang, July 15, 2014.

———. *Shen Zeyi shixuan* 沈泽宜诗选 (Selected Poems of Shen Zeyi). Guangzhou: Huacheng chubanshe, 2009.

———. "Wo xiang renmin qingzui" 我向人民请罪 (I Plead for Forgiveness from the People). In Zhang Yuanxun, *Beida, 1957*.

———. "Wu fu, wu xiang" 吾父，吾乡 (My Father and My Hometown). Unpublished memoir, 2012.

———. "Xuedi zhi deng—huainian Lin Zhao" (Lamplight in the Snowy Fields—Remembering Lin Zhao). In *Shen Zeyi shixuan*.

Shen Zhihua 沈志华. *Sikao yu xuanze: cong zhishi fenzi huiyi dao fanyoupai yundong (1956–1957)* 思考与选择：从知识分子会议到反右派运动 (1956–1957) (Reflections and Choices: The Consciousness of the Chinese Intellectuals and the Anti-Rightist Campaign [1956–1957]). Hong Kong: Chinese University of Hong Kong Press, 2008.

SHGY: Shanghai Shi Gaoji Renmin Fayuan 上海市高级人民法院 (Shanghai High People's Court). "Shanghai Shi Gaoji Renmin Fayuan xingshi panjueshu"上海市高级人民法院刑 事判决书 (Shanghai High People's Court Criminal Case Verdict), August 22, 1980. (80) Hu gaoxing fuzi di 435 hao（80）沪高刑复字第435号 (1980 Shanghai High People's Court Re-examination No. 435).

———. "Shanghai Shi Gaoji Renmin Fayuan xingshi panjueshu"上海市高级人民法院刑 事判决书 (Shanghai High People's Court Criminal Case Verdict), December 30, 1981. (81) Hu gaoxing shenzi di 2346 hao（81）沪高刑申字第2346号 (1981 Shanghai High People's Court Appeals No. 2346).

SHLGJ: Shanghai Shi Gong'anju Laogaiju 上海市公安局劳改局 (Reform through Labor Bureau of Shanghai Municipal Public Security Bureau). "Lin Zhao an jiaxing cailiao" 林昭案加刑材料 (Materials in Support of the Additional Penalty in Lin Zhao's Case), (December[?]) 1966.

Sikorski, Grazyna. *Jerzy Popieluszko: Victim of Communism*. Kindle edition. Catholic Truth Society, 2017.

SJRJY: Shanghai Shi Jing'anqu Renmin Jianchayuan 上海市静安区人民检察院 (People's Procuratorate of Jing'an District, the Municipality of Shanghai). "Qisushu" 起诉书 (64) (Indictment [64]), Hujingjiansuzi di 423 hao 沪静检诉字第四二三号 (Shanghai Jing'an District Procuratorate Indictment Document No. 423).

Snow, Edgar. *Red Star Over China*. Rev. and enl. ed. New York: Grove Press, 1968. First published 1938.

SNXZ: Su'nan Xinwen Zhuanke Xuexiao biye jiniance bianweihui 苏南新闻专科学校毕业纪念册编委会 (Editing Committee of South Jiangsu Journalism Vocational School Graduation Yearbook). *Su'nan Xinwen Zhuanke Xuexiao biye jiniance* 苏南新闻专科学校毕业纪念册 (South Jiangsu Journalism Vocational School Graduation Yearbook), n.d. (1950?). http://blog.sina.com.cn/s/blog_580296780102vpko.html.

Song Yongyi 宋永毅, ed. *Qianming Zhongguo youpai de chuli jielun he dang'an (1)* 千名中国右派的处理结论和个人档案 (1) (Conclusions on the Handling of One Thousand Chinese Rightists and Their Individual Files, No. 1). E-book. Guoshi chubanshe, 2015. www.mingjingnews.com/MIB/ebook/book.aspx?TID=1&ID=E00001463.

———. "Wenge zhong 'fei zhengchang siwang' le duoshao ren?" 文革中"非正常死亡"了多少人？ (How Many People Died "Abnormal Deaths" during the Cultural Revolution?). *Dongxiang* 动向 (The Trend), no. 9 (2011).

———, ed. *Wenhua Dageming: lishi zhenxiang he jiti jiyi* 文化大革命：历史真相和集体记忆 (The Great Cultural Revolution: Historical Truths and the Collective Memory). Vols. 1–2. Hong Kong: Tianyuan shuwu, 2010.

Song Yongyi et al., eds. *Zhongguo Fanyou Yundong shujuku* 中国反右运动数据库 (Chinese Anti-Rightist Campaign Database). Hong Kong: Universities Service Centre for China Studies, Chinese University of Hong Kong, 2013.

———. *Zhongguo Wenhua Dageming wenku* 中国文化大革命文库 (Chinese Cultural Revolution Database). Hong Kong: Universities Service Centre for China Studies, Chinese University of Hong Kong, 2013.

———. *Zhongguo wushi niandai chuzhongqi de zhengzhi yundong shujuku: cong tudi gaige dao gongsi heying* 中国五十年代初中期的政治运动数据库：从土地改革到公私合营，1949–1956 (Database of the Chinese Political Campaigns in the 1950s: From Land Reform to State-Private Partnership). Cambridge, MA: Fairbank Center for Chinese Studies, Harvard University, 2014.

Song Yongyi 宋永毅 and Sun Dajin 孙大进, eds. *Wenhua Dageming he tade yiduan sichao* 文化大革命和它的异端思潮 (Heterodox Thoughts during the Cultural Revolution). Hong Kong: Tianyuan shuwu, 1997.

Spence, Jonathan D. *The Gate of Heavenly Peace: The Chinese and Their Revolution, 1895–1980*. New York: Penguin Books, 1981.

———. *The Search for Modern China*. 2nd ed. New York and London: W. W. Norton, 1999.

Stuart, John Leighton. *Fifty Years in China: The Memoirs of John Leighton Stuart, Missionary and Ambassador*. New York: Random House, 1954.

Sun Wenshuo 孙文铄. "Xuejian luoqun zhidao cun—jinian Lin Zhao tongxue jiuyi sayi zhounian" 血溅罗裙直道存—纪念林昭同学就义卅一周年 (The Silk Skirt Is Spattered with Blood but the Path of the Upright Remains—Commemorating the Thirty-First Anniversary of the Martyrdom of My Classmate Lin Zhao). In *Lin Zhao, buzai bei yiwang*, edited by Xu Juemin.

Sun Yancheng 孙言诚. "Guo Moruo he Qin Shihuang" 郭沫若和秦始皇 (Guo Moruo and the First Emperor of Qin). *Lishi xuejia chazuo* 历史学家茶座 (Teahouse for Historians), 2009, no. 1. http://history.people.com.cn/GB /205396/17294309.html.

Sun Yingqing 孙迎庆. "Tiancizhuang: Peiyang shunü de Jinghai Nüshi" 天赐庄：培养淑女的景海女师 (Tianci Village: The Laura Haygood Memorial School for Girls That Cultivated Ladies). *Gusu Wanbao* 姑苏晚报 (Gusu Evening Newspaper), February 8, 2009.

Tan Chanxue 谭蝉雪. Interview with the author. Shanghai, July 16, 2014.

———. Interview with the author. Shanghai, April 27, 2015.

———. Interview with the author. Shanghai, June 13, 2017.

———. *Qiusuo: Lanzhou Daxue "Youpai fangeming jituan an" jishi* 求索—兰州大学 "右派反革命集团案"记实 (The Quest: An Account of the Lanzhou University "Rightist Counterrevolutionary Clique" Case). Hong Kong: Tianma chubanshe, 2010.

Tan Tianrong 谭天荣. "Di'er zhu ducao" 第二株毒草 (The Second Poison Weed). In *Yuanshang cao: jiyi zhong de fanyoupai yundong*, edited by Niu Han and Deng Jiuping.

———. "Yige meiyou qingjie de aiqing gushi—huiyi Lin Zhao" 一个没有情节的爱情故事—回忆林昭 (A Love Story without a Plot: Remembering Lin Zhao). In *Zoujin Lin Zhao*, edited by Xu Juemin.

Troeltsch, Ernst. *The Social Teaching of the Christian Churches*. 2 vols. Translated by Olive Wyon. Reprint. Louisville, KY: Westminster/John Knox Press, 1992. First published 1931.

Twitchett, Dennis, and John K. Fairbank, eds. *The Cambridge History of China*. Vol. 15: *The People's Republic of China, Part 2: Revolutions within the Chinese Revolution, 1966–1982*. Cambridge, UK: Cambridge University Press, 1991.

Unger, Jonathan. "Whither China? Yang Xiguang, Red Capitalists, and the Social Turmoil of the Cultural Revolution." *Modern China* 17, no. 1 (1991): 3–37.

Walder, Andrew G. *China Under Mao: A Revolution Derailed*. Cambridge, MA: Harvard University Press, 2015.

———. "Cultural Revolution Radicalism: Variations on a Stalinist Theme." In *New Perspectives on the Cultural Revolution*, edited by William A. Joseph,

Christine P. W. Wong, and David Zweig. Cambridge, MA: Council on East Asian Studies, Harvard University, 1991.

Wang Guoxiang 王国乡. "Beida minzhu yundong jishi" 北大民主运动纪事 (Documenting the Democratic Movement at Peking University). In *Yuanshang cao: jiyi zhong de fanyoupai yundong*, edited by Niu Han and Deng Jiuping.

Wang Ningsheng 汪宁生. "Lin Zhao yinxiang" 林昭印象 (Lin Zhao Impressions). *Lao Zhaopian* 老照片 (Old Photos), no. 79 (November 1, 2011). www.lzp1996.com/mrys/20111101/609_2.html.

Wang Rongfen 王容芬. "Wo zai yuzhong de rizi" 我在狱中的日子 (My Days in Prison). www.secretchina.com/news/gb/2017/03/20/817410.html.

Wang Rui 王锐. "Zhou Enlai yü 'Yida Sanfan' yundong" 周恩来与"一打三反"运动 (Zhou Enlai and the "One Strike, Three Anti" campaign). *Jiyi* 记忆 (Remembrance), no. 56 (September 13, 2010). http://prchistory.org/wp-content/uploads/2014/05/REMEMBRANCE-No-57-2010%E5%B9%B49%E6%9C%8813%E6%97%A5.pdf.

Wang Ruowang 王若望. "Lin Zhao zhi si" 林昭之死 (The Death of Lin Zhao). Excerpted from *Wang Ruowang zizhuan* 王若望自傳 (An Autobiography of Wang Ruowang). Hong Kong: Mingbao chubanshe, 1991. www.huanghuagang.org/hhgMagazine/issue11/big5/14.htm.

Wang Youqin 王友琴. "Cong shounanzhe kan fanyou he wenge de guanlian: yi Beijing Daxue weili" 从受难者看反右和文革的关联：以北京大学为例 (Examining the Connections between the Anti-Rightist Campaign and the Cultural Revolution by Looking at the Victims: Peking University as a Case Study), 2007. www.cnd.org/HXWK/author/WANG-Youqin/zk0709f-0.gb.html.

———. "Cuihui riji de geming" 摧毁日记 的革命 (The Revolution That Destroyed Diaries). *Huanghuagang zazhi* 黄花岗杂志 (Huanghuagang Magazine) 18 (2006, no. 3). www.huanghuagang.org/hhgMagazine/issue18/gb/17.htm.

———. "Kongbu de 'Hong bayue'" 恐怖的 "红八月" (The Terror-filled "Red August"). *Yanhuang chunqiu* 炎黄春秋 (China through the Ages), 2010, no. 10.

———. *Wenge shounanzhe: guanyu pohai, jianjin yu shalu de xunfang shilu* 文革受难者： 关于迫害、监禁与杀戮的寻访实录 (Victims of the Cultural Revolution: An Investigative Account of Persecution, Imprisonment, and Murder). Hong Kong: Kaifang zazhi chubanshe, 2004.

Wang Zhongxiao 王忠孝, ed. *Yi che dao zhan: jinian Wang Chunyi* 驿车到站： 纪念汪纯懿. (The Stagecoach Arriving at the Station: Remembering Wang Chunyi). Los Angeles: Private printing, 2007.

Weber, Max. *The Religion of China: Confucianism and Taoism.* Translated by Hans H. Gerth. Glencoe, IL: Free Press, 1951.

Wei Chengsi 魏承思. *Zhongguo zhishi fenzi de chenfu* 中国知识分子的沉浮 (The Ups and Downs of Intellectuals in China). Hong Kong: Oxford University Press, 2004.

Wei Zidan 魏紫丹. "Mao Zedong yinshe chudong kao" 毛泽东 "引蛇出洞"考 (On Mao Zedong's "enticing snakes out of their lairs"). http://blog.boxun .com/hero/200811/weizidan2005/1_1.shtml.

Wen Miao 文庙. "Lin Zhao baodi—wenxue dashi Peng Enhua chuanqi (shang, xia)" 林昭胞弟—文学大师彭恩华传奇 (The Legend of Peng Enhua, Lin Zhao's Brother and a Literary Master [1, 2]). www.creaders.net /m/blog/user_blog_diary.php?did=149497; http://blog.creaders.net/u /5129/201305/149752.html.

"'Wenge' ruhe fasheng: Mao Zedong cong tichang Hui Rui dao pipan *Hai Rui baguan* de zhuanbian" "文革" 如何发生：毛泽东从提倡海瑞到批判 "海瑞罢官" 的转变 (How the "Cultural Revolution" Happened: Mao Zedong's Switch from Promoting Hui Rui to Criticizing *Hui Rui Dismissed from Office*). http://history.people.com.cn/n/2015/0522/c372327-27043416-2.html. Excerpted from *Hu Qiaomu zhuan* 胡乔木传 (A Biography of Hu Qiaomu), compiled by Hu Qiaomu zhuanji bianxiezu 胡乔木传记编写组 (Compilers of the Biography of Hu Qiaomu). Beijing: Dangdai Zhongguo chubanshe and Renmin chubanshe, 2015.

West, Philip. *Yenching University and Sino-Western Relations, 1916–1952.* Cambridge, MA: Harvard University Press, 1976.

Wickeri, Philip L. *Reconstructing Christianity in China: K. H. Ting and the Chinese Church.* Maryknoll, NY: Orbis Books, 2007.

Wu Lengxi 吴冷西. *Yi Maozhuxi—wo suo qinshen jingli de ruogan zhongda lishi shijian pianduan* 忆毛主席—我亲身经历的若干重大历史事件片断 (Remembering Chairman Mao: Fragments of Major Historical Events I Personally Experienced). Beijing: Xinhua chubanshe, 1995.

Wu Rong 吴镕. "Xinjizhe de yaolan: yiwei Sunan Huazhong xinwen zhuanke xuexiao biyesheng de huiyi" 新记者的摇篮——一位苏南、华中新闻专科学校毕业生的回忆 (The Cradle for New Journalists: The Memory of a Graduate from South Jiangsu Journalism Vocational School). *Renmin Zhengxie wang* 人民政协网 (People's Political Consultative Conference Net), July 5, 2012. http://blog.sina.com.cn/s/blog_487d902d0102eh0e.html.

Wu Yaozong. *Meiyou ren kanjian guo Shangdi* 没有人看见过上帝 (Nobody Has Seen God). Shanghai: Qingnian xiehui shuju, 1947.

Xiao Donglian 萧冬连, et al. *Qiusuo Zhongguo: Wenge qian shinian shi* 求索中国：文革前十年史 (Searching for China: A History of Ten Years before the Cultural Revolution). Beijing: Zhonggong dangshi chubanshe, 2011.

Xie Yong 谢泳. "*Honglou* zazhi yanjiu" "红楼" 杂志研究 (A Study of the Journal *The Red Building*), 2008. *Ai sixiang* 爱思想 (In Love with Ideas). www.aisixiang.com/data/20984.html.

———. "*Honglou* zazhi zhong de Lin Zhao shiliao" "红楼" 杂志中的林昭史料 (Lin Zhao Materials in the Journal *The Red Building*). In *Lin Zhao zhi si*, edited by Fu Guoyong.

Xu Jiajun 徐家俊. Interview with the author. Shanghai, June 12, 2017.

———. *Shanghai jianyu de qianshi jinsheng* 上海监狱的前世今生 (Shanghai Prisons: Past and Present). Shanghai: Shanghai shehui kexueyuan chubanshe, 2015.

———. "Shanghai shi Tilanqiao jianyu" 上海市提篮桥监狱 (Shanghai Tilanqiao Prison). Beijing: Zhongguo wenshi chubanshe, 2011.

———. "Shanghai shi Tilanqiao jianyu" 上海市提篮桥监狱 (Shanghai Tilanqiao Prison). *Shanghai difang zhi* 上海地方志 (Chronicles of Shanghai). www.shtong.gov.cn/node2/node70393/node70403/node72472/node72476/userobject1ai80856.html.

"Xu Jinyuan" 许金元. *Jiangsusheng difangzhi* 江苏省地方志 (Chronicles of Jiangsu Province). www.jssdfz.com/book/jsrwz_rwz2/HTM/Noname0882.htm.

Xu Juemin 许觉民, ed. *Lin Zhao, buzai bei yiwang* 林昭，不再被遗忘 (Lin Zhao, No Longer Forgotten). Wuhan: Changjiang wenyi chubanshe, 2000.

———, ed. *Zhuixun Lin Zhao* 追寻林昭 (In Search of Lin Zhao). Wuhan: Changjiang wenyi chubanshe, 2000.

———, ed. *Zoujin Lin Zhao* 走近林昭 (Walking toward Lin Zhao). Hong Kong: Mingbao chubanshe, 2006.

Xu Wanyun 许宛云. Phone interview with Shen Liangmiao 沈良苗 and the author, June 13, 2017.

Xu Xianmin 许宪民. "Wo weishenme bei qinsheng erzi duda jiuci?" 我为什么被亲生儿子毒打九次？ (Why Was I Savagely Beaten by My Own Son Nine Times?). Personal written testimony entrusted to Yan Qianli 严倩莉 (wife of Feng Yingzi 冯英子), summer 1975. Disclosed and verified by Feng Yingzi, December 10, 1999.

Xu Yan 徐言. "Peiran 'Honglou' zuo shang ke jingshi 'Guangchang' muhouren: ruci Lin Zhao zhen mianmu" 翩然"红楼"座上客竟是"广场"幕后人：如此林昭真面目 (Fluttering into the "Red Building" as an Honored Guest, She Turned Out to Be the Wire Puller of "The Square": The True Face of Lin Zhao). *Honglou: Fan youpai douzheng tekan* 红楼：反右派斗争特刊 (The Red Building: Special Edition on the Anti-Rightist Struggle), 1957: 3. In *Lin Zhao zhi si*, edited by Fu Guoyong.

Xu Zhiyong 许志永. "Weile ziyou, gongyi, ai: wode fating chenci" 为了自由、公义、爱—我的法庭陈词 (For Freedom, Righteousness, and Love: My

Court Statement), January 22, 2014. *Human Rights in China*. www.hrichina
.org/chs/gong-min-yan-chang/xu-zhi-yong-zai-fa-ting-shang-de-zui
-hou-chen-shu.

———. "Ziyou Zhonghua de xundaozhe: du Lin Zhao 'shisiwan yan shu'" 自
由中华的殉道者—读林昭 "十四万言书" (A Martyr for a Free China—
Reading Lin Zhao's "140,000-Character Letter"), March 13, 2013. www.
epochtimes.com/gb/13/12/19/n4037695.htm.

Xue Liyong 薛理勇. "Lao Shanghai de jianyu" 老上海的監獄 (The Prisons of
Old Shanghai). www.baqu.org/article/15551673340/.

Yan Zhang 炎章 and Ling 苓 [Lin Zhao]. "Zongjie chengji, touru xin zhandou"
总结成绩，投入新战斗 (Summarize Achievements; Throw Ourselves
into the New Battle). *Changzhou Minbao* (Changzhou People News), January 3, 1954.

Yan Zuyou 严祖佑. Interview with the author. Shanghai, November 15, 2015.

———. "Jiaoshou fenggu—yuyou Sun Dayu" 教授风骨—狱友孙大雨
(The Professor's Strength of Character: My Prison Friend Sun Dayu),
2012. www.21ccom.net/articles/rwcq/article_2012090767163.html.

———. *Renqu* 人曲 (The Human Comedy). Shanghai: Dongfang chuban
zhongxin, 2012.

Yang, Guobin. *The Red Guard Generation and Political Activism in China*. New
York: Columbia University Press, 2016.

Yang Huarong 羊华荣. "Huishou wangshi" 回首往事 (Remembering Things
of the Past). In *Lin Zhao, buzai bei yiwang*, edited by Xu Juemin.

Yang Jisheng 杨继绳. "Daolu, lilun, zhidu—wo dui Wenhua Dageming de
sikao" 道路·理论·制度—我对文化大革命的思考 (The Way, Theories,
and the System: My Reflections on the Cultural Revolution). Jiyi 记忆
(Memories), no. 104 (November 30, 2013). www.boxun.com/news/gb/
pubvp/2015/08/201508040834.shtml#.Vo10qrerTIU.

———. *Mubei: Zhongguo liushi niandai da jihuang jishi* 墓碑: 中国六十年
代大饥荒纪实 (Tombstone: Records of the Great Chinese Famine of the
1960s). Rev. ed. Hong Kong: Tiandi tushu, 2009. First published 2007.

Yang Kuisong 杨奎松. "Xin Zhongguo 'zhenya fangeming' yundong yanjiu"
新中国 "镇压反革命"运动研究 (A Study of the "Suppression of Counterrevolutionaries" Campaign in New China). *Shixue yuekan* 史学月刊
(Journal of Historical Science), no. 1 (2006).

———. "Zhonggong tugai de ruogan wenti" 中共土改的若干问题 (Several
Problems in CCP's Land Reform), October 24, 2011. http://blog.sina.com.
cn/s/blog_56e72aa30102dzau.html.

Yanhuang chunqiu 炎黄春秋 (China through the Ages), 2000–2015.

Yao, Kevin Xiyi. *The Fundamentalist Movement among Protestant Missionaries
in China, 1920–1937*. Lanham, MD: University Press of America, 2003.

Yao Wenyuan 姚文元. "Ping 'Sanjiacun'—'Yanshan yehua,' 'sanjiacun zhaji' de fandong benzhi" 评"三家村"—"燕山夜话" "三家村札记" 的反动本质 (On "Three-Family Village"—The Reactionary Nature of "Evening Chats in the Yan Mountains" and "Notes from the Three-Family Village"). *Jiefang Ribao* 解放日报 (Liberation Daily), May 10, 1966.

———. "Ping xinbian lishiju *Hairui baguan*" 评新编历史剧 "海瑞罢官" (On the New Historical Play *Hai Rui Dismissed from Office*). *Wenhui bao* 文汇报, November 10, 1965.

Ye Jiefu 叶介甫. "Chuanqi mushi Dong Jianwu: Gaiming huanxing chengwei guogong liangdang de mimi teshi" 传奇牧师董健吾：改名换姓成为国共两党的秘密特使 (The Legendary Pastor Dong Jianwu: Being the Undercover Envoy for CCP and GMD). *Zhongguo Gongchandang xinwen wang* 中国共产党新闻网 (Chinese Communist Party News Net) September 8, 2010. http://dangshi.people.com.cn/GB/85038/12663526.html.

Yin Hongbiao 印红标. *Shizong zhe de zuji: Wenhua Dageming qijian de qingnian sichao* 失踪者的足迹—文化大革命期间的青年思潮 (Footprints of the Disappeared: Youth Thought Trends during the Cultural Revolution). Hong Kong: Chinese University Press, 2009.

———. "Wenge houxu jieduan de minjian sichao" 文革后续阶段的民间思潮 (Unofficial Ideological Trends during the Later Phase of the Cultural Revolution). *Ershiyi shiji* 二十一世纪 (Twenty-First Century) 117, no. 2 (February 2010).

Yin Shusheng 尹曙生. "Mao Zedong yu disanci quanguo gong'an huiyi" 毛泽东与第三次全国公安会议 (Mao Zedong and the Third National Meeting on Public Security). *Yanhuang chunqiu* 炎黄春秋 (China through the Ages), 2014, no. 5.

Yin Wenhan 尹文汉. "Zhongguo gudai cixue jingshu zhifeng" 中国古代刺血书经之风 (The Common Practice of Drawing Blood to Copy Sutras in Ancient China). *Zongjiao xue yanjiu* 宗教学研究 (Religious Studies), no. 1 (2016).

Yu Luoke 遇罗克. "Chushen lun" 出身论 (On Family Origins). *Zhongxue wenge bao* 中学文革报 (Middle School Cultural Revolution News). Red Guards Pamphlet, January 18, 1967. In *Wenhua Dageming he tade yiduan sichao*, edited by Song Yongyi and Sun Dajin.

Yu Meisun 俞梅荪. "Lin Zhao jiuyi sishi zhounian ji: Beida fanyou weihai jin youzai" 林昭就义四十周年祭：北大反右危害今犹在 (Commemorating the Fortieth Anniversary of Lin Zhao's Martyrdom: The Evil of Peking University Anti-Rightist Campaign Still Exists). *Canyu* 参与, May 31, 2008. www.canyu.org/n2233c11.aspx.

Yu Yingshi 余英时. "Cong chuantong 'shi' dao xiandai zhishiren" 从传统 '士' 到现代知识人 (From Conventional 'shi' to Modern Intellectuals). *Shi yu*

Zhongguo wenhua 士与中国文化 (The Literati and Chinese Culture), "Introduction." Shanghai: Shanghai renmin chubanshe, 2003.

Yuan Ling 袁凌. "Mao Zedong shidai de wuda zhuming laojiaoying"毛泽东时代的五大著名劳教营 (Five Well-known Re-education through Labor Camps of the Mao Zedong Era), January 15, 2014. www.shz100.com/portal_mobilep_mobile_view.html?aid=4480&page=2.

———. "Shanghai dang'an li de 'fangeming'"上海档案里的"反革命" ("Counterrevolutionaries" in Shanghai's Archives). *Yanhuang chunqiu* 炎黄春秋 (China through the Ages), 2015, no. 4.

———. "Tilanqiao li de qiutu"提篮里的囚徒"(上、下)(The Inmates of Tilanqiao [1–2]). http://magazine.caijing.com.cn/2013-09-08/113273360.html; http://doc.qkzz.net/article/f9404fcd-d24c-4051-b98e-f9e82d356b23.htm.

Zeng Yuhuai 曾毓淮. Interview with the author. Shanghai, May 31, 2016.

Zhang, Mr. (Given name omitted at his request. Suzhou scholar and Lin Zhao's former classmate.) "Guanyu 'wufenqian zidan fei' deng shuo de zhiyi" 关于"五分钱子弹费"等说的质疑 (Questions Concerning the "Five-Cent Bullet Fee" and Other Accounts). Unpublished paper, February 2014.

———. Interview with the author. Suzhou, June 11, 2017.

———. Telephone interview with the author. July 17, 2014.

———. Telephone interview with the author. July 12, 2016.

Zhang Ling 张玲. "Youming xinyu—yi Lin Zhao" 幽明心语—忆林昭 (Flickers and Murmurs from Inside: Remembering Lin Zhao). In *Lin Zhao, buzai bei yiwang*, edited by Xu Juemin.

Zhang Min 张敏. "Lin Zhao baomei Peng Lingfan fangtan lu" 林昭胞妹彭令范访谈录 (An Interview with Lin Zhao's Sister Peng Lingfan), September 4, 2004. www.chinesepen.org/Article/sxsy/200804/Article_20080429040845.shtml.

———. "Lin Zhao jiuyi 49 zhounian: huifang Lin Zhao qinyou yi Lin Zhao" 林昭就义49周年：回放林昭亲友忆林昭 (The Forty-Ninth Anniversary of Lin Zhao's Martyrdom: Rebroadcasting Remembrances of Lin Zhao by Her Family and Friends). *Radio Free Asia*, April 28, 2017. www.rfa.org/mandarin/zhuanlan/xinlingzhilyu/fanyouhuiyiyuyanjiu/mind-04282017152337.html.

Zhang Yihe 章诒和. *Zuihou de guizu* 最后的贵族 (The Last Nobility). Hong Kong: Oxford University Press, 2004.

Zhang Yuanxun 张元勋. *Beida, 1957* 北大一九五七 (Peking University, 1957). Hong Kong: Mingbao chubanshe, 2004.

———. "Beida wangshi yu Lin Zhao zhi si" 北大往事与林昭之死 (Peking University's Past Events and Lin Zhao's Death). In *Lin Zhao, buzai bei yiwang*, edited by Xu Juemin.

———. "*Guangchang* fakan ci" 广场发刊词 (Foreword to the Inaugural Issue of *The Square*). In *Yuanshang cao: jiyi zhong de fanyoupai yundong*, edited by Niu Han and Deng Jiuping.

Zhang Zhejun 张哲俊. "Peng Enhua qiren yu *Riben paiju shi*" 彭恩华其人与 "日本俳句史" (Peng Enhua and *The History of Japanese Haiku*), June 3, 2013. http://blog.sina.com.cn/s/blog_790520270101d8ak.html.

Zhao Rui 赵锐. *Jitan shang de shengnü: Lin Zhao zhuan* 祭坛上的圣女—林昭传 (The Female Saint on the Altar: A Biography of Lin Zhao). Taipei: Xiuwei zixun keji, 2009.

Zhengwuyuan 政务院 (Government Administration Council). "Renmin fating zuzhi tongze" 人民法庭组织通则 (General Principles for Structuring the People's Tribunals), July 14, 1950, *Renmin Wang* 人民网 (People's Daily Online). http://cpc.people.com.cn/GB/64184/64186/66655/4492599.html.

Zhu Yi 朱毅 (祭园守园人). "Chen Fengxiao, Wang Guoxiang, Wang Shuyao juyi Beida wuyijiu yundong" 陈奉孝、王国乡、王书瑶聚忆北大五一九运动 (Chen Fengxiao, Wang Guoxiang, and Wang Shuyao Gathered to Remember the May 19 Movement at Peking University), September 2008. http://beijingspring.com/bj2/2010/550/2014122201614.htm.

———. Interview with the author. Ganzhou, June 9, 2017.

———. "Lin Zhao: 'Ling'ou xuyu' jiaoduzhe shuoming" "林昭：灵耦絮语" 校读者说明 (A Word of Explanation about Lin Zhao's "Ling'ou xuyu" by the Proofreader). Preface to Lin Zhao, "Ling'ou xuyu."

INDEX

Page numbers in italics refer to illustrative material.

LIAN XI, a historian, is Professor of World Christianity at Duke Divinity School. The author of *Redeemed by Fire* and *The Conversion of Missionaries*, he lives in Chapel Hill, North Carolina.

Duke Photography